SERVICE WISDOM

CREATING AND MAINTAINING
THE CUSTOMER SERVICE EDGE

RON ZEMKE
AND CHIP R. BELL

Lakewood Books
50 S. Ninth Street
Minneapolis, MN 55402
(612)333-0471

Editorial Coordinator: **Julie Swiler**
Copy Editor: **Susan C. Jones**
Production Editor: **Helen Spielberg**
Design: **Pollock Haro**

With special thanks to **Klay DeVries.**

Second Printing, 1990.

Lakewood Publications Inc. is a subsidiary of Maclean Hunter Publishing Company. Lakewood publishes TRAINING, The Magazine of Human Resources Development, the Training Director's Forum Newsletter, Creative Training Techniques Newsletter, The Service Edge Newsletter, Airport Services Magazine, Potentials In Marketing Magazine, Recreation Resources Magazine, and other business periodicals and books. James P. Secord, president; Mary Hanson, Philip G. Jones, Linda Klemstein, Michael C. Miller, Jerry C. Noack, vice presidents.

ISBN 0-943210-08-9

Table Of Contents

Introduction

Listen and Respond to the Customer

Define a Service Strategy

Set Standards and Measure Performance

Train and Empower People

Recognize and Reward Accomplishment

Service Wisdom: The Glue Of Service Success

"The mind of man is capable of anything, because everything is in it, all the past, as well as all the future."

Joseph Conrad

The need to focus on customer care and the desirability of creating distinctive service quality are widely accepted today. Just try and find a company that isn't promising "Superior Service" or advertising "We care about you—our customers." And, of course, you and we and a hundred million or so other "once fooled, twice cynical" fellow consumers just shake our heads and believe little of it. Our skepticism is well-founded.

Nothing is as common today as the organization committed more to lip service than customer service; more interested in advertising than action. In a funny way, we sympathize with those organizations. As we and the other authors represented in this book can attest, moving an organization from self-centered to customer-centered is damned hard work. Creating a truly customer-focused, service-quality-obsessed organization takes time, patience, and dedication. And it takes wisdom—Service Wisdom.

SERVICE WISDOM—AT THE TOP

Service Wisdom in the executive suite is knowing and believing that a service-quality focus is a solid business strategy and not just an ephemeral marketing fad. Service Wisdom at the top is knowing that establishing a service edge in the marketplace means finding and focusing on a service "differentiator," some attribute that is both easy to describe and understand, yet unique in the eyes of the customer, worth a premium, and not a pale imitation of what everyone else in your business is doing. Service Wisdom at the helm is the willingness to spend on those things that are important to the customer— and to cut back or hold the line on things customers don't care about. And it is understanding the importance of having numbers, dollars and cents evidence in hand, to back up and reinforce your conviction that service quality is important.

Service Wisdom is understanding that managing the delivery of a service is the management of a "performing art" and, as such, is very different from managing the production of a product. It is understanding the importance of stage setting, scripts, props, and casting—and having an enthusiasm for the indirect and supportive nature of managing in such an environment.

And, for all that, Service Wisdom is also understanding and accepting as axiomatic the dictum that service quality is as much a management responsibility as it is a "front-line" responsibility. Service Wisdom is what drives the senior management team to take time to create an understandable and vivid "vision" of the distinctive level of service it believes the organization must commit to long-term.

And Service Wisdom is what motivates those same senior managers to demonstrate very publicly an obsession with service quality and to take a strong leadership role in removing barriers and making the changes necessary for the organization to serve customers better. Service Wisdom at the top is what comforts senior management when it must make trade-offs between strategic and financial goals, arbitrate internal cost-/quality arguments, and reassure doubting managers and investors that the course is sound.

SERVICE WISDOM—IN THE MIDDLE
Service Wisdom is hardly the sole property of senior management. Nor could it ever be. Service Wisdom in middle management is understanding that front-line employees and customers aren't going to believe the service-quality message—at first.

Service Wisdom in middle management is understanding the import of Will Rogers's simple dictum that "people learn from observation, not conversation" and that the manager front-line employees see is the model they emulate—for better or for worse. Service Wisdom in middle management is knowing that reluctance to champion a service-quality effort will be seen by the front-line troops as a rejection of that effort. And, conversely, it is believing and knowing that if you personally lead the way—set the example—and break your neck for customers day after day, front-line employees will do the same. Service Wisdom in middle management is understanding that only *you* can begin the process of removing the service-quality barriers that come between the front-line people and their customers.

It means taking the risk of trying to do things a little differently, of taking chances on behalf of the front-line employee and his/her customer and standing up for—supporting—the front-line employee when things get fouled up. Service Wisdom in middle management is understanding the critical impact that selection and training of front-line people have on customer satisfaction. And having the patience and skill to coach a faltering employee along toward superior performance. And Service Wisdom in middle management is about knowing when it is time to kick back and celebrate accomplishments, to salute the team for pulling together and succeeding.

SERVICE WISDOM—AT THE FRONT LINE
Last, but not least, Service Wisdom is having front-line people who are unflappable, bright, well-trained, and capable of getting things done for the customer. The Service-Wise front-line person knows the "red rules" from the "blue rules." Front-line Service Wisdom is knowing where, when, and how to be flexible and creative and to take a little risk on behalf of a customer. Front-line Service Wisdom means knowing how to solve problems for customers and solving them so well that customers—and competitors—marvel at the skill.

Service Wisdom at the front line also means knowing what your customers expect from your organization—and from you. And it is understanding that, sometimes, *how* a thing is done is as important as *what* gets done.

Service Wisdom at the front line also means knowing when it is time to give up and hand an unhappy customer to someone else and when it is time to get away from the front line and refresh mind, body, and soul. Service Wisdom at the front line is also understanding how customers act and think in 101 situations—and knowing 102 ways to respond. And it is understanding that those responses, no matter how pat and rehearsed they may be, must be delivered in a way that conveys caring and interest to the customer.

Most of all, Service Wisdom at the front line is about being smart, about knowing things and being able to piece information and knowledge together in a confident, convincing, and skillful way for the customer. It is also about caring enough about doing a good job that it motivates you to know more about the job and the organization and the customers and their businesses than you need to know just to "get by"—and being proud of that.

BECOMING SERVICE WISE

Service Wisdom—at the top, in the middle, and at the front line—is, perhaps more than anything else, about pride, about caring, about winning, about success and about how every one of us feels when we have tackled a tough job, come through for the customer, and seen the satisfaction and pleasure that brings. For ourselves and for others, as well. This book is about the things Service-Wise organizations—and managers—do to make themselves look terrific in their customers' eyes. It is organized around the major themes of those management activities.

At one point, we were sorely tempted to call these themes "The Imperatives of Service Quality" or "The Keys to Service-Quality Heaven" or "The Critical Building Blocks of Extraordinary Customer Satisfaction" or some such piece of pomposity. But that would not be in keeping with one of the critical attributes we find totally *lacking* in Service-Wise managers—dogmatism. The Service Wise, it seems, keep their options and their assumptions and operating principles pretty open. They consistently and continually examine the world around them for new and different ways to think about, and go about, improving the quality of the services they provide their customers.

Still, we needed a way to organize the 33 separate articles that constitute this book. So we stuck with our concept of major themes and created seven sections, each of which represents one of those sets of activities we routinely see managers engaging in at Service-Wise organizations.

- Listen and Respond to Customers
- Define a Service Strategy
- Set Standards and Measure Performance
- Train and Empower Employees
- Recognize and Reward Accomplishment
- Overcome Customer Disappointment
- Create a Service Culture

Hold on now. We know as well as you that these seven themes aren't exactly new news. You've undoubtedly seen them—or themes very much like them—before. But don't let that fool you into thinking the associated content is just a rehash of what you've read or heard before about service, service quality, and service excellence. It is not. What we've assembled here are the articles and ideas that have caused *us* to pause, have caused *us* consternation, and have made *us* think—and sometimes rethink—what we thought we knew about service quality, service delivery, service management, service marketing, service . . . everything.

For instance, the articles "What the Hell Is 'Market Oriented?'," by Ben Shapiro, and "Quality Work Doesn't Mean Quality Service," by David Maister, caused us to stop and think about the concepts of who is and isn't a customer, what quality in service really means, and how that all fits together with the idea of market segmentation.

A few of the articles, while instructive, are also just plain fun. "Love That Customer," by Stew Leonard, Sr., simply exudes passion, confidence, and determination and is exhilarating to read. It reconfirmed our belief that you have to like what you are doing if you are going to do it well. Others are contemporary classics that taught us so much we would have been remiss not to include them. Theodore Levitt's "After the Sale Is Over . . . ," and "The Service-Quality Puzzle," by Berry, Parasuraman and Zeithaml, easily fit that description.

And, yes, there are a number of articles (14 to be exact) by one or the other of *us*. Vanity? Perhaps. But we think not. For instance, the article "Supervising Service Workers," while written by Ron Zemke, is really a distillation of the ideas and experiences of a dozen or so managers and consultants who till the soil in that vineyard on a daily basis.

Do we *guarantee* you will be Service Wise when you finish this book? Absolutely not. Not even if you swear to quit smoking, take up jogging, lose 20 pounds, and eschew chocolate chip cookies 'til Christmas 1999.

Service Wisdom comes, first and foremost, from getting up everyday; going to the shop or office; being face-to-face, ear-to-ear, and mind-to-mind with the customer; and succeeding—and occasionally failing to succeed—at creating a 100% genuinely satisfied customer.

Books, articles, films, and speeches may—and do—give you ideas that you can use, that will lighten somewhat the load you carry. But, in the last analysis, it is your use of these ideas, your creative shaping and fitting of them to your unique and special situation, that really create Service Wisdom. Nothing more. So real Service Wisdom is in *your* actions and *your* thoughts and *your* results. If the articles and ideas in this book expedite in some way the getting and the keeping of that wisdom—they, and we, have done our job. Enjoy!

Ron Zemke
Minneapolis

Chip Bell
Charlotte, NC

April 1989

Listen And Respond To The Customer

"Customers perceive service in their own unique, idiosyncratic, emotional, erratic, irrational, end-of-the-day and totally human terms. Perception is all there is!"
Tom Peters

Service-wise organizations have learned that communication with the customer has at least two components. The first is listening. The winners in the service game devise countless means and opportunities to get input from customers. If the customer doesn't believe you are listening, your efforts are for naught. The goal is to listen in a manner that convinces customers you seek to understand their needs and expectations.

The second part of effective communication with customers is responding. Responding entails insuring there is linkage back to customers that they were heard. It also means insuring that the communication mattered by acting on what has been learned. As Fred Smith, president of Federal Express says: "Listening is useless unless it creates actions which realign efforts based on what is learned." Countless customers can cite cases that went something like this: "I complained, and they wrote me a nice letter. But they never bothered to correct what I complained about."

It is easy to get into the habit of assuming we know everything we need to know about our customers. But the longer we work in an organization, the easier it is to be out of touch, removed

1

from the customer. The "I used to work on the front line" type rationalizations can be particularly seductive. As Tom Peters says, *How to stay close to the customer is neither complex or difficult. And most companies say it is important. They just don't do it.*

In service-sensitive organizations, people listen to customers with a kind of naiveté, sincere openness with a sense of wonder. In doing so, they are more apt to hear the subtleties of customers' needs rather than hearing only what they expected to hear. The organization that listens without presumption or bias—listening to learn rather than listening to confirm what it thinks it knows —will hear more of what the customer is attempting to communicate about service needs and expectations.

Listening and responding have been the keys to success of many organizations. The Marriott Corporation's highly successful Courtyard hotel chain is a good example. In an attempt to create a business uniquely responsive to the needs of traveling businesspeople, they interviewed countless travelers to determine (down to the minute detail) what their target market wanted. For instance, while most moderately priced hotels offer their guests an assortment of toiletries (from hand lotion to several types of soap to a lint remover), most Courtyards have only soap and shampoo. On the other hand, while most moderately priced chains require a trip to the lobby or restaurant or a call to room service for a cup of coffee, Courtyards provide coffee-making apparatus (including a faucet that produces boiling water) in every room. Both provisions illustrate how listening can prompt actions based on what the customer wants as well as what the customer does not want.

First Union National Bank in Charlotte, North Carolina, established a strategy of exceeding customers' service expectations for branch banking service. Implementing such a strategy required finding out at every turn *exactly* what customers expected. They learned, for instance, that customers expected to wait (but no longer than four minutes) in branch teller lines. They established a three-minute wait as their "exceed expectations" standard and then staffed the branches to be able to implement the standard. Since this bank had greater profits than any other bank in America in 1987, obviously their efforts had significant economic payoff.

We have selected five readings to challenge your thinking about listening and responding to the customer. Their choice was driven by a desire to combine philosophy, practice, and technique in the same section. The philosophy reading is an article, "After the Sale Is Over . . . ," by Theodore Levitt that appeared in the September-October 1983 *Harvard Business*

Review. Levitt is a professor of marketing in the Harvard Business School and editor of the *Harvard Business Review.* The article, which compares service after the sale with marriage, makes a strong case for staying plugged in to customers' expectations.

The use of the marriage analogy recognizes the customer/service-provider relationship as a partnership. Says Levitt, "If the customer has not complained, he is either not being candid or not being contacted." Are customer complaints (or lack thereof) an appropriate barometer of the quality of a relationship? If customers are to be partners, how do we deal with those who are fickle, unreasonable, uncertain, overly demanding? Is service after the sale of a product different than person-to-person service during a sale? For the service provider, is "divorce" ever an appropriate ending to an untenable customer relationship?

The "practice" reading is a case study offered by Stew Leonard, CEO of the phenomenally successful Stew Leonard's Dairy Store in Norwalk, Connecticut. Stew Leonard's is in the *Guiness Book of World Records* for having the world's highest retail revenue per square foot. While most grocery stores average $200,000 per week on 16,000 items, Stew averages $1.5 million on about 750 items. Since the store opened, he has made 24 additions to accommodate growth, which he attributes to listening and responding to customers. Stew advocates the "customer is king" perspective. This suggests the service provider is more servant than partner. The granite stone outside his store proclaims, "Rule 1—The customer is always right. Rule 2—If the customer is ever wrong, reread rule #1."

Is the customer always right? If that philosophy is carried to its full measure, what happens to the self-esteem of front-line people who become the innocent victims of customers who take their "king" status to ruthless, despotic lengths? With an "always right" philosophy, how do you effectively deal with unrealistic customer demands that make no business sense? Is there a difference between a "servant" role (meaning subservience) and a "deferential" role (meaning to defer to the customer)?

Next, we offer two technique-type pieces. One is a brief article selected from the December 1986 issue of author and lecturer Tom Peters' *On Achieving Excellence* newsletter. Despite its brevity, the article is chock-full of useful techniques for listening to customers.

The other technique article is a short but powerful piece from the Fall 1988 issue of *Mobius,* the journal for the Society for Consumer Affairs Professionals. Its authors are John Goodman, Arlene Malech, and Gary Bargatze, three consultants from TARP Institute, a Washington, DC-based research and consulting firm. The article offers a variety of practical suggestions on how best to understand customers' needs and expectations. The authors' focus is a departure from traditional market research in that it concentrates on *people,* not segments. While they acknowledge the merits of learning the demographics and psychographics of a given target market, they recognize that, unless the input of real people forms the basis of decisions and responses, there is great danger of making inaccurate assumptions. In other words, they agree with Stanley Marcus of Neiman-Marcus, who is credited with saying, "A market never bought a thing in my stores, but a lot of customers came in and made me rich!"

The final article we have included is the counterpoint piece, an effort to push your thinking beyond traditional limits. David Bowen's "Managing Customers As Human Resources in Service Organizations" from the Fall 1986 issue of *Human Resource Management* encourages us to rethink the whole definition of "customer." He explores the idea of "putting the customer to work." We all have made our own salad, pumped our own gas, or filled our own drink cup. Here, Bowen explores these outer limits of service. At what point does the "customer as quasi-employee" begin to feel "worked" instead of "served"?

AFTER THE SALE
IS OVER...

Theodore Levitt

The relationship between a seller and a buyer seldom ends when a sale is made. Increasingly, the relationship intensifies after the sale and helps determine the buyer's choice the next time around. Such dynamics are found particularly with services and products dealt in a stream of transactions between seller and buyer—financial services, consulting, general contracting, military and space equipment, and capital goods.

The sale, then, merely consummates the courtship, at which point the marriage begins. How good the marriage is depends on how well the seller manages the relationship. The quality of the marriage determines whether there will be continued or expanded business, or troubles and divorce. In some cases divorce is impossible, as when a major construction or installation project is under way. If the marriage that remains is burdened, it tarnishes the seller's reputation.

Companies can avoid such troubles by recognizing at the outset the necessity of managing their relationships with customers. This takes special attention to an often ignored aspect of relationships: time.

The theory of supply and demand presumes that the work of the economic system is time-discrete and bare of human interaction—that an instantaneous, disembodied sales transaction clears the market at the intersection of supply and demand.

This was never completely accurate and has become less so as product complexity and interdependences have intensified. Buyers of automated machinery do not, like buyers at a flea market, walk home with purchases and take their chances. They expect installation services, application aids, parts, post purchase repair and maintenance, retrofitted enhancements, and vendor R&D to keep the products effective and up to date for as long as possible and to help the company stay competitive.

The buyer of a continuous stream of transactions, like a frozen-food manufacturer that buys its cartons from a packaging company and its

5
■

cash-management services from a bank, is concerned not only with completing transactions but also with maintaining the process. Due to the growing complexity of military equipment, even the Department of Defense makes most of it purchases in units of less than a hundred and therefore has to repeat transactions often.

Because purchase cycles of products and major components are increasingly stretched, needs that began tended to have changed. Consider the purchase cycles and the changing assurances backing purchases (see Exhibit I). Under these conditions, a purchase decision is not a decision to

Exhibit I
Purchase Cycles and Assurances

Item	Purchase cycle (in years)
Oil field installation	15 to 20
Chemical plant	10 to 15
EDP system	5 to 10
Weapons system	20 to 30
Major components of steel plant	5 to 10
Paper supply contract	5

Item	Previous Assurance	Present Assurance
Tankers	Spot	Charter
Apartments	Rentals	Coopertative
Auto warranties	10,000 miles	100,000 miles
Technology	Buy	Lease
Labor	Hire	Contracts
Supplies	Shopping	Contracting
Equipment	Repair	Maintenance

enter a bonded relationship (to get married). This requires of the would-be-seller a new orientation and a new strategy.

Selling by itself is no longer enough. Consider the compelling differences between the old and the new selling arrangements Exhibit II illustrates. In the selling scheme the seller is located at a distance from buyers and reaches out with a sales department to unload products on them. This is the basis for the notion that a salesperson needs charisma, because charisma rather than the product's qualities makes the sale.

Consider by contrast, marketing. Here the seller, being physically close to buyers, penetrates their domain to learn about their needs, desires, and fears and then designs and supplies the product with those considerations in mind. Instead of trying to get buyers to want what the seller has, the seller tries to have what they want. The "product" is no longer merely an item but a whole bundle of values that satisfy buyers—an "augmented" product.

Thanks to increasing interdependence, more and more of the world's economic work gets done through long-term relationships between sellers and buyers. It is not a matter of just getting and then holding on to customers. It is more a matter of giving the buyers what they want. Buyers

Exhibit II
The Change From Selling to Market

Selling

```
┌──────────┐   ┌──────────────┐   ┌──────────┐
│ Seller   │──▶│ Sales        │──▶│ Buyer    │
│          │   │ department   │   │          │
│          │   │              │   │          │
└──────────┘   └──────────────┘   └──────────┘
```

Marketing

```
┌──────────┐                      ┌──────────┐
│ Seller   │─────────────────────▶│ Buyer    │
│          │                      │          │
│          │                      │          │
└──────────┘                      └──────────┘
```

want vendors who keep promises, who'll keep supplying and standing behind what they promised. The era of the one-night stand is gone. Marriage is both necessary and more convenient. Products are too complicated, repeat negotiations too much of a hassle and too costly. Under these conditions, success in marketing is transformed into the inescapability of a relationship. Interface becomes interdependence.

Under these circumstances, being a good marketer in the conventional sense is not enough. When it takes five years of intensive work between seller and buyer to "deliver" an operating chemical plant or a telecommunication system, much more is required than the kind of marketing that simply lands the contract. The buyer needs assurance at the outset that the two parties can work well together during the long period in which the purchase gets transformed into delivery.

The seller and the buyer have different capital structures, competitive conditions, costs, and incentives driving the commitments they make to each other. The seller has made a sale that is expected to yield a profit. For the seller it is the end of the process; for the buyer, only the beginning. Yet their interdependence is inescapable and profound. To make these differently motivated dependencies work, the selling company must understand the relationship and plan its management in advance of the wedding. It can't get out the marriage manual only after trouble has begun.

THE PRODUCT'S CHANGING NATURE
The future will be marked by intense business relationships in all areas of marketing, including frequently purchased consumer goods. Proctor & Gamble, copying General Mills' Betty Crocker advisory service, has found that the installation of a consumer hot line to give advice on its products and their uses has cemented customer brand loyalty.

In the industrial setting we have only to review changing perceptions of various aspects of product characteristics to appreciate the new emphasis on relationships (see Exhibit III). The common characteristic of the terms in the "future" column of this exhibit is time. What is labeled "item" in the first column was in the past simply a product, something that was bought for its own value. More recently that simple product has not been enough. Instead, buyers have bought augmented products.

During the era we are entering the emphasis will be on systems contracts, and buyer-seller relationships will be characterized by continuous contact and evolving relationships to effect the systems. The "sale" will be not just a system but a system over time. The value at stake will be the advantages of that total system over time. As the customer gains experience, the technology will decline in importance relative to the system that enables the buyer to realize the benefits of the technology. Services, delivery, reliability, responsiveness, and the quality of the human and organizational interactions between seller and buyer will be more important than the technology itself.

The more complex the system and the more "software" (including operating procedures and protocols, management routines, service components) it requires, the greater the customer's anxieties and expectations. People buy expectations, not things. They buy the expectations of benefits promised by the vendor. When it takes a long time to fulfill the promise (to deliver a new custom-made automated work station, for example) or when fulfillment is continual over a long period (as it is in banking services, fuel deliveries, or shipments of components for assembly operations), the buyer's anxieties build up after the purchase decision is made. Will the delivery be prompt? Will it be smooth and regular? Did we select the best vendor?

DIFFERING EXPECTATIONS

When downstream realities loom larger than up-front promises, what do you do before, during, and after the sale? Who should be responsible for what?

Exhibit III
Perceptions of Product Values

Category	Past	Present	Future
Item	Product	Augmented product	System contracts
Sale	Unit	System	System over time
Value	Feature advantages	Technology advantages	System advantages
Leadtime	Short	Long	Lengthy
Service	Modest	Important	Vital
Delivery place	Local	National	Global
Delivery phase	Once	Often	Continually
Strategy	Sales	Marketing	Relationship

To answer these questions it helps to understand how the promises and behavior of the vendor before the sale is made shape the customer's expectations. It is reasonable for a customer who has been promised the moon to expect it to be delivered. But if those who make the promises are paid commissions before the customer gets everything he bargained for, they're not likely to feel compelled to ensure that the customer gets fully satisfied later. After the sale, they'll rush off to pursue other prey. If marketing plans the sale, sales makes it, manufacturing fulfills it, and service services it, who's in charge and who takes responsibility for the whole process?

Problems arise not only because those who do the selling, the marketing, the manufacturing, and the servicing have varying incentives and views of the customer but also because organizations are one-dimensional. People, with the exception of those who work in sales or marketing, seldom see beyond their company's walls. For those inside those walls, inside is where the work gets done, where the penalties and incentives are doled out, where the budgets and plans get made, where engineering and manufacturing are done, where performance is measured, where one's friends and associates gather, where things are managed and manageable. Outside "has nothing to do with me" and is where "you can't change things."

Many disjunctions exist between seller and buyer at various stages of the sales process. These may be simply illustrated, as in Exhibit IV.

AFTER THE FACT

The fact of buying changes the dynamics of the relationship. The buyer expects the seller to remember the purchase as having been a favor bestowed, not as something earned by the seller. Hence it is wrong to assume that getting an account gives you an advantage because you've got a foot in the door. The opposite is more often the case. The buyer that views the sale as a favor conferred on the seller in effect debits the seller's account. The seller owes the buyer one. He is in the position of having to rebuild the relationship from a deficit stance.

In the absence of good management, the relationship deteriorates because both organizations tend naturally to face inward rather than outward toward each other. The natural tendency of relationships, whether in marriage or in business, is toward erosion of sensitivity and attentiveness. Inward orientation by the selling organization leads to insensitivity and unresponsiveness in customer relations. At best the company substitutes bureaucratic formalities for authentic interaction.

Listen And Respond
To The Customer

A healthy relationship maintains, and preferably expands, the equity and the possibilities that were created during courtship. A healthy relationship requires a conscious and constant fight against the forces of decline. It becomes important for the seller regularly and seriously to consider whether the relationship is improving or deteriorating, whether the prom-

Exhibit IV
Varying Reactions and Perceptions
Before and During Sale Process

When the sale is first made

Seller	Buyer
Objective achieved	Judgement postponed applies test of time
Selling stops	Shopping continues
Focus goes elsewhere	Focus on purchase; wants affirmation that expectations have been met
Tension released	Tension increased
Relationship reduced or ended	Commitment made; relationship intensified

Throughout the process

	Stage of sale	Seller	Buyer
1	Before	Real hope	Vague need
2	Romance	Hot & heavy	Testing & hopeful
3	Sale	Fantasy: bed	Fantasy: board
4	After	Looks elsewhere for next sale	"You don't care"
5	Long after	Indifferent	"Can't this be made better?"
6	Next sale	"How about a new one?"	"Really?"

ises are being completely fulfilled, whether he is neglecting anything, and how he stands vis-a-vis his competitors. Exhibit V compares actions that affect—for better or worse—relationships with buyers.

BUILDING DEPENDENCIES

One of the surest signs of a bad or declining relationship is the absence of complaints from the customer. Nobody is ever *that* satisfied, especially not over an extended period of time. The customer is either not being candid or not being contacted. Probably both. The absence of candor reflects the

Exhibit V
Actions That Affect Relationships

Positive actions	Negative actions
Initiate postive phone calls	Make only call backs
Make recommendations	Make justifications
Use candid language	Use accommodative language
Use phone	Use correspondence
Show appreciation	Wait for misunderstanding
Make service suggestions	Wait for service requests
Use "we" problem-solving language	Use "owe us" legal language
Get to problems	Respond only to problems
Use jargon or shorthand	Use long-winded communications
Air personality problems	Hide personality problems
Talk of "our future together"	Talk about making good on the past
Routinize responses	Fire drill/emergency responsiveness
Accept responses	Shift blame
Plan the future	Rehash the past

decline of trust and the deterioration of the relationship. Bad things accumulate. Impaired communication is both a symptom and a cause of trouble. Things fester inside. When they finally erupt, it's usually too late or too costly to correct the situation.

We can invest in relationships and we can borrow from them. We all do both, but we seldom account for our actions and almost never manage them. Yet a company's most precious asset is its relationships with its customers. What matters is not whom you know but how you are known to them.

Not all relationships can or need be of the same duration or at the same level of intimacy. These factors depend on the extent of the actual or felt dependency between the buyer and the seller. And of course these dependencies can be extended or contracted through various direct links that can be established between the two parties. Thus, when Bergen Brunswig, the booming drug and health care products distributor, puts computer terminals in its customer's offices to enable them to order directly and get instant feedback regarding their sales and inventory, it creates a new link that helps tie the customer to the vendor.

At the same time, however, the seller can become dependent on the buyer in important ways. Most obvious is vendor reliance on the buyer for a certain percentage of its sales. More subtle is reliance on the buyer for important information, including how the buyer's business will change, how changes will affect future purchases, and what competitors are offering in the way of substitute products or materials, at what prices and including which services. The buyer can also answer questions like these for the vendor: How well is the vendor fulfilling the customer's needs? Is performance up to promises from headquarters? To what new uses is the customer putting the product?

The seller's ability to forecast the buyer's intentions rests on the quality of the overall relationship. In a good relationship the buyer shares plans and expectations with the vendor, or at least makes available relevant information. With that information the vendor can better serve the buyer. Surprises and bad forecasts are symptoms of bad relationships. In such instances, everybody—even the buyer—loses.

Thus, a system of reciprocal dependencies develops. It is up to the seller to nurture the relationship beyond its simple dollar value. In a proper relationship both the buyer and the seller will benefit or the relationship will not last.

Moreover, both parties should understand that the seller's expenses rarely end with acquisition costs. This means that the vendor should work at convincing the customer of the importance of maintaining the vendor's long-term profitability at a comfortable level instead of squeezing to get rock-bottom delivered prices. Unless the costs of the expected post-purchase services are reflected in the price, the buyer will end up paying extra in money, in delays, and in aggravation. The smart relationship manager in the selling company will help the buyer do long-term lifecycle costing to assess the vendor's offering.

BONDS THAT LAST

Professional partnerships in law, medicine, architecture, consulting, investment banking, and advertising rate and reward associates by their client relationships. Like any other assets, these relationships can appreciate or depreciate. Their maintenance and enhancement depend not so much on good manners, public relations, tact, charm, window dressing, or manipulation as they do on management. Relationship management requires company wide maintenance, investment, improvement, and even replacement programs. The results can be spectacular.

Examine the case of the North Sea oil and gas fields. Norway and Britain urged and facilitated exploration and development of those resources. They were eager and even generous hosts to the oil companies. The companies, though they spent hundreds of millions of dollars to do the work, didn't fully nurture their relationships. When oil and gas suddenly started to flow, the host countries levied taxes exceeding 90% of the market prices. No one was more surprised than the companies. Why should they have been surprised? Had they built sound relationships with the governments, the politicians, and the voters—by whatever means—so as to have created a sense of mutuality and partnership, they might have moderated the size of the taxes. What would it have been worth?

This is not an isolated occurrence. The same problem crops up in similar circumstances where vendors are required to make heavy expenditures to get accounts and develop products. Exhibit VI depicts cash flows to a vendor of this type during the life of the account. During the customer-getting and development period, cash flows are negative and the customer eagerly encourages the expenditures. When the product is delivered or the joint venture becomes operative, cumulative cash flows turn up and finally become positive. In the case of the North Sea, the surprising new high taxes represent the difference between what revenue to the oil companies might have been (the upper level of potential revenue) and what they actually became. With worse relationships they might, of course, have fallen to an even lower level of potential revenue.

Consider also the case of Gillette North America. It has four separate sales forces and special programs for major accounts to ensure Gillette's rapid

Exhibit VI
Cummulative Cash Flow History of An Account

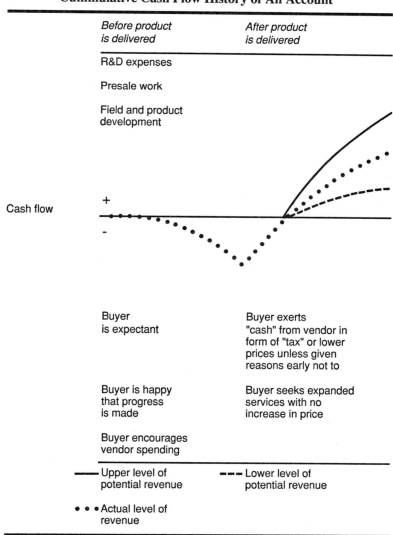

and smooth response to customers' requirements. Gillette also has a vice president of business relations who has among his major duties cultivation of relationships with major retailers and distributors. He carries out that responsibility via a vast array of ceremonial activities ranging from entertainment at trade association conventions to organization of special events for major accounts in connection with the annual All-Star baseball game, the World Series, the Superbowl, and the NCAA play offs. These activities establish bonds and affirm reciprocal obligations and benefits.

Some companies now require engineering and manufacturing people to spend time with customers and users in the field—not just to get product and design ideas or feedback regarding present products but also to get to know and to respond to customers in deep and abiding ways so as to build relationships and bonds that last. The Sperry Corporation's much-advertised "listening" campaign has included training employees to listen and communicate effectively with each other and with customers.

All too often company officials take action instead of spending time. It is all too easy to act first and later try to fix the relationship, instead of the other way around. It is all too simple to say, "We'll look into it and call you back" or "Let's get together for lunch sometime." These are tactics of diversion and delay, not of relationship building.

When a purchase cycle is long—as when a beer-making plant contracts with a can-making vendor to build a factory next door or when the U.S. Air Force commits itself to buying a jet engine with a life of 20 to 30 years—the people in the vendor organization who did the selling and those in the customer organization who did the buying will be replaced over the course of those relationships. So, in all likelihood, will the entire upper levels of management on both sides. What must the seller do to ensure continuity of good relations? What is expected of the customer when people who did the buying are changed and gone? Clearly the idea is to build bonds that last no matter who comes and goes.

MAKING IT HAPPEN
To effectively manage relationships, managers must meet four requirements:

1. *Awareness.* Understand both the problem and the opportunity areas.
2. *Assessment.* Determine where the company now stands, especially in terms of what's necessary to get the desired results.

3. *Accountability.* Establish regular reporting on individual relationships, and then on group relationships, so that these can be
weighed against other measures of performance.
4. *Actions.* Make decisions and allocations and establish routines
and communications on the basis of their impact on the
targeted relationships. Constantly reinforce awareness and actions.

Relationship management can be institutionalized, but in the process it
must also be humanized. One company has regular sensitivity sessions and
role-playing seminars in which sales officials assume the buyer role. It also
conducts debriefings on meeting with customers. And it requires its
customer-contact people (including those who make deliveries and handle
receivables) to regularly ask of various accounts the seminal questions:
How are we doing in the relationship? Is it going up or down? Are we talking
with the right people about the right issues? What have we not done lately?

The emphasis on "lately" is not incidental. It reflects the recognition that
relationships naturally degrade and have to be reinvigorated. If I owe you a
favor, I forget—but you don't. And when I've done you a favor, you feel
obligated—but not for long. You ask, "What have you done for me lately?"
A relationship credit must be cashed in or it expires, and it must be used
soon or it depreciates.

Another way companies can institutionalize relationship management is by
establishing routines that ensure the right kinds of customer contacts. A
well-known Wall Street investment firm requires its security analysts and
salespeople to make regular "constructive" contacts with their institutional
customers. Constructive is defined as conveying useful information to
them. The firm has set up a regular Monday-morning investment strategy
"commentary" that analysts and salespeople can convey by telephone to
their customers. In addition, each analyst must develop periodic industry
commentaries and updates, to be mailed or telephoned to customers.
Analysts and salespeople are required to keep logs of these contacts, which
are compiled, counted, and communicated to all in a weekly company-
wide report. Those salespeople and analysts making the fewest contacts
have to explain their inaction to supervisors.

The firm allocates end-of-year bonuses on the basis of not only commissions earned from the various institutions but also the number and types
of contacts initiated and maintained. Meanwhile, the firm conducts regular
sensitivity-training sessions to enhance the contacts and the quality of the
relationships. The results, which show that the efforts have been highly

successful, are analyzed and made known to all, thus reinforcing the importance of the process.

Relationship management is a special field all its own and is as important to preserving and enhancing the intangible asset commonly known as "goodwill" as is the management of hard assets. The fact that it is probably more difficult makes hard work at it that much more important.

LOVE THAT CUSTOMER

Stew Leonard

My wife Marianne and I risked everything we owned in the world when we opened our small dairy store back in 1969. About a week after opening day, I was standing at the entrance when a customer angrily said, "This eggnog is sour." I took the half-gallon carton, opened it, and tasted it. It tasted all right to me, so I said, "You're wrong, it's perfect."

Then, to prove the customer really was wrong, I said, "We sold over 300 half-gallons of eggnog this week, and you're the only one who's complained." The customer was boiling mad and demanded her money back. I reached into my pocket and gave it to her. She grabbed the money, and as she was heading out the door, the last thing I heard her say was, "I'm never coming back to this store again!"

That night, at home, I couldn't get the incident out of my head. As I carefully analyzed it, I realized that I was in the wrong. First, I didn't listen. Second, I contradicted the customer and told her she was wrong. Third, I humiliated her and practically called her a liar by saying 300 other customers had not complained.

CHISELLED IN STONE

This incident has had a great impact on our business. I learned two important lessons that have been chiselled into a 6,000-pound rock next to the front door of our store in Norwalk, Connecticut, where our 100,000 customers can read it each week. (We call it our rock of commitment.) It states:

OUR POLICY

Rule 1—The customer is always right.
Rule 2—If the customer is ever wrong, reread rule 1.

It's chiselled in stone because it's never going to change. These rules are the main reasons why we built our business from a 1,000-square foot "mom and pop" store into a 100,000-square foot "world's largest dairy store," with annual sales now approaching $100 million.

Reprinted by permission of publisher, from *Management Review*, October 1987. © 1987 American Management
Association, New York. All rights reserved.

19
■

Now we're actually glad when customers complain. We feel they're our friends because they care enough to give us the opportunity to improve. The customers you have to worry about are not the ones who complain, but the ones who don't—because they don't come back either!

We begin to instill our spirit of customer service the moment an applicant sits down for a job interview. The main thing Jill Tavello, our director of personnel, looks for is a good attitude—above experience, skills, training, education, or appearance. If applicants have a good attitude, we can do the rest: give them extensive training, send them to business seminars, give them audiotapes and books, and set an example by our actions. But if they have a bad attitude to start with, everything we try to do seems to fail. Usually, Jill has to interview 15 to 25 applicants to find the exact person she's looking for.

Our goal is to instill a team spirit in every new applicant. With team spirit, we can instill pride, and with pride, we can instill a desire for excellence. And, of course, excellence is the very foundation of success.

CHICKEN TO GO

Tom Leonard is in charge of what will someday be our second store: a farmer's market in a circus tent in Danbury, Connecticut. He has a customer suggestion box which he often opens two or three times a day. In so doing, he's taking our customer's pulse.

At about 6:00 p.m. one evening, Tom found a note that had been written only a half an hour earlier: "I'm upset. I made a special stop on my way home from work to buy chicken breasts for dinner, but you're sold out and now I'll have to eat a TV dinner instead." As Tom was reading the note, Les Slater, our Norwalk front-end manager who lives in Danbury, stopped by on his way home to say hello. Just then, the big white Perdue chicken truck backed into the loading dock to make a delivery. Tom and Les got an idea. Five minutes later, Les was in his car taking a little detour.

You can imagine the smile on the customer's face when he answered the door at 6:20 p.m. and found Les Slater with a complimentary two-pound package of fresh Perdue chicken breasts—just in time for supper!

THINK YES

The moral of the story? Customer service cannot be a sometimes thing. It must be earned and re-earned every single day, in a hundred little ways. It's important that all employees react toward customers with empathy. That's why we use the acronym, "Think YES."

The Y in YES stands for you. We tell employees, "Pretend you are the customer. Put yourself in the customer's place."

The E stands for encourage. We encourage the customers to talk about their problems with the store's products, services, or employees. The more we listen, the better the customer will begin to feel and the more we'll learn about the cause of the complaint.

The S stands for support. Management will support its employees. We should never let a customer leave the store unhappy, because we look at each customer as a potential $50,000 asset. An average customer spends $100 a week on food shopping. That's more than $5,000 a year, and more than $50,000 over ten years. Customer service is big business when you look at the long-term picture.

Here's an example of how our "Think YES" program works. At five minutes before closing one Sunday night, a customer said to cashier Betsy Mucci, "We've just returned from vacation and are so happy you're open. Our refrigerator is empty, and we needed this bread and milk for breakfast and the kid's school lunches tomorrow." When the total of $37.12 was rung up, the customer panicked and said, "Oh my gosh, I forgot my wallet. I don't have any money!"

Betsy just smiled and said, "That's okay, just give me your name and address." Betsy wrote the information down, put a void slip in the register drawer, and said, "Don't worry, next time you're in the store you can pay for your groceries." The customer asked, "Do you have the authority to let me walk out without paying for all these groceries?" Betsy said yes, but the customer still wasn't convinced and asked to see the manager.

When the manager appeared and the customer explained the problem, he said, "When it comes to keeping our customers happy, we have no hard and fast rules. Each of us has the authority to use our own best judgement and treat every customer the way we'd like to be treated our self."

Two weeks later, I ran into a friend at a local restaurant. He came up to me all excited and said, "Stew, you won't believe this story!" He proceeded to tell me how his wife had been the customer who forgot her wallet, and how she had been telling the tale to everyone she met. "But what I don't understand," he said, "is how you can afford to do it. Aren't you afraid cashiers will use poor judgement and you'll lose money?"

I responded, "How can we afford not to do it?" Ninety-nine percent of the people in our store at any given moment are repeat customers. They're back because we satisfied them the last time they shopped with us. Our attitude is that everybody's honest. If we occasionally run into someone who isn't, we just take it on the chin. But the important point is that 999 out of 1,000 customers are honest. We simply refuse to let the one dishonest customer determine how we are going to treat the other 999.

LETTING EMPLOYEES CLIMB THE LADDER

We give the responsibility of customer satisfaction to the people on the firing line, because we are training them for future management positions. I once had the opportunity to meet the chairman of a large chain of supermarkets. I told him I admired his organization but wondered why there often were long lines at the registers in his stores. He said, "I can't afford to keep all the registers open just to eliminate lines. Some of our cashiers have been working at the registers for 15 years straight and by now are earning $20.00 an hour; we have to control our labor costs, even at the expense of customer service."

I wondered how he could keep someone on staff for 15 years without training them and promoting them to a job equal in value to their earnings. To this day I don't understand it. It seems to me that everybody involved loses. The cashiers resent being in the same job all those years, and you can be sure their resentment comes across to customers. The company loses because of inefficiency of having to pay $20.00 an hour strictly on the basis of tenure, not contribution. The customers lose because they have to wait in long lines, waste valuable time, and become frustrated.

Good leaders look for growth potential in their people. They want to be surrounded by people who want to better themselves and get ahead. When we hire employees, we should ask ourselves about each one, "How would I like to work for this person?" Then, when some day they're being paid $20.00 per hour, they'll be worth every penny.

The people who start at the bottom and work their way up to the top are the backbone of any business. They make good managers because they know what it's like to be on the firing line. A big sign hanging in our employee cafeteria reads, "If you're training someone to do your job as well or better than you, you're one of the most valuable people in our company—and one of the most likely to be promoted."

Nothing motivates employees more than the knowledge that you believe in promoting from within. Our hallways are lined with evidence of this policy. We call them our "ladders of success" photos. Mike Hughes, our director of purchasing, started out shucking corn and stocking shelves. Doug Hempstead started by unloading truckloads of watermelons. Now he has total responsibility for receiving over 100 trailer truckloads of products each week as director of our receiving department.

ATTITUDE IS THE SECRET

The longer I'm in business, the more I'm convinced that the real secret of success is our attitude toward our customer. The bottom line is that "like attracts like." If you treat the unreasonable customer the same way you treat the reasonable one, it's amazing how often you can turn a frown into a smile.

Marion Murphy works at our customer service desk. A very unreasonable customer came up to her and slammed two cases of empty soda cans on the counter and said, "Look lady, I'm not going to put these 24 cans in those automatic can-refund machines of yours one at time. I want my money back . . . now!"

Marion replied, "Sir, this is not the can return department, and we don't take cans here. But I can see that you're in a hurry, so let me give you your refund out of my pocketbook. I'll put the cans in the machine on my lunch hour and get reimbursed."

The customer's expression changed and he said, "You'd do that?" Marion answered, "It's no problem, that's my job—to create happy customers." The man blushed and said, "I can't let you do that for me. If you've got the time, I've got the time."

ARE YOUR MANAGERS READY FOR THESE BLOOD OATHS?

Tom Peters

Our five-day Skunk Camps (executive seminars) are organized around a series of so-called "blood oaths" or "promises." At the top of the list of the original seven oaths is this:

> "Develop and use hard-nosed, quantitative, systematic customer satisfaction measures (focusing on relative, perceived product quality and responsiveness); tie the measures directly to performance evaluation and compensation, preferably for all functions at all levels in the organization."

This is easier said than done. So we have developed the following list to help you make and keep such a commitment:

1. *Customer feedback must be frequent,* with no more than 30 days between surveys. Thorough image surveys and customer debriefings should be done by a third party at least once a year, and preferably twice a year.
2. *All surveys must be done relative to "best competitors" in any marketplace.* And best competitors must surely include foreign competitors. (Companies tend to focus on last year's winners, rather than the smaller firms or international firms that are knocking our socks off today.)
3. *Surveys must focus on what would ordinarily be called perception and intangibles.* This onerous task means leaving one's own expertise and preconceptions behind, in pursuit of understanding the customers' business in the customers' terms. That is, our notion of responsiveness in one part of the delivery process may not match critical factors that customers look at, given the configuration of their plants, machines, receiving departments or corporate cultures.
4. *All hands in all functions*—order entry, MIS, accounting, personnel—must be involved in the process: in forming questions, executing the survey, analyzing results and taking corrective action.

SERVICE—SECTOR SERVICE

Measuring customers' perception of quality for products can be difficult at best. If your company is the provider of an intangible service, the job might seem downright impossible. For one thing, your clients' evaluations don't just depend on the outcome of the service, but also rely on how they feel about the process of the service delivery, whether it be a haircut or a doctor's visit.

Three professors of marketing at Texas A&M University have studied and surveyed several service sectors from both the providers' and consumers' perspectives. And they have devised a list of ten traits of service that customers use to rate the quality of service they receive. These traits are reliability, responsiveness, competence, access, courtesy, communication, credibility, security, understanding/knowing the customer and tangibles (such as the physical facilities and appearance of personnel).

1. *The measures must be tied directly to compensation and evaluation* of all people at all levels. Customer satisfaction, not budgetary nor profit measures, should determine a large share of discretionary compensation and performance evaluation.
2. *Customer satisfaction should not be massaged into averages or median measures.* Rather, they always should deal with the most abused five or ten percent of the population. It is of no interest that the average customer has to make 1.3 trips to a repair facility. What's happening to the bottom ten percent? Odds are the number is 3.6 or 4.8 trips, totally unacceptable, given the power of word of mouth mentioned earlier.
3. *All people, at all levels, seniority and functions, should become "customer people."* IBM spells out a "customer connection" in every job description in the company. And this doesn't mean the internal or intermediate customer—but the ultimate end user.
4. *Customer surveys should include all customers*—distributors, retailers, suppliers, franchises—and the ultimate, end user.

Optimally, you should do all the above. Realistically, focus on at least four steps you can implement—now.

CUSTOMER-BASED RESEARCH: MOVING FROM RESEARCH TO ACTION

John A. Goodman, Arlene R. Malech, Ph.D.
and Gary F. Bargatze

Consumer affairs departments often conduct useful, innovative studies and analyses. When the data is presented to corporate decision makers, however, three basic problems often ensue: the report is not read, the report is read and ignored, or the report is read and attacked as invalid. The original course of action is ultimately endorsed and implemented. Why? In most cases, the lack of impact is not because of the data itself or because it comes from consumer affairs. It is, rather, because of the way the original data was interpreted and presented.

The following article is designed to help consumer affairs personnel collect and use data to gain maximum impact. A primary way to gaining such impact is to go beyond complaint/inquiry analysis and to conduct customer-based research. This article begins with a definition of customer-based research and outlines the types of such research typically used by the business community. It then describes the context in which customer-based research takes place and discusses its relative impact vis-a-vis that of other sources of quality/satisfaction data. Finally, it offers suggestions for improving the impact of the data.

CUSTOMER-BASED RESEARCH DEFINED AND OUTLINED

Customer-based research is, very simply, that research conducted with one or more segments of the existing customer base in order to determine the attitudes and opinions about the products and service offered by the company. It differs from the traditional view of market research in that the focus is on existing products and service. Each of the types of customer-based research outlined below is appropriate whether the customer is a business or a consumer.

■ *Customer Surveys*—Mail or telephone surveys which ask current customers a structured set of questions. The focus may be on either the entire customer base or on a particular segment of customers (e.g., those who have recently purchased, those who have recently had a service contact, or those who have purchased a particular product). This type of research is easiest when customer identity is known. However, research with purchasers of a particular product may be conducted using techniques such as national panels or random digit dialing to identify customers.

- ■ *Cancellation Surveys*—Mail or telephone surveys of customers who have recently cancelled an account. This type of research also uses a structured set of questions and is designed to determine why the customer cancelled. Cancellation surveys are possible only in environments where customer identity is known.

- ■ *Focus Groups*—A group of up to 10 customers, led by a facilitator, discusses one or more aspects of existing products and service. This type of research is less structured than either customer or cancellation surveys and is considered qualitative in nature. It is often a preliminary step to more formal customer-based research.

- ■ *Caller Interviews*—A sample of callers who meet a defined set of criteria (e.g., have purchased a particular product or experienced a particular problem) is asked a short set of structured questions about product use and/or service expectations. This is the fastest and least expensive way to obtain limited customer-based data.

- ■ *Comment Cards*—Postcards with a structured set of questions are included with the product or available in retail outlets. This type of research is susceptible to manipulation by local management. Therefore, while a good mechanism for soliciting complaints, comment cards are not effective as a basis for research.

THE CONTEXT IN WHICH CUSTOMER-BASED RESEARCH IS CONDUCTED

Customer-based research is one piece of information available to the company. It is not designed to replace the internal measures typically used (e.g., quality inspections, warranty data, service call data, etc.). Rather, it is designed to provide the company with data which is either unobtainable from internal measures or which strengthens the meaning of internal data.

Consumer affairs is a key player in providing the company with customer-based data. The complaint and inquiry data captured by consumer affairs is, of course, one necessary piece of customer-based data. Customer-based research information supplements and gives additional strength to that data. For example, while consumer affairs records the number of complaints in a particular area, customer-based research helps consumer affairs determine what that means in terms of problem incidence in the marketplace. Chart 1 outlines the types of information which can be used by consumer affairs in order to build a complete case, the types of data which can be obtained from each, and a suggested methodology for obtaining the data.

THE RELATIVE CONTRIBUTION OF CUSTOMER-BASED RESEARCH

Both internal and external (customer-based) measures can contribute to corporate knowledge about a product. However, there are instances when one or the other type of information is either more relevant or more appropriate. Chart 2 defines the relative contribution of customer-based research as compared to that of two internal measures—quality inspections and warranty/service data. The relative contribution of each type of data is defined in terms of the three causes of problems: employee-caused problems, company-caused problems and customer-caused problems.

The chart shows that internal measures are a much more valuable source of data on employee-caused problems than are external measures. Conversely, customer-based research can provide details on customer-caused problems that cannot be obtained from internal measures. Finally, while both types of data are important sources of information about product-design problems, customer-based research is essential to determining information about marketing-related problems, and internal measures are far more useful in obtaining details about production-process errors.

MAKING YOUR DATA ACTIONABLE

Consumer affairs is only one source of information for the company. Quality assurance, warranty, and service personnel, for example, also provide management with data on the current situation. Therefore, if consumer affairs is to have maximum impact from its data, it needs to coordinate the analysis of production/manufacturing data with these personnel. In this way, consumer affairs will not be at odds with other departments in the company. Further, consumer affairs should emphasize the analysis of customer-caused, design and marketing-caused problems, since customer-based research data is of better quality than other data available in identifying these problems. In addition, the following are also aids to ensuring that data from consumer affairs gets the necessary attention from corporate management:

■ Report only those things that require management's attention.

Don't include issues which don't require action. Report the information in a straightforward and easy-to-read format. Large tables are typically ignored by the reader.

■ Suggest the incidence in the marketplace which is implied by the number of cases reported by the analysis. Suggest the cause of the problem-qualified as a "best guess"—and invite alternative analysis by the reader. Suggest a solution to the problem and estimate the market damage/cost of not correcting the problem (e.g., during each quarter, 1,000 customers will be lost unless this problem is corrected).

■ Involve the market research department in any customer-based studies which are done (at least in an informal advisory capacity). In this way, market research will be an ally when the data is presented and will not attack the research as either not credible or invalid.

■ Educate management about the source of the data and the underlying concepts of the customer's long-term value, the impact of problem experience on customer loyalty, and customer-complaint behavior.

■ Consider yourself in the role of an internal consultant to the remainder of the company. Give department management an opportunity to correct a problem before senior management is told, unless the problem is extremely serious and/or potentially life threatening.

CONCLUSION
By adopting some of the research techniques outlined in this article and integrating their findings into the analysis of complaint/inquiry data, consumer affairs can improve the impact and action-ability of their data.

■

Listen And Respond
To The Customer

Chart 1
Customer Research

Information Source	Type of Data Obtained	Suggested Methodology+	Suggested Use
Customer Surveys*			
Baseline Customer	Identifies levels of satisfaction within customer base and provides estimates of overall level of complaint behavior	Mail/phone survey to at least 1,500 customers	Once at beginning of service improvement program
Baseline Service Contact	Identifies levels of satisfaction with most recent service contact and identifies market impact of service system	Mail survey to 500 customers who *recently* requested assistance (i.e., ideally, within the past 3 months)	Ongoing
Expectations	Identifies relative importance of different dimensions of product/service delivery acceptable to the customer	Mail survey to 1,000-1,500 customers	Once at beginning of service improvement program
Cancellation Survey	Identifies those factors which drive customers to the competition	Mail/phone survey to 500-750 customers who *recently* cancelled (i.e., Ideally, within the past 3 months)	Every 2 years
Focus Group	Identifies complaint behavior and areas of customer confusion arising from lack of customer education	3 groups of 10 customers	Every 2 years
Caller Interview	Identifies customer problems and their root causes(s)	Phone interview of 150 users who have experienced problems	Ongoing
Employee Survey	Identifies key system and customer-caused problems	Survey of employees in sales, production quality, and service (50 each)	Annually
Complaint and Inquiry Data Analysis	Identifies emerging problems before they appear in surveys or in warranty/service data	Using detailed codes, identify clusters of problems and then extrapolate to the marketplace based on baseline customer survey	Ongoing

+ Sample size projections are based on ensuring sufficient number of response to enable detailed data analysis.

* Many people also include exit interviews and comment cards in this category. Exit interviews are simply a different methodology. Comment cards are ineffective for research.

■

Listen And Respond
To The Customer

Chart 2
Relative Contribution of Customer-Based Research
and Internal Measures of Quality in
Defining the Cause of Customers Problems

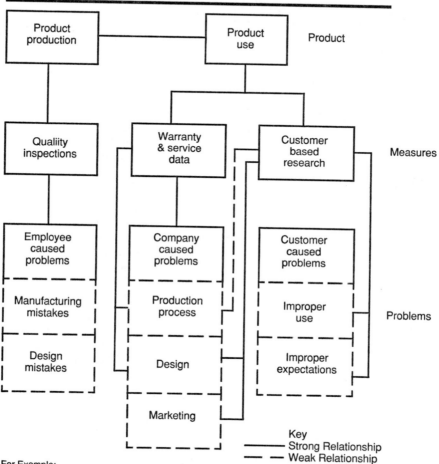

For Example:

In an electronic product environment (e.g. VCRs), the company may receive the following data concerning problems:

Internal measures will include 1) quality inspection information on manufacturing defects such as employee assembly errors, 2) warranty and service data identifying design problems (e.g. if an interlock is lacking, the VCR can erase tapes while rewinding them), and 3) warranty and service data indentifying customer difficulty in using the product (e.g. nothing wrong is found in a product submitted for repair).

External measures (Customer-based research) will include 1) complaint and inquiry data indentifying confusion with hookup directions and 2) satisfaction tracking data (customer surveys) highlighting general problems with use, service and product performance as well as the market damage resulting from these problems.

MANAGING CUSTOMERS AS HUMAN RESOURCES IN SERVICE ORGANIZATIONS

David E. Bowen

On-site service encounters blur the organizational boundary between employees and customers. The strategic tradeoffs involved in having customers on-site, and the HRM practices that can influence the satisfaction and performance of customers within the organization, are described. Central points include the HRM practices that foster a climate for service and that provide customers the role clarity, ability and motivation they require to contribute to service production and delivery.

> *"No existing management theory helps much in explaining the role of the customer in the prototypical excellent company."*
>
> **Peters and Waterman**
> **In Search of Excellence**

> *"Using industrial models to manage service-based corporations makes as little sense as using farm models to run factories."*
>
> **Stanley Davis**
> **New Management**

Two relatively ignored actors in management thought are customers and service organizations. Peters and Waterman (1982) correctly point out that management theory has not developed the vital role customers play in the organizational dynamics of companies. Davis' (1983) comment follows his observation that most of what is known about how companies operate has evolved from the study of manufacturing organizations. He added his voice to others, who argue that management principles derived from studying manufacturing organizations may not provide managers the tools needed for being effective in service organizations, given how products and services differ (Czepiel et al., 1985). A central difference between service and manufacturing firms is that customers are often physically present as the service is offered, quite unlike manufacturing firms where customers are only rarely present during production. When this occurs, both customers and employees constitute the human resources of the service organization. Consequently, service organizations face the unique human re-source challenge of what management practices can lead to customers being satisfied and productive during the time they spend within the company.

This article describes how service managers can effectively manage customers as human resources within their organizations. After expanding further on the observation that customers and service businesses have been largely overlooked in the management literature, we will examine three central human resources management issues surrounding the on-site customer. The first issue concerns the strategic tradeoffs involved in even having customers on-site as opposed to having them off-site. The second issue involves the development of strategies for ensuring the customers' satisfaction with their organizational surroundings. Strategies are offered for managing the firms's climate for service, i.e., shaping the cues in the organizational setting that customers use to evaluate service quality. A central focus is what employee human resource practices are associated with customer satisfaction. Third, we consider strategies for managing the behavior of customers in helping to create the service they receive. For example, how can fast-food restaurants get customers to bus their own tables? How can retail banks get customers to fill out the right deposit slips before approaching the teller window or to operate the ATM correctly? We suggest that answers to how to manage the behavior of on-site customers can be found in models used to manage employee behavior. That is, "lessons learned" about employee selection, motivation, and training can be applied to influencing customer behavior as well.

CUSTOMERS AND SERVICE BUSINESSES: MISSING LINKS IN THE CHAIN OF MANAGEMENT THOUGHT

Management theory typically refers to customers as passive consumers of goods and services, interfacing with the company in fleeting, faceless exchanges. When the customer is described as more proactive, it is in unflattering terms. Customers have been portrayed as disrupting organizational routines and failing to comply with procedures; as constraining potential operating efficiency when they become involved in service operations; and as being an interest group with whom employees identify at the expense of corporate goals (Aldrich and Herker, 1977; Chase, 1978; Danet, 1981). Consequently, the literature prescribes organizational designs that seal the company's operations off from the customer. J.D. Thompson (1967) offered the now classical concept of buffering a company's core technology from environmental disturbances, e.g., customers. Against this backdrop, it is not surprising that Peters and Waterman did not find an elaboration of the customer's role in management thought or textbooks.

Service businesses have been ignored as theorists and practitioners have focused on developing strategies for managing manufacturing firms. Furthermore, it has been assumed that the principles of organization developed from studying manufacturing firms apply to all organizations. This assumption can be attributed, in part, to the tendency in comparative management to focus on similarities of organizational phenomena rather than on differences, and to assume that organizations are essentially "brothers under the skin" (Lammers and Hickson, 1979). However, differences in organizational dynamics that may exist between manufacturing and service organizations have received recent attention to both the management and marketing literatures. In the management literature, the emphasis has been on the implications of structuring organizations for the delivery of the prototypical service which differs from the prototypical good by being less tangible, requiring greater participation from customers in the production of what they receive, and involving less delay between output production and customer consumption. In the marketing literature, the concern has been with how these characteristics of services may require different marketing strategies than those used with goods.

In what follows, we do not view manufacturing and service organizations as brothers under the same skin-due largely to differences in the roles played by customers in each of them. These differences are neatly summarized by two metaphors in Daniel Bell's (1973) book, *The Coming of Post-Industrial Society*. Bell described the nature of work in industrial society as a "game against fabricated nature" in which man and machine turn out goods. Customers are typically only distant spectators in this game. In contrast, he labeled work in a service-based society as a "game between persons"— between bureaucrat and client, teacher and student, hairdresser and patron, and so on. Consequently, service businesses entail a potential for more frequent and intense on-site interaction between employees and customers than exists in the production of goods. Whereas Peters and Waterman urge companies explore ways of getting "close to the customer," service firms must find ways to effectively manage the closeness to the customer that exists when customers are stepping through their doorstep.

HRM AND ON-SITE CUSTOMERS
IN SERVICE ORGANIZATIONS
Three key issues relative to customer presence confront managers in service firms. First, there is the issue of whether or not it is desirable to even have the customer physically present. Face-to-face exchanges be-

tween service employees and customers typify many services, which have no middle men between production and consumption. Nevertheless, services can also be produced for, and delivered to, physically off-site customers as well. Retail stores that use mail order catalogues are one example; schools and universities that offer correspondence degrees are another. These same services could have been offered to customers on-site, so the question is: How do service managers make the strategic choice between off-site vs. on-site customer services?

Second, when customers are present, service firms must manage all the attributes of the organizational setting because much of what is visible to employees is visible to customers as well. Customers are there within the physical bounds of the business and their on-site perceptions will influence their satisfaction with the service and their intention to keep using that service or seek other alternatives.

Third, on-site service customers often are expected to do things to help create the service they receive. In other words, the purchase of many services involves both consumption and production on the part of the customer. As examples, consulting firms often expect their clients to help design and deliver training programs; supermarkets have customers fill their own carts. Service firm managers must decide what behaviors they expect of customers and how to get customers to perform those desired behaviors. In these cases, service firm managers must manage not only employee behavior, but customer behavior as well.

THE CUSTOMER AS HUMAN RESOURCE:
ESTABLISHING THE ORGANIZATIONAL BOUNDARY

Criteria favoring on-site production and delivery strategies have been suggested by Chase et al. (1984). Customer presence is desirable when:

1. Service production and delivery are absolutely inseparable. This is a nearly inescapable imperative for customer presence. A barber is an example where it is impossible to produce or deliver the service without the customer's presence. Also, there are services in which customer presence could possibly be avoided, but such a strategy would likely compromise service quality. Psychological counseling, for example, could be conducted by telephone or letter, but probably not as successfully as face-to-face.

2. Marketing benefits are afforded by on-site contact with the customer. Here customer contact is not required, but is desirable in that customer contact provides the service organization an opportunity to sell additional services. Mail-order retailing rules out the "add-on sales" possible when the customer comes to the store.

Given the marketing advantages of having the customer present, why would service businesses choose, nevertheless, to keep the customer off-site? There is a delicate balancing act involved here, as Chase points out, that goes like this: Direct customer contact is negatively correlated with production efficiency and positively correlated with marketing effectiveness. Service management must consider which of the two objectives it wants to pursue with its off-site vs. on-site choice.

We would add a third criterion to these two:

3. It is desirable to have customers physically present when they can supplement, or substitute for, the labor and information provided by employees. The strategy of having customers on-site, participating in service production and delivery, can be a means of enhancing productivity not available to most manufacturing organizations. In this spirit, Lovelock and Young (1979) encourage service managers "to look to customers to increase productivity." They suggest that companies typically have three means available for increasing productivity: (1) improve the quality of employees, (2) invest in more efficient capital equipment, and (3) automate tasks previously undertaken by labor. A fourth is available in service organizations—having customers perform certain service operation tasks. Gartner and Reissman (1974) term this strategy increasing the "customer intensiveness" of service operations. When this occurs, customers do not diminish service system efficiency, they enhance it.

CUSTOMER SATISFACTION:
HRM PRACTICES AND THE CLIMATE FOR SERVICE

Once customers arrive in the service facility, their on-site attitudes and behaviors are added to employee's as ingredients affecting organizational effectiveness. In order for customers to positively experience their organizational surroundings, service firms need to manage the climate for service.

Climate for service refers to the summary perceptions that customers have of the service-related attributes and practices of the business. This can include everything from how customer-contact employees behave, the cleanliness of the facility, and the materials customers use. We can suggest four strategies for creating a favorable climate for service:

1. Service businesses must be careful to manage all the "evidence" visible to the customer. The customer's definition of what's "real" about a service is arrived at by deductions drawn from two kinds of service evidence. First there is "peripheral" evidence that the service customer can possess, such as an airline ticket. Secondly, there is "essential" evidence that the customer cannot possess (Shostack, 1977). Examples include office appearance, employees' dress, and manner of speaking. In similar terms, Sasser et al. (1978) have differentiated the characteristics of a service environment into the service concept (i.e., the good that accompanies the service) and the service delivery system (i.e., the image of the facilities, the attitudes of employees, and so on). All this evidence must be carefully designed as the service itself because customers rely on this evidence for clues in forming their own personal mental "reality" of what the service is.

The way this evidence shapes customers' service perceptions was explored in a study of branch banks by Schneider and Bowen (1985). They found that how service was delivered on climate dimensions including courtesy/competency, "tellers care about customers as people in my branch"; adequate staff, "my branch seems to have enough employees to handle its customers"; and employee morale, "employees complain about the branch," was strongly related to customer evaluations of the service they received and their intentions to continue using the service. The results also revealed considerable agreement between employee descriptions of what happens in their branch with respect to customer service and what customers say about the service they receive. First, the correlation between employee and customer views of service quality was substantial (r = .63, p (.01). Second, there were numerous strong relationships between the way employees described the climate for service and both the customers' views of various dimensions of climate and their views of overall service quality.

The agreement between employee and customer service views indicates that on-site service encounters bring employees close to the customer both physically and psychologically. Employees appear to listen to, and sympathize with, customers. There is an important lesson here for managers to service firms: Front-line employees can be valuable sources of information about customer preferences when decisions are being made about what new services to offer and how to deliver them.

2. A second strategy for management to pursue in creating a favorable climate for service is to treat its customer contact personnel not only as employees, but as "partial customers", individuals deserving the same courteous treatment that management wants the organization's customers to receive. This translates into management developing and applying a set of human resource management practices, from selection to training to career counseling, that support front-line service providers. In the same sense, Berry (1981), past president of American Marketing Association, has suggested that service management view their front-line employees as "internal customers", using survey research and market segmentation strategies, internally, to offer customerized jobs, flexible work hours, and cafeteria benefits that satisfy the needs of employees who, in turn, are responsible for satisfying the needs of external customers.

A strategy of treating employees as partial customers is supported by research indicating that when service employees feel that management is meeting their needs they, in turn, feel free to concentrate on meeting the needs of customers. In the Schneider and Bowen (1985) study, employees were asked to assess the bank's human resource practices and customers were asked to evaluate the quality of service they receive in the branch. When employees reported positively about how well they were trained, supervised, and so on, customers also had favorable views of the quality of service they received. In other words, what employees experience on their jobs as front-line service employees seems to affect the quality of the on-site experience for customers. Specifically, management's human resource practices can favorably influence the on-site experience of both employees and customers.

3. In order for a favorable climate for service to be present, customer contact personnel should possess the interpersonal skills needed to be effective players in the "Game Between Persons". Unfortunately, service organizations often prepare employees to only play a "Game Against Fabricated Nature." Service businesses focus their training on technical skills, e.g., how to run the cash register, fill out guest reports, etc., and often fail to train employees in customer service techniques. Unfortunately, most validated selections tests tap cognitive and motor aptitudes, to the relative exclusion of interpersonal skills. Also, training programs for interpersonal skill development have been used primarily with managers, not first-line employees. Overall, many personnel practices are still geared to the needs of manufacturing firms, where it is less important for first-line employees to possess interpersonal skills to perform their production tasks well.

4. Finally, the more intangible the service provided, the more attention service managers need to pay to the preceding three strategies (managing all the evidence, treating employees as partial customers, equipping service providers with interpersonal skills). The more intangible the service provided, the more customers will rely upon contextual cues surrounding service delivery in evaluating the quality of service they receive. Intangibility increases as services become more complex and less associated with a facilitating good. Thus, banking and insurance are services that are more intangible than dry cleaning and retailing. When a product is not present to influence customer satisfaction with the service, service firms must increasingly rely on managing tangibles such as characteristics of setting, and contact personnel to create a positive image of their intangible offering.

A summary word on managing climate for service is that the different strategies respond to the same core service organization reality: In service settings where the customer is present, human resource management practices relate to both employee and customer satisfaction more strongly than in work settings where the two parties are separate, e.g., durable goods factories. On-site encounters blur the organizational boundary between employees and customers. Consequently, employee and customer perceptions and behaviors are shaped by the same set of organizational practices and they become strongly intertwined with one another.

CUSTOMER PERFORMANCE: SHAPING
CUSTOMER ROLE CLARITY, ABILITY, AND MOTIVATION

On-site customers are not just attentive spectators in the Game Between Persons; they are often active players as well, supplying labor and knowledge to the service creation process.

This has led to the suggestion that customers be viewed as "partial employees" of the service organization (Mills, 1983). Customers act as "partial employees" at numerous points during service creation. At the front-end, customers need to plan for their encounters with service employees. Clients of tax accountants are encouraged to bring their records; retail customers are expected to bring their receipts with them when they return unwanted merchandise. During the actual service encounter, customers may need to make decisions about alternative service items. Finally, customers may still be performing for the organizations even after service delivery. For example, postoperative exercises may be required of the hospital patient.

Services will vary considerably in whether customers or employees are the principal performers. In some services, the customer as "partial employee" acts only as a "co-producer" with employees, having responsibility ranging from banks where employees provide most of the labor for customers who essentially need only arrive at the window, to supermarkets where customers provide most of the labor while employees handle only checkout. In other services, the customer as "partial employee" becomes the sole producer. Examples here include automated teller machines and laundromats.

These examples illustrate that service management is free within techno-logical constraints to assign various "partial employee" roles to customers. An important strategic issue for service managers is determining the optimal size role for customers to play in their operations. This involves weighing the productivity increases possible with an expanded customer role vs. the productivity increases possible with other alternatives, e.g., increased automation. However, service managers may be reluctant to formulate a customer intensive service production strategy, given uncer-tainty as to how to implement a strategy of using customers as partial employees, i.e., they are unclear about how to insure that customers will perform their roles as the firm desires.

We suggest that strategies for managing customer behavior in service production and delivery can be drawn from models of employee behavior. A general model of the determinants of employee behavior attributes their behavior to three ingredients: role clarity, ability, and motivation (e.g. Vroom 1964). In other words, employees behave the way they do based largely on three considerations:

1. Do they understand how they are expected to perform?
2. Are they able to perform as expected?
3. Are there valued rewards for performing as expected?

Customer behavior can be viewed as being shaped by these same three ingredients. Therefore, the key to managing customer performance in-volves developing HRM practices that influence customers to answer "yes" to these three questions for any "partial employee" behaviors expected of them.

Do customers understand how they are expected to perform? An initial role expectation of the on-site service customer is to "go to the right spot or person." In other words, the customer must have the proper "orientation" to the setting. Researchers in environmental psychology argue that orien-tation is a compelling behavioral need of individuals upon entering a setting (Wener, 1985). Any customer who has stood in the wrong line at the Post Office, Department of Motor Vehicles, checkout lines at a retail store, etc., can appreciate how disorientation, together with time constraints, is annoying and stressful. Disorientation can also result in employees spend-ing more time answering directional questions for customers than actually providing the service.

On-site customers require two kinds of orientation. "Place Orientation" answers their questions of "where am I" or "how do I get from here to there." "Function orientation" deals with the question of "how does this organization work." Customers turn to several sources for answering these questions. One source is the experiences they bring to the setting. Repeat customers and customers of comparable services require less orientation than first time users of any unknown service. Another service is the inherent legibility of the system. Is the service facility design, itself, comprehensive or maze-like? Thirdly, customers turn to "orientation aids" provided by the service firm. Airports can hire guides to direct passengers to proper terminals and gates; banks can use floor managers to direct customers to the proper windows and officers. Orientation can also take the form of rules governing customer behavior: for safety (airlines), dress (restaurants), noise levels (hotels).

Service organizations face the challenge, then, of providing orientation for not only their employees, but their on-site customers as well. Some do this superbly. McDonalds, with their highly visible multiple trash cans and tray racks ensures that customers quickly "learn the ropes" about bussing their own tables after eating; numerous orthodontic offices show prospective patients videos describing what it is like to have braces put on—providing the patient a "realistic service preview" of their role in service production and delivery; managers of self-service operations, e.g., gasoline stations, have learned that more explicit instructions regarding what is expected of customers (e.g., whether or not to pay first, which handles and dials work the pump) lead to more customers using their service and using it correctly. These are all examples of helping the customer to be in the right place, at the right time doing all the right things.

Are customers able to perform as expected? Firms can guarantee that customers have the abilities necessary to perform their roles by using the same approaches that work with employees. Recruitment, selection, and training can be used to acquire on-site customers who are able to perform as expected.

A study of self-service alternatives demonstrates how service organizations can identify customers who are willing and able to perform as partial employees (Langeard et al., 1981). In the study, customers completed surveys that presented alternative "service scenarios" at a bank, gasoline service station, hotel, airport, restaurant, and travelers' checks outlet. For each, service customers were presented a choice between a less partici-pative (full-service) and more participative (self-service) alternative. For example, the bank scenario posed the following question:

It is 10 a.m. and you wish to withdraw $50 from your checking account. You have a card which would enable you to use an automatic teller machine or you could go to a human teller with your checkbook. So your choices are:

Either use the automatic teller machine or use the human teller.

There are equally short lines of people waiting to use the machine and at the teller window.

Customers who were generally participative in all scenarios were more likely to be younger, male, and more educated; to be impatient and to dislike waiting in line; and to like to play with machines more than those in the nonparticipative segment. Firms pursuing customer intensive production strategies might focus their advertising on recruiting and selecting this participative market segment. Relatedly, many professional service organizations, e.g., universities, only select students/customers who have demonstrated their ability to perform effectively via standardized test scores and prior work experience. However, certain classes of potential customers, e.g., the poor, minority groups, may not possess the abilities necessary for performing a production role. In these cases, service managers need choose between excluding these customers, on efficiency grounds, or including them for social responsibility reasons and then providing them the necessary training.

In addition to trying to select the "right type" of performing customer, customers can be trained to perform as expected. For example, when self-service alternatives are introduced, service employees may need to demonstrate the equipment and answer questions, particularly when there is potential customer resistance to change. Resistance may stem from customers having learned over the years how to behave as a consumer in the service encounter, but not as a producer. Consumer behavior research on how customers acquire their perceptions of their consumption and production roles may benefit service managers trying to develop able partial employees.

Are there valued rewards for customers performing as expected? Models of employee motivation offer two keys for how managers can energize their employees. One key is to base rewards upon performance and to make the connection between them visible. The second key is to offer rewards that employees value.

Customers, too, can be motivated to perform by providing them visible performance-contingent rewards. When customers participate in service creation they acquire benefits such as increased control over the terms of service delivery, time savings, and monetary savings. However, customers may not realize these benefits are possible unless service management makes their existence visible through marketing. In other words, service managers need to clarify the performance-contingent rewards for their customers, as they do for their employees.

Deciding what rewards customers will value should take into account that customers, like employees, satisfy diverse needs via their organizational presence. Customers are not driven exclusively by economic needs; for example, they may value interacting with service employees or even the sheer enjoyment of the service experience. Also, service managers too often have a theory X view of customers as being sneaky, troublesome, and motivated exclusively by narrow self-interests. A more theory Y view of customers would see them as trustworthy collaborators in the service creation process who can creatively fashion their own service roles and be internally motivated to perform them well.

We have claimed that strategies for managing customer performance can draw on the same management techniques appropriate for employees. As a closing thought on this notion, we recommend that service managers conduct performance appraisals of how customers are doing as partial employees. Regularly monitor if customer use of self-service alternatives is increasing or decreasing; if customers are performing ably as co-producers. For example, do Department of Motor Vehicle customers use self-service options for "change of address"? Do they bring the proper records to the counter clerks? If they do not, they may lack role clarity, the first performance ingredient; ability, the second; or motivation, the third. Diagnosing which ingredient is responsible can indicate which prescriptions (better orientation, recruitment, selection, training, or rewards) are most likely to remedy poor customer performance.

SERVICE ORGANIZATIONS, CUSTOMERS, AND HRM: SOME FUTURE DIRECTIONS

This paper has dealt with two relatively unknown actors in the management literature, service organizations and customers, and HRM issues involved in their interaction. We have looked at only some of the issues involved in managing customers as human resources. There is a real need to continue developing models and techniques that service managers can apply to the unique HRM concerns in this area, including:

Do employees and customers prefer face-to-face or face-to-machine service production and delivery strategies? That is, do they prefer a "game between persons" or a "game against fabricated nature?" For employees, the opportunities for customer contact may be one of the primary attractions of a service job. However, customer contact also involves stressful "emotional labor", where employees must express pretended feelings of warmth for difficult customers rather than showing their true feelings (Hochschild, 1983). From the customer's viewpoint, Naisbitt (1982), in *Megatrends*, suggested that high-tech customers also need high touch, i.e., an interpersonal dimension, to be satisfied. How can service operations be designed to accommodate these varied preferences?

What do service operations lose when involving customers as producers? Might highly participative customers reject the idea of doing the work and paying for it, too, or elect to create the service at home? Might they contest management for control of the service creation process?

What other roles might customers play in the service organization in addition to their roles as consumers and producers? One possibility is to use feedback from on-site customers in appraising the performance of front-line service personnel.

We believe that both the consumption and production demands of our economy are well-served through understanding of the issues we have raised. We acquire more satisfied consumers as HRM practices for managing the climate for service are implemented more effectively. We respond to the lagging productivity of the service sector as we develop HRM practices for utilizing the information and labor supplied by customers. These are some of the gains possible from managing customers as human resources in service organizations.

Define A
Service Strategy

"Developing a competitive strategy is developing a broad formula for how a business is going to compete, what its goals should be, and what policies will be needed to carry out those goals."

Michael Porter
Competitive Strategy:
Techniques for Analyzing
Industries and Companies

We looked for a suitable analogy to capture and convey the essence of service strategy. Unable to choose between two possibilities, we opted for both.

The first: If the act of serving a customer is compared to the act of photographing a scene, the service strategy can be seen as serving the same purpose as the lens of a camera—to clarify and focus, to balance the close up and the far away. A service strategy is a means to make clear, to put things in perspective; it is a device for giving meaning to, and testing the value and importance of, day-to-day tasks.

The second metaphor is that of herding cattle. As any rancher or farmer knows, when driving a herd of cows from one pasture to another, it is important to keep a close watch on the feisty cows immediately in front, the ones most likely to double back from the herd. But if the herder devotes all his attention to the behavior of the cows immediately in front of him, he risks completely missing the distant gate.

A service strategy provides a view of the

"distant gate." It reminds everyone in the "drive" where the "cattle" are headed and why and how we are going to get them there. In addition to communicating and focusing our attention on where we are going and why, the well-designed service strategy is aimed at differentiation, at telling everyone in the organization what makes that organization unique in the eyes of the customer. A service strategy is a distinctive formula for delivering service; such a strategy is keyed to a well-chosen benefit premise that is valuable to the customer and that establishes an effective competitive position. It is the vision of what the organization is trying to become in the eyes of both internal and external customers. It provides managers and workers with a common focus: to maximize the quality of the customer's experience.

A service strategy is a nontrivial statement of intent, a promise made to yourself on behalf of the customer. Done effectively, the service strategy makes you unique in the eyes of your customer. What you promise or intend must be valued by the customer, and it also must be credible to your service people, those folks who will align their efforts with the strategy.

Finally, the service strategy must be deliverable. The service strategy is not public relations pap or ad copy or catchy lines dreamed up by corporate headquarters. It is a serious commitment backed by synchronized action and congruent tactics. It is the perpetual battle cry that is sounded year after year, not the "project of the month" or "theme of the year." Clever lip service won't create consistent customer service.

"*Unique* and *valued* in the eyes of the customer" is an important asset of an effective service strategy. The bank promising the "greenest money," the hospital promising the "cleanest operating rooms," or the insurance company touting the "most peace of mind" would probably elicit customer—and employee—yawns. A superior service strategy helps set the organization apart in a believable way. The selection of such a strategy, therefore, is best achieved, first, by understanding the target market and, second, by examining the organization's strengths, weaknesses, opportunities, history, and values.

We have included three articles we think evoke the essence of what a service strategy is all about. We chose the first article "Focusing on Distinctive Customer Serivce," (portions of which were adapted from Ron Zemke's *The Service Edge: 101 Companies That Profit from Customer Care*) to communicate the philosophy of a service strategy—the rationale for having one and the dimensions that will make it effective.

The December 3, 1987, issue of the *Wall Street Journal* carried an unusual piece on cab drivers in Japan. Written by then *WSJ* staff reporter Karl Schoenberger, it describes how a serious statement of service intent plays out in the daily actions of Japan's top hacks. The MK Taxi company couples an institutionalized service philosophy with sound employee relations. Cabbies are treated like jet pilots!

Finally, we picked an article by Ron Zemke and Karl Albrecht titled "Instilling a Service Mentality: Like Teaching an Elephant to Dance." It is adapted from their book *Service America!* and appeared in the November 1985 issue of the British journal, *International Management.* The article makes the point that service excellence—that which brings customers back, with their friends—depends upon a demonstrated commitment from the top of the organization on down. A visible management that talks service routinely can turn a theme into a service-minded culture and a campaign into a way of life that translates into a powerful competitive weapon.

To follow our three "essence" articles, we chose a counterpoint article by Benson P. Shapiro "What the Hell Is 'Market Oriented'?" from the November-December 1988 issue of *Harvard Business Review.* Shapiro contends there is a lot more to being market-oriented than accepting the clichés about getting close to the customer. In his view, market oriented is not a state of being; it is a set of "processes that touch all aspects of an organization." He makes a strong point that, in service-oriented, market-driven organizations, managers *must* stick their noses in each other's business. Every group that has an interest in the way a product or service will look and act should have a say in the process of bringing it to the marketplace. His views run completely counter to the way most companies are organized and managed.

FOCUSING ON DISTINCTIVE CUSTOMER SERVICE

Ron Zemke and Chip R. Bell

We are in the middle of a vision quest. Everywhere corporate leaders turn, they are reminded of the crucial importance of vision, of being clear on corporate purpose or in alignment with mission. Is this just the latest fashion on mahogany row, or is there merit in worrying over a common, corporate focus? Though the title reveals our bias, we are cautious about asking that inordinate energy be devoted to wordsmithing followed by a paltry effort at blacksmithing.

The concept of a service focus is more about synchronized sinews than sounds. It is far easier to craft a beautifully worded, drum-roll statement of purpose than to live in sync with it. The challenge is not in finding better ways to say the words but, rather, more authentic ways to live the words, to "walk the talk."

But perhaps it *starts* with words, the tools for transmitting our meaning. We use language to clarify the pictures we hold in our heads. Wise consultants believe that the *process* of crafting vision is equal in importance to, if not far more important than, the statement that ends up on the page. For it is the struggle to communicate service mission, the messy meshing of individual dreams into a consensual focus, that links team members in congruent toil. Such struggle is hard won through experience and thinking. It is not something you "get" from lying on a conference-room floor chanting a mantra.

At its most basic core, focus is an agreed-upon, clear-eyed view and understanding of what is and is not important to creating a desired end. If you've ever gone to a library in search of a specific journal article or technical book and ended up sidetracked by a bound volume of 20-year-old *Life* magazines, you know the price of wavering focus.

A service focus serves in two ways: alignment and grounding. Focus is the means by which individual work is kept in sync with the work of others. Alignment means laser-point direction of energy rather than scattered effort, the basis for work performed in a deliberate, efficient, precise, and intentional manner. Focus is also a boon to grounding—as in having one's feet on the ground and knowing what one is about.

Focus is not just a synonym for vision, mission, and strategy; it also is often substituted for the word *purpose*. The oft-quoted "working on purpose" is an attempt to cleverly capture the double meaning of focus—(on PUR-POSE), i.e., aligned or precise and (ON purpose), i.e., grounded or relevant. In a sentence: Focus lends meaning to an enterprise.

What does a clear service focus *do* for you and *how* is it crafted and communicated? An organization can elect any focus. Ford Motor elected quality (" . . . is job one"), and the Marine Corps chose elitism (" . . . a few good men"). Or so, at least, it seems from their ads. A service focus (or service strategy, mission, or vision), however, is not about ad copy; it is about that which employees worry, talk, and get excited. A service focus is not a slogan, though slogans can call attention to the focus. It is the definition, the "image," of good service you want everyone to have in mind every time they face—or think about—the customer.

There are some intriguing litmus tests for a service focus. Ask the janitor leaning on the broom what is most important to the company. Janitors usually know! Or reflect on the last several meetings and try to recall the overriding theme—the subjects capturing air time. Or examine what type of error or mistake is likely to produce the most rapid ire or "wind sucking." Or notice the subject of most reports circulated and dissected. What gets delighted comments or disdainful cusses? The net of all the answers to these questions can be useful indicators of whether your organization has a service focus and what it might be.

A solid service focus is not—or, at least, need not be—complex, academic, vague, or esoteric. The example below is the Country Kitchen service focus.

"We make a very simple promise to all our guests . . . that our Country Kitchen is a warm, friendly place where you'll always feel welcome . . . just like in your mom's kitchen. Come in any time of the day for meals cooked the way you like them . . . made from only the finest ingredients . . . and always served with a smile. Good food . . . satisfying helpings . . . and fair prices. Thanks for coming in to our Kitchen."

Such a clear service pledge leaves little doubt about what the organization is trying to deliver or how management wants the organization to be perceived by the customer. After reading it, you would hardly expect a

Country Kitchen restaurant to look, smell, or feel like a McDonald's or Chez Panisse.

A good service focus reflects the values of your organization. During a discussion we were leading on what a service focus or strategy should and should not do and say, an executive of the Dayton Hudson Department Store Company cut through the techniqueeze with blinding brilliance. "In other words," he offered patiently, "a service strategy is the 'bear any burden, pay any price promise' we make to *ourselves* on behalf of our customers, isn't it?" Though he took a considerable amount of wind out of our overblown, overlong lecture, he touched the essence of a service focus. It is a statement of what you intend to do—*must* do, really—for the customer if you are to be successful in the business—whatever form the business may take—of distinguishing yourself through service quality.

A service focus isn't necessarily a single, brilliant blanket statement covering all actions and applying to all people in the organization. In many organizations, trying to wrap a blanket service focus around multiple businesses and diverse products is foolish and winds up in the publication of an embarrassing banality like "Service is our number one mission." At worst, such watered-down, all-encompassing efforts to fit all forums fails to pass the snicker test with the troops; at best, they fail to aid in directing effort or inspiring excellence.

Deluxe Corporation in St. Paul prints checks for banks, brokerage firms, and savings and loan institutions nationwide. Careful study of their customers' needs and expectations revealed the need for these organizations to provide blinding speed and efficiency to their customers. It became clear that, when financial-services customers opened a new checking account, they did not want to wait an inordinate amount of time to receive their checks.

Deluxe crafted a service focus that promised error-free financial instruments in a timely manner. "Error-free" translated to absolutely zero defects; "timely" meant a 48-hour turnaround. Armed with such clarity and convinced of its tantamount importance, Deluxe employees from printer to president could, if required, go to extraordinary means to uphold the two-pronged promise.

Some organizations develop a service focus or strategy that gets wired into their ads. Eddie Bauer is a major mail-order catalog and chain of retail stores similar to the popular L.L. Bean Company. Eddie Bauer professes, "Our creed is to give you such outstanding quality, value, service, and guarantee that we may be worthy of your high esteem. We guarantee every item we sell will give you complete satisfaction, or you may return it for a full refund."

Precision LensCrafters, a fast-growing Cincinnati-based chain of optical-supplies stores, couples a promise on behalf of their customers with one made to employees. "PLC exists to develop enthusiastically satisfied customers all the time and to provide associates with a working environment which supports and encourages the development and achievement of their personal goals." LensCrafters follows its service focus with a set of ten "commands" ranging from "Demand highest possible quality" to "Accept mistakes" to "Have fun!"

ANATOMY OF A SERVICE FOCUS
We would gladly give you a definitive formula for creating a service focus, if such a thing existed. But it does not. There is, however, guidance available. It is our observation that an effective service focus has four characteristics. Specifically, an effective service strategy is:

- A nontrivial statement of intent
- that noticeably differentiates you from others,
- has value in your customers' eyes,
- and is deliverable by the organization.

The service focus functions first and foremost as an internal focus of effort. It is based on your understanding of a combination of organizational values, customer expectations of your products and services, customer expectations of the process of doing business with you, and your analysis of the strengths and weaknesses of your organization and the opportunities and threats in your current marketplace. That whole swirl of information and ideas must be distilled to a form that can be understood by employee and customer alike.

Let us examine an example of these elements played out in real, concrete terms. In Charlotte, North Carolina, First Union Corporation, the second largest bank in the South, decided several years ago to make superior service a key focus. According to CEO Ed Crutchfield, " . . . we could not expect much excitement from the customer by promising that our bank would have the greenest money, the lowest price, most convenient branches, or least hassle."

The bank's specific service focus evolved from mounds of research on what the customer wanted and expected in a bank. Such data also pointed the way on a path to help First Union stand out from "all the other banks in town."

The strategy was also in sync with a culture that, for many years, had honored humanistic management. The acronym for the bank portion of the Corporation (First Union National Bank) was frequently altered by employees and customers to "FUN Bank"—a characterization highlighting the bank's upbeat, original style in the marketplace, as well as its cadre of employees often described as more optimistic, confident, and creative than the garden-variety banker.

The operational side of the First Union focus played heavily on their analysis of how customers characterized superior service. If, for instance, the customer said he or she considered four minutes to be a reasonable wait in line in a branch to cash a check, then FUNB set three minutes as their "we want to be more" internal standard. First Union recognized that, while they were by no means the least-expensive bank in town, they could compensate by keying on the "value-added" dimension. Explosive, high-tech, and dramatic ads, for example, were created to promote the perception in the consumer's mind that "the price of admission may be a bit higher than at some other banks, but the 'show' will knock your socks off." Finally, First Union's service focus was made tangible through a highly publicized service guarantee: " . . . if you are not completely satisfied within six months of opening an account, we will refund the monthly service charges."

The FUNB's service commitment is continually reinforced. At least every quarter, customer-contact people are "shopped" by a professional third party, who, under the guise of "customer," evaluates the customer-contact person. Excellent performers receive financial rewards; poor performers are coached, counseled, and often trained; repeat poor performers are placed in non-customer-contact roles or "made available to the industry."

In short, a workable service focus or strategy must include a concept or mission that people can understand and support through concrete actions. It must include benefits important to the customer that differentiate the organization from its competitors in a meaningful way. The bank promising the "greenest money," the hospital with "the cleanest rooms," or the insurance company (or funeral home) guaranteeing "the most peace of mind" may not get many points for differentiation in the marketplace. A service focus must aid in making you unique, must help you stand apart from others in similar endeavors.

You cannot form a service focus instantly. It is not just a slogan you dream up in a half-day creative-problem-solving or "visioning" workshop. The service focus must be created, or evolve, using the answers to questions like these:

- What is our business?
- What counts most to our customers?
- What will count most tomorrow?
- What can we do with our service that customers will really notice and pay for?
- How do our customers see us right now?
- What actions can we take to improve our service and the customer perception of our service and of our organization?

It is important for an organization to take pains to describe its service focus to employees and customers alike. Defining and communicating the service focus is as important as training employees, developing delivery systems, measuring organizational performance and managing the sales and marketing budget. A well-defined service focus declares an organization's competitive direction and must become its gospel. That means it has to be communicated over and over again, until everyone in the organization can hum it right along with you.

One test of completeness for a service focus is the form below. A service focus or strategy will be complete if it answers the following three questions: 1. What is your core contribution? 2. To whom do we provide this service? 3. What distinction do we want them to perceive about us?

A SERVICE FOCUS FRAMEWORK
To provide _____ (our core contribution) to _____ (our key customers) so that we are perceived by them as _____ (our distinction).

As an example, an elevator company might complete the framework this way:

To provide a means of moving people and things up, down, and sideways over short distances to individuals and organizations everywhere with higher reliability than any comparable company in the world.

The transportation-services department of a company might word its framework in this manner:

To provide all vehicle users in XYZ company with the ability to improve their services, increase their productivity, and reduce their costs. Our users write our performance appraisals; our competition is their expectation of what we should be. We will be successful if *they* say we have significantly added value to their efforts.

Ponderosa Steakhouse Restaurants were content to define their service focus thusly: "To provide a reasonably priced meal in a pleasant, family-oriented environment." And McDonald's leans on its short and to the point "Q.S.V.C.—Quality, Service, Value and Cleanliness."

GETTING IT SAID AND KEEPING IT SAID

Communicating a service focus is less like surgery and more like taking a bath: You have to do it all over again frequently if you are going to stay clean. To "take it out to the troops" once and expect the message to stay "heard" is to expect more of the human condition than is realistic. Unlike a heart-valve repair or a tonsil removal, the communication of the service focus is something that must be done over again to remain effective. The message must be repeated again and again in a variety of ways at a variety of times if it is to become a norm, an organizational way of life.

The Distributions and Logistics Division of Gillette uses a portion of each management meeting to examine their critical success factors for service to internal customers and to readjust efforts counter to those factors. At Multicare Medical in Tacoma, Washington, the service focus or strategy and performance pledge of each functional unit is revisited at goal-setting time. People in individual units work at finding unique and unusual ways of making their commitment a reality.

Quad Graphics, a high-quality printing company headquartered in Pewaukee, Wisconsin, annually spends several days in a conference setting with *customers*—listening, learning, and aligning their efforts with customer expectations. First Union incorporates some aspect of customer service or service management into practically every training program offered. Not only are customer-contact people monitored and measured on service quality, other employees are evaluated on service to internal customers. At Disney World, cast-member (employee) relations standards are parallel to guest (customer) relations standards.

Service is not an extra; it is a central focus and a way of life. A service focus is not a slogan; it is a serious, value-based business proposition. It is created by means of careful analysis of customer needs and a realistic assessment of corporate capacity. The sound of service need not be melodious or catchy. But it must be clear and unmistakable. Communicating the service message internally is not a program or an event. If it is to be believed and honored by those who must act in sync with its substance, it must be told and retold. And the actions of those who are watched and modeled must be consistent with what is told. The service focus is an ongoing effort that never stays done.

THE CABBIES IN JAPAN DO NOT LOOK OR ACT LIKE ORDINARY HACKS

Karl Schoenberger

Kyoto, Japan—Picture this in New York, say, or Los Angeles. You hail a cab, it pulls up to the curb and the driver hops out and runs around toward you. If you are a New Yorker, you probably think he is about to assault you for a reason known only to him. But instead, here in Japan's sixth-largest city, the cabby is racing to *open the passenger door for you.*

"Thank your for riding MK Taxi," he chirps in honorific Japanese. "Where may I take your, Mr. Passenger?" He is so polite that you brace for a scam. But the Japanese know he is not a con artist or even a clever cabby angling for a bigger tip (the Japanese don't tip taxi drivers). They know before he says it that he is from MK Taxi, a company that is revolutionizing Kyoto's cab culture.

The driver, Yasuhiko Kumio, not only doesn't act like a typical hack but also doesn't look like one. In contrast to cities like New York, Boston and Houston, where many drivers look so shabby that regulators have instituted dress codes banning t-shirts and tattered shorts, Japan's cabbies have always taken pride in their dress. Traditionally, many even wear white gloves, which would get a New York cabby drummed out of the fraternity.

But Mr. Kumoi and MK's 1000 other drivers now are absolute fashion plates, wearing uniforms created by designer Hanae Mori: airline captain's hat, striped shirts, tie and collarless blazer with brass buttons and winged insignia on the breast pocket. MK's drivers at first thought this was carrying things a bit too far, especially since rival cabbies were branding them *chirdinya,* or roughly "clowns."

Competitor cabbies also taunted MK drivers for getting out to open the door for passengers, an extreme step even for Japanese hacks, and for not refusing short-haul fares. But the rivals have stopped taunting and started imitating, out of competitive necessity.

The 34-year-old Mr. Kumoi, like many a cabby elsewhere, got behind the wheel of a cab because of misfortune—the kimono wholesaler he worked for went bankrupt. He now wears his high-fashion suit with awkward pride and says he no longer feels silly in public, just conspicuous.

He motors around this ancient city of temples and teahouses in a sleek, black sedan rather than the company's tradition red-and-white taxi. He and his colleagues have been meticulously trained in the fine art of haute hacking.

Behind the MK miracle is the company's 59-year-old chairman, Sadao Aoki, an immigrant from Korea who got his start in business 31 years ago peddling gasoline on a bicycle. MK (the initials stand for two predecessor cab companies) has since diversified into the development and leisure businesses and plans to expand its taxi business to Tokyo and Osaka.

Expounding on his taxi philosophy, Mr. Aoki says, "You take care of your passengers by taking care of your drivers. The drivers are important, and they should feel that way. They're like land pilots."

Sometimes they are also like nursemaids, providing paramedical attention for a passenger or helping a drunken businessman get home safely after he has missed his last train. In fact, Japanese cabdrivers play a significant role in getting drunks home at night, partly because of stringent drunk-driving laws. Legend has it that Japanese breath-analyzing devices are sensitive enough to detect when a driver has eaten narazuke, pickles cured in rice-wine, and that drivers with that amount of alcohol in their blood-stream risk arrest. MK drivers, with their reputation for courtesy and dependability, have built up a loyal customer base in bars.

Without any prompting, Chairman Aoki goes into an evangelical lecture and slide show he has repeated hundreds of times to businessmen. He relates how he built subsidized housing for his employees, reasoning that if they sleep better they would have fewer accidents and make more money. To increase capitalist incentive, he raised the drivers's share of meter proceeds to 60% from the standard 40%. And he ordered them never to refuse a passenger, even on short rides.

When Mr. Aoki started requiring his drivers to open doors for passengers and to repeat a standard set of gushingly polite phrases, a plaque mounted in the back of the cab once informed customers that if the driver didn't go by the script, they didn't have to pay the fare. Mr. Aoki says he removed the plaque when it wasn't necessary anymore.

Now, the MK philosophy has been institutionalized, but MK drivers must take refresher courses to stay on the road. Mr. Aoki, who still has tea with his drivers, dreams of establishing Japan's first "taxi university."

He angered his competitors five years ago by applying for permission to lower government-set fares, arguing that cheaper rides would reverse a national trend of falling taxi use. The Transport Ministry rejected his request, so he sued the government, which sets uniform fares by region— and won. Kyoto's taxi fares, which start at 430 yen, or more than $3.25, at the drop of the meter flag, remain frozen at 1981 levels pending a government appeal of an Osaka court ruling. An appellate verdict is expected by the end of the year.

"If you look at him from outside the business, he seems unique," says Daisuke Matsuura, the director of the Kyoto Taxi Operators Association, a group of cab companies. "But to those of us inside the industry, he's been a real nuisance."

Mr. Matsuura grudgingly concedes that Mr. Aoki has had a positive influence on local taxi etiquette. "He's got zeal. He's got a lot of ideas," Mr. Matsuura says. "He's really stimulated us to improve our service."

Mr. Aoki was born in Korea, then a Japanese colony, and he came to Kyoto during Would War II at age 15 to study. He remembers crying at night because he was so hungry. After the war, Mr. Aoki remained in Kyoto and entered the Ritsumeikan University law school. He later dropped out to do odd jobs and eventually bought a bankrupt service station that he has transformed into his conglomerate. Consolidated sales in the year ending last March 31 were 30 billion yen ($227 million).

Though Koreans generally constitute a downtrodden minority in Japan, Mr. Aoki says he has never suffered from discrimination. "There's no nationality when it comes to high quality and good service," he says. "The people of Kyoto value modesty and diligence. They don't care what nationality I am."

Indeed, MK Taxi is a household word in this city—largely owing to Mr. Aoki's flair for publicity. He converted his drivers' cafeteria into an inexpensive smorgasbord open to the public. He started an "ambulance taxi" service, training many of his drivers in first aid. He startled authorities by proposing to make private Kyoto's public-transport system and replace inefficient buses with low-priced taxis. That plan was quietly shelved after some polite study by the city fathers.

Thwarted by authorities when he applied to increase his fleet to 1000 cabs from 451, Mr. Aoki recently has been cultivating the black sedans to create a kind of mass-market limousine service. He has recruited a stable of English-speaking drivers to offer tours to foreign visitors.

Elevating the status of cab drivers hasn't been easy. Mr. Aoki says it took him four years to persuade Ms. Mori to agree to design his uniforms. "She said taxi drivers were the wrong image for her designers," Mr. Aoki says.

"He was very earnest," recalls Yasuko Suita, the managing director of Hanae Mori International. "Mr. Aoki told us that taxi drivers have a very prestigious job, that their status should be the same as jet pilots."

Having failed to win lower fares, he sought and got government approval to sell discount coupons that, in effect, reduced the fares 5%. The Transport Ministry skirted the issue by calling the discount a rebate for interest lost on the advance payment.

MK's latest innovation is the "moving department store," a sales program in which cabbies hawk furniture and other catalog goods to captive shoppers in the back seat. MK drivers get a commission for passing interested customers's names along to the manufacturers.

"If something is good, cheap and the service is good, you can't stop it," Mr. Aoki says. "It's like water flowing downhill."

INSTILLING A SERVICE MENTALITY: LIKE TEACHING AN ELEPHANT TO DANCE

Karl Albrecht and Ron Zemke

A friend of ours was traveling alone in Japan on a extended vacation. He inquired in his limited Japanese which train he should take to go from Sapporo, where he was at the moment, to Tokyo. The man behind the counter wrote out all the information for him—times, trains numbers and track numbers. He even took the trouble to write it in both English and Japanese, in case our friend should lose his way and later need to show the note to some other Japanese person.

This is a "moment of truth," one of many that happened that day. At that instant our friend had an opportunity to form an impression of the train company, or at least of that one employee. He came away thinking, "That was a nice experience. There's somebody who really takes the trouble to help people."

But the story goes even a bit further. Pleased and gratified, our friend thanked the information man and walked down the corridor to the waiting area, to sit and wait for the departure time. A half-hour later he saw the information man come bustling through the crowded waiting hall, looking for him. Locating him at last, the man gestured for the return of the paper. He wrote something on it, gave it back, bowed quickly, and hurried back to his post. He had figured out a faster, more convenient sequence of trains, and came back to correct the note.

CUSTOMERS REMEMBER

A powerful new wave is washing over the already turbulent business world, the wave of service. People are getting more and more critical of the quality of service they experience in their everyday lives, and they want something done about it. And when they have a good experience, they remember.

We no longer live in a manufacturing economy. We now live in a very new economy, a service economy, where "relationships" are starting to become more important than physical products.

This new service imperative will mean that the old customer service department will probably fade into obscurity as managers work to transform their entire organizations into customer-driven business entities. The quality of the customer's experience is becoming a hot topic in boardrooms and executive suites, not only in the United States but in many other countries as well. This is a worldwide phenomenon affecting manufacturing companies as much as service firms.

High-quality service at the front line starts in the minds of top management. This service concept must find its way into the structure and operation of the organization. There must be a customer-oriented culture in the organization, and it is the leaders of the enterprise who must build and maintain this culture.

Management itself is a service, and this point of view will become more and more prevalent as competition gets tougher and service becomes more and more a competitive weapon. Managers need to see their roles as helping service people do their jobs better. The role of management in a service-driven organization is to enhance the culture, set expectations of quality, provide a motivating climate, furnish the necessary resources, help solve problems, remove obstacles, and make sure high quality job performance pays off.

This new era of service management will call for a return to the most fundamental principles of leadership and in many cases to a rethinking of the organization's basic reasons for being.

Managing service means having as many of the moments of truth as possible come out well. As Donald Porter, director of customer service quality assurance for British Airways, points out:

"If you're a service person, and you get it wrong at your point in the customer's chain of experience, you are very likely erasing from the customer's mind all the memories of the good treatment he or she may have had up until you. But if you get it right, you have a chance to undo all the wrongs that may have happened before the customer got you."

Every time a service organization performs for a customer, the customer makes an assessment of the quality of the service, even if unconsciously. The sum total of the repeated assessments by this customer and the collective assessments by all customers establish in their minds the organization's image in service quality.

INVISIBLE REPORT CARD

We can think of the customer as carrying around a kind of "report card," which is the basis of a grading system that leads the customer to decide whether to partake of the service again or to go elsewhere. It is crucial for us to find out as much as we possibly can about this invisible report card. We can only score consistently high grades on the customer's report card by knowing what evaluation factors the customer is applying when he thinks about our organization and what we offer.

A story shared by Porter of British Airways foreshadows the answer to the question of why service quality is so frequently low. "When we launched our Customer First campaign," Porter reports, "we wanted to find out where we were in our market at the time. What did our customers think of us, compared with other airline companies? We conducted a market research study to try to find out.

"Our study aimed at answering two questions: first, what factors did people really consider most important in the flying experiences; and second, how did British Airways stack up against the other airlines in those factors?

"After some extensive interviewing and data analysis, we discovered some very interesting facts. Of all the statements made by the air travellers we interviewed, four factors stood out from all the rest as being vitally important. What took us aback was the fact that two of the four factors came more or less as a surprise to us."

According to BA's findings, says Porter, customers seemed to be responding to four factors as they moved through the chain experience:

- *Care and Concern*—"We knew about this one."
- *Spontaneity*—"We hadn't thought much about this one."
- *Problem solving*—"We were conscious of this one."
- *Recovery*—"We hadn't thought about this one at all."

'Care and concern' are fairly clear, I thought," says Porter. "We weren't surprised by finding this a key factor, although I think we have to confess that we couldn't claim very high levels of performance on it.

'Spontaneity' made us stop and scratch our heads a bit. Customers were saying, "We want to know that your front line people are authorized to think. When a problem comes up that doesn't fit the procedure book, can a service person use some discretion—find a way to jockey the system on the customer's behalf? Or does he or she simply shrug shoulders and brush the customer off?"

'Problem Solving' was pretty clear, we knew customers thought our people should by qualified at working out the intricacies of travel schedules, handling complicated logistics, and in general getting them smoothly on their way.

"The fourth factor sort of threw us. It had never really occurred to us in any concrete way. 'Recovery' was the term we coined to describe a very frequently repeated concern: if something goes wrong, as it often does, will anybody make a special effort to set it right? Will someone go out of his or her way to make amends to the customer? Does anybody make an effort to offset the negative effects of a screw-up? Does anyone even know how to deliver a simple apology?

"We were struck by a rather chilling thought: if two of these four primary evaluation factors were things we had never consciously considered, what were the changes that our people in the service areas were paying attention to them? For the first time we were really beginning to understand and come to terms with the real motivational factors that are embedded in our customer's nervous system."

The market research project also came up with some other interesting findings. When the interviewers asked air travelers to rate British Airways in comparison with other airlines they had personally dealt with, they found some interesting statistics. About 20% of the respondents considered British Airways inferior to others. The remaining expressed no strong opinions one way or the other.

The initial reaction of company management to the figures was guardedly optimistic. One executive offered the interpretation that "it seems like 85% of the people interviewed think we're OK". But as the implications of the data began to soak in, the attitude changed to one of mild concern. Another observer volunteered, "There's another interpretation that one could make. It seems that 65% of the respondents don't see any important difference between us and the other airlines. That doesn't strike me as very good news."

This, indeed, was bad news, when considered in the light of a specific directive for Colin Marshall, chief executive of British Airways. "I want British Airways to be the best airline in the world," he said, "and I'm willing to do whatever it takes to make it that." With 65% of the people apparently evaluating the company as just so-so in quality of service, there seemed to be quite a distance to go.

From many of our everyday experiences, as well as from the British Airways case, we can draw a fairly mundane conclusion, one that we believe can be stated as an out-and-out principle of service management: "When the moments of truth go unmanaged, the quality of service regresses to mediocrity."

To survive and prosper in a service industry requires *differentiation*. An effective service company must show evidence that it really does have something special to offer. Especially in industries where customers don't readily see important differences in the choices of service offered them, "average" really equates to "mediocre," at least in the mind of the customer.

One of the most common symptoms of mediocrity in service is when the customer finds it necessary to run through an organizational maze to get his or her needs met.

Most telephone monopolies around the world are notorious for this customer runaround process. A person would call up the company with the need to have a telephone installed, or a service changed, and end up dealing with three or more departments. In each case calling the department a second time got a completely different person, who had no prior knowledge of the order at all.

DEADLY COMPARTMENTALIZATION
Banks often operate this way. Many branch banks are so compartmentalized and regimented in an attempt to eliminate all evidence of human judgment and initiative that very few people can steer a customer through the maze on their own. It is very common practice in dealing with banks to deal with people who know only one microscopic function, and who cannot offer help with any other.

Service people can become so robotized in their actions that they greet any customer request with a standardized response, even if the response is only marginally effective.

It also helps to invite the "non-service" people in the company to think of themselves as really being in service roles. Administrative people, accountants, computer specialists, engineers, contracts people and staff people of various kinds tend to think of themselves as somehow removed from the din of battle. All too often they look upon service people as the ones who deal the *hoi polloi*. They are sometimes tempted to think of themselves as "above" the level of service roles. A strong and determined chief executive can disabuse them of this elitist viewpoint, and get them to thinking of service as a highly valued role.

When Robert Townsend took over as head of Avis Corp. and instituted its famous "We Try Harder" campaign, he decided that a bit of time behind the counter was therapeutic for every manager in the company. He issued a decree that even vice presidents were expected to do duty face-to-face with the customer.

He wanted all key people in the company to have first-hand knowledge of the needs and experiences of people who were using rental cars. He also wanted to dispel the connotation that the really important people were back at headquarters. The message, according to Townsend, was that the survival and prosperity of the company were in the hands of the people at the retail counters and in the maintenance shops, and that was where the action was.

Elitist attitudes and factional interests die hard in most organizations. Sometimes the accounting people act as if they think the organization exists so they can keep books on it. Some engineering people act as if the organization exists to support their intellectual hobbies. Some physicians act as if the hospital exists to cater to their overfed egos. It takes a very strong management to get the people in these various camps to see themselves as supporting the people and processes that deliver the quality of experiences the customer considers important.

If managing the moments of truth is the essence of service management, then the essential process in managing the moments of truth is building a service-minded culture in the organization. If the moments of truth go unmanaged and service quality regresses to mediocrity, there is usually a concomitant poverty of spirit among the people in the company overall. A "don't-give-a-damn" attitude creeps into the collective psyche.

OLD WINE IN NEW BOTTLES?
In briefing hundreds of managers in a number of countries on the service management concept, we have frequently had to field the question, "So what's new? This is just the same old 'customer satisfaction' stuff that we've known about for years. Isn't service management just putting old wine in new bottles?"

Perhaps, but let's take a closer look at the bottles. We have been fond of saying, "The customer is always right." And yet there has not been until now a clear-cut model of thinking about the management of service. Managers have tended to leave the matter of customer satisfaction to the customer service department. They typically assure that someone is taking proper care of the customer, unless the number of complaints begins to get too high. Then it becomes time for corrective action.

But leading companies today are placing more emphasis on service, beginning with an effort to understand customer preferences.

We live in a service economy and an increasingly service-conscious society, Service accounts for 71% of the gross national product and 75% of the jobs in the United States. Other developed countries are experiencing the same trends and patterns. Many more organizations are getting serious about the quality of the customer's experience, and more and more are finding ways to improve it.

Further, we have concluded that a high quality service orientation is such a powerful competitive weapon that it is coming to be regarded as an essential part of business strategy. Organizations that cannot demonstrate a significant commitment to the needs of their customers will be left behind. Quality of service is the do-or-die management issue of the decade.

INDICATIONS OF EXCELLENCE
Organizations that have achieved excellence in service are easy to spot, and their internal characteristics are fairly easy to identify. Successful service organizations share the following characteristics:

1. They have a strong vision—a strategy for service that is clearly developed and clearly communicated.
2. They practice visible management.
3. They "take" service routinely.
4. They have customer-friendly service systems.
5. They balance high tech with high touch. They temper their systems and methods with the personal factor.
6. They recruit, hire, train and promote for service.
7. They market service to their customers.
8. They market service internally to their employees.
9. They measure service quality and make the results available to the service people.

The process of reorienting a large organization towards its market is like trying to teach an elephant to dance. Many of the same challenges are involved. At least two things have to happen in order for an elephant to dance or for a large organization to change its ways. First, somebody has to demonstrate that it's possible to do so. Second, there must be a motivating factor sufficiently powerful to generate commitment.

Service management offers a way to create and communicate a vision of service, and to make that vision a reality in the day-to-day business of the company. In the sense of making an organization a customer-driven business entity, service management can be the means of teaching the elephant to dance.

WHAT THE HELL IS 'MARKET ORIENTED?'

Benson P. Shapiro

The air hung heavy in French Lick, Indiana. A tornado watch was in effect that morning, and the sky was black. In a meeting room in one of the local resort hotels, where top management of the Wolverine Controller Company had gathered, the atmosphere matched the weather. Recent results had been poor for the Indianapolis-based producer of flow controllers for process industries like chemicals, paper, and food. Sales were off, but earnings were off even more. Market share was down in all product lines.

As the president called the meeting to order he had fire in his eyes. "The situation can't get much more serious," he proclaimed. "As you all know, over the past couple of years everything has gone to hell in a handbasket. We're in deep trouble, with both domestic and foreign competition preempting us at every turn. The only way to get out of this mess is for us to become customer driven or market oriented. I'm not even sure what that means, but I'm damn sure that we want to be there. I don't even know whether there's a difference between being market driven and customer oriented or customer driven and market oriented or whatever. We've just got to do a hell of a lot better."

"I couldn't agree with you more, Frank," the marketing vice president put in. "I've been saying all along that we've got to be more marketing oriented. The marketing department has to be more involved in everything that goes on because we represent the customer and we've got an integrated view of the company."

The CEO scowled at him. "I said *market* oriented, not marketing oriented! It's unclear to me what we get for all the overhead we have in marketing. Those sexy brochures of yours sure haven't been doing the job."

There followed a lively, often acrimonious discussion of what was wrong and what was needed. Each vice president defended his or her function or unit and set out solutions from that particular standpoint. I will draw a curtain over their heedless and profane bickering, but here are paraphrases of their positions.

Sales VP: "We need more salespeople. *We're* the ones who are close to the customers. We have to have more call capacity in the sales force so we can provide better service and get new product ideas into the company faster."

Manufacturing VP: "We all know that our customers want quality. We need more automated machinery so we can work to closer tolerances and give them better quality. Also, we ought to send our whole manufacturing team to Crosby's Quality College."

Research and development VP: "Clearly we could do much better at both making and selling our products. But the fundamental problem is a lack of *new* products. They're the heart of our business. Our technology is getting old because we aren't investing enough in R&D."

Finance VP: "The problem isn't not enough resources; it's too many resources misspent. We've got too much overhead. Our variable costs are out of control. Our marketing and sales expenses are unreasonable. And we spend too much on R&D. We don't need more, we need less."

The general manager of the Electronic Flow Controls Division: "We aren't organized in the right way—that's the fundamental problem. If each division had its own sales force, we would have better coordination between sales and the other functions."

Her counterpart in the Pneumatic Controls Division: "We don't need our own sales forces anywhere near as much as we need our own engineering group so we can develop designs tailored to our customers. As long as we have a central R&D group that owns all the engineers, the divisions can't do their jobs."

As the group adjourned for lunch, the president interjected a last word. "You all put in a lot of time talking past each other and defending your own turf. Some of that's all right. You're supposed to represent your own departments and sell your own perspectives. If you didn't work hard for your own organizations, you wouldn't have lasted long at Wolverine, and you couldn't have made the contributions that you have.

"But enough is enough! You aren't just representatives of your own shops. You're the corporate executives at Wolverine and you have to take a more integrated, global view. It's my job to get all of you coordinated, but it's also the job of each of you. I don't have the knowledge, and nothing can replace direct, lateral communication across departments. Let's figure out how to do that after we get some lunch."

ALL RIGHT, WHAT IS IT?

Leaving the Wolverine bunch to its meal, I want to make a start in dispelling the president's uncertainty. After years of research, I'm convinced that the term "market oriented" represents a set of processes touching on all aspects of the company. It's a great deal more than the cliche "getting close to the customer." Since most companies sell to a variety of customers with varying and even conflicting desires and needs, the goal of getting close to the customer is meaningless. I've also found no meaningful difference between "market driven" and "customer oriented," so I use the phrases interchangeably. In my view, three characteristics make a company market driven.

Information on all important buying influences permeates every corporate function. A company can be market oriented only if it completely understands its markets and the people who decide whether to buy its products or services.

In some industries, wholesalers, retailers, and other parts of the distribution channels have a profound influence on the choices customers make. So it's important to understand "the trade." In other markets, nonbuying influences specify the product, although they neither purchase it nor use it. These include architects, consulting engineers, and doctors. In still other markets, one person may buy the product and another may use it; family situations are an obvious illustration. In commercial and industrial marketplaces, a professional procurement organization may actually purchase the product, while a manufacturing or operational function uses it.

To be of greatest use, customer information must move beyond the market research, sales, and marketing functions and "permeate every corporate function"—the R&D scientists and engineers, the manufacturing people, and the field-service specialists. When the technologists, for example, get unvarnished feedback on the way customers use the product, they can better develop improvements on the product and the production processes. If, on the other hand, market research or marketing people predigest the information, technologists may miss opportunities.

Of course, regular cross-functional meetings to discuss customer needs and to analyze feedback from buying influences are very important. At least once a year, the top functional officers should spend a full day or more to consider what is happening with key buying influences.

Corporate officers and functions should have access to all useful market research reports. If company staff appends summaries to regular customer surveys, like the Greenwich commercial and investment banking reports or the numerous consumer package-goods industry sales analyses, top officers are more likely to study them. That approach lets top management get the sales and marketing departments opinions as well as those of less-biased observers.

Some companies that have customer response phones—toll-free 800 numbers that consumers or distributors call to ask questions or make comments—distribute selected cassette recordings of calls to a wide range of executives, line and staff. The cassettes stimulate new ideas for products, product improvements, packaging, and service.

Reports to read and cassettes to hear are useful—but insufficient. High-level executives need to make visits to important customers to see them using their industrial and commercial products, consuming their services, or retailing their consumer goods. When, say, top manufacturing executives understand how a customer factory uses their products, they will have a more solid appreciation of customer needs for quality and close toler-ances. Trade show visits provide valuable opportunities for operations and technical people to talk with customers and visit competitors' booths (if allowed by industry custom and show rules).

In my statement on the first characteristic, I referred to "important" buying influences. Because different customers have different needs, a marketer cannot effectively satisfy a wide range of them equally. The most important strategic decision is to choose the important customers. All customers are important, but invariably some are more important to the company than others. Collaboration among the various functions is important when pinpointing the key target accounts and market segments. Then the salespeople know whom to call on first and most often, the people who schedule production runs know who gets favored treatment, and those who make service calls know who rates special attention. If the priorities are not clear in the calm of planning meetings, they certainly won't be when the sales production scheduling, and service dispatching processes get hectic.

The choice of customers influences the way decisions are made. During a marketing meeting at Wolverine Controller, one senior marketing person said, "Sales and marketing will pick out the customers they want to do business with, and then we'll sit down with the manufacturing and technical people and manage the product mix." Too late! Once you have a certain group of customers, the product mix is pretty much set; you must make the types of products they want. If sales and marketing choose the customers, they have undue power over decisions. Customer selection must involve all operating functions.

Strategic and tactical decisions are made interfunctionally and interdivisionally. Functions and divisions will inevitably have conflicting objectives that mirror distinctions in cultures and in modes of operation. The glimpse into the meeting at French Lick demonstrates that. The customer-oriented company possesses mechanisms to get these differences out on the table for candid discussion and to make trade-offs that reconcile the various points of view. Each function and division must have the ear of the others and must be encouraged to lay out its ideas and requirements honestly and vigorously.

To make wise decisions, functions and units must recognize their differences. A big part of being market driven is the way different jurisdictions deal with one another. The marketing department may ask the R&D department to develop a product with a certain specification by a certain date. If R&D thinks the request is unreasonable but doesn't say so, it may develop a phony plan that the company will never achieve. Or R&D may make changes in the specifications and the delivery date without talking to marketing. The result: a missed deadline and an overrun budget. If, on the other hand, the two functions get together, they are in a position to make intelligent technological and marketing trade-offs. They can change a specification or extend a delivery date with the benefit of both points of view.

An alternative to integrated decision making, of course, is to kick the decision upstairs to the CEO or at least the division general manager. But though the higher executives have unbiased views, they lack the close knowledge of the specialists. An open decision making process gets the best of both worlds, exploiting the evenhandedness of the general manager and the functional skills of the specialists.

Divisions and functions make well-coordinated decisions and execute them with a sense of commitment. An open dialogue on strategic and tactical trade-offs is the best way to engender commitment to meet goals. When the implementers also do the planning, the commitment will be strong and clear.

The depth of the biases revealed at the French Lick gathering demonstrated the difficulty of implementing cross-functional programs. But there's nothing wrong with that. In fact, the strength of those biases had a lot to do with Wolverine's past success. If the R&D vice president thought like the financial vice president, she wouldn't be effective in her job. On the other hand, if each function is marching to its own drum, implementation will be weak regardless of the competence and devotion of each function.

Serial communication, when one function passes an idea or request to another routinely without interaction—like tossing a brick with a message tied to it over the wall—can't build the commitment needed in the customer-driven company. Successful new products don't, for example, emerge out of a process in which marketing sends a set of specifications to R&D, which sends finished blueprints and designs to manufacturing. But joint opportunity analysis, in which functional and divisional people share ideas and discuss alternative solutions and approaches, leverages the different strengths of each party. Powerful internal connections make communication clear, coordination strong, and commitment high.

Poor coordination leads to misapplication of resources and failure to make the most of market opportunities. At one point in the meeting at French Lick, the vice president for human resources spoke up in this fashion: "Remember how impressed everyone was in '86 with the new pulp-bleaching control we developed? Not just us, but the whole industry—especially with our fast response rate. Even though the technology was the best, the product flopped. Why? Because the industry changed its process so that the response rate was less important then the ability to handle tough operating conditions and higher temperatures and pressures. Plus we couldn't manufacture to the right tolerances the industry needed. We wasted a lot of talent on the wrong problem."

Probably the salespeople, and perhaps the technical service people, knew about the evolving customer needs. By working together, manufacturing and R&D could have designed a manufacturable product. But the company lacked the coordination that a focused market orientation stimulates.

ACTION AT WOLVERINE
Just about every company thinks of itself as market oriented. It's confident it has the strength to compete with the wolf pack, but in reality it's often weak and tends to follow the shepherd. In marketing efforts, businesses are particularly vulnerable to this delusion. Let's return to French Lick to hear of such a sheep in wolf's clothing.

"Look at Mutton Machinery," the vice president of manufacturing was saying. "They've done worse than we have. And their ads and brochures brag about them being customer oriented! At the trade show last year, they had a huge booth with the theme 'The Customer is King.' They had a sales contest that sent a salesperson and customer to tour the major castles of Europe."

The sales vice president piped up. "They should send their salespeople for technical training, not to look at castles. We interviewed two of their better people, and they didn't measure up technically. The glitzy trade show stuff and the sexy contest don't make them customer oriented."

No, slogans and glossy programs don't give a company a market orientation. It takes a philosophy and a culture that go deep in the organization. Let's take a look at Wolverine's approach.

It's unlikely that any company ever became market oriented with a bottom-up approach; to make it happen, you need the commitment and power of those at the top. In gathering everybody who mattered at French Lick, Wolverine was taking the right step at the start. And from what we have heard, clearly they were not sugarcoating their concerns.

By the end of the first day, the executives had decided that they knew too little about their own industry, particularly customers and competitors. After a mostly social dinner meeting and a good night's sleep, they began at breakfast on day two to develop a plan to learn more. They listed 20 major customers they wanted to understand better. They designated each of the ten executives at the meeting (CEO, six functional heads, and three division general managers) to visit the customers in pairs in the next two months; the sales force would coordinate the visits. All ten agreed to attend the next big trade show.

They assigned the marketing vice president to prepare dossiers on the 20 customers plus another 10, as well as prospects selected by the group. Besides data on the customer or prospect, each dossier was to include an examination of Wolverine's relationship with it.

Finally, the group singled out seven competitors for close scrutiny. The marketing vice president agreed to gather market data on them. The R&D vice president committed herself to drawing up technical reviews of them, and the financial vice president was to prepare analyses of financial performance. The seven remaining executives each agreed to analyze the relative strengths and weaknesses of one competitor.

Spurred by the president, the group concluded on day two that barriers had arisen among Wolverine's functional departments. Each was on its own little island. The human resources vice president took on the responsibility of scrutinizing cross-functional communication and identifying ways to improve it.

Back at headquarters in Indianapolis, the top brass did another smart thing: it involved all functional leadership so that line as well as staff chieftains would contribute to the effort. Top management quickly pinpointed the management information system as a major point of leverage for shaping a more integrated company view. Therefore, the president invited the MIS director to join the team.

Top management also decided that the bonus plan encouraged each function to pursue its own objectives instead of corporate wide goals. So the controller teamed up with the human resources vice president to devise a better plan, which won the approval of top management.

As a new interest in communication and cooperation developed, the president perceived the need to make changes in structure and process. Chief among these were the establishment of a process engineering department to help production and R&D move new products from design into manufacturing and the redesign of managerial reports to emphasize the total company perspective.

The management group, more sensitive now to the ways people deal with each other, awoke to the power of informal social systems. To make the salespeople more accessible to headquarters staff, the sales office at a nearby location moved to headquarters (over the objections of the vice president of sales). The effort to promote interfunctional teamwork even extended to the restructuring of the bowling league. Wolverine had divided its teams by function or division. Now, however, each team had members from various functions. some old-timers snorted that that was taking the new market orientation too far. But in a conversation during a bowling league party, the head of technical field service and a customer-service manager came up with an idea for a program to improve customer responsiveness. Then even the skeptics began to understand.

The analyses of customers and competitors identified an important market opportunity for Wolverine. The management group diverted resources to it, and under the direction of the Pneumatic Controls Division general manager, a multifunctional task force launched an effort to exploit it. Top management viewed this undertaking as a laboratory for the development of new approaches and as a showcase to demonstrate the company's new philosophy and culture. Headquarters maintained an intense interest in the project.

As the project gained momentum, support for the underlying philosophy grew. Gradually, the tone of interfunctional relationships changed. People evinced more trust in each other and were much more willing to admit responsibility for mistakes and to expose shortcomings.

Unfortunately, some people found it difficult to change. The sales vice president resisted the idea that a big part of his job was bringing customers and data about them into the company as well as encouraging all functions to deal with customers. He became irate when the vice president of manufacturing worked directly with several major customers, and he told the president that he wouldn't stand for other people dealing with *his* customers. His colleagues couldn't alter his attitude, so the president replaced him.

Wolverine's sales and earnings slowly began to improve. The market price of its stock edged upward. Internally, decision making became more integrative. Some early victories helped build momentum. Implementation improved through cooperation very low in the ranks, where most of the real work was done.

IMITATE LARRY BIRD
A year after Wolverine's first meeting in the French Lick hotel, the management group gathered there again. A new sales vice president was present, and the newly promoted MIS vice president/controller was also there.

This time the executives focused on two concerns. The first was how to handle the inordinate demands on the company resulting from the new push to satisfy important customers. The second was how to maintain Wolverine's momentum toward achieving a market orientation.

Attacking the first item, the group agreed to set major customer priorities. At hand was the information gathered during the year via industry analysis and executives' visits to top accounts. Available to the executives also were several frameworks for analysis.[1] Some accounts fit together in unexpected ways. In some situations, a series of accounts used similar products similarly. In others, the accounts competed for Wolverine's resources.

It took several meetings to set priorities on customers. The hardest part was resolving a dispute over whether to raise prices drastically on the custom products made for the third largest account. Wolverine was losing money on these. "Maybe not all business is good business," the R&D vice president suggested. That notion was pretty hard for the team to accept.

But the CEO pushed hard for a decision. Ultimately, the group agreed to drop the account if it did not accede to price increases within the next six to eight months.

On the second matter, the management group decided it needed a way to measure the company's progress. The approach, everybody understood, had to be grounded in unrelieved emphasis on information gathering, on interfunctional decision making, and on a vigorous sense of commitment throughout the organization. They recognized how easy it is to get complacent and lose detachment when examining one's own performance. Nevertheless, the executives drew up a checklist of customer-focused questions for the organization to ask itself. It appears in the insert.

Two years after the company changed its direction, a major customer asked the president about his impressions of Wolverine's efforts to become market oriented. Here is his response:

"It's proved to be harder than I had imagined. I had to really drive people to think about customers and the corporation as a whole, not just what's good for their own departments. It's also proved to be more worthwhile. We have a different tone in our outlook and a different way of dealing with each other.

"We use all kinds of customer data and bring it into all functions. We do much more interfunctional decision making. The hardest part of all was account selection, and that really paid off for us. It also had the most impact. Our implementation has improved through what we call the three Cs, communication, coordination, and commitment. We're getting smooth, but we sure aren't flawless yet.

"Last night I watched the Pacers play the Boston Celtics on TV. The Celtics won. Sure they've got more talent, but the real edge the Celtics have is their teamwork. At one point in the game, the Indiana team got impatient with each other. They seemed to forget that the Celtics were the competition.

"That's the way we used to be too — each department competing with each other. A few years ago we had a meeting down at French Lick where everything came to a head, and I was feeling pretty desperate. There's a real irony here because French Lick is the hometown of Larry Bird.

"When I think about the Celtics and Bird, what working together means becomes clear. If each Wolverine manager only helps his or her department do its job well, we're going to lose. Back when the company was small, products were simple, competition was unsophisticated, and customers were less demanding, we could afford to work separately. But now, our individual best isn't good enough; we've got to work as a unit. Bird is the epitome. He subverts his own interest and ego for the sake of the team. That's what I want to see at Wolverine."

SELF-EXAMINATION CHECKLIST
1. Are we easy to do business with?
   Easy to contact?
   Fast to provide information?
   Easy to order from?
   Make reasonable promises?
2. Do we keep our promises?
   On product performance?
   Delivery?
   Installation?
   Training?
   Service?
3. Do we meet the standards we set?
   Specifics?
   General tone?
   Do we even know the standards?
4. Are we responsive?
   Do we listen?
   Do we follow up?
   Do we ask "why not," not "why?"
   Do we treat customers as individual companies and individual people?
5. Do we work together?
   Share blame?
   Share information?
   Make joint decisions?
   Provide satisfaction?

---

1. They used the account profitability matrix described by Benson P. Shapiro, V. Kasturi Rangan, Rowland T. Moriarty, and Elliot B. Ross in "Manage Customers for Profits (Not Just Sales)," *HBR* September-October 1987. p.101.

Set Standards And Measure Performance

"We put a microscope on our branches and ask, 'What has to happen here for our customers to get excellent service?' Then we developed the standards of performance and trained our people to meet them."

Edward Crutchfield
Chairman of the Board
First Union Corporation

To say that it is possible to create distinctive service quality by setting service standards almost sounds like an oxymoron, a contradiction in terms—like jumbo shrimp, military intelligence, and postal express. Part of the dilemma lies in the language. Quality, for instance, means "conformance to specifications"—a license to impose tight control and strict discipline. The word "standards" also conjures up images of uniformity and sameness. Yet, in the world of pure service, the customer (not the organization) determines how quality is spelled. And, while uniformity in service quality is a virtue, the customer also wants uniqueness. How do you standardize quality and still create unique experiences for this fickle, demanding evaluator?

The nature of service is that of a performing art—more like experimental theater than a controlled assembly line. Given this special nature, what place do standards and measures have? Shouldn't service managers just hire super-friendly people (like picking the best actors); train them to know the products, policies and procedures (like having them learn the script of a play); tell them to "always do your best for the customers"; and just let the show begin? Absolutely not! Total license is no more likely to lead to service satisfaction (or great theater) than is rigid control. It takes the communication of clear performance expectations plus a means for the performer to compare the performance given to the performance expected. Service standards—and associated measurement—are tools for this communication. And, like in theater, it also takes the guidance of a leader who can encourage, correct, coach and support to pull off a successful service performance.

Yet, we know superior service combines uniqueness with uniformity. We know that consistency in service performance requires some common set of parameters for the performer; it needs some method of measurement to allow effective coaching, feedback, evaluation, and rewards. Even art has its tools—albeit more qualitative than quantitative—for judging excellence. How are we to escape this dilemma? In a world that worships bottom-line, balance-sheet-related yardsticks, how can we, with equal fervor, adopt the evaluative tools of a gymnastics judge or a movie critic?

Perhaps a route out of the box lies in revisiting the meaning of service. Service is a deferential act. No, it is not synonymous with servile, servitude, or doormat. But it does imply the act of being responsive to and supportive of the customer and his or her needs.

Service might be characterized by the childhood story of the lion and the mouse. Listen to the story and be patient! Our societal allegiance to achievement, excelling, and being on top has filled our heads with the kinds of images that leave little room for thoughts of deferring to another. Somehow, such thoughts sound downright weak and wimpy.

The king of beasts was roaming through the jungle, roaring at each animal he encountered. Suddenly, he emerged from a thicket in great pain: a thorn had deeply pierced his right front paw. Frantically, he tried to remove the thorn with his sharp teeth. But, because the thorn was lodged between two toes, he only pushed it deeper. He knew he would need the help of some other animal to remove the thorn.

The lion's reputation, always an asset in getting his choice of the kill, suddenly became a liability in soliciting a fellow animal to be of service. In pain, he roamed the jungle seeking help. All the animals fled like department-store clerks at lunch hour! Finally, he came upon a field mouse who elected to substitute service for survival. With great care, the field mouse dug between the lion's toes and pulled free the painful thorn. The lion was grateful and left to resume his kingly procession through the jungle.

Some months later, the lion and the mouse again met as the lion was trolling for food. The lion failed to recognize the mouse, but the mouse quickly alerted the lion of his identity just in time to be spared. The grateful lion, reminded of the past deed, became friends with the field mouse.

The service of the mouse was, in the full sense of the term, an "act of giving," *unrequited* giving. The mouse gave without requiring reciprocity. The fact that the lion reciprocated by later sparing the mouse's life was purely coincidental. Like most good service acts, it gave the story a happy ending. But the gift carried no requirement for later payment.

What's more, the mouse took some risks to serve, even though escape was a more comfortable route. So it is with service. Each time a service person encounters a customer, there are risks of rebuttal, rebuke, or rejection. But, in the little fable, as in all service situations, the lion (or "customer") was the sole judge of service quality. Standards for customer service (and thorn removal) must begin with the customer's needs and expectations.

The customer *is* the king, and the service person *is* the subject, but *not* the slave. The challenge of effective service management is to help service people understand the difference and carry out the service role in a manner that bolsters (rather than banishes) self-esteem. And, while neither real kings nor kingly customers are always right, we can never take for granted their position as *the* one with the need to be served and *the* one whose expectations and experiences are the criteria for service excellence.

Service standards and measurements begin and end with customers. It is their expectations that shape what ought to happen; their reactions and experiences that determine how well we did. If we are successful in the process of serving, we emerge fulfilled; if we get a special reward in the arena of the jeering marketplace, it is icing on the cake!

We begin this chapter with an article we wrote especially for this book. Titled "Crafting Customer Service Standards: Replication without Robotics," the article explores the interpersonal side of service standards. Since the business world is enthralled with standards that lend themselves to counting—"time, length of . . . , speed, number of . . ."—this piece focuses on setting standards around those aspects of service that are interpersonal in nature. But how does the service manager sell captains of the bottom line on emotion-based service standards?

The second article, "Organization and Customer: Managing Design and Coordination of Services" by Rikard Larsson and David Bowen, appeared in the April, 1989 issue of the *Academy of Management Review*. Written for an university audience, the article is prepared in an academic style. While it may test your patience as a reader, it addresses the difficulty in using production logic to create service delivery systems in a powerful manner.

Since customers share with front-line service people in the creation of a service (Larsson and Bowen refer to customers and service employees as co-producers), the uncertainty in the service-creation process of the customers' input expectations and their willingness to participate add unique challenges to an enterprise's quest for predictability in the "production" effort. The authors explore in depth the issue of input uncertainty (What will the customer expect?, Will the customer's request or feedback offer information with sufficient accuracy and specificity? or How unique will the customer's demand be?) as well as the issue of interdependence (How balanced will the work load be between customer and employee? and How customization versus standardization will be required?). The interaction of these two issues enables the authors to construct a model for discussion which yields a set of propositions useful in designing service processes.

Our third article, "The Service-Quality Puzzle" by Leonard L. Berry, A. Parasuraman, and Valarie A. Zeithaml, appeared in the September-October 1988 issue of *Business Horizons*. Berry is well-known for his writings on service management. The article reaffirms the case that the customer's expectations should be the bedrock of standards and measures and then offers a bridge from standards to measurement by articulating the authors' researched core expectations of customers. "Customers," assert Berry *et al,* "look to reliability, responsiveness, assurance, empathy, and tangibles to form their evaluation of service."

The authors state that service standards help clarify work roles and communicate the organization's priorities. They also provide the benchmark against which performance can be evaluated. The measures recommended by the authors go beyond the isolated "shopping" visits, customer-complaint analyses, image tracking, and other typical approaches. It is as important to keep in touch with the attitudes and insights of service providers as it is to track those of customers. "Customer studies reveal what is happening," say the authors. "Employee studies help explain why."

We've also included a short article—"10 Steps for Measuring Customer Perception of Your Service"—that Ron Zemke wrote for the August-

September 1988 issue of "The Service Edge" newsletter. Like the Tom Peters' article on listening to customers in the first section, this piece offers pragmatic ways to ascertain how your customers evaluate your service efforts.

The chapter ends with our counterpoint piece. "Developing Client-Sponsored Satisfaction Measures" by Matt Elbeck appeared in the Summer 1987 issue of *Health Care Management Review* (originally titled "An Approach to Client Satisfaction Measurement As an Attribute of Health Service Quality"). A warning is in order: Be prepared for more philosophy than pragmatics. While Elbeck is to be lauded for his attempt to take apart a slippery concept like "customer (client) satisfaction" in order to offer ideas for measurement, his claim that such a thing actually can be done is unconvincing. Can concepts like perception and feeling be quantified? Or is this another example of trying to "drive a nail with a B flat"—the wrong tool for the context?

Can, for example, "attitude" be completely dissected as the combination of cognition (awareness), affect (preference), conation (intention), and evaluative beliefs (containing judgments about similarities)? We encourage you to wade through the Elbeck article. While it may come up short as an instructive piece, it invites you to join the search for useful ways to measure an art form.

CRAFTING CUSTOMER SERVICE STANDARDS: REPLICATION WITHOUT ROBOTICS

Chip R. Bell and Ron Zemke

"Mr. Rainey, we're delighted to see you again at the Marriott Long Wharf. We've made a few changes since you were here, and I'd like to tell you about them." The bellhop enthusiastically updates the returning guest while their elevator rises twelve floors from the lobby. The guest is pleased to be remembered and grateful he again made the wise decision to return to this Marriott. "How does this hotel find such thoughtful, efficient people?" he wonders.

Selection wizardry? Absolutely—at least, in part. The front-line employee with a definitive knack for chatting with people, putting them at ease when they are upset, and a disposition to be of service is a special resource to be carefully culled from the stream of more ordinary applicants. The right person in the right job can turn lead into gold for customer and company alike.

But selection alone isn't the whole answer, although it is necessary for creating high-quality front-line performance over a sustained period. Talent—untutored, untrained, undeveloped—is potential, not performance. Add incentive and reward to selection and training, and we still come up short. It is critical that service people, charged with serving and satisfying customers, work within a framework or system of carefully crafted service quality and performance standards that are grounded both by the organization's service strategy and by customer expectations of that organization.

Not all service standards relate directly to actions service people take with the customer. In a theme park, for instance, it is generally important that customers experience scary rides, hot food and cold drinks, funny clowns, and an attractive setting. Along with those experiences comes the matter of standing in line. No one visits theme parks for the purpose of waiting in lines; it just happens. And when it does, we are not surprised; we anticipated it might happen. But when the wait is perceived as too long, too uncomfortable, or too boring, it has a major dampening effect on the quality of the experience. So theme parks work on making lines move quickly—both in fact and in perception. They do this in several ways: 1. The line weaves around to provide changes of scene and a sense of progress; 2. sidewalk entertainment distracts customers from concentrating on the wait, and 3. reminders are posted—"20" minutes from this sign," "10 minutes from this sign"—to let customers know how much longer they will have to wait.

THE GOAL OF A SERVICE SYSTEM

The Marriott hotel and the theme park have in common the goal of making a repeat client of the here-and-now customer. Strategically, they accomplish this by creating a service-delivery system that focuses on providing an important—for the guest—outcome: "a good night's rest at a reasonable price," on the one hand, and "a fun, family-entertainment experience" on the other. The actual service outcome can, however, be just what the customer wanted—in a narrow technical sense—but still be unsatisfactory or displeasing. How? By making the process the customer must endure to arrive at the desired outcome a painful, unpleasant, or otherwise noxious experience. The auto-repair customer expects to have his or her mechanical problems corrected. But, at the same time, he or she expects to be treated as a valued client, not put off, stalled, patronized, or otherwise abused or offended. What we need, therefore, is a system of delivery and a framework of performance standards that consider both outcomes *and* process, ends *and* means.

DISTINCTIVE SERVICE THROUGH SERVICE STANDARDS

Standards for superior service begin with a clear understanding of the customer's expectations of service outcomes and processes. From this array of insight, management fashions performance expectations for service providers. These service expectations are crafted both around what the customer thinks "ought to happen" in getting service plus the unique service vision of the organization. This service vision is an amalgam of a service strategy or focus ("Our nontrivial statement of intent, the promise we make to ourselves on behalf of our customers") plus a service philosophy or set of values about how the organization treats customers and what the organization believes is important to do for customers. The "in living color" character of the service strategy is a vital foundation if service expectations are to become standards.

Service standards grow logically and directly from the organization's service strategy. At its core, a service standard is a set of instructions designed for and communicated to service people to promote consistency in how service is to be delivered to customers. The manager who tells front-line service people always to "act enthusiastically" is communicating a service standard, albeit a vague one. Likewise, the manager who tells new hires to ask "How may I help you?" when answering the telephone is also telegraphing a service standard. The set of instructions might be broad and imprecise, or the instructions might be very specific. But they all relay expectations to those whose professional performances affect the customer's experience of service.

Service standards come in three forms—transactional, outcome, and status. Transactional standards, like the examples given above, pertain to the human-to-human dimensions of customer contact: for example, "Greet all customers with a warm smile, eye contact, and a handshake." Outcome standards communicate the nature of a completed service: "The guest has been satisfactorily checked into the hotel when . . . " Status standards cover those conditions that affect (directly or indirectly) the customer's experience but do not involve a personal exchange. Two examples might be: "The customer-service-center in the lobby will always be stocked with appropriate literature" or "The parking lot will be bused for trash every hour and as needed."

Outcome and status standards frequently involve actions below the line of the customer's visibility. The training center of a major New England bank always offers freshly baked bread and hot coffee before eight o'clock of each business morning. Providing these amenities to the center's participants no doubt involves some transactional standards. However, the status service standard that requires the delivery of freshly baked bread by the neighborhood bakery between 7:30 and 7:45 each morning is no less important to the customer's ultimate experience. (Before 7:30, there might be no one at the center to receive the delivery; after 7:45 would not allow sufficient time for the bread to be sliced and displayed in the break area prior to the arrival of participants (customers of the center) for 8:00 or 8:30 a.m. classes.)

While the "customer" of the training center may never actually witness a bread delivery, the precise status service standard works with transactional service standards to insure that center customers experience this particular service encounter positively.

Service standards help the organization replicate customer experiences with some level of consistency and predictability. The excellent service companies promote uniform quality delivered in a manner customers experience as unique. To paraphrase a famous beer advertisement, "Customers want every Budweiser to taste the same, and they also want to feel that 'this Bud's for you!' "

Service standards enable the service provider to deliver the quality of service that customers expect. Organizations can use service standards to telegraph the amount of latitude or freedom the service person has in determining how service is to be delivered. At times, existing service standards are altered to increase the service person's freedom to act on behalf of the customer.

A major telephone company in the Midwest was required by the public utilities commission always to advise residential customers who reported a phone problem that, if an on-site inspection revealed the problem was with the telephone or the wires in the wall, that customer would be charged a visit repair fee. The telephone company implemented the requirement by giving telephone operators in customer-inquiry centers a script to follow when a customer requested an on-site repair person.

The utilities commission was satisfied. But customer-focus-group interviews revealed that many customers felt "Mirandized" by the cue-card reading; to them, it sounded like a police officer advising a criminal of his or her rights. So the telephone company, anxious to improve its customer-service ratings, altered its service standard's "Read this cue card" and encouraged operators to use their own approach when advising the customer about a possible charge. Customer reaction to the more adaptable, less routinized approach produced higher service-satisfaction ratings.

STANDARDS FOR THE ARTISTIC SIDE OF SERVICE

Most observers of Olympic figure-skating or gymnastic events are grateful to be on the sidelines, evaluating the performances with comments like "fantastic," "shaky," "beautiful," or "she was better than the last one." Pity the poor judges who are trying to choose between the "eight" card and the "nine" card. Ever wonder what it would feel like if, as an Olympic judge, you chose a five card when all your fellow judges held up an eight or a nine? It must be a lot easier to judge running or swimming.

Service is performed, not produced. The intangible, interpersonal dimension of service makes its creation far more art than science. Service performance is more like figure skating than running the 100-yard dash. Style may help the runner go faster, but speed is the only determination of who has won. While it is true that some aspects of the service effort can be quantified—length of time to process a form, customer wait time, or the number of rings allowed before the phone must be answered—the service actions that make a major impact on the customer's experience are subjective. In the Olympics, some of the judges' "eights" look like "tens" to us on the sidelines. In the service Olympics, where customers are the judge, some of their decisions are every bit as mystifying.

Most service managers have little difficulty quantifying the outcome and status dimensions of service; we are better at counting scientifically than appreciating esthetically. Yet, the qualitative side of the service performance is as integral to customers' evaluations as the quantifiable side, perhaps more so. Thus, we run great risks when our quantification (e.g., number of calls handled) results in customers qualitatively voting with their checkbook because "they made me feel I was just a number."

How is the manager to escape this quagmire? In a business world that, for years, has worshipped bottom-line objectivity, to tell the boss we now want to make changes based on customers' whims or feelings sounds like a kamikaze dive into the boardroom table. And, since service rewards are determined by service performance, how in the world can one base pay raises on the subjectivity of a gymnastics judge? Won't this provoke intense boss-subordinate verbal dueling over definitions of terms? "What do you mean, I'm not *enthusiastic*?"! "I DID demonstrate *empathy* to that customer!"

While style is key to excelling in figure-skating, as well as service, performances, you *do* get points for some of the more quantifiable dimensions. Politely answer a phone that has just rung off the wall, and you probably are not going to get a "ten" on the customer's score card. But most managers have had lots of practice making performance standards measurable, quantifiable, and objective. It is the "artsy," interpersonal parts of service focus that leave most service managers scratching their heads. Interpersonal service standards can fall along a continuum from being very general and broad to very specific and precise. "Be friendly" is general; "Say 'Thanks for banking with us' " is precise. Both extremes can be appropriate, depending on the circumstance and the customer's expectations. The service manager's first task vis-à-vis service standards is to decide where service standards are appropriate—that is, where consistency is a virtue in promoting the customer's overall positive memory with getting this service.

The service manager's second responsibility is to decide at what level of preciseness service standards should be developed and communicated. The more precise the service standard, the more exactly is the service to be delivered. With an increasing level of preciseness, however, comes a greater potential for "robotics"—that insincere, rote, mechanically delivered service response. We all can recall phone solicitations that clearly were being read from a script or a cue card. Likewise, we can remember the flat-sounding "Have a nice day," the mechanical "Thank you for shopping at K-Mart," or the insincere "Enjoy" parroted by a restaurant host. Nonetheless, precise service standards may be appropriate to provide the consistency needed for customers to experience service excellence.

The model below outlines three different types of transactional service standards. The most precise type of standard is a "prescription," which prescribes in minute detail how the service person is to act. In a few service settings,the prescription might become a script that outlines exactly what the service person is to say. The "prescription" service standard might be relevant when the service provider wants the customers' experiences to be practically identical each time. This might occur in a theme park when the tour guide repeats the same words to each tour group.

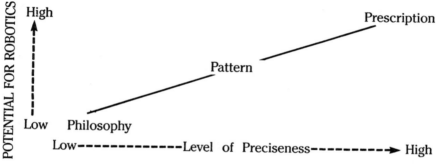

The level of preciseness sought with a "prescription" service standard also might be appropriate under tense or emotional customer encounters when the service person's confidence is bolstered by having consistent lines to guide his or her efforts. The gate attendant of an overbooked flight who has to deal with customers who have tickets or the front-desk clerk who encounters a customer with a guaranteed reservation checking in late at an overbooked hotel might well appreciate a "prescription" for handling these sticky service situations.

The moderate level of preciseness is referred to as "pattern." This level encompasses actions that are similar but not the same. The "pattern" service standard might suggest an array of similar actions without prescribing exactly how they are to occur. An airline might have a service standard for pilots that states: "A member of the cockpit crew will stand in the cockpit door and give deplaning passengers a friendly greeting as they exit the plane." Implicit but not stated is that the individual will say something like "Thank you for flying Piedmont Airlines."

Some banks give their branch customer-service representatives a service pattern to be used when encountering a customer who needs service. The standard communicates that the rep should "always stand, warmly greet the customer, and sincerely apologize if the customer has had to wait more than a few minutes." Such a pattern is often adequate to insure that all bank customers have a consistently positive experience when encountering a customer-service representative. Again, the goal is service consistency at a given customer encounter.

The point at the bottom left corner of the figure is a level of preciseness we refer to as "philosophy." This level is often achieved simply by communicating to service people how they are to "be." This "way of being" is typically the mirror image of "the way we want our customers to feel." If the airline simply told its pilots always to "be friendly" to passengers, standing in the cockpit door to greet exiting passengers might or might not occur.

The advantage of the "philosophy" level of preciseness is that it affords service people considerable freedom to respond to their customers in ways unique to that customer and that situation. The down side is that it poses the risk of inconsistent service performance. A New York pilot's interpretation of "always be friendly" might be vastly different from an Atlanta pilot's interpretation!

As part of its service strategy and core values, a major hotel chain strives to "insure that all guests have a pleasurable experience when staying at our properties." A woman on the housekeeping staff who notices a cracked electrical receptacle in the bathroom and contacts the engineering crew is acting beyond her "job instructions" but consistently with the hotel's strategy, or philosophy. Without allegiance to that philosophy, the house-keeper might smugly say, "I do windows and rooms; I don't do receptacles!" and refuse to take an extra step. The acclaimed Nordstrom, Inc., a department store chain based in Seattle, is known for having the "world's thinnest employee handbook." Except for "Use your good judgment in all situations," there are no rules or patterns outlining what to do or prescriptions communicating what to say; there is only a clear philosophy that directs the service person. In actuality, there are coaching sessions after-the-fact to help service people learn some patterns that are consistent with this pervasive philosophy. In fact, that famously thin handbook encourages employees to "feel free to ask your department manager, store manager, or division general manager any question at any time." But, by and large, service people are guided by the company's philosophy, and customers line up at Nordstrom for its unique brand of service excellence.

RESISTING ROBOTICS

It is easy to see how simply communicating a service philosophy to guide the actions of service people offers great potential for myriad interpretations. How are service standards made more precise without fostering mechanical, or robotic, behavior in those who adhere to such standards? Is there a way to make a "thank you for shopping at . . . " type prescription work for both the organization desiring uniformity *and* for the customer desiring uniqueness?

The solution to this dilemma may be found in the world of theater. Most of us have had the experience of seeing the same play performed by a different cast of actors. Although the script remains the same, the playgoer's experience is altered by the "new" performers and their unique interpretations of those lines with which we are so familiar. In a similar way, so it is with effective service standards. The script in a prescribed service performance may not vary from situation to situation but the customer-oriented philosophy and service values instilled in the service worker and conveyed to the customer during that performance keep a replicated effort from being experienced as a robotic one. If I am to mouth "Thank you for shopping at . . . " *and* I also "Greet every customer with sincerity and authenticity," it will be difficult for me to deliver the prescribed performance rotely. Like actors who use their interpretation of a role to make a script feel fresh, service people use a service philosophy/value to make uniform service performance feel unique.

Walt Disney World uses its "Traditions One" orientation program to acquaint all new hires with the tailor-made Disney philosophy that insures that guests are on the receiving end of the organization's "make people happy" focus. Language and symbolism underscore this show-business philosophy. Customers are guests, rides are attractions, uniforms are costumes, and employees are hosts hired by central casting to work "on stage." This entire thought-out-in-advance process reinforces a central philosophy to give guests a consistently value-added experience when they come to Walt Disney World.

Service standards should be guidelines for performance. Done effectively, they reflect the customers' expectations of what ought to happen; done with distinction, they surprise customers by exceeding expectations. Wise service enterprises seek to insure consistency by crafting service standards that clearly communicate performance expectations to service people. Such organizations also have learned that mechanical motions can be muted by making certain all employees also act in ways that honor the service values manifested in the service strategy of the organization.

ORGANIZATION AND CUSTOMER: MANGING DESIGN AND COORDINATION OF SERVICES

Rikard Larsson and David E. Bowen

Customer participation in the operations of service organizations can be a major source of input uncertainty. A framework for analyzing service organizations is presented in which different conditions of input uncertainty are matched with the design of different interdependence patterns which, in turn, are matched to different portfolios of coordination mechanisms. The composition of portfolios draws on both the conventional organizational literature and recent work on control mechanisms at the client/service firm interface.

The organization-customer interface deserves to be an important focus of analysis within organizational theory, particularly given the shift from a manufacturing-oriented economy to one that is more service dominated (Davis, 1983). The production and delivery of services typically involves considerable contact between the organization and customers; customers frequently participate in service production tasks performed at the organization-customer interface (Bowen & Schneider, 1988; Lovelock, 1984; Mills, 1986). Nevertheless, the tendency remains for authors to depict customers as being buffered from the core technology and to treat them only as consumers, not as producers.

This paper examines how varying forms of co-production by employees and customers affect the design and coordination of service systems. First, we review alternative perspectives on the service organization-customer interface. Then we develop a framework for coordinating service interdependencies that integrates organizational contingency theory (e.g. Lawrence & Lorsch, 1967; Thompson, 1967) and the emergent services literature (e.g. Czepiel, Solomon, & Surprenant, 1985). This is done with some support from the areas of marketing and economics. Our framework treats customer participation in service production and delivery as a source of input uncertainty (Argote, 1982), a concept that we elaborate on relative to prior treatments of the uncertainty concept (e.g., Brass, 1985; Galbraith, 1973; Slocum & Sims, 1980; Thompson, 1967). Next, we present

a typology of four service interdependence patterns that matches alternative designs of the service system to alternative conditions of input
uncertainty. Finally, we match these alternative interdependence patterns
of the typology to appropriate portfolios of coordination mechanisms (cf.
McGann & Galbraith, 1981), which have been drawn from the conventional
intraorganizational coordination literature and the service literature's
description of the control mechanisms at the organization-customer
interface. We conclude with research propositions that are indicated by the
framework and implications for strategic management and marketing.

THE SERVICE ORGANIZATION-CUSTOMER INTERFACE: AN OVERVIEW OF DIFFERENT PERSPECTIVES

Organization-customer relationships have been conceptualized from diverse perspectives. In economics they are viewed in terms of aggregated
meetings of supply and demand coordinated by the invisible hand of the
price mechanism (Smith, 1937 cf. Scherer, 1980). In organization theory an
open systems perspective is applied in which organizations adapt to
conditions of the environment of which customers are components
(Lawrence & Lorsch, 1967; Scott, 1981; Thompson, 1967). In marketing, an
organization reactively adapts to customers through the marketing concept, and actively influences customers through product, place, promotion, and price variables (Borden, 1964; Houston, 1986; Kotler, 1980).

Many works in the literature on services claim that these established
perspectives include a bias toward manufacturing that limits their appli-
cability to service organizations, given the differences between goods and
services (Berry, 1980; Mills & Margulies, 1980; Sasser, 1976; Shostack, 1977;
Thomas, 1978; Zeithaml, Parasuraman, & Berry, 1985). Indeed the phenomenon of customers participating in the production of services (more so
than goods) is not easily addressed through established perspectives. For
example, in economics the focus is on the market coordination of
organizational supply of output and the customer demand for it. However,
in services, customers are not simply a source of demand, they also are a
source of production inputs in the form of information, their bodies, or
their labor (Fuchs, 1968; Hill, 1977; Lovelock, 1983; Mills, 1986). Thus, in
order to be effective, the price mechanism would require complete
contracting of not only organizational supply of output but also customer
supply of inputs and the coordination of co-production (i.e., joint production by service employees and customers). However, customer supply of
inputs introduces substantial uncertainty in service production that pro-
hibits complete contracting and restricts the utility of a market governance
mechanism (cf. Arrow, 1974; Mills, 1986; Williamson, 1975, 1979). Organization theory is limited given the noted tendency to view production as

internal conversion processes by employees who are sealed off/buffered from environmental uncertainty, for example, customers (Mills & Moberg, 1982; Thompson, 1967). With respect to marketing, traditionally, its functions are viewed as separate from production. However, service coproduction tends to merge the two (Gronroos, 1982; Gummesson, 1979; Northcraft & Chase, 1985).

Recognizing these limitations, a number of researchers in the services literature have explicitly addressed the service organization interface, yet their works also have limitations, which are understandable because these were initial attempts to explain a relatively ignored issue. The customer-contact model (Chase, 1978, 1981: Chase & Tansik, 1983) differentiated between high-and low-customer-contact services and suggested some of the possible organizational design implications of each. However, the model has limitations because it is based on only one dimension, customer contact, and this dimension also fails to differentiate between active versus passive customer presence (Schmenner, 1986). Several two-dimentional typologies have been developed that, at least implicitly, extended Chase's customer-contact model. For example, the two dimensions, extent of customer contact and extent of customer contact and extent of customization, were used by Lovelock (1983) and Maister and Lovelock (1982); the two dimensions, degree of interaction, and degree of customization, were used by Schmenner (1986).

The most visible service organization typology, however, is found in Mills work (Mills, 1986; Mills & Margulies, 1980; Mills & Morris, 1986), which presents three types of service organizations that are classified based on various low-, medium-, or high-level combinations of seven service organization-customer interface variables (e.g., information exchange at the interface, time spent interfacing). Although this framework offers a more finely grained treatment of the interface, it also is burdened with how the resulting complexity compromises the typology. For example, the typology is not exhaustive because the three types do not cover all possible combinations of the seven interface variables, and it is not mutually exclusive (as noted by Snyder, Cox, & Jesse, 1982) because any service organization could include characteristics of more than one of the three alternative types of organizations.

Another limitation of most service organization typologies is that they are developed as definitional classifications of alternative designs that are outside of a contingency framework. That is, the characteristics of the interface are themselves the characteristics used to type organizations— the interface characteristics are not treated as contingencies faced by the organization which, in turn, suggest a separate set of design characteristics which then become the basis for labeling alternative types of service organizations. An analogous approach to the one used in such typologies would have been if Burns and Stalker (1961) specified the characteristics of organic and mechanistic organizational designs without stating that they are most appropriate in turbulent and stable environments, as described by a different set of characteristics.

Mills (1986), who mixed both environmental and organizational character-istics in his typology, may be viewed as an exception to this non-contingency rule in service frameworks. A clear exception is the transac-tion cost analysis of service organization-customer exchange offered by Bowen and Jones (1986), which presented four different types of service organizations that were based on matching the use of different governance mechanisms at the organization-customer interface to varying conditions of performance ambiguity and goal congruence faced by the organization.

Another limitation of these prior service perspectives is that they were focused primarily on coordination issues at the service organization-customer interface without researchers developing the implications of this unique interface for the overall coordination of the service system. Although the customer-contact model (Chase, 1978, 1981; Chase & Tansik, 1983) stresses the importance of coordinating back-office and front-office operations, it offers little guidance on how to do so. Even though the works of Lovelock (1983), Maister and Lovelock (1982), and Schmenner (1986) raise management issues relevant to each of their types, they generally ignore coordination concerns and totally ignore a systematic, theoretical development of the issues. Clearly, Mills' typology (Mills, 1986; Mills & Margulies, 1980; Mills & Morris, 1986) is based on characteristics of the service organization-customer interface, and only recently does some empirical work begin to address the relationship between that interface and organization technology and structure (Mills & Turk, 1986).

Although there are individual exceptions to each of the above cited limitations of previous service typologies, very few efforts handle most of them and no single typology appears to overcome them all. In what follows, we address these limitations by offering a contingency framework for examining the total system design and coordination implications of the service organization-customer interface. The focus is on how the relation-ship between the service organization and customers influences the management of differentiation and integration across the entire system (cf. Lawrence & Lorsch, 1967). We attempt to integrate the explanatory power of established frameworks, particularly organizational contingency theory, with the more recent frameworks of the services literature, rather than contributing to the apparent development of allegedly separate traditional manufacturing and service theories. The starting point is the development of the concept of input uncertainty.

A FRAMEWORK FOR THE DESIGN AND COORDINATION OF SERVICE INTERDEPENDENCIES

Figure 1 offers a model to guide the design and coordination of service operations in which differing conditions of input uncertainty are matched with alternative interdependence patterns which, in turn, are matched to different coordination mechanisms, consistent with the contingency framework of the organizational literature on coordination.

Input Uncertainty In Service Operations In general, uncertainty is conceptualized as incomplete information about varying foci, including tasks (e.g., customer demands), and inputs to production (e.g., raw material quality). For instance, Galbraith (1973, p.5) defined *uncertainty* as "the difference between the amount of information required to perform the task and the amount of information already possessed by the organization." The task, as with any instrumental action, can be seen as rooted in desired outcomes and beliefs of cause/effect relationships (Thompson, 1967). Thus, organizations can have incomplete information about what outcomes are desired and how to accomplish the tasks that produce them.

Slocum and Sims (1980) further specified the uncertainty concept by

Figure 1
A Framework for the Design and Coordination
of Service Interdependencies

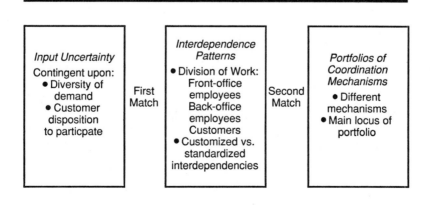

identifying two sources; task uncertainty, which is incomplete information about when input will arrive to be processed. Brass (1985) identified three sources; input uncertainty, conversion uncertainty, and output uncertainty. Brass's input uncertainty resembles Slocum and Sims's (1980) work flow uncertainty, and conversion uncertainty resembles task uncertainty. Brass's output uncertainty resembles the desired outcome uncertainty at least implied by Thompson (1967). However, Brass's output uncertainty is restricted to knowledge of when and where outputs will be distributed and not what outputs to distribute.

The relationship among these various sources of uncertainty is depicted in Table 1, which also indicates how they can be extended to a service setting. Extending Slocum and Sims's (1980) and Brass's (1985) conceptions of uncertainty to a service setting is complicated because they did not distinguish whether their sources of uncertainty stem directly from the environment or from within the organization. Yet this distinction is crucial to how organizations approach different sources of uncertainty (cf. Thompson's, 1967, environmental contingencies versus internal interdependence). Furthermore, their separation of the input and conversion subsystems is more relevant to manufacturing than to service industries due to customer input of labor and information during the service operation.

Argote's (1982) concept of input uncertainty offered researchers a means by which to integrate these sources of uncertainty relative to the service organization-customer interface. She suggested a movement "from diffuse characterizations of an organizations environment or task to more precise descriptions of the uncertainty characterizing a particular element of an organization's task environment" (1982, p. 422). Thus, in her study of hospital emergency units, Argote presented patient inputs as the principle source of uncertainty and developed the concept of input uncertainty differently from Brass (1985) in that it "bridges the somewhat artificial distinction between environmental and task-related uncertainty. Input uncertainty stems from the external environment with which the various units are in continuous contact, yet it has an immediate impact on the tasks that the units perform" (1982, p. 422).

We suggest that Argote's view of input uncertainty generally is a useful conceptualization of service operations. Bridging environmental and task uncertainty is the essence of boundary operations in service production (cf. Rousseau, 1979). Customer inputs can be (a) his/her specification of desired outcomes; (b) his/her body, mind, and/or goods to be serviced; and (c) his/her actions participating in the service production. These inputs, controlled by the customers, are relatively unknown to the service organization before the specific service performance (Thompson, 1962). Thus, customer inputs are environmental sources of incomplete information for the service organization's performance of specific service tasks, at least until the actual service encounter. There are, of course, internal sources of uncertainty, for example, incomplete employee knowledge of how to perform a specific task, given high task difficulty. However, we can expect an organization to have more complete knowledge about the tasks it offers with supposed expertise than about what customer input it will face because in this latter case it has far less authority (Thompson, 1962).

Building on these prior treatments, we offer the following definition: *Customer-induced input uncertainty is the organization's incomplete information about what, where, when, and how customer input is going to be processed to produce desired outcomes.* This includes the full set of uncertainty sources in Table 1. Overall, this concept of input uncertainty is different from conventional concepts of environmental uncertainty, which can be buffered from the technical core, and task uncertainty, which includes internal sources of uncertainty under hierarchical control of the organization. Although buffering and hierarchical control are present to

Table 1
General and Service Sources of Uncertainty

Sources of Uncertainity	General Concepts			Service Concepts
Incomplete information about:	Siocum & Sims 1980	Brass 1985	Thompson 1967	Input uncertainty stemming from the customer (/environment building on Argote, 1982)
what to process				Customer's supply (of object)
where to process it,	Input uncertainity			Customer's supply (place)
when to process it,	Workflow uncertainity			Customer's supply (time)
how to process it,	Task uncertainity	Conversion uncertainity	Cause-effect relationships	Customer's supply (of labor)
into what,				Customer's desired (object) outcome
distributed where,	Output uncertainity		Desired outcomes	Customer's desired (place) outcome
distributed when.				Customer's desired (time) outcome

some extent, these options, which are readily available in manufacturing operations, are limited in services by the predominance of customer input and boundary operations.

Conditions Of Input Uncertainty We can expect the input uncertainty that the customer poses for service operations to vary with two environmental variables: the diversity of customer demand and the tendency of customers to participate in the performance of the service (Bowen & Jones, 1986). Customers present the service organization with incomplete information regarding either what (customer mind, body, and/or goods) is to be serviced toward which desired outcomes or what actions they will contribute in service coproduction. Thus, these two sources can be used for a two-dimensional framework of different conditions of input uncertainty in service production.

Diversity of demand refers to the uniqueness of customers' demands. This includes both the uniqueness of the customer's supply of goods and/or self that is to be serviced and the uniqueness of the desired outcome. It corresponds to how wide a range of patient conditions/inputs the emergency unites faced in Argote's (1982) study. The wider the range of unique customer demands, the greater the specific information not possessed by the organization before the actual service encounter and, thereby, the higher the input uncertainty faced by the organization. Also, high diversity refers to qualitative differences in demand, for example, different car problems; demand of the same service in different quantities is viewed as low diversity, for example different amounts of deposits in similar bank accounts. Thus, the dimension is related to the customization-standardization distinction found in the literature on service organizations (Berry, 1980; Levitt, 1976; Matteis, 1979), but it represents environmental conditions *facing organizations* to which they can respond with more or less customized service designs. Therefore, customization-standardization can be seen as the designed diversity of service supply that can be matched to the diversity of demand.

Customer disposition to participate refers to the extent the customer tends to play an active role in supplying labor or information inputs to the service production process. The more actions the customers tend to contribute, the higher the input uncertainty because the organization has incomplete information about what the customer actually will do before the service encounter (Thompson, 1962). This dimension stresses the degree of active customer participation as opposed to Chase's (1978, 1981) high versus low contact dimension, which depends only on the customer's presence.

The disposition to participate is driven primarily by customer motivation, which, in turn, stems from at least two sources: (a) Customers find doing it for themselves intrinsically attractive (Bateson, 1983), which means customers prefer to be involved in serving themselves even without a price reduction, and (b) customers may feel that their active involvement is necessary to guarantee quality. This is in line with the agency theory rationale for the customer principal to monitor the service agent's fulfillment of the service contract (Mills, 1986). It also includes the possibility of unique customer competencies, such as information about the financial, legal, psychological, or physical situations that the customer may need to supply, firsthand, during service production.

Customer disposition to participate can be constrained by insufficient ability (in terms of knowledge, physical strength and skills, and time) or role clarity (in terms of understanding their role in the service co-production). In other words, customers may lack the competence and role readiness necessary to participate (Mills & Morris, 1986). Thus, this dimension represents how willing the customers are to actively participate, given that they are capable of handling what the role entails and are clear about it (Bowen, 1986; cf. Vroom, 1964).

In sum, customers are a source of input uncertainty relative to the diversity of their demands and their disposition to participate. These variables are customer characteristics external to the organization, constituting constraints and contingencies to which the design of the organization must adapt (Thompson, 1967). This adaptation can be both anticipatory in start-up designs and reactive as the service operations evolve over time. It should be observed that the service organization can also actively influence these environmental variables. Advertising can increase customer awareness of, and positive attitudes toward, product differences, thereby raising diversity of demand (e.g., Kotler, 1980). Also, lowering prices can induce customers to sacrifice more expensive customized product differentiation and/or motivate customers to provide some of the service labor themselves. For instance, banks can impose service charges for transactions using bank tellers but not for transactions using automatic teller machines. For the sake of clarity, first, we will present the reactive contingency framework, and second, we will address how to influence these environmental contingencies in the discussion.

Interdependence Patterns The design of service operations can be viewed in terms of different interdependence patterns consisting of (a) division of service work between employees and customers and (b) customization versus standardization of service actions and interdependencies. The design of service production includes the division of work not only among employees but also between employees and customers. Traditionally, organizational theorists have focused on the division of work among employees (which is natural from a manufacturing standpoint). Yet in service organizations, Chase's (1978, 1981) twofold division of labor between front and back offices can be elaborated on to more fully identify the customer's place in the division of service work. According to Chase, front-office work is performed by service employees in contact with customers and/or it is performed by the customers themselves; back-office employees perform functions separate from customers. Whereas Chase's work addressed the implications of only front-versus back-office activity, the present discussion develops the implications of service work divided among three parties: back-office (low contact) employees, front-office (high-contact) employees, and customers.

This division of work creates interdependencies among the actions of the three parties. The character of these interdependencies can be more or less customized or standardized. The more customized the service, the more unique (highly differentiated) the interdependencies between the actions of the divided service work. (Differentiation, here, refers to providing unique products to meet customer needs (Porter, 1985). It should not be confused with structural differentiation in relation to division or work and decoupling.) Correspondingly, the more standardized the service, the more repetitive and the less differentiated the actions and the interdependencies.

Matching Input Uncertainty And Interdependence Patterns
Dichotomizing the two customer input dimensions yields four basic conditions of input uncertainty facing the service organization. The contingency logic of the first match in Figure 1 is that organization attempt to adapt the design of service interdependence patterns to the conditions they face. This design determines the input uncertainty *allowed* in the service production. Conceivably, a service organization that faces both high demand diversity and high customer disposition to participate could design a highly standardized and nonparticipative service system. This would reduce customer-induced uncertainty in the production. However, we suggest that this would be counterproductive because it can be expected to frustrate customer demands. Thus, the underlying rationale of the proposed contingency relationship is that of the marketing concept: to achieve organizational goals by adapting the organization to satisfy target customer desires (Houston, 1986; Keith, 1960; Kotler, 1980). Also, it would be unnecessarily costly to allow for more diversity and/or participation

than the service organization typically faces (cf. Chase, 1978, 1981; Levitt, 1972, 1976).

Different conditions of input uncertainty can be matched with different designs of service interdependence patterns. First, customization follows the logic that the higher the demand diversity, the greater the need for customization rather than standardization, and vice versa. if customers want uniqueness, they are willing to pay a premium price for differentiated services (Porter, 1985). This conclusion is consistent with the economic notion of product differentiation in which the seller can raise prices without sacrificing the entire sales volume, as opposed to the case of product homogeneity (Scherer, 1980). If this customization is less important to the customer, then "speed, consistency, and price savings (through standardized mass production) may be more important to many customers than customized service" (Lovelock, 1984, p. 57).

Regarding the match to division of work, the less customer disposition to participate, the more work can be shifted from customers to service employees. Further, the lower the customer disposition to participate, the greater the amount of work that can be shifted to the more efficient operations of the back office decoupled from the more disruptive front office (Chase, 1978, 1981; Danet, 1981; Levitt, 1976). Conversely, the more the customer disposition to participate, the greater the amount of work that can be shifted to the customer. This is in line with suggestions to utilize customers as partial employees in order to take advantage of customer motivation, competencies, and labor (Bowen, 1986; Eiglier & Langeard, 1977; Lovelock & Young, 1979; Mills & Morris, 1986). It seems more appropriate to decouple front-and back-office operations when the service design is standardized because customization requires more coupling/interaction between customer/front office and back office to ensure accurate performance of unique demand (cf. Chase & Tansik, 1983). Therefore, decoupled divisions can be expected to accompany standardized service designs matching low demand diversity. These decoupled divisions allow either the customers or back-office employees to do most of the service work. Conversely, coupled divisions between two of the three parties that work more interactively are likely to accompany customized service designs matching high demand diversity.

Figure 2 shows how the two contingencies governing input uncertainty— diversity of demand and customer disposition to participate—create four distinct conditions of input uncertainty. Combining the matching logic above gives rise to four different service design configurations (cf. Mintzberg, 1979) with distinct interdependence patterns that match these four conditions. The interdependence patterns are symbolized in the figure in terms of the three parties of the service work division (Back-and Front-office employees and Customers) and the main locus of interdependencies. The latter is centered around the dominant party(ies) of the division of service work (i.e., where the most interdependencies are located). The labels of the interdependence patterns are discussed in the next section.

Figure 2
A Typology of Service Interdependence Patterns
Matching Input Uncertainity

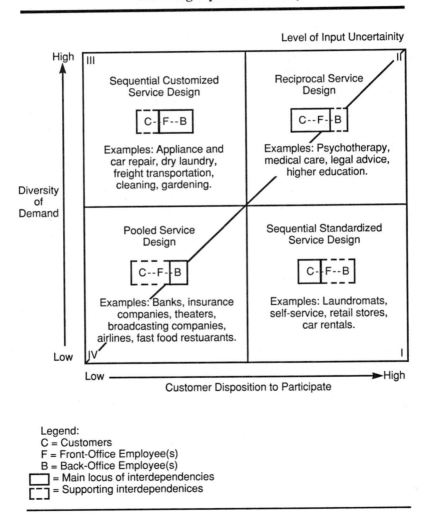

Level of Input Uncertainity

III Sequential Customized Service Design

C- F--B

Examples: Appliance and car repair, dry laundry, freight transportation, cleaning, gardening.

II Reciprocal Service Design

C--F-B

Examples: Psychotherapy, medical care, legal advice, higher education.

IV Pooled Service Design

C--F-B

Examples: Banks, insurance companies, theaters, broadcasting companies, airlines, fast food restuarants.

I Sequential Standardized Service Design

C-F--B

Examples: Laundromats, self-service, retail stores, car rentals.

Diversity of Demand (High / Low)

Customer Disposition to Participate (Low → High)

Legend:
C = Customers
F = Front-Office Employee(s)
B = Back-Office Employee(s)
☐ = Main locus of interdependencies
⌐⌐ = Supporting interdependenices

Four Alternative Service Interdependence Patterns *Quadrant I.*

In situations of high customer disposition to participate and low diversity of demand, the bulk of the workload can be placed on customers if they have adequate ability and are clear about their roles. Here, customers are expected to be more sensitive to prices since they forgo customization and provide most of the labor themselves. By standardizing the supply of goods, facilities, and so forth, organizations can mass-produce inexpensive services. (If not, these may be services that customers will perform for themselves.) This also means that employees' work is held to a minimum to keep costs down, while the organization utilizes customer disposition to participate. Some customers may simply enjoy serving themselves. It is unlikely that their participation will be motivated by a need to monitor service quality, given the clarity of standardized options (Mills, 1986). Furthermore, standardization allows extensive decoupling between front and back office for efficient delivery of service. Typical examples of this design include laundromats, car rentals, and self-service retail stores, that is, businesses that have relatively standardized options.

Quadrant II. If customers have complex and unique problems (i.e., high demand diversity), then it can be expected that they will be less price sensitive and will want expertise for customized solutions to their problems. The customer's self, rather than his or her goods, is often the focus of these complex services. This can be a strong source of motivation for them to actively participate in order either to obtain intrinsic rewards or to monitor the quality of the service. The high disposition to participate also can stem from the need for the customer to provide information for adequate problem solving throughout service production. This leads to interactive service production between mainly customer and front-office employees that is typically found in professional services such as psychotherapy, medical care, legal advice, and higher education (cf. Sasser, Olsen, & Wyckoff, 1978).

Quadrant III. High diversity of demand also can be accompanied by low customer disposition to participate. Many unique services are purchased for mere convenience when customers prefer to have others perform the services for them (without necessarily lacking the expertise as in the case of professional services). This could be because of the lack of time (cf. Fuchs, 1968) or the customer's low intrinsic motivation to participate in menial services. Here, the bulk of the workload is placed on service employees. Front-office employees take in the customer's specifications of the service, and it is performed by back-office employees. Examples include tailoring of clothes and repair services. The separation of high-and low-contact functions allows for the specialization of interpersonal versus technical skills of front-and back-office employees because front-office employees have received the customer's unique specifications. In many services of this design, this coupling is achieved by front-and back-office functions being performed by the same employees, particularly when the service is performed at the customer's location (e.g., gardening and cleaning).

Quadrant IV. This last quadrant represents low demand diversity and low customer disposition to participate in the service production. Low disposition of customers to participate can stem, for example, from their low need to monitor standardized services or their inability to perform large-scale services (e.g., handling insurance needs). This allows for allocating most of the work to efficient back-office operations composed of standardized interdependencies and decoupling from most front-office disturbances (Chase, 1981). Here, division of work between back-office employees can result in advantages of specialization because the repetitiveness of standardized operations creates a higher tolerance for interdependencies (March & Simon, 1958). Standardization also can utilize economies of scale in the form of low-cost, mass-service production for relatively price-sensitive customers with low demand diversity. Examples of this are mass-services with quantitative rather than qualitative differences in demand such as banks, insurance companies, mass-passenger transportation, theaters, broadcasting companies, and fast-food restaurants.

These four interdependence patterns represent different combinations of the customization and customer participation allowed in different service designs. Thus, these two design parameters constitute the defining dimensions of our typology of service interdependence patterns. Dichotomization of the design dimensions into high or low allowed customization and participation creates a two-by-two service design framework. It is proposed to correspond to the faced conditions of the input uncertainty matrix in Figure 2, thereby giving the framework its contingency basis. Furthermore, it covers all possible combinations of different degrees of customization and participation with one of the four specific service designs. Therefore, it overcomes the limitation of not being mutually exhaustive and exclusive that compromises some other service typologies. The interdependence patterns could be labeled with their respective combinations of high or low customization and participation, but this would be awkward and repetitive. Instead, we will next identify/label four alternative service designs that can both add to the description of the interdependence patterns and relate them to the literature on coordination.

A SERVICE DESIGN TYPOLOGY OF INTERDEPENDENCE PATTERNS

Consistent with how the coordination literature prescribes coordination mechanisms based on degree of input and task uncertainty (e.g., Argote, 1982; Galbraith, 1973), typing the four interdependence patterns relative to their level of input uncertainty can guide researchers in selecting the appropriate coordination mechanisms developed in the second match in Figure 1. This typology can be created through using a diagonal in the matrix in a manner analogous to Perrow's (1967) use of a diagonal to represent routineness in his technology matrix. The highest level of input uncertainty is Quadrant II, in the upper right-hand corner (high demand diversity, high customer disposition to participate), and vice versa. Similar to Perrow's schema, the two off-diagonal quadrants represent viable, distinct cases of intermediate levels of input uncertainty in service operations: Quadrant III has high demand diversity and low customer disposition to participate, and Quadrant I low demand diversity and high customer disposition to participate.

Furthermore, Thompson's (1967) interdependence typology can be aligned in order of complexity (pooled—> sequential—> reciprocal) along the same diagonal. This further connects our framework to the coordination literature, especially since significant similarities can be seen between Thompson's typology and the service interdependence patterns. The customized interactive service design between customers and front-office employees in Quadrant II seems to correspond to his reciprocal type of interdependence "referring to the situation in which the output of each becomes the input for the others" (1967, p. 55). Also, the standardized, decoupled, and back-office-dominated service design in Quadrant III is similar to his pooled type of interdependence in which "each part renders a discrete contribution to the whole and each is supported by the whole: (1967, p. 54), in the sense that each customer does not extensively interact with service employees (or fellow customers being served simultaneously) while, at the same time, engaging in the sharing of resources that makes the mass-service possible. This pooling allows large-scale operations to provide low-cost, standardized services such as linking customers who indirectly want to be interdependent (e.g., depositors and borrowers, insurance pooling of risks, and sharing costs of air transportation and broadcasting).

Basically, the different off-diagonal interdependence patterns have sequential characteristics corresponding to Thompson's intermediate type of interdependence as well as intermediate levels of input uncertainty. The self-service character of the decoupled customer-dominated design in

Quadrant I is mainly sequential in the sense that customers serve themselves after service employees have provided the goods and facilities needed for the self-service. The opposite seriality is found in the customized front-and back-office interactive design in Quadrant III. Here, customer specification of the demanded services *precedes* employee performance of the service.

Thus, we label the diagonal patterns *reciprocal service design* (II) and *pooled service design* (IV). The different off-diagonal patterns are labeled *sequential customized service design* (III) and *sequential standardized service design* (I). It should be emphasized that this is a typology of service interdependence patterns, not a typology of service organizations per se. Consequently, the examples of different service businesses offered in Figure 2 are only illustrations of services that typically apply the service design indicated.

It should also be emphasized that this application of Thompson's interdependence types refers only to the main type of interdependence characterizing each service interdependence pattern. It can be expected that the other types will be found to some extent in the patterns. This is, in a sense, represented by the alignment of Thompson's three types along the diagonal, with the intermediate sequential types being placed in the center, thereby making it to some extent relevant to all four designs. The Guttman scale character of Thompson's typology further supports the notion of one interdependence pattern also containing interdependencies of lower complexity (i.e., reciprocal service design also contains sequential and pooled while sequential designs also include pooled). Indeed, this coexistence of more than one interdependence type in a pattern is necessary because our concept of interdependence *patterns* goes beyond Thompson's simple classification of *single* types of interdependence between two parts (indirect, one-way, or two-way). We address the whole configuration of a number of interdependencies between three or more parts of the service production, and the labels indicate the dominant type of interdependence within a pattern. Thus, one interdependence pattern consists of many single interdependencies, but the patterns themselves are distinct from one another (due primarily to their underlying differences in either high or low allowed customization and participation).

MATCHING SERVICE INTERDEPENDENCE PATTERNS AND COORDINATION PORTFOLIOS

The second match in Figure 1 can now be developed, consistent with the logic that specific types of interdependence can be matched by specific coordination mechanisms to achieve concerted action (Thompson, 1967).

Since no mechanism can coordinate all the interdependencies of an organization (Galbraith, 1973; Lawrence & Lorsch, 1967), a *portfolio* of coordination mechanisms, or what McCann and Galbraith (1981) call a portfolio of control and coordination strategies, is required. McCann and Galbraith emphasized "the importance of organizations using multiple strategies (i.e., coordination mechanisms), selected in an explicit conscious manner. These strategies should not interfere with each other too much, but, instead, complement each other as much as possible: (p.79). Their call for more research on the selection process of these coordination portfolios has been left mainly unheeded.

The framework presented here develops this selection process by relating different configurations of mechanisms in terms of coordination portfolios that match different interdependence patterns. This perspective extends conventional coordination frameworks that match individual coordination mechanisms to specific interdependencies and that ignore the mechanisms necessary for coordinating customer activities.

A description of the portfolios of coordination mechanisms that match alternative patterns of service interdependencies requires the resolution of two issues: (a) determining the mechanisms to be included and (b) identifying the emphasis of the portfolio.

Alternative Coordination Mechanisms The organization literature on coordination provides numerous lists of possibilities, building largely on classic works by March and Simon (1958) and Thompson (1967). Thompson's seminal work proposed that pooled interdependence was coordinated through standardization, sequential interdependence through planning, and reciprocal interdependence through mutual adjustment. More recently researchers have developed comprehensive and sophisticated lists of coordination mechanisms, including lateral relations, the design of work, and different human resource management practices (e.g., Galbraith, 1973; McCann & Galbraith, 1981; Mintzberg, 1979; Van de Ven, Delbecq & Koenig, 1976).

The present focus is only to note two summary characteristics of this literature, not to fully review it. First, this literature has an internal focus that does not address the role of customers in operations. Second, most coordination mechanisms rest on the assumption of hierarchical control, which applies only to customers in exceptional circumstances (e.g., prisons and monopolies without substitute products). Relative to both these points, it is worth repeating that price, in the absence of complete contracting, cannot coordinate the actual co-production of services (cf. Arrow, 1974).

Service organizations, then, have a need to coordinate the inputs of participating customers that cannot be filled by the conventional coordination literature. Here, the emerging service literature is helpful. A particularly promising contribution is the application of the dramaturgical metaphor to *script* the service encounter (Solomon, Surprenant, Czepiel, & Gutman, 1985; Smith & Houston, 1983). Abelson (1976, p. 33) defined a script as "a coherent sequence of events expected by the individual, involving him either as a participant or an observer." Relative to services, customers can be thought of as possessing cognitive scripts for a wide variety of service encounters that reflect the individuals' learned (or imagined) conception of the prototypical service experience.

The importance of customer scripts is that they represent customers' knowledge of what to do for effective participation in the service production. Missing or inadequate knowledge of what to do leaves customers with two options: either they must successfully invent what to do or they must be told what to do in order to participate in a well-coordinated manner. But relying on customers' creativity or complete acceptance of employee instructions seems risky for both the customers and the service organization.

Service organizations need to influence the scripts customers follow as a mechanism for coordinating customer participation. Given that customers can retain a variety of potentially relevant scripts in memory, the organization needs to offer cues to the customer to indicate which script fits the given setting. For example, McDonalds presents the customer with an overall restaurant staging, but it also uses highly visible tray racks and garbage cans to inform the customer of what particular script to follow (i.e., one busses one's table after eating).

The notion of shaping customer scripts in-use is similar to the concept of socializing customers as partial employees of the service organization (Mills, 1986; Mills & Morris, 1986). This socialization can reduce uncertainty in service operations through developing conformity to role requirements. Customers also can be selected on the basis of the organizations' suppositions about what scripts customers would be likely to follow. It may even be possible to provide customers with a realistic service preview of the behaviors expected of them during service production (Mills & Morris, 1986). In a similar vein, Bowen (1986) described how to manage customers as human resources in service organizations. A central focus here is ensuring that customers clearly understand their roles so they can perform them effectively.

In this discussion, we suggest that how suitable different customer scripts are is contingent upon the characteristics of the service design. Thus, service organizations can be expected to foster and cue different types of customer scripts for different interdependence patterns of service operations. These scripts can be expected to differ on two dimensions that are best described in the language of the dramaturgical metaphor (Goffman, 1961; Grove & Fisk, 1983; Solomon et al., 1985). The first dimension is the size of the role, or part, that the organization wants the customer to play in the service production. The script can offer either a large or limited role. The second dimension is the flexibility, or freedom to ad-lib, afforded the customer in how to play the role. This dimension is the same as the degree to which the terms of the service encounter are loosely or tightly specified (Chase & Bowen, in press). It is also similar to the concept of the customer engaging in some role making, rather than simply role taking (Mills & Morris, 1986). Overall, organizations need to cue large roles when confronted with high customer motivation to participate; also, organizations cue loose scripts for conditions of high diversity of demand.

Main Locus Of Portfolio The main locus of the portfolio can be considered in the context of which of the three areas of coordination arising from the division of work poses the most critical coordination requirements: (a) front-office coordination of service interaction between front-office employees and customers, (b) front-and back-office coordination of the service support between front-and back-office employees, and (c) back-office coordination of the processing of service support by back-office employees.

Thompson (1967) suggested that coordination costs can be minimized by giving first priority to the more complex interdependencies in order to localize the more difficult and costly coordination mechanisms. In line with this, we suggest that the main locus of the coordination portfolio (i.e., the area with most critical/frequent mechanisms) needs to center around the most complex area of coordination. This area is the most complex part(s) of the interdependence pattern (i.e., most numerous exchanges), and it is identified as the main locus of interdependencies in Figure 2. In this way, coordinative efforts become focused where they are most needed, rather than on less complex interdependencies.

Portfolios Of Coordination Mechanisms Table 2 displays the portfolios of coordination mechanisms that match each of the four designs of interdependence patterns. Specifically, a portfolio for a given design is composed of the row of mechanisms, with the main locus indicated by the highlighted cell.

In the *sequential standardized service design* the main locus is the front office. Coordination mechanisms include, foremostly, customer *self*-adjustment of his or her service-producing actions to presupplied facilities and goods. The presupply provides the customer with different standardized options that are supported by employee maintenance of service facilities and storage of goods. This back-office processing (i.e., decoupled from the customers) can be coordinated by traditional mechanisms such as logistic planning (Chase, 1981) routines for maintenance, refilling shelves with goods, and so forth. Customer scripts for this self-service-oriented design must be tightly specified. Customers need a clear definition of their central

Table 2
Portfolios of Coordination Mechanisms for Alternative Designs of Service Interdependence Patterns

Design of Service Interdependence Patterns	Area of Coordination		
	Front-office coordination of service interaction	Front/back-office coordination of service support	Back-office coordination of support processing
Sequential Standardized Service Design (Customer dominated)	Customer self-adjustment to presupply Large, tightly specified scripts	Routines for presupply Decoupling	Logoistic Planning
Reciprocal Service Design (Customized customer/ employee interactive)	Customer/ employee mutual adjustment Large, loosely specified scripts	Communication Limited decoupling	Programming
Sequential Customized Service Design (Front/back-office employees interactive)	Communication and agreement Limited, loosely specified scripts	Adjusting customer orders and input to agreed performances	Planning
Pooled Service Design (Standardized back-office dominated)	Standardization Limited, tightly specified scripts	Information systems Decoupling	Standardized pooling

role in producing and delivering the service, within the limits of the preadjusted routines for delivering a set of standardized services. The dominant self-serving role of customers casts them in a large role in service performance. This allows customers some role-making discretion for innovative and spontaneous behavior (Mills & Morris, 1986).

In *reciprocal service design*, the main locus of interdependencies is also in the front office. However *mutual* adjustment is the primary mechanism of coordination between front-office employee and customer (Thompson, 1967). This mutual adjustment cannot be preadjusted because it involves the continuous transmission of new information or feedback (March & Simon, 1958); it is impossible to specify a priori the full range of idiosyncratic demands that could arise in this type of service encounter (Mills, Chase, & Margulies, 1983); nonprogrammed coordination mechanisms are appropriate (Argote, 1982). The mutual adjustment of the service production is generally led by the professional expertise of the front-office employee in relation to the often unique and complex problem input from the customer.

Here the script guiding the service encounter customers can be only loosely specified a priori. Still, the customer plays a large part in helping the service employee to diagnose the problem. Thus, the script must emphasize the customer's assisting role (cf. Mills, Hall, Leidecker, & Margulies, 1983) in terms of acceptance of instructions for how to participate effectively in the problem solving. Although this acceptance cannot be based on hierarchical authority over the customer, it can rest on (a) the legitimacy afforded professionals based on expertise or tradition (Weber, 1947) and (b) the customer's dependence on the professional (McCallum & Harrison, 1985). Indeed, it will be likely that the customer's need for the service provider's expertise brought them together (Lefton & Rosengren, 1966).

Relative to the employee's role in mutual adjustment, professional service employees are similar to customers because their behavior is also difficult to control through hierarchical mechanisms. Research indicates that professional service employees exercise self-management (Mills & Posner, 1982); self-management involves employees taking responsibility for the management of their task-related activities rather than having their task activities closely monitored by a supervisor (Mills, 1986). Also, these professionals may rely on substitutes for leadership (Kerr & Jermier, 1977), such as professional norms and cohesive work groups.

Lastly, even though most of the work in this service design is done in the front office, activities, such as the processing of tests, can be decoupled and delegated to the back office. Again, the back-office processing of the service support can be coordinated with conventional mechanisms such as programming (Argote, 1982). Both delegation and decoupling are limited by the unique nature of interdependencies. Customization requires communicating the particularities of each customer problem in the coordination of the service support between front and back offices.

In *sequential customized service design*, the main locus is between the front and back offices. The main coordination task is to adjust unique customer requests communicated to front-office employees to the performance of back-office employees. One means for making this adjustment is to have the same employees assume both front-and back-office roles. The front-office activities of receiving the customer orders and input are mainly coordinated through communication and agreement of specific service performance. Loosely specified customer scripts geared to giving relevant performance instructions to the service employees are expected to adequately allow for demand diversity and clear communication for correct customization. Given low disposition to participate, the customer plays a limited part in the service performance for his/her convenience.

The actual transformation of the customer input is done primarily through back-office activities coordinated by planning of tools and personnel and other internal mechanisms. Even if these front-and back-office activities can be physically separated, such decoupling leads to risks of wrong service performances due to miscommunication between decoupled front and back offices.

Finally, *pooled service design* of interdependence patterns have the back office as the main locus of interdependencies and coordination. The pooled mass-service-oriented design is mainly coordinated by standardization of both front and back offices (Thompson, 1967). The customer contact is standardized through the use of preadjusted options (e.g., bank accounts and insurance policies), forms, programs, routines, and so forth. This allows for decoupling of the back office for efficient operations (Chase, 1978, 1981) and using preadjusted information systems (Galbraith, 1973) as links between the front and back office. The back office coordinates its operations through standardized pooling of customer input for mediating and large scale purposes. Here, it is likely that tightly specified customer scripts will be useful because they provide narrowly specified action sequences corresponding to the standardized options. Limited customer scripts accommodate both low motivation to participate and large-scale specialization by back-office employees. Furthermore, the mass character of this service design will benefit from imitative customer role behavior in order to standardize customer conduct and to utilize interacting customers as role models (Mills, 1986).

IMPLICATIONS

This contingency framework for service production can be summarized in terms of a set of research propositions that focus on the various proposed matches. This provides a coherent, relatively parsimonious framework integrating some hypotheses similar to propositions found scattered throughout the organizational and services literatures with some hypotheses unique to the present proposed typology. First, the overall *design* proposition is that service organizations tend more to use, and to be more effective when using, service designs that match the demand diversity and customer disposition to participate they face. Specifically, the design of service production matches input uncertainty as follows:

> *Proposition 1A: The higher the demand diversity, the higher the degree of customization.*

> *Proposition 1B: The higher the customer disposition to participate, the greater the amount of service work shifted to the customer: the lower the customer disposition to participate, the greater the amount of service work shifted to back-office employees.*

> *Proposition 1C: The higher the demand diversity, the greater the amount of service work shifted to front-office employees in interaction with either the customer or back-office employees, depending on the customer disposition to participate (as in Proposition 1B).*

> *Proposition 1D: The lower demand diversity is, the more decoupled are service designs between the front and back office.*

Proposition 1 breaks down the service design into hypothesized main effects. But the design of the overall service interdependence patterns is likely to also include interaction effects between the two input uncertainty variables. For instance, on the one hand, the mere question of who does the main part of the service work is proposed to depend on the simultaneous main effects of Propositions 1B and 1C. On the other hand, the overall question of *how* the service production is designed also includes the possibly changing nature of service work itself. For example, moving from Quadrant I to Quadrant II in Figure 2 does not simply add front-office employees to the customer as dominating parties of the division of service work. It can also be expected to change the nature of the service work to be divided due to the interactive design between these parties (as compared with customer self-service in Quadrant I or front-and back-office employee interaction in Quadrant III). Thus, viewing service work as a dynamic rather than static set of activities can provide a rationale for hypothesizing interaction effects, but their specification needs further research.

> *Proposition 2: Service organizations are more effective if they design their service production according to Proposition 1 than those service organizations that do not, all other things being constant.*

Turning to the second matching process between interdependence patterns and *coordination* portfolios, we propose that the selection of service organizations' portfolios of coordination mechanisms depends on the following:

> *Proposition 3A: The more complex the interdependence pattern (i.e., the closer to the upper right-hand corner in Figure 2), the more nonprogrammed mechanisms are utilized, and vice versa.*

> *Proposition 3B: The more standardized the service design, the more decoupled the coordination between front and back offices, and vice versa.*

> *Proposition 3C: Back-office activities are primarily coordinated by programmed mechanisms, whereas front-office activities are more coordinated by nonprogrammed mechanisms.*

> *Proposition 3D: The emphasis of the coordination portfolio (i.e., main coordinative effort) follows the main locus of interdependencies of the service design (indicated in Figure 2).*

> *Proposition 4: Service organizations that match their interdependence patterns with their coordination portfolios according to Proposition 3 are more effective than those that do not, all other things being constant.*

Finally, the overall matching of these two design and coordination matching processes is addressed as follows:

> *Proposition 5: Service organizations match both their design of*

interdependence patterns to faced conditions of input uncertainty and their selection of coordination portfolios according to Propositions 1 and 3 (illustrated by Figure 1).

Proposition 6: Service organizations with the overall match between design and coordination according to Proposition 5 are more effective than those without, all other things being constant.

This set of propositions expresses the often intertwined prescriptive and descriptive statements of contingency relationships. The matching rationales *prescribe* certain fits between designs and situations as being more effective than misfits. At the same time, these fits are likely to *describe* most organizations because a given organization "may be driven toward configuration in order to achieve consistency in its internal characteristics, synergy (or mutual complementarity) in its processes, and fit with its situation" (Miller & Mintzberg, 1983, p. 69). This can occur through both strategic adaptation and environmental selection (cf. Child, 1972; Hannan & Freeman, 1977; Hrebreniak & Joyce, 1985). The testing of both the frequency and the effectiveness of these fits can empirically disentangle descriptive and prescriptive aspects of the contingency framework, and this can have potentially interesting implications. For instance, findings of proposed fits being more effective but not more frequent than misfits would suggest either a lack of competitive pressure (cf. Pfeffer & Leblebici, 1973; Rushing, 1976) or a lack of rationality and/or knowledge on the part of organization designers (Argote, 1982; cf. Thompson, 1967). Alternatively, the effectiveness measure may be inappropriate (Argote, 1982); for example, it may not include external assessment criteria as legitimacy needed for success in institutionalized environments (Meyer & Rowan, 1977).

Finally, additional specification to the basics of the framework may be needed before its effectiveness is fully realized in research or practice. For example, researchers in this area should address how to coordinate the different mechanisms that constitute a portfolio. That is, what strategies and mechanisms can be used to coordinate the interdependence that exists *across* the three cells in the row of a portfolio? Compatibility of strategies is required within a portfolio because one mechanism can nullify or reinforce another (McCann & Galbraith, 1981). The portfolio selection process can be viewed partly as coordination of interdependent coordination mechanisms. This leads us to Ashby's (1960) concept of *amplification* in the context of how the overall coordination capacity of an organization can be amplified through coordination of interdependent coordination mechanisms. For example, in pooled service design, it is necessary to coordinate the standardized forms, routines, and so forth, of the front-office interaction; the information system between front and back office; and the main coordination effort of standardized back-office processing of the customer pool. Propositions should be developed that will help us to understand this amplification process.

Strategic Management And Marketing Implications A second area for future analysis involves the strategic and marketing implications of the presented framework. One strategic concern involves the service organization's distinctive coordination competencies. For instance, if an organization has great back-office strength in dealing with large-scale standardized operations, then a pooled service design may be appropriate not only for conditions of low input uncertainty, assuming the organization is weak in implementing sequential designs. In a broader context, the organization's coordination competence may provide a rationale for not pursuing reactive adaptation to environmental conditions emphasized in the framework and, instead, actively influencing the demand diversity and customer disposition to participate it faces. For example, an organization that has distinctive programming capability could utilize price size product homogeneity, thereby decreasing demand diversity so that there would be a match with standardized service offerings. Another example would be that front-office strengths can be capitalized upon by inducing customers to participate more actively through price reductions, intrinsic rewards, and/or customer socialization toward role readiness and requisite ability.

Another strategic and marketing implication is that the framework can guide the market segmentation of customers and the provision to these segments of suitable service designs. This is possible because a service organization can use several different service designs simultaneously, especially if it faces different uncertainty conditions. For instance, a bank that has a predominantly pooled service design via automatic teller machines that fit a market segment of customers who are disposed to participate and who have low demand diversity. The bank also could use a reciprocal service design by offering a broader range of professionalized financial services to fit a segment of customers who have diverse demands and a disposition to participate. In all, the reactive marketing concept rationale for the contingency framework, together with these active marketing influences on the customer/environmental variables, provides a conceptual vehicle for jointly optimizing the organization and marketing of services.

CONCLUSION
We have offered a framework for analyzing design and coordination issues at the service organization—customer interface. The attention this inter-

■

Set Standards And
Measure Performance

face should receive in organizational theory is clearly indicated by the growth of the service sector. Yet the importance of service operations to manufacturing firms is also a growing concern. (Bowen, Siehl, & Schneider, 1989). There is a need, then, to better understand the management of service interdependencies in the economy as a whole—a need that we hope this framework begins to address.

Abelson, R.P., (1976) Script Processing in Attitude Formation and Decision Making. In J.S. Carroll & J.W. Payne (Eds.), *Cognition and Social Behavior,* pp. 33-46. Hillsdale, NJ: Erlbaum.

Argote, L., (1982) Input Uncertainty and Organizational Coordination in Hospital Emergency Units. *Administrative Science Quarterly,* 27, pp. 420-434.

Arrow, K.J., (1974) *The Limits of Organization,* New York: Norton.

Ashby, W.R., (1960) *Design for a Brain,* London; Chapman and Hall.

Bateson, J.E.G., (1983) The Self Service Customer: Empirical Findings. In L. Berry, L. Shostack, & G. Upah (eds.), *Emerging Perspectives in Services Marketing,* pp. 50-53). Chicago: American Marketing Association.

Berry, Leonard L., (1980, May-June) *Services Marketing Is Different.* Business, pp. 24-28.

Borden, N.H., (1964, June) The Concept of Marketing Mix. *Journal of Advertising Research,* 4, 2-7.

Bowen, David E., (Fall 1986) Managing Customers As Human Resources in Service Organizations. *Human Resource Management,* pp. 371-383.

Bowen, David E. and Jones, Gareth R., (Vol. 11, No. 2, 1986) Transaction Cost Analysis of Service Organization-Customer Exchange. *Academy of Management Review,* pp. 428-441.

Bowen, David E. and Schneider, B., (1988) Services Marketing and Management: Implications for Organizational Behavior. In B.M. Staw & L.L. Cummings (Eds.), *Research in Organizational Behavior,* (Vol. 10, pp. 43-80). Greenwich, CT: JAI Press.

Bowen, David E., Siehl, C., & Schneider, B., (1989) A Framework for Analyzing Customer Service Orientations in Manufacturing. *Academy of Management Review,* 14, 75-95.

Brass, D.J., (1984) Technology and the Structuring of Jobs: Employee Satisfaction, Performance, and Influence. *Organizational Behavior and Human Decision Processes,* 35, pp. 216-240.

Chase, Richard B., (Winter 1981) The Customer Contact Approach to Services: Theoretical Bases and Practical Extensions. *Operations Research,* pp. 37-43.

Chase, Richard B., (Vol. 56, 1978) Where Does the Customer Fit in a Service Operation? *Harvard Business Review,* pp. 137-142.

Chase, Richard B. and Tansik, David A., (September 1983) The Customer Contact Model for Organization Design. *Management Science,* pp. 1037-1049.

Chase, Richard B. and Bowen, David E., (in press) Integrating Operations and Human Resource Management in the Service Sector. In C.C. Snow (Ed.), *Strategy, Organization Design, and Human Resource Management,* Greenwich, CT: JAI Press.

Czepiel, J.A., Solomon, M.R., & Suprenant, C.F., (1985) *The Service Encounter,* Lexington, MA: Heath.

Danet, B., (1981) Client-Organizational Relationships. In P.C. Nystrom & W.H. Starbuck (Eds.), *Handbook of Organizational Design,* pp. 382-428. New York: Oxford University Press.

Davis, S., (1983, Spring) Management Models for the Future. *New Management,* pp. 12-15.

Eiglier, P., & Langeard, E., (1977) A New Approach to Service Marketing. In E.E. Langeard, C. Lovelock, J. Bateson, & R. Young (Eds.), *Marketing Consumer Services: New Insights,* (Report 77-115) pp. 37-41, Boston: Marketing Science Institute.

Fuchs, V.R., (1968) *The Service Economy,* New York: Columbia University Press.

Galbraith, J., (1973) *Designing Complex Organizations,* Reading, MA: Addison-Wesley.

Goffman, E., (1961) *Encounters: Two Studies in the Sociology of Interaction,* Indianapolis: Bobbs-Merrill.

Grove, S.J., & Fisk, R.P., (1983) The Dramaturgy of Services Exchange: An Analytical Framework for Services Marketing. In L.L. Berry, G. L. Shostack, & G. Upah (Eds.), *Emerging Perspectives in Services Marketing,* pp. 45-49. Chicago: American Marketing Association.

Gronroos, C., (1982) An Applied Service Marketing Theory. *European Journal of Marketing,* 16(7), pp. 30-41.

Gummesson, E., (1979) The Marketing of Professional Services: An Organizational Dilemma. *European Journal of Marketing,* 13(5), pp. 308-318.

Hannan, M.T., & Freeman, J., (1977) The Population Ecology of Organizations. *American Journal of Sociology,* 82, pp. 929-964.

Hill, T.P., (1977) On Goods and Services. *Review of Income and Wealth,* 23, pp. 315-338.

Houston, F.S., (1986) The Marketing Concept: What It Is and What It Is Not. *Journal of Marketing,* 50(2), pp. 81-87.

Hrebiniak, L.G., & Joyce, W.F., (1985) Organizational Adaptation: Strategic Choice and Environmental Determinism. *Administrative Science Quarterly,* 30, pp. 336-349.

Keith, R.J., (1960, January) The Marketing Revolution. *Journal of Marketing,* 24, pp. 35-38.

Karr, S., & Jermier, J., (1977) Substitutes for Leadership: Their Meaning and Measurement. *Organizational Behavior and Human Performance,* 22, pp. 375-403.

Kotler, P., (1980) *Marketing Management: Analysis, Planning and Control* (4th Ed.), Englewood Cliffs, NJ: Prentice-Hall.

Lawrence, P.R., & Lorsch, J.W., (1967) *Organization and Environment: Managing Differentiation and Integration,* Boston: Harvard University Press.

Lefton, M., & Rosengren, W.R., (1966) Organizations and Clients: Lateral and Longitudinal Dimensions. *American Sociological Review,* 31, pp. 802-810.

Levitt, T., (1972) Production-Line Approach to Service. *Harvard Business Review,* 54(5), 41-52.

Lovelock, C.H., (1983) Classifying Services to Gain Strategic Marketing Insights. *Journal of Marketing,* 47(3), pp. 9-20.

Lovelock, C.H., (1984) *Services Marketing,* Englewood Cliffs, NJ: Prenctice-Hall.

Maister, D.H., & Lovelock, C.H., (1982) Managing Facilitator Services. *Sloan Management Review,* 23(2), pp. 19-32.

March, J.G., & Simon, H.A., (1958) *Organizations,* New York: Wiley.

Matteis, R.J., (1979) The New Back Office Focuses on Customer Service. *Harvard Business Review,* 57(2), pp. 146-159.

McCallum, J.R., & Harrison, W., (1985) Interdependence in the Service Encounter. In J.A. Czepiel, M.R. Solomon, & C.F. Suprenant (Eds.), *The Service Encounter,* pp. 35-48. Lexington, MA: Heath.

McCann J., & Galbraith, J.R., (1981) Interdepartmental Relations. In P.C. Nystrom & W.H. Starbuck (Eds.), *Handbook of Organizational Design*, (Vol. 2), pp. 60-84. New York: Oxford University Press.

Meyer, J.W., & Rowan, B., (1977) Institutionalized Organizations: Formal Structure As Myth and Ceremony. *American Journal of Sociology*, 83, pp. 340-363.

Miller, D., & Mintzberg, H., (1983) The Case for Configuration. In G. Morgan (Ed.), *Beyond Method: Strategies for Social Research*, pp. 57-73. Beverly Hills, CA: Sage.

Mills, P.K., (1986) *Managing Service Industries: Organizational Practices in a Post-Industrial Economy*, Cambridge, MA: Ballinger.

Mills, P.K., Chase, R. B., & Margulies, N., (1983) Motivating the Client/Employee System As a Production Strategy. *Academy of Management Review*, 8, pp. 301-310.

Mills, P.K., Hall J. L., Leidecker, J.K., & Margulies, N., (1983) Flexiform: A Model for Professional Service Organizations. *Academy of Management Review*, 8, pp. 118-131.

Mills, P.K. & Margulies, N., (1980) Toward a Core Typology of Service Organizations. *Academy of Management Review*, 5, pp. 255-265.

Mills, P.K., & Moberg, D.J., (1982) Perspectives on the Technology of Service Operations. *Academy of Management Review*, 7, pp. 487-478.

Mills, P.K., & Posner, B.Z., (1982) The Relationships Among Self-Supervision, Structure, and Technology in Professional Organizations. *Academy of Management Journal*, 25, pp. 437-441.

Mills, P.K. & Turk, T., (1986) a Preliminary Investigation into the Influence of Customer-Firm Interface on Information Processing and Task Activities in Service Organizations. *Journal of Management*, 12(1), pp. 91-104.

Mintzberg, H., (1979) *The Structuring of Organizations*, Englewood Cliffs, NJ: Prentice-Hall.

Northcraft, G.B., & Chase, R.B., (1985) Managing Service Demand at the Point of Delivery. *Academy of Management Review*, 10, pp. 66-75.

Perrow, C., (1967) A Framework for the Comparative Analysis of Organizations. *American Sociological Review*, 32. pp. 194-208.

Pfeffer, J., & Leblebici, H., (1973) The Effect of Competition on Some Dimensions of Organizational Structure. *Social Forces*, 52, pp. 268-279.

Porter, M.E., (1985) *Competitive Advantage: Creating and Sustaining Superior Performance*, New York: Free Press.

Rousseau, D. M., (1979) Assessment of Technology in Organizations: Closed Versus Open Systems Approaches. *Academy of Management Review*, 4, pp. 531-542.

Rushing, W.A., (1976) Profit and Nonprofit Orientations and the Differentiation-Coordination Hypothesis for Organizations: A Study of Small General Hospitals. *American Sociological Review*, 41, pp. 676-691.

Sasser, W.E., (1976) Match Supply and Demand in Service Industries. *Harvard Business Review*, 54(6), pp. 133-140.

Sasser, W.E., Olsen, R.P., & Wyckoff, D.D., (1978) *Management of Service Operations*, Boston: Allyn & Bacon.

Scherer, F.M., (1980)*Industrial Market Structure and Economic Performance*, Chicago: Rand McNally.

Schmenner, R.W., (1986) How Can Service Businesses Survive and Prosper? *Sloan Management Review*, (3), pp. 21-32.

Scott, W.R., (1981) *Organizations: Rational, Natural, and Open Systems*, Englewood Cliffs, NJ: Prentice-Hall.

Shostack, G.L., (1977)Breaking Free From Product Marketing. *Journal of Marketing*, 41(2), 73-80.

Slocum, J.W., & Sims, H., (1980) A Typology for Integrating Technology, Organization, and Job Design. *Human Relations*, 33, pp. 193-212.

Smith, A., (1937) *An Inquiry into the Nature and Causes of the Wealth of Nations*, New York: The Modern Library (Original work published 1776).

Smith R.A., & Houston, M.J., (1983) Script-Based Evaluations of Satisfaction with Services. In L.L. Berry, G.L. Shostack, & G. Upah (Eds.), *Emerging Perspectives in Services Marketing*, (pp. 59-62). Chicago: American Marketing Association.

Snyder, C.A., Cox, J.F., & Jesse, R.R., (1982) A Dependent Demand Approach to Service Organization Planning and Control. *Academy of Management Review*, 7, pp. 455-466.

Solomon, M.R., Suprenant, C., Czepiel, J.A., & Gutman, E.G., (1985) A Role Theory of Dyadic Interactions: The Service Encounter. *Journal of Marketing*, 49(1), pp. 99-111.

Thomas, D.R.E., (1978) Strategy Is Different in Service Businesses. *Harvard Business Review*, 56(4), pp. 158-165.

Thompson, J.D., (1962) Organizations and Output Transactions. *American Journal of Sociology*, 68, pp. 309-324.

Van de Ven, A.H., Delbecq, A.L., & Koenig, R., Jr., (1976) Determinants of Coordination Modes Within Organizations. *American Sociological Review*, 41, pp. 322-338.

Vroom, V., (1964) *Work and Motivation*, New York: Wiley.

Weber, M., (1947 *The Theory of Social and Economic Organization*, New York: Free Press.

Williamson, O.E., (1975) *Markets and Hierarchies: Analysis and Antitrust Implications*, New York: Free Press.

Williamson, O.E., (1979) Transaction-Cost Economics: The Governance of Contractual Relations. *Journal of Law and Economics*, 22, pp. 233-262.

Zeithaml, V.A., Parasuraman, A., & Berry, L.L., (1985) Problems and Strategies in Services Marketing. *Journal of Marketing*, 49(2), pp. 33-45.

THE SERVICE-QUALITY PUZZLE

Leonard L. Berry, A. Parasuraman,
and Valarie A. Zeithaml

Competing organizations provide the same *types* of service—airline transportation to Chicago, tax-return preparation, shampoo and blow-dry services—but they do not provide the same *quality* of service. No one knows this better than customers. To customers, competing service enterprises may look alike, but they do not feel alike.

In fact, service quality has become the great differentiator, the most powerful competitive weapon most service organizations possess. As Stanley Marcus once remarked to a group of bankers, "The dollar bills the customer gets from the tellers in four banks are the same. What is different are the tellers." What, however, makes the tellers different? Quality has received much attention, but many service firms continue to have trouble delivering, even defining it.

We have studied the issue of service quality since 1983 to try to answer three fundamental questions:

- What is service quality?
- What causes service-quality problems?
- What can service organizations do to improve quality?

Our work has included both qualitative and quantitative research on customers, employees, and managers of businesses offering retail banking, securities brokerage, product repair-and-maintainance, bank credit-card, and long-distance telephone services.

This article outlines our most important findings. We will begin at the beginning by defining the components of service quality. We will then explain some of the organizational factors that can undermine service quality and illustrate these points with a case study of a large U.S. bank. Finally, we will recommend ways to enhance quality throughout a service organization.

123

■

WHAT IS SERVICE QUALITY?

Quality is often defined as "conformance to specifications, "[1] but this phrase can be misleading. Quality is conformance to customer specifications; it is the customer's definition of quality, not management's, that counts.

Customers assess service quality by comparing what they want or expect to what they actually get or perceive they are getting. To earn a reputation for quality, an organization must meet—or exceed—customer expectations.

And what do service customers expect? Our research suggests these expectations cover five areas:

- *Tangibles:* the physical facilities, equipment, appearance of personnel;
- *Reliability:* the ability to perform the desired service dependably, accurately, and consistently;
- *Responsiveness:* the willingness to provide prompt service and help customers;
- *Assurance:* employees' knowledge, courtesy, and ability to convey trust and confidence; and
- *Empathy:* the provision of caring, individualized attention to customers.

We asked users of credit-card, repair-and-maintenance, long-distance telephone, and retail banking services to rate the importance of each of these dimensions on a scale of 1 (not at all important) to 10 (extremely important). We found—not surprisingly—that all were considered important. The scores for tangibles, however, ranged from a relatively low 7.14 to 8.56, while reliability, responsiveness, assurance, and empathy received average scores well above 9 for all the services studied. These results are presented in Table 1.

Reliability clearly emerged as the most important dimension, regardless of the service being studied. As shown in the table, 61 percent of the long-distance telephone customers, 57 percent of the repair-service customers, 49 percent of the credit-card customers, and 42 percent of the bank customers considered this dimension most important. When we used the same questionnaire with a second sample of bank customers, the results were similar: 58 percent chose reliability as the most important dimension of service.

Set Standards And
Measure Performance

The customer's message to service providers is clear: Be responsive, be reassuring, be empathetic, and most of all, be reliable—*do what you say you are going to do.* This is more easily acknowledged and understood than accomplished.

There is another message: human performance plays a major role in customers' perceptions of service quality. Three of the five—dimension,

Table 1
Importance of Service-Quality Dimensions
in Four Service Sections

	Mean Importance Rating on 10-point Scale*	Percentage of Respondents Indicating Dimension is Most Important
Credit-Card Customers (n=187)		
Tangibles	7.43	0.6
Reliability	9.45	48.6
Responsiveness	9.37	19.8
Assurance	9.25	17.5
Empathy	9.09	13.6
Repair-and-Maintenance Customers (n=183)		
Tangibles	8.48	1.2
Reliability	9.64	57.2
Responsiveness	9.54	19.9
Assurance	9.62	12.0
Empathy	9.30	9.6
Long-Distance Telelphone Customers (n=184)		
Tangibles	7.14	0.6
Reliability	9.67	60.6
Responsiveness	9.57	16.0
Assurance	9.29	12.6
Empathy	9.25	10.3
Bank Customers (n=177)		
Tangibles	8.56	1.1
Reliability	9.44	42.1
Responsiveness	9.34	18.0
Assurance	9.18	13.6
Empathy	9.30	25.1

*Scale ranges from 1 (not all important) to 10 (extremely important).

assurance, and empathy—result *directly* from human performance. Clearly, if one is to understand and avoid service-quality problems one must contend with the people factor.

WHAT CAUSES SERVICE-QUALITY PROBLEMS?

Customers' expectations for a particular service shape their assessment of the quality of that service. When there is a discrepancy between customers' expectations and management's *understanding* of customer expectations, perceived service quality will suffer. Management's failure to identify customer desires accurately is one kind of quality gap.

Even when management fully understands customer expectations, service-quality problems may occur. For one thing, management may believe that it is impossible or impractical to meet all of the expectations. We interviewed executives at a repair-and-maintenance firm who knew they would have trouble meeting customer demand for prompt service during the summer months, when air conditioners, lawn mowers, and bicycles are in heavy use. Yet they said they could not increase staff for the demand peak. Asked why, one executive answered, "Summer is when our technicians like to take their vacations." The firm did not set its service specifications according to customer needs; instead, it allowed service to suffer because of an assumption about the work force.

The Service-Performance Gap In some cases, however, management does understand customer expectations and does set appropriate specifications (either informally or formally), and still the service delivered by the organization falls short. The difference between service specifications and the actual service is the service-performance gap. Unfortunately, it is common in service businesses.[2] Organizations offering services that are highly interactive, labor-intensive, and performed in multiple locations are especially vulnerable to this gap.

There are many opportunities for something to go wrong when the service provider and the customer interact, when both parties experience and respond to each other's mannerisms, attitude, competence, mood, dress, language, and so forth. Similarly, there is more variability among service outcomes in labor-intensive services than when machines dominate service delivery; bank customers who use human tellers will experience far more service variability than those using automatic teller machines. Finally, decentralized service production through a chain of outlets complicates quality control, because the organizational layers between senior management and front-line service providers hinder two-way communication and make it more difficult to assess individual employees' performance.

The People Factor Service quality suffers when employees are unwilling or unable to perform a service at the level required. Willingness to perform may be described in terms of discretionary effort, the difference "between the maximum amount of effort and care that an individual could bring to his or her job, and the minimum amount of effort required to avoid being fired or penalized."[3] Employees who begin a new job giving 100 percent discretionary effort may be giving far less within weeks or months. This can happen because they have had to deal with too many long lines, too many unreasonable customers, too many rules and regulations, and too few pats on the back; it can also happen when they observe that few of their associates are giving the job their all.

In other cases service providers may simply not have the ability to perform at specified levels. An organization may offer wage rates insufficient to attract skilled workers, or it may fail to train personnel adequately, or both. In addition, as a result of high turnover, workers may be moved into higher-level positions before they are ready. These factors are typical of many service industries, and all can lead to poor service quality.

Maintaining service quality, then, depends not only on recognizing customer desires and establishing appropriate standards but also on maintaining a work force of people both willing and able to perform at specified levels. Factors that can contribute to the service-performance gap are illustrated in the story of one large bank.

THE CASE OF ALPHA BANK
To investigate the service-performance gap in more detail, we studied a large U.S. branch bank we will call Alpha Bank. All of the service-business traits mentioned earlier—extensive interaction between service personnel and customers, labor-intensiveness, and multiple service locations—were present in Alpha Bank.

Like many other banking organizations, Alpha Bank had responded to deregulation by adding new services. At the time of our study, it had also centralized the branch-lending function in an attempt to boost productivity. In research with customers, employees, and managers, however, it became apparent that there was a sizable gap between the level of performance Alpha Bank's management wanted and what was actually occurring in the branches. Ironically, we found that management was bringing some of its service headaches upon itself. Many of Alpha's service problems could be traced to three organizational factors that influenced workers' willingness and ability to perform: role conflict, inadequate role support, and inadequate role environment. Figure 1 illustrates the relationships of these factors to the service-performance gap.

Role Conflict Alpha Bank's problem with role conflict (a poor fit among different elements of a service provider's job) stemmed from a failure to set appropriate service specifications.

Alpha had decided to introduce more aggressive personal selling at the branch level by emphasizing the sales component of branch employees' responsibilities. Many service providers viewed the sales and service elements of their jobs as conflicting. A teller observed, "If I'm trying to cross-sell when there's a long line, the customers waiting in line give me that look" 'When is this girl going to shut up?' " One service representative said, "You are torn sometimes between giving the customer what he or she wants and bringing money into the bank."

The service-versus-sales dichotomy was not the only conflict branch employees experienced. There were also too many demands on the employees' attention. The following comment was typical: "You are supposed to give your customer your undivided attention, but you have already been interrupted seven times by telephone calls. You can't put the telephone caller on hold or send him elsewhere, because once I did that and the caller was a 'shopper' and my [performance] score was lowered."

For branch lenders, another source of role conflict was a loss of personal control over the quality of service rendered. Branch lenders had processed and approved loans in the past. Now, however, loan processing was handled

Figure 1
Causes of the Service-Performance Gap at Alpha Bank

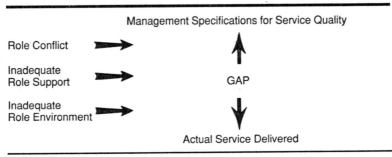

at operations centers; as a result, loans moved more slowly and branch employees were not able to give customers timely information on the status of their applications. One branch lender said, "My number-one problem is working with other units over which I have no control." A branch manager put it this way: "We're offering terrible service now. We used to have control and now we don't. We used to know where everything was and now we don't."

Inadequate Role Support Alpha employees suffered from a lack of adequate role support—hiring practices, training programs, and support services, functions that directly affect employees' ability to perform. Focus-group discussions revealed perceived deficiencies in all three areas.

In regard to hiring, the overriding sentiment among disgruntled Alpha employees was that you get what you pay for, and Alpha wasn't paying for much. One branch manager said, "We draw from the bottom of the barrel because that's the way we compensate."

The status of training was equally bleak—a case of too little, too late. A customer-service representative commented, "It's really embarrassing—customers know about new products before we do. We're the bank. We should know things before the customer does. But the training classes may be scheduled after the product comes out." During a focus group, a lending officer expressed a similar complaint: "The bank will put out a product we don't understand—especially loans—and not tell us enough about it, not train us enough to sell it. With 'XYZ,' for example, I still have to get out the book [to look up how the loan works] and it takes me a good ten minutes." At this point, another participant in the group chimed in, "I just found out two weeks ago that we had the book." Then another said, "I just found out now that we had 'XYZ'!"

Employees were also frustrated about support services, particularly because of the centralization of the loan function. Whereas role conflict concerns the question, "Do I control my own destiny?" with role support the question is, "Do others in the organization come through for me when I don't control my own destiny?" At Alpha the answer to the latter appeared to be no. One employee said, "We're having a breakdown in our support services. It goes all the way from bookkeeping to loans. I have had a home equity loan in there for a month. The customer gets upset—he can go next door and get the same thing in three days."

Inadequate Role Environment Alpha Bank employees were also hampered by an inadequate role environment (organizational climate and culture). Strong belief in an organization and in the importance of one's contribution to it can inspire strong discretionary effort by workers; weak belief (what we observed Alpha) can have the opposite effect.

The principal role-environment issue at Alpha Bank was branch employees widespread impression that individual performance went unnoticed and unrewarded. A lending officer said, "You feel like management doesn't know what you are doing. We need more support and recognition." A teller echoed this thought: "They should give recognition to people who are really performing. So many times you are judged by your immediate supervisor. That person may not like you. I wish other managers, higher up, would know how people are performing."

Employee And Customer Surveys We obtained further information on attitudes at Alpha Bank through a structured employee questionnaire, comprising 30 statements about working in Alpha's branch system. Employees rated these statements on a scale of 1 (strongly disagree) to 7 (strongly agree). Mean responses to 12 representative statements are shown in Table 2.

The scores in the table hover around the midpoint of the scale—"neither agree or disagree." Ideally, Alpha Bank's management would like to see the mean scores on the negatively worded statements in the 1-2 range (indicating strong and consistent disagreement) and scores on the positively worded statements of 6-7 (indicating strong and consistent agreement). In fact, not one score falls into either category.

We also surveyed some of Alpha Bank's customers. As one would expect, the survey data indicated that the problems mentioned by employees were damaging the bank's perceived service quality.

We computed customers' mean ratings of Alpha's service quality in each of the five areas mentioned earlier—tangibles, reliability, responsiveness, empathy, and assurance—on an overall scale of $+6$ to -6. A score of zero would imply that the bank's performance, as perceived by customers, just met their expectations; positive scores would indicate that perceived performance exceeded expectations, and negative scores would indicate that performance fell short of expectations.

Alpha Bank's mean score on reliability—the most important dimension from the customer's standpoint—was -1.35. Its mean scores on responsiveness, assurance, and empathy were -0.63, -1.32, and -1.51. Even on the tangibles dimension Alpha's mean score was negative, although not as

Table 2
Alpha Bank Employee Survey Results
Concerning Realities of Working in the Branch System

Selected Statements	Mean Score		
	Strongly Disagree (1)	Neither Disagree Nor Agree (4)	Strongly Agree (7)
Role Conflict			
The bank emphasizes quality of service to customers as much as or more than it emphasizes being a salesperson.		4.4 ●	
Trying to be a salesperson makes it more difficult for me to deliver quality service to my customers.		4.7 ●	
I am often interrupted by other branch personnel, the telephone, or something else when I am trying to service my customers.		4.2 ●	
I spend a lot of time in my job trying to resolve problems over which I have little control.		3.9 ●	
Indequate Role Support			
All in all, the bank seems to hire competent and able people to work in the branches.		4.2 ●	
I do not feel well-prepared in terms of product knowledge training.		3.8 ●	
I feel that I have been well trained by the bank in how to interact effectively with customers.			5.3 ●
The centralization of certain bank functions that used to be performed in the branches has made it easier for me to give quality service to my customers.		4.0 ●	
Inadequate Role Environment			
Branch employees who do the best job serving their customers are more likely to be recognized and rewarded for their efforts than employees doing a mediocre job.		4.5 ●	
Making a special effort to serve customer well does not result in more pay or recognition.			5.3 ●
Everyone in our branch contributes to a team effort in servicing customers.			5.2 ●
The branch manager is a "role model" for other branch personnel concerning the importance of quality of service.			5.5 ●

n=237
These 12 statements were selected from a group of 30 statements rated by 237 Alpha Bank employees. The mean scores for the statements included in this exhibit are illustrative of the patterns of scores for the entire group of statements. For the entire group of statements, scores fell between 3.3 and 5.9.

negative as on the other dimensions (-0.24). In short, customer perceptions of Alpha's performance fell short of expectations across the board.

Lessons From Alpha Bank Alpha Bank's experience holds lessons for many different kinds of service organizations. The bank's first fundamental error was its failure to define service providers' roles in terms of customer expectations. By asking tellers to be sellers, Alpha's management jeopardized the quality of its most visible service. It is certainly tempting for banks to ask tellers to sell, since tellers see more customers than other bank personnel do. But from the customer's standpoint selling is not part of the teller's job; most customers want their tellers to be accurate, friendly, and fast. Tellers' cross-selling compromised responsiveness.

The bank's decision to centralize elements of the lending function compromised responsiveness, reliability, and assurance. The loan decision and its timing were no longer in the hands of those interacting with the customer. Branch lenders who had once controlled this service were now dependent on personnel in a distant facility. The centralization complicated service delivery, leading to paperwork snafus and backlogs. More important, perhaps, branch lenders lost esteem and clout in customers' eyes. The human cost of the new system was clearly expressed by one executive: "The branch people used to be bankers but aren't anymore. All of their status, all of their recognition, is gone." It is reasonable to speculate that over the long term these conditions will reduce branch lenders' willingness to give full discretionary effort and the bank's ability to attract able workers. The lesson for service firms is to keep control over the service as close to the customer as possible.

Alpha Bank made yet another mistake by underestimating the importance to service quality of support services—"from bookkeeping to loans," as one employee observed. While customer-contact personnel are obvious targets for quality-improvement efforts, the providers of internal support services are also important. Poor service to customer-contact personnel will result in poor service by those personnel. The importance of internal support services, however, is often overlooked. One Alpha Bank executive noted, "Our loan centers are overcrowded, overworked, and have some poor people. A manager will say, 'I want to get rid of Susie—I'll send her to work at the loan center.'" In this respect, as in others, Alpha Bank is hardly unique; we have heard similar comments from managers in numerous service companies.

WHAT CAN SERVICE ORGANIZATIONS DO TO IMPROVE QUALITY?

Having examined some of the causes of poor service quality, we now turn our attention to some of the cures. Service quality is a puzzle with many pieces, pieces that need to be assembled carefully. Service can be improved only through a systematic, step-by-step journey that enhances employees' ability and willingness to provide service by creating an organization that supports quality service in every area.

Institutionalize And Symbolize Quality The first step in any quality-improvement effort is to define the organization's service standards on the basis of customer expectations. Service standards help clarify work roles and communicate the organization's priorities. They also provide the benchmark against which performance can be evaluated. Service organizations need not establish a large number of standards. It is more manageable to identify a few standards that relate to the most important customer expectations—accuracy of transactions, allowable waiting time, and appropriate treatment of customers, for example. Setting the standards is really a matter of defining customer expectations so service personnel fully understand them. This is important because quality improvement requires that those who perform services assume responsibility for their quality.

Another key to quality improvement is to provide a structural means for good ideas to become tangible actions. The organization need not establish quality circles involving every employee, but some formal vehicle for voicing and evaluating quality-improvement ideas is necessary. One possibility is a rotating quality-assurance board composed of both managerial and nonmanagerial personnel (including both customer-contact personnel and intermediate service providers).

Such a board can provide several important benefits. For one, it forces participating employees to think continually about service-quality issues. It also provides an effective mechanism for generating, evaluating, and recommending service-improvement ideas. Ultimately, it symbolizes the organization's commitment to quality service.

Indeed, symbols can be a powerful tool. The symbolic representation of quality can take many forms: from placing unit managers in offices close to the action so that they can see and be seen, to publishing an annual employees' report that features workers who have gone to great lengths to protect the integrity of the organization's service commitment. Symbols alone cannot change a company's culture, but if backed up by policy, strategy, and organizational changes they can have material effects on culture, encouraging greater discretionary effort by adding meaning to employees' work.

Include Managers In Quality-Improvement Efforts Quality-improvement efforts should be focused not only on customer-contact personnel and providers of internal support services but also on managers, as Figure 2 illustrates. One of the toughest service-quality challenges is sustaining high quality over time. A person key to meeting this challenge is the operating-unit manager.

The manager sets the tone in the work unit and is in the best position to champion quality. Too often, however, service organizations place people with technical skills, not human-relations skills, in managerial jobs. Many organizations could dramatically improve their quality of service by assessing the commitment to service and the people skills of operating managers, and retooling (or replacing) those who do not pass muster. Moreover, all actions taken to improve service quality in the organization as a whole—training, performance measurement, and incentives, for example—must include managers.

Figure 2
Targets for Service-Quality Improvement Efforts

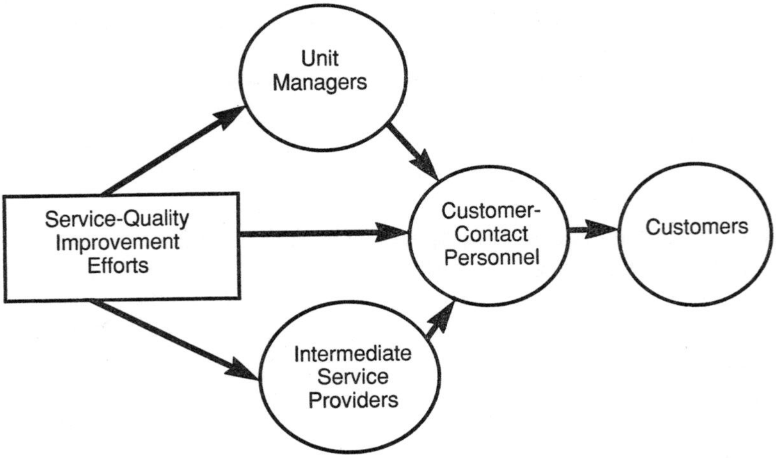

Improvement efforts are often focused on customer-contact personnel, but it is equally important to involve unit managers and providers of intermediary services. The service provided to customer-contact employees strongly affects the service provided by these employees.

View Knowledge And Skills Development As A Process Quality-improvement efforts must increase not only employees' willingness to perform but also their ability to perform. The efforts should focus on improving employees' knowledge and skills, because reliability and assurance are directly related to employee competence.

In many service organizations, there is a tendency to think of knowledge and skills development in terms of events—a three-day training session here, a special presentation there. It is better to think of this development as a never-ending process, including refresher, practice, and more advanced sessions. Service workers risk going stale, getting sloppy, and losing motivation when they stop growing in knowledge and skills.

We recommend decentralized as well as centralized approaches to knowledge and skills development. Employees within operating units can lead and participate in regular sessions to demonstrate and practice customer-service techniques, explain specific services, and raise service-quality issues. These sessions will not replace those led by experts from headquarters but complement them, fostering team building within work units and emphasizing employees' responsibility for their own development.

Close The Quality Loop Another vital service-quality ingredient is the recognition of performance. After service standards have been established, performance should be continually compared with those standards and outstanding performance should be rewarded. Completing this quality loop is the best way to build a strong service-minded culture.

A performance-measurement system can be very motivating, especially when workers know that others will learn how well they are performing and when measurement is tied to an effective reward system. It also helps management determine the specific effects of policy and personnel changes on operating performance and weed out individuals who deliver substandard performance. Finally, it symbolizes management commitment to service quality.

Performance measurement should extend beyond image tracking, isolated "shopping" visits, customer-complaint analyses, and other traditional approaches. While useful, these studies are insufficient for service organizations. It is just as important to track the attitudes and insights of service providers as it is to track those of customers. Customer studies reveal what is happening; employee studies help explain why.

For example, service organizations should explore employee perceptions of such factors as role conflict and role support. They could also benefit from regularly asking employees two questions we found particularly revealing at Alpha Bank.

- What is the biggest problem you face in trying to deliver quality service, day in and day out?
- If you were president and could make only one change to improve service quality here, what change would you make?

A performance-measurement system will get employees' attention. A well-executed reward system will keep it. Workers realize that management is serious about quality when management is willing to pay for it. A good reward system, like a good measurement system, is one that is meaningful, timely, simple, accurate, and fair.

We recommend using a reward system under which employees are expected to meet quality standards and are rewarded for outstanding performance. Rewards can take three basic forms: direct financial rewards (merit salary increases and bonuses), career advancement, and recognition. The most effective system is one that incorporates all three approaches for both individuals and work groups. Singling out high-performing work units can energize peer pressure and lead to better teamwork.

Invest In Problem Resolution An organization is judged not only on how well it delivers its regular services but also on the way it deals with problems: if the "repaired" appliance still doesn't work properly; if the stockbroker sold 1,000 shares when the customer instructed him to sell 100; if there is a mistake on the monthly statement. It is in handling problems such as these that an organization's service quality is most tested. But the organization also has the greatest leverage on customer perceptions when dealing with these problems.

Investment in quick, competent, and courteous problem resolution is one of the most effective steps a service organization can take to build a quality reputation. Customers are used to experiencing additional problems when they attempt to have a problem resolved, so problem resolution gives organizations an excellent opportunity to impress customers.

Being great at problem resolution is simpler in concept than in execution. It requires educating the customer about what to do when a problem occurs. It requires having enough staff, and the right kind of staff: talented, resilient, well-trained. It requires pushing authority downward so the problem can be solved at the first contact with the customer. It requires nurturing a core corporate value of being easy to do business with. Finally, it requires taking a long view toward building a business, rather than taking the short view of maximizing profits next quarter.[4]

A long-term view is essential for service quality. There are no ways to change the attitudes, habits, knowledge, and skills of human beings quickly. It is more useful to think in terms of organizational evolution than revolution.

Businesses need leaders who can envision and build a service-oriented culture to overcome the many obstacles that stand in the way of service excellence. Quality of service is more than a set of activities; it is, in the final analysis, primarily an attitude. Only leaders who insist upon service quality and are obsessed with it will stay the course through the pitfalls, the short-term financial pressures, and the discouragements, and succeed in meeting customers' expectations.

RESEARCH METHODOLOGY

Our research on service quality consisted of two distinct, sequential phases. The first phase was qualitative and focused on how both customers and service-firm executives perceive and evaluate service quality.

To learn about customers' views on service quality, we conducted 12 focus-group interviews, three for each of four selected services: retail banking, credit cards, securities brokerage, and appliance repair and maintenance. To ascertain how service-firm executives view service quality, we conducted in-depth, face-to-face interviews with marketing, operations, and customer-relations executives in each of four nationally recognized companies—one from each of the four service categories we investigated.

The first phase of the research indicated that customers evaluate service quality by mentally comparing their perceptions of delivered services with their expectations of the service firms. They do this along ten distinct dimensions (reliability, responsiveness, competence, access, courtesy, communication, credibility, security, understanding/knowing the customer, tangibles). This inquiry also revealed key gaps within service firms (such as the inability of customer-contact personnel to meet service-quality specifications laid down by management) that could have a bearing on service quality as perceived by customers.

The second phase of our research, which was more empirical, focused on two objectives: developing a comprehensive but parsimonious instrument for measuring customer perceptions of service quality, and gaining a more in-depth understanding of organizational shortfalls that have an impact on service quality and how such shortfalls can be corrected. To accomplish the first objective, we followed well-established procedures for developing structured instruments to measure constructs that are not directly observable.[5] We developed 97 items, fleshing out the 10 dimensions of service quality identified in our first phase. We then recast each item into a pair of statements—one to measure expectations about firms in general within the service category being investigated (sample statement: "When these firms promise to do something by a certain time, they should do so"), and the other to measure perceptions about the particular firm whose service quality was being assessed (sample statement: "When XYZ promises to do something by a certain time, it does so"). A seven-point scale ranging from 7 (strongly agree) to 1 (strongly disagree) accompanied each statement.

We refined and shortened the 97-item instrument through a series of iterative data-collection and-analysis steps. We performed this instrument purification to eliminate items that failed to discriminate well among respondents with differing quality perceptions about firms in several service categories. We gathered data for the initial refinement of the 97-item instrument from a quota sample of 200 customers, divided equally between males and females and representing recent users of one of the following five services: appliance repair and maintenance, retail banking, long-distance telephone, securities brokerage, and credit cards. We converted the raw questionnaire data into perception-minus-expectation scores for the various items. These difference scores could range from $+6$ to -6, with more-positive scores representing higher perceived service quality. We analyzed the difference scores using item-to-total correlation analysis and factor analysis. These analyses resulted in the elimination of roughly two-thirds of the original items and the consolidation of several overlapping quality dimensions into new, combined dimensions. To verify the reliability and validity of the condensed scale, we administered it to four independent samples of approximately 190 customers each to gather data on the service quality of four nationally known firms: a bank, a credit-card issuer, an appliance repair-and-maintenance firm, and a long-distance telephone company. Analysis of data from the four samples led to additional refinement of the instrument and confirmed its reliability and validity. The final instrument consisted of 22 items, spanning the five dimensions of service quality described in the article: tangibles, reliability, responsiveness, assurance, and empathy.

To accomplish our second research objective we conducted a comprehensive case study of a nationally known bank. We selected three bank regions (with about 12 branches per region) and did separate focus-group interviews with tellers, customer-service representatives, lending personnel, and branch managers from within the regions (a total of seven focus-group interviews). We also conducted in-depth interviews with more than a dozen middle and senior managers having responsibilities for the branch system. From the focus-group and in-depth-interview data we developed a structured questionnaire that was sent to all customer-contact personnel in the three regions. We received completed questionnaires from 237 employees, or 55 percent of the sample. Finally, we mailed the service-quality questionnnaire to a random sample of the bank's customers within the regions. We received completed questionnaires from 138 customers, 14 percent of this sample.

1. Philip B. Crosby, *Quality is Free* (New York: McGraw-Hill, 1979), p. 17.

2. We have developed a model that incorporates these discrepancies or "gaps." See A. Parasuraman, Valarie A. Zeithaml, and Leonard L. Berry, "A Conceptual Model of Service Quality and Its Implications for Future Research," *Journal of Marketing,* Fall 1985, pp. 41-50.

3. Daniel Yankelovich and John Immerwahr, *Putting the Work Ethnic to Work* (New York: Public Agenda Foundation, 1983) p. 1.

4. Leonard L. Berry, "Big Ideas in Services Marketing," *Journal of Consumer Marketing,* Spring 1986, pp. 47-51.

5. Conceptual and technical details of this procedure can be found in Gilbert A. Churchill, Jr., "A Paradigm for Developing Better Measures of Marketing Constructs," *Journal of Marketing Research,* February 1979, pp. 64-73.

TEN STEPS FOR MEASURING CUSTOMER PERCEPTION OF YOUR SERVICE

Ron Zemke

Beginning or refining a system for measuring customer service performance is not a task to take lightly. A marketplace reputation for distinctive service can quickly translate into market share today, but that distinction is most often only earned through a philosophical commitment to service backed by diligent attention to the nitty gritty of what customers want and need.

The Service Edge suggests considering these 10 steps in developing methods to help determine how customers perceive your service:

1. Begin with your service strategy. What promises are implied in your service strategy, and what measurement points and questions are implicit? If you promise 24-hour turnaround on orders and zero defects, you can measure the turnaround time internally, but tracking defects will involve communicating with customers. When service falls short of expectations, where do the breakdowns occur? What happens to the customer?

2. Measure frequently. Measure at least monthly so information is fresh. Domino's, the king of speedy pizza delivery, measures weekly. Embassy Suites, which is setting new standards in the hotel industry, requires managers to interview five guests a day.

3. Ask customer-based questions that are fair. Ask customers not only what happened during their transaction with your company, but how they felt about it. Be specific, and ask about things that your people can act upon.

4. Collect group and individual data. Get information that can help work groups as well as individual performers.

5. Benchmark. Collect information regarding your competitors' sales, market share, and customer satisfaction at least three times a year.

6. Collect quantitative and qualitative data. Collect numerical ratings (on a scale of 10, customers say we rate . . .) and specific customer comments.

7. Make the results visible. Display the results of your measuring to emphasize their importance, and to actively involve front-line employees in the process.

8. Make the results employee friendly. Simple, straightforward numbers work best. People are more comfortable knowing that "87 percent of all customers said . . . " or "nearly nine out of 10 customers surveyed feel . . ." than they are trying to understand the statistical significance of medians or weighted averages.

9. Make the results believable. Don't pass information down from the top of your organization after some invisible outside firm has conducted surveys and expect your employees to swallow it. Involve employees in the process—at least make them aware of how the information is gathered and assure them it comes from their customers—and they'll be more likely to act on it.

10. Use the results. It's not enough to send out a memo listing results or complaints compiled in a customer survey. Discuss the survey widely. Use the results as the basis for problem-solving meetings and to celebrate successes, and people will regard the information as important.

DEVELOPING CLIENT-SPONSORED SATISFACTION MEASURES

Matt Elbeck

Health service quality encompasses a broad area of research that questions the meaning and measurement of "quality." Quality may be considered the achievement of health service delivery that attains both external (accreditation) and internal (institutional) standards as they apply to the duties performed by health services personnel in terms of management's perception (risk management); employees' perception (quality of working life); and clients' perception (quality assurance) with regard to the institution's resources and manner of service delivery (quality control).

Brook and Williams suggest that health care is composed of three elements:

1. *Technical Care:* adequacy of the diagnostic and therapeutic processes;
2. *Art of Care:* milieu, manner, and behavior of care providers; and
3. *E:* error term containing unidentifiable and residual elements describing health care.

Donabedian adds that care is a function of perspective taken from the provider or from the user's point of view, whether the relationship is personalized, aggregate (social), or absolutist, that is, unless any aspect of care can be unequivocally related to service improvement, it must be dismissed.

One of the first user-oriented studies suggested that clients perceive "good" patients as autonomous or totally submissive. These dichotomies were further researched and it was concluded that clients demand equality with and interest from a physician, with all clients objecting to mechanical, routinized, and impersonal handling. In essence, clients desire a physician who manifests a personal interest in the patient and who exhibits competence. The apparent rationale behind this conclusion is that personal interest on the part of the physician provides the assurance that the practitioner's competence is fully used in the interest of the client.

Reprinted from *Health Care Management Review*, Vol. 12, No. 3, pp. 47-52, with permission of Aspen Publishers, Inc., © Summer 1987.

A study of 24 administrative officers in U.S. metropolitan hospitals indicated that providers discriminate between good and bad clinics based on the clinics' concern for patient satisfaction more so than the clinics' medical skills and facilities. Donabedian's interpretation of this study questions the absence of client teaching/counseling, stressing that this is done poorly in both good and bad clinics.

Sanazaro and Williamson surveyed 2,350 physicians in full-time private practice who were also faculty members at one of 20 U.S. medical schools. The study revealed that physician *concern over health services costs is minimal,* and the physicians' belief that actions responsible for the benefits and harmful effects to patient care services were due to technical problems (70%), interpersonal problems (20%), and access, coordination, and continuity of care problems (10%). A study of Sussman et al. noted that clients perceive all elements of care to be important while physicians seem to limit the importance for health care to technical care, as shown by Sanazaro and Williamson.

The above studies delineate the differing perceptions between providers and users of health care services about what constitutes quality of care. The problem seems to invoke a lack of concern over areas other than a "technical" orientation toward care, considering and utilizing patient attitudes as part of health services quality assessment.

THE IMPORTANCE OF CLIENT ATTITUDE
As with more types of service industries, information concerning consumer attitudes regarding the quality of health care service received is critically important to the strategic survival of the organization. Society today demands that consumers and their organized representatives be educated in order to appraise the quality of service offered and to decide whether to support a particular service delivery system. Awareness of client satisfaction with the quality and methods used to provide health care services can assist with institutional survival.

Medical science has long veiled its activities as sacrosanct, shrouded in unbending faith that medical associations and their members "know best." Times have changed; client satisfaction is now a core issue to the survival of health care institutions. In order to provide a relevant base of knowledge, the components of attitude and methods of measurement must be examined.

Constructs Of Attitude There is wide agreement that attitudes (perceptions) determine the choice of one item among a set of alternatives.

There is less agreement among psychologists as to whether attitudes also have a dynamic (energizing) influence, that is, whether a favorable attitude toward health care will influence the overall need to enhance one's own health, reactively or proactively. Attitude is therefore a readiness to respond in a preferential manner.

The supposition that the intervening state between stimulus and behavior is richer than affect (or liking) is widely supported. The availability of a tricomponent model to explain and interrelated attitude constructs allows a richer and more flexible model. The components are:

1. a cognitive or perceptual component;
2. an affective or feeling component; and
3. a conative or intentions component.

Cognition The measurement of satisfaction with an object (e.g., nursing care) can occur only if awareness (cognition) exists. The need to measure awareness is best illustrated by the frustrations psychiatric institutions have with public perceptions. Without knowledge of what the public knows, an effective publicity program cannot be generated to ensure public comprehension; therefore, the measurement of effect (like-dislike) and conation (support for a funding drive) is needed.

A client's information about an object, in terms of beliefs in the *existence* of an object, or *evaluative* beliefs about the object make up the cognitive component. Existential beliefs are composed of awareness measures (aided and unaided recall of names, functions, etc.) Evaluative beliefs are comparative measures composed of *attribute* judgment (which is bigger, tastes better, last longer) and *similarity* judgments (are the objects the same or different?). Both existential beliefs (exB) and evaluative beliefs (evB) as an attribute judgment [aj] and/or similarity judgment [sj] may be illustrated as follows:

■ exB—physicians exist to cure disease;
■ exB—nurses exist to aid client recovery;
■ evB(aj)—nurses are friendlier than physicians; and
■ evB(sj)—nurses and physicians both work in hospitals.

Affect Affect concerns a client's overall liking or disliking of a situation, object, person or concept (unidimensional element). Most theorists regard affect as the core of the attitude concept and believe that it is derived from the more specific cognitive elements. Debate exists whether to distinguish between affect (like-dislike) and cognition (object is good-bad, harmful-beneficial, etc.). This form of nonsyllogism (nondeductive reasoning) may be explained as follows: "Cigarettes taste terrible, cause cancer, make me cough, and offend others (cognition). I dislike terrible tastes, cancer, coughing and offending others (affect), but I will likely smoke cigarettes."

Therefore, cognition (evaluation) concerns a client's assessment with respect to an object's ideal point (sweeter, bigger, juicier) while affect (preference) will indicate client selection with respect to some benchmark, and not merely relative rankings. In many cases one prefers that which is evaluated highly, but evaluation and affect are not necessarily synonymous. Affect (Af) may be illustrated as follows; Af—"I prefer nurses to physicians."

Conation Conation is comprised of a client's gross behavioral expectations (intentions) regarding the object. Is he or she "very, somewhat, or not at all likely" to use the outpatient service of a particular hospital in the evening hours? Consequently, behavioral intentions are limited to a finite time period and are probabilistic measures of behavior. Conation (Cn) may be illustrated as follows: Cn—"I would respond more readily to a physician's orders than to a nurse's orders."

Attitude Specificity Attitudes do not exist independently, but are linked in complex ways to a hierarchy of increasingly fundamental beliefs and attitudes. Must fundamental are *values,* which are attitudes toward end states of existence (equality, self-fulfillment) or modes of conduct (honesty, friendship). Deep-seated values and attitudes are often unconsciously held and are difficult to unambiguously identify with the usual projective methods and related clinical techniques. Their remoteness from the specific attitudes and behaviors of interest to researchers has reduced their usefulness for diagnostic purposes.

Attitude In A Nutshell A client's attitude, a predisposition to behave in a certain way, is composed of these components:

- Cognition: exB:Nurses exist to aid client recovery.
- evB(sj):Nurses are friendlier than physicians.
- evB(sj):Nurses and physicians both work in hospitals.
- Affect:Af:I prefer nurses to physicians.
- Conation:Cn:I would respond more readily to a physician's orders than to a nurse's orders.

THE USE OF ATTITUDE SCALES
Attitudes are measured as responses to statements. They are not absolute or dichotomous in nature (e.g., yes/no; on/off) but instead are continuous

and are measured with attitude scales. The following three attitude measurement scales represent the more commonly used forms.

Likert Scale A Likert scale requires a client to indicate a degree of agreement or disagreement (in this case using a 5-point scale, that is, 1 = Totally agree, 2 = Agree, 3 = Unsure, 4 = Disagree, 5 = Totally disagree) with statements related to an attitude object (e.g., nurses) in a unidirectional manner:

1. The nurses are very helpful: 1 2 3 4 5

2. The nurses are very happy to help me: 1 2 3 4 5

3. The nurses are not nervous: 1 2 3 4 5

Semantic Differential Scale A semantic differential scale requires the client to rate the attitude object on seven-point rating scales bounded at each end by one of two bipolar adjectives:

Nurses

■ Helpful ————————————————— Selfish

■ Happy ————————————————— Sad

■ Soothing ————————————————— Nervous

Stapel Scale The Stapel scale is a simplified version of the semantic differential scale and is a unipolar six-point nonverbal rating scale that simultaneously measures direction and intensity. Unlike the semantic differential, the Stapel scale values are used to indicate how one adjective describes the attitude object in question (see the box).

	Nurses	
+3	+3	+3
+2	+2	+2
+1	+1	+1
Helpful	Happy	Soothing
-1	-1	-1
-2	-2	-2
-3	-3	-3

Although the above-mentioned scales are in common use, others exist such as a percentage scale (0% to 100% agreement), categorical scale (the response categories are positioned in a series of boxes), and graphic rating scales (faces or similar graphic forms are used to portray a continuum of agreement, e.g., from a happy face to sad face.)

The drawback of the semantic differential scale concerns semantic consistency (is the opposite of man boy, woman, or God?) although it is useful to identify evaluative information (as well as potency and activity). The Likert scale has the advantage of ease of construction and simplicity of administration. The Stapel scale can reproduce results equivalent to the semantic differential scale, is easy to administer and requires no pretesting of adjectives or phrases to ensure true bipolarity.

The selection of a scaling technique should depend on the nature of the information required, the cost of the technique, how well the technique adapts to the preferred method of administration, and most importantly, the ease of use for the client. Drug treatment, a foreign environment and pre-or postoperative anxiety are among the variables causing lowered cognitive powers in a client. The attitude scaling technique should reflect this predicament and therefore the simplest and most commonly used form would be appropriate—the Likert scale. Early results from one of the author's ongoing studies designed to establish attitude scale preference from clients in an extended care hospital suggests strongly that elderly clients prefer a graphic response scale, which middle-aged clients indicate equal preference for the Likert, percentage, and categorical scales.

GENERATING AN ATTITUDE SURVEY

Comprehension of the nature of attitude and the selection of an appropriate measurement scale allow the researcher to search for the actual statements to be included in an attitude measuring survey, in this case, a client satisfaction survey.

One of the more attractive methods to uncover client satisfaction with a health care service is the focus group interview, which is composed of 10 to 12 clients with common experience regarding the subject of the interview (e.g., service in a radiotherapy nursing unit). The interviewer, or moderator, is a skilled individual with background in psychology. Using appropriate forms of verbal and nonverbal behavior, the moderator encourages and directs the group of clients along the intended direction of discussion by initially explaining the nature of the subject matter to be discussed. In this case, the subject of discussion is the perception of an ideal radiotherapy unit's service within a tricomponent framework, that is, client level of awareness (cognition), feelings of like-dislike (affect), and behavioral intentions (conation).

The focus group interview should be taped (for postinterview analysis) and should last no more than two hours. Following is a focus group interview procedure.

- Identify attitude object (client satisfaction, hospital image, staff quality of working life, etc.) to a sample (8 to 12 participants) of the health service population to be surveyed.
- Request that focus group participants discuss the criteria relevant to the identified attitude object. The discussion may be enhanced if an example is provided by the moderator, such as the criteria one would use to describe an ideal vacation.
- Arrange the generated statements into a questionnaire format by placing an attitude response scale (e.g., Likert scale) adjacent to each statement. For example: physicians treat you as an individual. 1 2 3 4 5
- Pilot test the questionnaire to a sample (10 to 15 persons) of the survey population to identify statements that are ambiguous, difficult to understand, overly intimidating, or which might encourage response bias (i.e., that may generate an "acceptable" response that may be far from the truth of the matter.)
- Administer a refined version of the scale questionnaire to a large

sample of clients using the same response categories (e.g., 5-point Likert scale). Identify which statements best discriminate between high total attitude scores. Eliminate statements with responses not substantially correlated with high and low total attitude scores.

■ For each client add all the discriminating statement responses algebraically, the result being total client attitude score toward the attitude object.

The end product is a unit-specific client satisfaction survey that is administered to patients before discharge from the hospital, thus ensuring familiarity with the unit in question and spontaneity of responses.

This approach allows for a client-generated list of statements that reflect cultural and environmental congruency. If two attitude response scales for each statement are included, one measuring ideal levels of importance and one measuring actual levels of satisfaction, a comparison can be made of ideal and actual scores, thus allowing health services decision makers to establish what is important to the client and how well the important areas score.

To identify the criteria by which clients describe health care services, the evaluation of client attitudes should be practical. In other words, the surveys should be conducted on a unit basis (inpatient, outpatient, admissions, ambulatory) thus allowing for organizational congruency and simplified managerial action related to client health status. Such information gauges client satisfaction with the service supplied and serves as a teaching tool to inform health service personnel about client perceptions of multi-disciplinary health services delivery, thus allowing providers to improve their own service delivery.

Client satisfaction transforms into some form of (positive) behavior, such as positive word-of-mouth communication describing the exemplary standards of an institution's health service; a belief that providers can and do deliver excellence in health services; the feeling that one need not fear a stay in a particular nursing unit; and tangible community support for health services funding. More importantly, a content and relaxed client might well be easier to treat in clinical terms, because contentment may have the virtue of enhancing the recovery process.

The researcher is able to evaluate the degree of health care service excellence in terms of criteria developed by clients themselves. The degree of satisfaction (positive attitude scoring) is not necessarily a reflection of what *actually* happened, but is more a reflection of what the client *perceived* as happening. After all, it is patient well-being and recovery that are important, and whatever causes an improvement, stabilization, or cure in client health status must concern health service providers.

Cynics may argue that the art of care is no substitute for technical care. This is presumably true in the less-developed nations where culture does not consider art of care as a manifestation of health service; technical care is absolute. However, Western societies, and North America in particular, exhibit a culture that demands consumer satisfaction. Accepting that culture is pervasive and all embracing, it would be premature to suggest that technical care is all that health service stands for—both technical and art forms coexist in a synergistic form. Client involvement in health care service, via positive responses on service surveys, allows for the perception that health care services regard the client highly and that these services are following a culturally harmonious application of health care service delivery.

Train And Empower People

"Autonomy is the attitude that my actions are my own choices and the organization I am a part of is in many ways my own creation. It puts us in the center and in charge of what is happening at the moment. We are the cause, not the effect."

Peter Block
The Empowered Manager

Service wisdom is the byproduct of extraordinary competence and exceptional courage. Extraordinary competence means the service person has the capacity to go beyond the straight-line application of learned skills. Such service people can creatively serve the customer through the application of more than ordinary competence gained through ordinary training.

Exceptional courage means the exercise of risk in service situations that do not fit the rules and procedures. Such service people can act "with power" in making an exception on behalf of the customer. While typically this does not mean unlimited license, most empowered service people will act with reasonable restraint and exercise a corporate conscience. In fact, most organizations find they must encourage service people to use more freedom, not exercise more restraint.

Training and empowerment are familiar bedfellows: the more one is trained, the more one feels empowered. Conscious competence is the path to courageous confidence. Likewise, the more frequently service people act in an empowered fashion, the more they learn for use in future service situations. Since necessity, in the form of an "exception," is the mother of invention, the inventive side of empowerment can yield insights that are useful again and again.

Training and empowerment also can be strange bedfellows. Training that teaches only "the right way" can be a deterrent to the creativity associated with "wisdom." Wise people generally are not those with the most courses or degrees. They are those with breadth, whose learning helps them expand their options rather than narrow them. Likewise, empowerment can be a deterrent to training. Often, the more people are rewarded for their skills of improvisation, the less tolerant and patient they are for training.

The training-empowerment realm poses unique challenges for the service manager. How much training is adequate? Walt Disney World provides street sweepers with four days of training because these employees field many more questions from guests than the guest-relations hosts. Would they be even more effective with six days? How do you find the point of diminishing returns? If wisdom requires breadth or "overtraining," how can such excess be cost-justified and sold to a bottom-line-driven management that can act miserly even toward requests for basic, plain-vanilla training?

And what of empowerment? How much is enough? As earlier noted, Nordstroms is famous for their one-line policy book: "Use Your Good Judgement in All Situations." How would the Federal Deposit Insurance Corporation react to bank tellers given the same policy? Or how would the Nuclear Regulatory Commission like customer-service people employed by utilities companies to follow the route of exceptional courage? Are there areas in which empowered service people are a liability to the organization? At what point does the "they'll give away the shop" fear seem justified?

Some authors of the following articles raise more questions than they answer. But that is the path to service wisdom. It is a matter of perpetual querying, of chewing on far more ideas and issues than you could possibly swallow and digest. When you surface from this exploration, you will be in a much stronger position to make judgments and decisions that are right for you and your customers.

We begin with Ron Zemke's article "Contact! Training Employees to Meet the Public," which appeared in the August 1986 issue of *TRAINING* Magazine. Perhaps the most instructive feature of this inclusion is the real-life examples. They not only affirm that "training is vital" to service excellence; they also describe *how* it is vital.

Service wisdom begets service wisdom! From Walt Disney World to Scandinavian Airlines, service sages share their knowledge. Super service entails hard work and a never-ending allegiance to training—in good times and bad, during feast or famine.

The second selection is "Coaching for Distinctive Service," an article that appeared in the May 1989 issue of *Management Review*. Since creating service excellence is an interpersonal performance, the world of athletics and performing arts can be a fruitful domain for insights. The front-line supervisors in that world are the sideline and behind-the-scenes coaches who use their skills to sharpen the expression of talents and/or tendons. We hope this reading makes you question your present-day ideas. Is customer service primarily an art form? Is managing, as author Peter Vaill suggests, a performing art? As managers, must we trade in our bottom-line orientations for "Academy Award" or "Olympic gold" recognition?

Empowerment means placing extraordinary authority in the hands of people nearest the service problems to be solved. Typically, empowerment is more complex than simply saying, "Use your best judgment." There are legitimate "yes, but's" that must be carefully considered in order for empowerment to be a relevant balancing act.

Many supervisors get concerned about relinquishing their power to their subordinates. Will subordinates use added power responsibly? Will they "give away the shop" if they are allowed to exercise their own judgment in handling customer problems? To address the empowerment issues, we chose "Terms of Empowerment," an article we wrote under the title "Do Service Procedures Tie Employees' Hands?" for the September 1987 issue of *Personnel Journal*.

The fourth of five articles we chose for this section is another by Ron Zemke from *TRAINING* Magazine titled "Supervising Service Workers." The more we work in this arena, the more we realize there is a major difference between *performing* and *producing*. If you ask people to contrast the two, you may hear these distinctions: "soft versus hard," "subjective versus objective," "art versus science," "abstract versus concrete," "emotional versus rational," "style versus substance," or "process versus outcome." Such contrasts provide an insight into the differences between supervising people who produce a tangible product and those who perform an intangible service. One major difference is that, while self-esteem is always important in any working arrangement, it is critical when feelings about one's self affect how one treats others.

Our counterpoint article is David Maister's "Quality Work Doesn't Mean Quality Service," which raises serious questions about the goal of training. The article, which appeared in the April 1984 issue of *The American Lawyer,* makes an interesting case. When customers (clients) are unable to distinguish between outstanding technical work and simply competent work (such as in legal, accounting, or consulting services or car repair), the personal relationship between buyer and provider (client and consultant) takes on great significance. The article raises the question "Why train?" Since the lion's share of training is technical, not interpersonal, do we risk increasing the distance between the customer and the service provider?

According to Maister, "Because of the proclivity of professionals to become more fascinated with the intellectual challenge of their craft than with being responsive to clients, all too often clients are mocked for their lack of professional knowledge, despised because of their demands, and resented because they control the purse strings and hence the autonomy of the professional." If *effectiveness* is, to a large measure, determined by what the customer experiences, where does technical elegance or professional prowess enter the picture as a critical criterion?

CONTACT! TRAINING EMPLOYEES TO MEET THE PUBLIC

Ron Zemke

The word is out: Customer service is in. The reason is simple: The American economy is now dominated by industries that perform rather than produce. As a result, service and satisfaction have become broad responsibilities that relate very directly to bottom-line success. And as more and more organizations get the word that efficient, consistent "doing" plus first-class customer treatment equal repeat business, the calls for broad-scale customer-service training get louder.

Even the medical establishment is talking about customer service. One recent report suggests that doctors and dentists are realigning their hours to suit customer's work schedules; nurses and dental technicians are being selected not only for their technical skills but for their people-handling ability as well. And there is hardly a hospital left in the United States that hasn't begun training its staff in 'guest relations' skills.

On top of all that, organizations are coming to believe that the management and delivery of service requires a very special breed of cat—a species only remotely resembling that which oversees the production and delivery of widgets.

UCLA professor William Ouchi, author of *Theory Z: How American Business Can Meet the Japanese Challenge,* points out that "you can't build up an inventory of services the way you can build up an inventory of products. If you can't produce the service the moment it is needed, you lose the sale." The successful delivery of service, Ouchi contends, "requires people to perform an unnatural act: to work at an extraordinarily high level of interdependence, working not only for their own ends but toward a successful outcome for the customer."

Encouraged by such pronouncements, contemporary management theorists enjoy talking about customer service as "everybody's business," which it is. And they define "service" broadly, as every aspect of dealing with the public outside of selling. That makes sense as well. It makes sense,

Reprinted by permission of publisher, from *TRAINING*, The Magazine of Human Resources Development.

but not much difference, for customer service in the United States—to be succinct—stinks.

HOW BAD IS IT?

The Conference Board, a New York-based business research group, recently polled consumers—us—and asked us to rate our satisfaction with 19 products and 19 services. We reported that generally we're happy with the value and quality of the products we buy and use. We found only three types of products wanting—or greatly below our expectations: used cars, pet food and children's toys. On the other hand, we decreed that only two services give us acceptable value for our money: air travel and electricity. Every other service that we consumers rated, from health care to hotels to educational and legal services, we judged overpriced and under-delivered.

If you're looking for the culprits—the reasons that service is so bad—there are plenty to go around. For one thing, service is seen as servile work in the New World and treated as a necessary evil—a lesser child than manufacturing and building and inventing and financing—never mind the fact that 75% of the jobs in the United States and 71% of the GNP derives from services, not products.

Then there's the matter of managing service—we don't. But the management of service is as different from the management of production as the farm is from the factory. Finally, there is the training of service people: again, the simple fact is that we don't. We rely instead on entreaties to "smile," on brightly colored wall posters proclaiming our undying (and nonexistent) loyalty to customer care, and on short-term incentive programs, hoping that these will do the trick. And they don't.

MAKING SERVICE MATTER

What *does* work? First and foremost is management attention: attention to service as a desirable outcome and attention to systems—and a culture— that value service.

That focus is critically important to trainers and managers at Walt Disney World in Lake Buena Vista, FL, and it shows. Deede Sharp, former manager of educational program development at Disney World, laughs when you ask her the secret behind the theme park's reputation for unparalleled customer courtesy. "the secret," she insists, "is that there *is* no secret."

That's a slight over simplification, but it is a fact that in bits and pieces, the Disney approach to customer service contains nothing surprising. What distinguishes it is its thoroughness.

"Our guest courtesy (training course) is only a half-day program," Sharp says, "but it is only one part of what we do to make sure our guests receive the quality of customer service we expect." The number and detail of those other parts are mind-boggling.

Every issue of the company newspaper talks about some aspect of the service mission. Recruiting emphasizes the service focus, as do employee-relations standards and the training of managers. "Training, I guess you could say, starts with our culture. Our first task is to make (new employees) partners in the corporate culture. And the culture is focused on one thing: making sure our guests have an enjoyable experience," Sharp says.

The Disney culture, in fact, has two focal points—customers, called "guests," and employees, referred to as "cast members." "We have a belief that our guests will only receive the kind of treatment we want them to receive if the cast members receive that same kind of treatment," Sharp explains. "So some of our training is geared toward dealing with fellow cast members as guests."

Adds Sue Rye, manager of human resources development for Disney World's administration/support division, "We make a very real effort to help employees see that they are in show business and that our job is to create a fantasy for the guests. They (employees) are a critical part of that fantasy and have a role to play that has to be picture perfect. You know, sweeping up after the horses on Main Street isn't a fun job—we work hard at making sure the employee knows it's an important job and one that is respected and appreciated."

Catharina Wohlecke-Haglund, president of the Scandinavian Service School in New York City, puts a similar perspective on good service, "I sometimes tell people you can do all the customer-service training you need in four minutes—the hard part is fixing the organization so that it supports and promotes good service."

Wohlecke-Haglund worked as a trainer in the Scandinavian Airline System (SAS) passenger services department in Copenhagen before opening the Scandinavian Service School, an SAS subsidiary, in 1983. She is emphatic about the importance of management support and attention to good customer service. "At SAS we taught our front-line people you have to do what's right for the customer—that's our only rule. But management had to support that, yes? Suppose a passenger has a new bag torn or damaged. We wanted our gate agents to just take care of that. Arrange them a new bag— on forms, on investigation, just do it. Do it right now; that's where the impact is. But management had to trust the people and support them doing things like that or the system will never change. Management's role is very, very critical."

After mentioning management commitment and support, customer service pros voice a second theme: selection. At Disney the selection of front-line service people is taken extremely seriously. Says Sharp, "During our recruiting and selection cycle we make the importance of service and our expectations very clear. We do a one-hour presentation on what Disney stands for, what our values are and what working at Disney is like. We want people to back out before they ever see a guest if there is any doubt that they will like this kind of work."

A similar view comes from Maggie Hanson, vice president of sales and in-flight services for Air Atlanta. "Who you hire for customer contact is very important. So we do very extensive screening. We hold a three-hour group interview with prospective in-flight people. We give them role plays to do and present problems for them to solve. We try to get a look at them from the customer's perspective. We make it clear that we are tough on performance but easy on people. One other thing. We work to make sure *they* enjoy the selection and interview process. We have to remember that the people we *don't* hire are potential customers, and we want them to have a positive memory of the experience."

THE TRAINING CONNECTION
As critical as selection and management commitment are, they are only part of the customer-service puzzle. Good training is critical to good front-line service.

Dee Atkinson, consumer relations manager for the Long Grove, IL-based Kemper Group, emphasizes dealing with customer's feelings. Atkinson designed and delivered a customer-service training program for her organization that won an award from the Society of Consumer Affairs Professionals. "I want people to know now the customer thinks and feels and how they are to deal with those feelings," she says. "It's important that we listen to the customer on several levels."

Shannon Johnston of Kaset, Inc. of Tampa, FL, a customer service consulting company, sounds a similar theme. "We place an emphasis on customer sensitivity. You see, there are two parts to every customer interaction—the business side and the human side. Both are there, and they exert themselves more or less at the same time. Most people want to—at least try to—ignore the human side. My rule of thumb is that if you teach people to handle the human side first, the business side goes much quicker."

Air Atlanta's Hanson talks about attitude-shaping as well as people-handling skills. "Most airlines are good at teaching the technical skills, from serving soup to safety. When we set up our training—we're a small, new company and don't have all the resources in the world—we talked about asking other airlines to train our in-flight people. We realize though, that even if we just had the technical training done by someone else, that would have an impact on attitudes. So we decided to do it all ourselves."

Hanson says that her training emphasizes two things—the organization's view of the customer and flexibility. "We tell our new in-flight people that while it may seem harmless to make jokes at the customers' expense, the danger is that we'll start to treat the customer in accordance with some unfair label—like stupid or nasty. We try to instill specific values, like 'There is never an excuse for being rude to a customer,' and 'You'll never get in trouble trying to help a customer.' "

She stresses, however, that "it takes a lot of discussion and dialogue to make those living ideas and not just cliches. For instance, anyone can walk up to a passenger and give them the lecture on checking a bag that's too large to fit under the seat in front of them. It takes a lot of skill to make that a positive, to position the need to do something else with the bag in a way that doesn't offend or embarrass the customer. We tell our in-flight people that they are hired to think on their feet, not enforce a rule book. That's harder to train people to do. It takes time and talking.

Kaset's Johnston also brings up the subject of thinking on one's feet. "We use the work recovery. You aren't always going to be letter perfect. You're going to make mistakes. So you have to have recovery skills."

What does recovery look like? "One of our people sent out a letter that misspelled a client's name three times in two pages." Johnston answers. "The customer wrote back, saying that he expects a lot more from someone in the customer-service business. Our person called a caucus of her team to figure a way to make it a positive, to turn the incident around. They sent him a dozen roses with a note saying, 'No excuses. You're exactly right. I should not have made that mistake. I'm terribly sorry.' He's our customer yet today."

HANDLING HOTHEADS
Perhaps the most daunting task customer-service people face, and one of

the toughest when it comes to training, is dealing with upset customers—people who believe, rightly or wrongly, that they have been cheated, abused, yanked around or otherwise mistreated by the service person's organization. Upset customers are frequently irrational, erratic, rude and downright nasty. And those who don't scream and shout are likely to cry or pout.

Many of these people are aggravating and some of them are just plain jerks. But tempting as it may be to install trapdoors in the floor, upset customers are also one of your organization's key assets. According to Washington, DC-based Technical Assistance Research Programs (TARP Institute), one in four of your customers is unhappy enough with your organization right now to stop doing business with you. Worse yet, only 4% of those disgruntled customers are likely to complain—preferring to switch rather than fight.

Why is that worse? Because according to TARP, simply encouraging unhappy customers to complain changes the probability they will do business with you again from 30% to 50%. Listen to the unhappy customer and promise to look into the matter, and that probability goes to 72%. Respond immediately to the complaint, apologize for the problem and guarantee a "fix," and the probability goes to 95% that the customer will *remain* a customer.

Ask your marketing department how much it costs your organization to develop a new customer compared to the cost of keeping an old one. You will agree there is never an excuse for alienating a customer, and few for dropping the net on a nasty one.

Customer-service experts seem unanimous in suggesting that the first step in training employees to deal with unhappy customers is to put the customer in context. Disney's Sharp emphasizes that the angry customer is a rarity, given the number of people a front-line employee meets in a day, a week or a year. "We tell our cast members that 90% of the people they will deal with are nice people, easy and eager to *be* pleased, fun to do things for. But that can't affect the way we are. It's just a challenge we have to step up to when it happens."

Prudy Tweed, vice president of Tweed Corp. of Oil City, PA, a company that teaches a special course in dealing with upset customers, emphasizes understanding the disgruntled customer's mind-set. "You have to realize that 95% of the people you deal with are the same sort of honest, hard-working people you are. They get upset when they think they have been had or have made a mistake. Sometimes they lack confidence, so they come on strong and forceful. They don't like admitting mistakes. They sometimes panic when things seem to be other than they expected, so they can't see obvious solutions to their problems. And it is really important to understand that most of the time they aren't attacking you; it is the company and the situation they are upset with.

Shannon Johnston recommends dealing with the nasty customer's anger up front and directly. "It sounds funny, perhaps, but we say that you need to lead them out of anger into rapport. A bank customer, say, comes in to pay an overdraft charge and hollers, 'I've been banking here three years, you dammed well should have called me!' You could ignore it and go about your business. But if you take it as an opportunity to get the customer back into rapport by doing something special, you form a lasting impression with the customer—one he'll never forget, and that will *increase* loyalty."

Both Tweed and Johnston emphasize the need to involve the customer in the solution to unusual situations. Says Tweed, "It's hard, but you have to stay friendly and build trust. After that, it's critically important to build collaboration in solving the problem. You need to make clear what the problem really is, and get agreement about what you'll do to clear things up and what the customer has to do. You certainly want to avoid power plays, but before you conclude with a customer who has been really upset, you've got to go over the solution you've agreed upon, repeat what you'll do and what they agree to do to make the solution work."

SELF-PRESERVATION
Another piece of training needed by customer-service people is in self-preservation: how to suffer the slings and arrows, go on smiling and not come unwound in the effort.

It is becoming more and more accepted that public-contact jobs are wearing—just like ditch-digging (although it's true you don't see a lot of people turning in the smiles, blazers and air-conditioned surroundings for picks and shovels). The term that seems to be evolving to convey the nature of the stress load that people in service jobs encounter is "emotional labor." Some experts suggest that jobs with a high emotional labor content, jobs where the performer persona goes on the line time and time again at the customer interface, should be treated as combat. And like combat soldiers, people in high-stress service jobs need to be rotated off the front line frequently—and sometimes permanently. As one expert puts it, "In Vietnam we *knew*, come hell or high water, that after so many months, we were out of there. You need to do that for service people. They have to know there is a light at the end of that tunnel—and it isn't from an oncoming train."

Another extreme view is that only those with rhino hides and temperaments tough enough to deal with the nastiest of the nasty should ever be put in a high-stress customer-contact job. Between these two extreme positions are a multitude of options. Plain old stress-management training is one option many experts propose.

At Disney, several strategies are in play. First there is self-image. According to Sharp, "We tell our people that they are cast members playing a role in a show. And like an actor, they can walk away from the role at the end of the day. Even the most upset guest is only attacking the role the employee plays, not the employee." A second stress reducer at Disney is job rotation. Customer-contact people are encouraged to learn multiple roles and are provided with formal cross-training.

In the customer-service arena, self-preservation is becoming an issue for organizations as well for individual employees. Buck Blessing, cofounder and partner in Blessing/White, Inc., a Princeton, NJ, consulting firm specializing in career development, suggests that a realistic look at labor-force demographics is in order. "Just look at how hard it is to find a kid to mow your lawn today. Multiply that by the number of 7-Eleven stores and fast-food chains in this country and ask how they are going to find people to fill the service jobs and supply jobs. What you'll realize is that we are going to have to learn to treat service people and support people very differently."

Blessing argues that part of that difference has to be the way service people—and their employers—view their jobs. "The organization has to acknowledge the value of these jobs and help the employees see value in them." His formula for motivating service people and helping them deal with stress centers on improving four job factors: mastery, autonomy, relationships and variety. Specifically, Blessing suggests increasing skill and control over the job (mastery and autonomy); helping employees and their supervisors get along better (relationships); and introducing variety into job assignments on an individualized basis, according to the strengths, weaknesses and interests of the employee.

Scandinavian Service School's Wohlecke-Haglund stresses the need to build pride, self-confidence and teamwork. "Don't train front-line people alone," she cautions. "Service involves more than the front-line people who are visible to the public. Service people need to know that the organization and the people they depend on are trying to accomplish the same things with the customer." When people feel they have rear-echelon support, are part of a team and know what's expected of them, they will perform better and be less prone to stress, she says.

"You have to let them—help them—have confidence in their own decision making, in the decisions they make on behalf of the customer. When they know they are trusted and have support, they are more secure and less anxious," Wohlecke-Haglund says, adding that service people have to know that their jobs are indeed stress prone, where that stress comes from and how to develop strategies to deal with it.

As more organizations become convinced that quality service is *the* competitive edge of the 1980's and beyond, finding, developing and retaining topnotch service people becomes a more critical task. Managers who can manage the delivery of superior service, and trainers who can help create service-centered values, appear destined to be the corporate stars of tomorrow—and their organizations the star performers of the decade ahead.

COACHING FOR DISTINCTIVE SERVICE

Chip R. Bell and Ron Zemke

One of the surprises of the emerging service-focused business era is the realization that management of service delivery is, in many ways, a different art form than the management of product production. That management difference stems from the diverse nature of the work itself. The sale, production, and consumption of a service take place almost simultaneously; there is no stockpiling of resources, no opportunity to catch a faulty product before it reaches the public. The service deliverer frequently creates the service in front of the client, sometimes even enlisting the client's help in the production process.

The customer's evaluation of service quality depends as much on the delivery process the customer sees as on an actual end result. We don't go back to restaurants where those who wait on us are rude, we don't shop regularly at department stores where the clerks know less about the merchandise than we do, and we don't take our cars back to service stations where the mechanics suggest that we, not the car, are the ones with the problem.

In any of these instances, the core service may have been fine—the food tasty, the clothes fashionable, the car tuned to perfect running condition— but the delivery, the critical second half of the standard we use to assess the performance of the service, was unacceptable. Service managers must manage not only the outcomes but the delivery process as well.

Directing the performance of a service, rather than managing the production of a product, calls for a new management orientation. Leading the service performer requires skills most often associated with indirect management—coaching, teaching, conducting an orchestra, directing a play—essentially the same skills needed to bring out the best in a performing artist or athlete.

The context for service performance is more akin to that found in the theater and the sports arena than in the factory. Think about Walt Disney World. Thanks to books like *A Passion For Excellence* (Peters and Austin,

■

1987) and videos like *In Search of Excellence: The Film* (Nathan/Tyler, 1985), most of us are familiar with the fact that the young men and women who make the Disneyland and Walt Disney World rides and attractions "go" work from well-written and memorized scripts, complete with acceptance, situational variations, and approved modifications. The Disney service deliverer practices a performance art. The front-line service person is seen by and interacts with an audience—the customer. Managing behind the scenes, in the wings, or in the dugout, is the director or coach. It is a well-oiled, supporting relationship that keeps the "performance" running on course.

Consider the greatest coaches you can think of, but don't limit yourself to athletics: coaching is a critical part of any and every performance art. In sports, we have Vince Lombardi, Don Shula, Red Auerbach. Add to that list the Stephen Spielbergs, Leonard Bernsteins, Ron Howards, plus the less-public coaches who have produced such greats as Martina Navratilova, Katherine Hepburn, Edwin Moses, Van Cliburn, and Mike Tyson. What qualities did they share? What practices did they have in common? While their ring/court/set/field-side manners may have differed, their approaches were similar.

We believe the similarities of their talents, which recognize the importance of self-esteem in artistic and athletic expression, offer a model for any manager of front-line service people. What follows is a look at the varied practices of world-class performance coaches.

SELECTION BASED ON THE SUBJECTIVE
"She or he has that certain something" is a comment frequently made by performance coaches. It is an articulation that selection is based as much on the intuitive honoring of feelings as the analytical judgment of fact. Service excellence is an interpersonal profession. Heroes are often more affective than objective, more compassionate than calculating, and more heart-lead than head-driven.

There are risks associated with selection based more on the subjective than the objective, more on the vibes than the facts. Vibe-driven choices are more susceptible to inappropriate bias and prejudice. The "I have a gut feeling you just won't fit in here" rationale has slammed the door on candidates who were denied entry solely due to the color or shape of their skin. It has been the justification for the bigotry, old boys' networks, and anti-race, -color, -creed, -gender, -national origin, -age, -handicap, -veteran or -sexual-preference myopia that has excluded employees ready, willing, and able to perform with excellence.

Overkill and overboard efforts that exclude selection information that is personal to focus instead solely on information that is objective (applicant as object rather than person) leads to selection decisions that are fair and stupid (rather than fair and smart). We are strong advocates of equity and fairness. But we also believe that selection efforts should acknowledge the imprecise means of evaluating "a service-oriented personality." Work hard to pick people in service roles who have interpersonal skills and personalities consistent with what is needed to give customers an experience so effective they are pleasantly surprised.

So, just how does the service coach choose service people? The quest for the potential service star begins with a clear view of the service role you are seeking to fill. Treat the vacancy as an opening in a play. If you select an ideal (the applicant who comes closest to embodying the qualities best suited for the service role) rather than choosing someone "just like me," you may skirt the lure of choice that results in an unfair personnel practice. At Disney, central casting (also known as the personnel department) knows that one important quality for all its service roles is the ability to get along well with others. To help judge potential cast members—the Disney term for employees—central casting uses group interviews. If an applicant is not interested in what other interviewees have to say, chances are he or she will not be attentive to the needs and wants of Disney guests.

The interviewer should project an attitude of mutual exploration (rather than playing detective or hard-selling the role). If the applicant is treated as an important customer with a need for candid, accurate information to make a fully informed decision, that applicant will more likely respond with like candor and parallel authenticity.

Solicit stories. "Tell me about a time you had a particularly irate customer and how you handled it." Seek to understand the applicant's service values, not just résumé facts. "What does superior customer service mean to you?" "Describe ways you work to achieve superior customer service." We think it appropriate to simulate typical service encounters in an interview. "Now, I will be a customer with a problem about how my account was handled. You be the service rep I encounter first . . . " *How* the person works out the answer is far more important than having the right answer.

Customer service is, first and foremost, an interpersonal encounter. Just as an actor auditions by reading from a scene in a play and an athlete tries out in a practice scrimmage, an applicant should participate in an "encountering"-type interview. His or her "performance" will help you accurately gauge how well that applicant will fill a service role.

FOCUSING ON SERVICE EXCELLENCE

A colleague of ours who does consulting work with a major airline recently asked, "As a frequent flyer, how do you like the practice of the pilot standing in the cockpit door to greet passengers as they exit the plane?" We acknowledged that we thought it was a positive and thoughtful gesture. "It's not just a courteous gesture," our friend informed us. "It's a written standard by which pilots in some airlines are evaluated." Those airlines, such as Piedmont, that do not have it as a precise, written standard have it as a strong cultural norm.

It reminded us that consistently good service is not the result of some accidental happening. It is deliberately created, crafted to cause the customer to experience service that is remembered positively. In the final analysis, one way service performers differ from product producers is that customers walk away with memories rather than objects. The more fond the memories, the more the customer ascribes "excellence" to the encounter. Those are the moments of truth when the consumer remembers being well served.

Achieving this replication of experiences requires some ritual and much focus. Rarely is superior service a matter of routinely following a script. Even for the stage performer, the script is not used as a limiting factor; instead, it is a parameter to insure performance that is true to the author's intent—in our case, to the organization's service standard—within which there is great creative latitude. Thus, each time we see *Hamlet* or *The Glass Menagerie,* we hear the same words and see the same scenes, and yet we experience something unique, recreated just for us.

The extraordinarily attentive and responsive front-desk person at a Four Seasons or Ritz Hotel is not relying upon a learned script. He or she is acting consistently with a clear unit (or, in this case, property) focus that is unyielding in its devotion to serving customers. At the macro level, this requires the service coach constantly to remind the service person that service to customers is preeminent. At the micro level, it requires the service coach to act consistently with that message and to invest inordinate attention and energy, into those aspects of the unit that affect service quality.

Superior service focus begins with a service strategy or mission. This is the theme or concept of the play, the object of the game. If Deluxe Corporation says its service strategy is "the delivery of error-free financial instruments (i.e., zero defects) to the financial industry in a timely (i.e., 48-hour turnaround) fashion," the properly coached service person takes note of how that focus translates to his or her individual accountabilities. It is that cathedral-building-to-bricklaying linkage that coaches use to instill purpose and laser-focused employee energy. The hotel housekeeper conscientiously cleans rooms toward the goal of customer pleasure, not just for hygiene. If that individual focuses on the *customer* while the cleaning rag is in the sink, then he or she more likely will report the broken light socket to the engineering staff instead of leaving it with a "not my job" smirk.

Insuring focus requires repetition and reminder—repetitive redundance, if you will. If customer service is relegated to banners, buttons, and brass bands heard and seen only at the annual meeting, then folks are smart enough to realize it is not a serious intent. Focus takes perpetual underscoring through word and deed. As Ed Crutchfield, CEO of the highly successful First Union Corporation, says, "Service sinks in when managers talk and act service, service, service—day in and day out—in obvious and subtle ways." Service is a central focus if it gets major air time in meetings and ink in reports. Service is a central focus if service excellence is *the* ticket to mahogany row and if service quality—or lack of it—is the trigger behind the smiles—or frowns—of the organizational leaders.

The superior service coach takes an overall service strategy or focus and helps service people translate it into monthly goals, weekly objectives, and daily actions. A service strategy shapes standards of performance; it lends relevance to what gets measured and monitored. The hospital that interviews guests toward the end of their stay regarding hospital service communicates to employees that service quality is a strategic direction. The Will Rogers quote: "It's observation, not conversation that matters" serves as reminder of the tactile dimension of a true service focus.

THE COACH AS SERVICE MENTOR
Homer's character Mentor was chosen as the inspiration for the word we use to mean "a trusted advisor." Mentor was the surrogate parent whom Odysseus (Ulysses in Latin) hired to tutor his heir and son Telemachus while Ulysses was off fighting the Trojan War. Mentor, the tutor, combined worldly wisdom with sensitivity and freshness—a perfect job description for a kingmaker. The description offers inspiration for all service coaches who wish to teach and advise their service people.

Mentoring entails the provision of advice and training, both delivered with sensitivity. That last phrase—delivered with sensitivity—is an important one. At the very core of the delivery of service is an interpersonal relationship between service deliverer and service receiver. The quality of that interpersonal exchange is directly proportionate to the self-esteem of the service person. When self-esteem is a variable, sensitivity is a critical quality.

Advising is an act loaded with potential for resistance. Remember how you felt the last time you were on the receiving end of "let me give you some advice"? Such declarations get our backs up and serve as telling reminders of the authority hang-ups we have yet to reconcile. For a coach, advice giving is quicksand. We feel we need to give it, we want it to be heard, and we hope it will be heeded. Yet, too often we give it and are left with that sinking feeling we have just wasted wise words on deaf ears.

Two small additions to our advice-giving efforts greatly enhance receptivity: Get the receiver's permission to give advice, and couch the advice in an "I statement."

Service managers sometimes bristle at the idea of soliciting permission to give advice, but performance coaches do it all the time. Getting permission does not mean asking the front line if you can do your job or would they rather you just went away and stopped bothering them. Instead, it is a recognition that the service person may actually know what needs to be done. The "I have a suggestion that may be helpful" approach may involve "doing some discovery" with the service person so that he or she clearly understands the goal of the service encounter and can see the same service problems about which you are concerned. If service people think your advice is unneeded, it probably will be unheeded as well.

Giving advice as an "I statement" ("What I have found helpful is to . . . ") keeps you, as coach, out of the telling, judgmental posture. Most service people resent being told what to do. The "you should, you ought to" mode courts resistance. You want to be the trusted advisor to your service people, not the hanging judge!

Mentoring also involves encouragement—inspiration without criticism. The service person who hears "Jack, you're doing great on this, but you need to do better on that" focuses only on the "do better" part. Communications experts tell us "yes, but's" have the effect of erasing the "yes!" If we separate the inspiring/encouraging part of coaching from the critiquing/judging part, we enable the service person to glow and grow. If we don't, we risk losing the power of the reward as well as the focus on the improvement.

A part of the mentoring process is grounded in the Pygmalion effect—the power the coach's expectations have on the service person's performance.

While the self-fulfilling prophecy is a phenomenon not fully understood, it seems that demonstrated belief in the service person makes it work. If you think a subordinate will succeed and treat him or her that way, you generally are not disappointed. The reverse is equally true.

If you don't believe it, think about these actual examples. A teacher mistook students' locker numbers in a grade book for those students' I.Q.'s. Students with average I.Q.'s (but high locker numbers) made great gains in the intelligence-test scores at the year's end. Expectations, and the subtle actions they triggered, spoke louder than words in these Pygmalion transformations.

Although Villanova basketball guard Dwight Wilbur had sunk only two shots out of fifteen attempts in the NCAA tournament, Coach Rollie Massimino started him again against Memphis State. "I've talked with Dwight," Massimino said before the game. "There is more to the Final Four than worrying about 3, 4, or 5 more points in a half. Dwight *will* start. And I hope it restores his confidence." Villanova beat Memphis State 52-45 and went on to defeat Georgetown in the final game of the 1985 NCAA championship. Clearly, demonstrated belief is a key part of mentoring.

THE SERVICE COACH AS PERFORMANCE ANALYST
Sometimes, service people falter in their performance, leaving only vague clues about the reason for the stumble. The coach must analyze performance to ascertain the right coaching stance. The following considerations may help unearth gaps between the service performance expected and that which is delivered.

1. *Role-Person Match.* Reexamine whether the service person would be more successful in a different role. Just as an actor cast in the wrong role lacks believability (imagine Ronald Reagan in *Casablanca* or Sylvester Stallone in *Beverly Hills Cop,* roles for which both were considered), a service person who is incorrectly cast will fall short of customer expectations.
2. *Task Clarity.* Perhaps the service person is not clear on the service standards or expectations you require. Would you bet next year's salary on it? Said one well-known hockey coach, "You can't expect a player to make the right moves if that player doesn't know what 'right moves' means!"
3. *Task Priority.* Sometimes failure is due to the service person's perception that the performance you expect is not really very important.
4. *Competence.* Failure can sometimes be due to a skill deficiency.

Players can't do well if they don't know how. Robert Mager suggests asking, "Could they do it if their life depended on it?" This tactic helps separate skill deficiency from will deficiency.

5. *Obstacles.* The coach might address real or imagined barriers interfering with good service performance.

6. *Reward for Failure.* The service person may perceive more reward for poor or average performance than good or excellent performance. Service people who get attention (albeit negative attention) when they do poorly and are ignored when they do well sometimes stop doing well.

7. *Performance Feedback.* Does the service person receive clear, timely information that enables that person to focus his or her energy accurately? As Tom Landry, former coach of the Dallas Cowboys, says, "I try to find ways for players to measure what they can do, to measure what they can have confidence in—and what price they must pay for success."

8. *Valued Outcomes.* The service person who is not performing well may fail to experience positive outcomes (or rewards) for excellent performance. Part of the coaching responsibility is to figure out what outcomes are valued by the service person. One service coach decided to reward her best front line performer with lunch in the executive dining room with the company president—something she herself would have enjoyed. She later discovered that the lucky performer spent the morning in the bathroom in nervous dread of the event.

THE SERVICE COACH AS ROLE MODEL

One final thing: To move performance from competent and workmanlike to the realm of inspired and excellent requires the intervention of a dedicated leader, a competent "coach plus." In *The Service Edge* (New American Library, 1989), we profiled 101 companies that have profited through a commitment to customer care, companies that are service exemplars for their industries. As we stood back and looked at those profiles as a whole, we found several significant similarities—one of which was highly visible, inspiring leadership. Like the aspiring artistic director, the aspiring service coach should not lack for examples to emulate. People like Fred Smith of Federal Express, Bill Marriott, and the legendary Walt Disney come readily to mind.

A sampling of some of the others follows. They don't all jump on tables and deliver Knute Rockne-type speeches, but they all, in their own ways, make clear just what they are trying to do for their customers and that they mean to do it through other people—their front line. These service leaders are committed to coaching, advising, training, and managing what happens behind the scenes so that their service deliverers can give the best possible performance.

Paul Orafalea, founder of the Kinko's copy centers that bear his nickname, personifies the concept of service leader and coach as mentor. By continually focusing on the imperative of combining quality work, prompt and personal attention, reasonable prices, and innovative service, Orafalea has kept Kinko's a pacesetter in its field. The over 500 Kinko's around the country and abroad are run not by franchises but by regional partners who operate with a great deal of autonomy within a specific territory and under a fluid set of "minimum expectations."

One of the keys to Kinko's success is the tone Orafalea sets. "Keeping the music playing" is his chosen image for illustrating the harmony, teamwork, and delivery of a pleasing customer experience that a well-run Kinko's shop exhibits externally as well as internally.

At the store level, Kinko's employees make a point of listening to customers and asking their opinions on the quality of the work done and the service provided. Every finished order is sent out with a survey attached. As a result of a customer's suggestion, most stores now sell stamps and act as a mail drop. The logic? Easy! Most Kinko's are located near university campuses, where one of the big job items is copying proposals and résumés. Hence, the suggestion; thus, the service.

Mystery shoppers visit each store at least twice a year; their detailed readings are checked against expectations, and the results broadly discussed at the store level. "Discussion" in this case is not a euphemism for "chew 'em out and beat 'em up." There's an almost Scandinavian sense of industrial democracy in the fairly free and uninhibited discussion of minimum standards, system benefits, tips, and tricks that result in delivering better customer service and considering new ideas. "We learn from each other" is both a basic Kinko's tenet and the founder's explicit mind set.

Ben Edwards, chairman and CEO of A.G. Edwards and Sons, a brokerage company now entering its second century of business, "has run this retail-oriented firm from the standpoint of satisfying their customers first, rather than making a profit," the *Wall Street Transcript* reported last year— though profits have never been far behind. Edwards exemplifies his firm's service commitment through his constant attention to both customers and front-line personnel, spending much of his time visiting branch offices and mingling with customers at branch open houses.

"[Edwards] has run this retail-oriented firm from the standpoint of satisfying their customers first, rather than making a profit," the publication noted in explaining the 1987 citation. "The relationship with the customer is very important to the company and, therefore, to Edwards. Cultivating this association is what makes the CEO so outstanding."

The authors of the book *The 100 Best Companies to Work for in America* (1984, Addison-Wesley) also marvel at Edwards' unabashedly unselfish culture where "you are supposed to be accomplishing something for the firm, not for yourself. This is one reason they are able to run a successful branch network. They put a great deal of emphasis on servicing those branches . . . . Edwards is also old-fashioned in that it hasn't built up a huge institutional customer base, and the like. Its focus is still the little guy."

Service performance is an intangible. Service excellence—the measure of success—is exclusively in the eye of the beholder (that is, the customer). Service excellence more than product production is dependent on high employee self-esteem, a consideration that requires unique practices from the service leader. By understanding the context of service delivery—that it is a *performance* art—the service leader can focus on creating the best stage or playing field and on honing in rehearsal the skilled performance needed for his or her players to succeed when the curtain goes up, the gun sounds, and the action begins.

TERMS OF EMPOWERMENT

Chip R. Bell and Ron Zemke

The customer walked into a crowded fast-food restaurant at noon to order a sandwich, small order of french fries and soft drink to go. Upon reaching the front of the line and placing his order, he was informed that the sandwiches were being prepared and it would be a short wait.

His patience noticeably turned to anger as the sixth customer behind him received her order, and he was still waiting. The cashier earnestly checked the order and prodded her co-workers to hurry with the sandwich. Finally, she presented the customer with his order. "I'm very sorry," she said, "and you were in a hurry. Because you had to wait, I gave you a large order of fries." His anger instantly faded.

How did this 11th grader have such power? What gave her the confidence and clout to make a judgment that favored the customer, but also put the register receipts out of balance with the potato inventory? Didn't her manager worry about excesses—today she gave away extra fries. What tomorrow, a franchise?

We are on the edge of an era marked by rising consumer expectations for service quality. The familiar adage "If you always do what you've always done, you'll always get what you've always gotten" has proven false in the service industry. Because the industry's standards for quality are increasing daily, an individual doing next year what was done last year, no matter how successful, will put him or her one down from the competition.

Customer satisfaction is not a lofty goal. It simply means that customers are getting exactly what they expect—no more, no less. Too frequently this translates to invisible, taken-for-granted service, which is often forgotten. In addition, it rarely creates the tell-your-neighbor reviews required for word-of-mouth advertising. The successful enterprise goes for the gold by creating customer experiences that exceed customer expectations.

The process of delivering superior service generally includes some human effort, such as a service provider working (or not working) to respond to a customer need or request. The bank machine (surrogate teller) or the automatic airline ticket dispenser (surrogate reservations clerk) are the exceptions. Most service delivery involves human encounter, and how that encounter unfolds can determine whether the customer walks away feeling pleased, satisfied, annoyed or victimized.

Although the customer's expectations entering the process help shape his or her service report card, the interpersonal encounter can heavily weigh the grade given at the end. How does a service-providing enterprise ensure its service deliverers handle encounters so the company gets straight A's?

SERVICE PROVIDERS MUST BE ALLOWED TO SOLVE PROBLEMS AS THEY HAPPEN

Empowerment—the act of vesting substantial responsibility in the hands of people nearest the problems to be solved—is both exhilarating and awesome for managers with a healthy respect for Murphy's Law to contemplate. Nonetheless, the pressure for improved productivity in goods and services, accentuated by the thinning of middle management ranks, is leading more managers to rely on decisions and judgments made by the line worker.

The quality of the person-to-person relationship in the delivery of service is a function of many variables. It includes such important practices as selecting people with a service-orientation personality that engenders trust, reliability and supportiveness. Other variables include clarifying service expectations—the goals, objections, norms and values—that enable service providers to know where to focus their energy, as well as the priority superior service has among the other activities required of them. It also entails providing the rewards and experienced consequences that incent superior service delivery and discourage actions and attitudes contrary to quality service.

One critical ingredient in getting service providers to go the extra mile on behalf of the customer is empowerment. This internal clout results in the service deliverer acting with responsible competence and assertive confidence to take actions not covered by the firm's rules, regulations or procedures. Empowerment is the self-generated exercising of judgments. It's doing what needs to be done rather than doing what one is told.

It's unlikely the fast-food clerk was following a procedure that read: Give extra french fries to customers who have a long wait for an order. The clerk demonstrated empowerment by reading the situation and, following a philosophy of giving the customer a pleasurable experience by making a judgment to include extra french fries.

Empowerment is the process of releasing the expression of personal power; it's the opposite of enslavement. Because personal power is already present within the individual, empowerment is not a gift one gives to another individual. Therefore, power is released by removing the barriers that prevent its expression.

The concept of releasing power is important because it focuses us more on what we take away than what we give. It reminds us that the service deliverer is somehow bound and could be more responsive and attentive if unbound. Instead of asking what we can provide that will make this person feel more powerful, it leads us to think about what exists that prevents the person from feeling powerful.

SERVICE WISDOM CAN BE FOSTERED IN MANY WAYS

Most trainers have heard of or used the conscious/unconscious-competence/incompetence window model. Part of the explanation of the model is that while everyone has areas of unconscious competence, the highest performance emerges out of the conscious competence quadrant: I know and I know I know. Competence realized is the springboard of confidence, courage and proactivity.

Many organizations have learned that the bonds of psychological enslavement can be unshackled through improved competence. Walt Disney World, for example, provides four days of training to street sweepers, not because it takes that long to learn to pick up trash, but because the entertainment giant has learned that guests are more likely to direct questions to a kid on the business end of a broom than to ask the squeaky clean assistant wearing "Ask me, I'm in Guest Relations" lapel buttons. Walt Disney World wants the street sweepers to react to the myriad of questions with attentiveness and confidence, and not say, "Gee, I dunno, ask her."

Empowerment doesn't occur with training: it simply begins to unfold with training. The ultimate goal is service wisdom, which entails knowing more than what is required to perform a service role, and being capable of handling issues and incidents not covered in the procedure manual.

Think of the people you consider to be wise. Part of their wisdom lies in the fact that they are able to make intuitive leaps, not simply logical conclusions. They make connections and derive insight not readily apparent based simply on following rote procedures, memorized facts or obvious observations. There's common-sense richness borne out of their depth of experience.

Service wisdom can be fostered in many ways. For example, cross training is one obvious approach. If service providers are trained in roles around them, the bigger-picture perspective gained will bolster the confidence needed to respond to unusual customer requests.

For example, each year Quad Graphics has all its supervisors and lead operators attend Quad University—a learning opportunity held over several days on a nearby college campus. The Pewaukee, Wisconsin-based printer of such magazines as *Newsweek, Playboy, Inc.,* and *Ms.* allows its attendees (including company President Harry Quadracci) to select as many as four mini-courses, covering subjects ranging from personal growth to management skills. The company has found that the learning experience "pays off in many ways," says training officer Sue Barrett, "not the least of which is their confidence in how they respond to customers when those customers come into the plants."

Malcolm Knowles often tells the story of the medium-size electronics manufacturer of radios and televisions. The company realized the electronics industry was on the eve of sizable transition from a vacuum-tube technology to a transistor technology. The company began to train heavily—even in courses that would not be approved according to most tuition refund policies. When the industry began to change over to transistor, this company quickly grabbed the dominant market share in the electronic appliance world. The company is Sony.

One reason Sony's top brass gave for their meteoric rise was learning. They reasoned that the more people learned, the better learners they would become and the more likely they would want to learn. Therefore, Sony employees learned new transistor skills at much faster pace than their competitors. In addition, the more they learned, the more empowerment employees felt. They had the courage needed to risk new techniques and develop alternative approaches.

Many organizations are relaxing their educational rules to fund almost any academic course, regardless of job relatedness. Some are building what-if simulations into training programs targeted at helping learners feel prepared for almost any contingency.

First Union National Bank, headquartered in Charlotte, North Carolina, incorporates service stories into customer service training for branch managers. They encourage participants in their Consumer Bank Sales Academy to share experiences of exemplary beyond-the-call-of-duty services to customers.

American Express' annual Great Performers awards achieve much the same end. The company awards extraordinary effort while expanding the service wisdom through stories that then become models of how it can (and should) be done well.

Service wisdom is the beyond-competence state that is achieved through experience and breadth. Experience can be acquired directly by years of seeing it all or it can be gained vicariously through shared stories and selected simulations. Breadth comes via training in the whole process, as well as receiving explanations and directives that are faced with rationales. If the service provider knows why, his capacity to respond creatively and wisely climbs quickly.

EMPLOYEES LEARN SELF-DISCIPLINE AND RESPONSIBILITY THROUGH FREEDOM, NOT RESTRICTION

Freedom, Not License, is the title of A.S. Neill's best-selling book. The thesis of the book is that everyone, including children, can learn to be self-disciplined and responsible only by getting freedom, not restriction. However, Neill was quick to point out that freedom did not mean you can do absolutely whatever you like. There are boundaries. And, if the boundaries are examined regularly to ensure appropriateness, as well as a lot of breathing room, people will act responsibly.

Managers quickly learn there is power in control. Similar to the old-fashioned school marm, however, oppressiveness and unreasonable bridling not only substitute motivation for movement and commitment for compliance, it often encourages rebellious, aberrant behavior. The early days of assembly-line sabotage were classic examples of reactions to enslavement. The by-product in the service field can be devastating. The mentality that believes "They do it to me in here, I'm going to do it to them out there" turns poor employee relations into poor customer relations.

How can balance be struck between appropriate freedom and inappropriate license? How do we create systems in which it's appropriate for a fast-food employee to elect to give away a large order for french fries and inappropriate to give away a franchise, or cause illegal shrinkage?

In his book *The Renewal Factor,* Robert Waterman leans on a metaphor from higher mathematics to describe the process of gaining control by giving up control, which is the heart of directed autonomy. Many math problems have a variety of possible solutions contained inside a set of boundaries. It's the same with business problems. The manager's job is to decide the boundaries; the subordinate's responsibility is to find the best way of performing the job within the space.

There is no real optimum answer other than what employees suggest. If service deliverers' suggestions fit within the solution space and management likes the suggestions, that's about as close to optimum as you can get.

Bill Lee, chairman of Charlotte, North Carolina-based Duke Power Co., is fond of saying "Ask why, and if the answer to the question is not compelling, do what you think is right and it probably will be." The symbolic switch to solution space—you can do whatever you like as long as you stay in this space—provides a freeing experience while at the same time it offers the latitude to challenge and therefore, understand the boundaries.

Neill taught us much about the spirit and energy that comes from release. "Think of your role as that of a release valve, not that of restraining force. We need more green flags and less yellow; more rivers and less dams," he said.

Along the same train of thought, Tom Peters enjoyed telling the story of an experiment to determine the impact certain environmental factors had on productivity. Two groups of people were asked to complete several tasks, such as solving puzzles and proofreading, while listening to a tape recorder playing very distracting noise.

One group was instructed they could turn off the noise if it became too distracting; the other group was given no such permission. Although no one ever actually turned off the noise, the group with permission had much higher productivity. It's not the freedom people *use* that makes the difference, it's the freedom they *have*.

A major part of freedom is encouraging service providers to test the system. The barriers that bind often are illusory, as illustrated in the story of the barracuda in a tank with bite-size tropical fish.

Separated from the fish by a clear glass barrier, the barracuda continually dove at the tropical fish, only to get a bruised nose. As soon as the barracuda gave up, the partition was removed from the tank, which allowed the barracuda and the tropical fish to swim together. The hungry barracuda starved to death rather than risk a bruised nose.

The moral of the story? Although the barriers to giving good service can be real, often they are mythical barriers created by a painful past.

Take the time to audit service delivery from the inside. Asking service providers to identify barriers to providing superior service achieves two ends. In addition to surfacing useful information about clogs in the systems and procedures, it dramatizes a clear concern for removing the obstacles that enslave service people. It amplifies omissions.

A good example of service delivery occurred during a January snowstorm in which several thousand people were stranded overnight in a Charlotte, North Carolina terminal. The employees of Piedmont Airlines (now USAir) repeatedly made major judgments without supervisors' approval. "We let them know that customers comes ahead of everything," says Supervisor Sharon Eserling. "We let them make their own decisions and then we back them."

What if they make a bad judgment? "There are boundaries," she continues, "but it's pretty much common sense." Piedmont Airlines believes that if what their employees do is for the customer's welfare, and it's done using common sense, which, she says, is "how you'd expect a good airline to treat you," their employees won't make a bad judgment.

If a bad call is made, the company talks with the employee in an effort to figure out what happened. "Sometimes," adds Eserling, "meeting customers is just not for them."

A major division of a large telephone company conducted a barriers study aimed at identifying the internal obstacles that impacted quality of service in residential telephone repair. One repairman sheepishly acknowledged that if the customer was located in a remote area with telephone service and he determined that the trouble was in the customer's owned (not leased) instrument, he gave him or her a telephone. Although the repairman said he knew it was against company policy, his responsibility, he said, was to his customers.

On hearing about the incident in the report, the management team lauded his efforts, saying that was the attitude they wanted. However, they quickly realized that the system typically bruised such customer-driven actions and began to work on ways to reward such judgments without running the risk of giving away the shop.

Customers like to deal with a service person who has the power and confidence to act on their behalf. This is very important because the service deliverer may be the only company representative the customer encounters in his or her dealings with the organization.

Donald Porter, director of customer service quality assurance of British Airways, was quoted in *Service America* as saying, "If you're a service person and you get it wrong at your point in the customer's chain of experience, you are very likely erasing from the customer's mind all the memories of the good treatment he or she may have had up until you. But if you get it right you have a chance to undo all the wrong that may have happened before the customer got to you.

FEEDBACK IS A VALUABLE TOOL FOR EMPOWERMENT

When chairmen of IBM, Tom Watson put a young executive in charge of a new venture. Despite the executive's meritorious effort, the venture lost $8 million in the first few months. Watson asked to meet with the executive, who presumed he had been summoned to tender his resignation. The chairman, however, immediately responded that he couldn't afford to fire the executive because IBM had just spent several million dollars training him! This story stands in the culture-shaping archives of IBM as a belief that mistakes are treated as opportunities for growth and problem solving, not rebuke and disdain.

Feedback is a valuable tool for empowerment if the focus is on information for improvement rather than evaluation for punishment. Too often, service feedback is used to spotlight what went wrong, not to underscore what went right.

When a famous tennis player was learning a new technique, she became frustrated with her inability to quickly achieve perfection. "What am I doing wrong?" she asked her coach. His wise response was, "Why, do you want to do it again?"

The manager of a repair answering center for a major telephone company said, "We don't pay much attention to the percentage of "fairs" and "poors" we get from customer phone surveys. But, we study the dickens out of the percentage of 'excellents' we get. Our staff meetings are almost entirely devoted to what we can do to get more." Their ratings have become among the highest in the industry.

Likewise, Ken Blanchard's "Catch people doing things right" is more than a quip. It bespeaks of a philosophy that treats feedback as a technique to get more of the best rather than less of the worst. Such a flywheel effort mobilizes energy toward getting more information instead of avoiding the bad news.

If service providers are trusted and presumed to be responsible, they typically act in trustful, responsible ways. When mistakes occur, they feel disappointed rather than remorseful or guilty. They demonstrate a curiosity about how things go wrong, which then becomes a platform for growth and self-directed change. It's a wise manager who asks, "What did you learn and how will you do things differently next time?"

Our society has reinforced feedback as a search for negative information. We get back performance reviews and inspect them much as we did term papers in high school by looking for our mistakes. If the scale is tipped toward close scrutiny of the minus with only tacit review of the praise, it erodes self-esteem. Self-esteem among service deliverers is the premium ingredient for positive, superior customer relations.

"It takes happy employees to make happy customers," says J. Willard Marriott Sr. His giant hotel legacy was founded on a management philosophy of employees with high self-esteem.

Note that there can be an aloneness to customer service. When a product fails, the purchaser's wrath is typically directed toward the craftsmanship of the object. But when service fails, the ire is zeroed in on an individual. Even if the employee did nothing to cause the breakdown, he or she is treated as if the fault was due to his or her personal failure. In such a case, the potential for stress and burnout is significant.

The feeling of support manifested in the authority to act as a responsible adult can be a powerful antidote to service wear out. It can free the supervisor to put energies into tasks other than employee control. In addition, it can communicate to the customer that he or she is dealing with someone with the latitude to act as the company when they are in the field, on the telephone or eye to eye with the customer. Everybody wins and the customer walks away feeling his or her experience exceeded expectations. The terms of empowerment are the tools of service excellence.

SUPERVISING SERVICE WORKERS

Ron Zemke

The difference between managing the delivery of a service and managing the construction of a product is as great as the gap between farm and factory. Or so an old shibboleth contends. But it's a maxim that makes some sense. Services have unique characteristics that are different from products and require unique managing. For one thing, a service is an intangible. A haircut, for example, takes up no shelf space, has no shelf life and can't be inventoried or produced in advance of delivery. The customer is right there as an active participant in, and witness to, the production of the outcome: "Hey! Not so much off the top. I want to look just like this, right here on page 52."

Quality control of a service is as much a matter of monitoring a process as inspecting an outcome. Errors have very different consequences in service delivery than they do in the manufacture of products. The workman who lays down a bad weld creates a rejected product. His workmanship is important but his personality is of marginal concern to management. George may be a grumpy old goat, but if he can hang doors or tighten transmissions to specifications, it all works out. It is the quality of the outcome, of the finished automobile, that the customer judges.

On the other hand, the waiter who dumps a bowl of hot soup in a diner's lap ruins an entire meal and loses a customer. A surly nurse, teller, broker, waitress or flight attendant has a direct impact on customer satisfaction— and on repeat business. In today's service-sensitive marketplace, the consumer is increasingly inclined to avoid hospitals that treat him like an inconvenience or an idiot. Furthermore, the customer will stay away despite the quality of the products carried or the skill with which the core service is delivered.

It's not just logic and personal experience that substantiate the maxim that service delivery has to be managed differently from product production; we're beginning to see supporting research as well. Texas A&M marketing professor Leonard Berry, one of the first to research service distinctions systematically, concluded that, "Consumer perception of service quality results from comparing expectations prior to receiving the service and actual experiences with the service. Quality evaluations derive from the service process as well as the service outcome."

Another early investigator, management professor Benjamin Schneider at Michigan State University, looked at the relationship between management practices, employee satisfaction and customer satisfaction. Working in the retail division of a large East Coast bank, Schneider found that customers reported superior service at those branches where employees said their management had a strong commitment to service and their branch manager backed up that commitment with actions. Schneider also found that turnover and morale among employees strongly correlated with customers' satisfaction with service quality.

One of the most recent studies, conducted last year by Boston-based Forum Corp., discovered even more evidence that service management is unique and that there is a strong tie between good service management and customer satisfaction. According to Forum president Richard Whitely, there are at least three factors that make the service manager's job different from other managerial jobs. "There is an extra dimension to the job. The manager has to ensure that both the technical and the interpersonal aspects are done well. But beyond that, the manager has to do both well himself. People in service organizations are very conscious of what their managers do. They look up and say, 'Is my manager practicing what she preaches?' If the answer is no . . ."

"So the manager has to be very disciplined, very well self-managed," Whitely says, "The third dimension," he continues, "is espousing good service, being the translator of the overall service commitment to the work of the local unit. That's not something a manufacturing supervisor has to be concerned with."

MEANWHILE, BACK AT THE FRONT LINE . . .
Charlotte Wagenberg, assistant vice president of human resource development at St. Luke's-Roosevelt Hospital Center in New York City, sees daily evidence of the unique aspects of the service supervisors' job. "In health care, and probably all other service occupations as well, how you do the job is as important as what you do. That means the supervisor must be able to give feedback and correction not only on technical quality but on interpersonal style or skill as well. A technician who gives great X-rays but leaves the patient feeling like a slab of meat isn't doing the whole job. The supervisor has to be able to spot and correct that."

On that point, supervisory training expert Martin Broadwell, a consultant in Decatur, GA, adds an "amen" and an emphatic assertion: "I am convinced beyond a shadow of a doubt that what is rewarded—and the message about what is important [that] the supervisor sends to the front line—is the critical difference between good and poor service."

Both Wagenberg and Whitely agree with Broadwell's emphasis on the supervisor as someone who must set standards and give feedback to the front-line service provider. Says Whitely, "If there is one piece of advice I would give to a supervisor—one thing I would say, 'above all else do this'— it would be 'translate the mission of the organization into local terms.' If I'm a front-line service person, I want to be able to say I had a great day; but it's not always clear what that means in a service organization. You can't count the widgets produced and decide you have done good job. My supervisor has to help me do that, to see what a good job means."

Wagenberg says managers need to coach and counsel as well as see the broader context. "I emphasize that the manager has to help the front-line person keep a good focus. The job is to keep the consciousness high about total customer care."

Monica Jenks, a consultant with TARP Institute, a Washington, DC-based research firm that specializes in customer-satisfaction research, points out another unique service-supervision role, that of trainer. Jenks, who concentrates on training front-line service people to handle customer complaints, emphasizes that trained front-line workers *stay* trained only with help from their supervisors. "Service people are under a lot of pressure, especially when they are dealing with angry customers. The supervisor must monitor, evaluate and give them feedback on how they are doing," she says. "Doing weekly follow-up workshops after you've introduced new skills to the front line is important. They need a lot of support and feedback in the use of the new skill. The supervisor is the only one close enough to the day-to-day performance to do that well."

Broadwell agrees: "The goal for the supervisor is to be sure that the front-line people know what behaviors the customer translates as 'good customer service,' and ensure that they are doing those things. Because of the intensity of service jobs, they need that feedback much more frequently. If a person who is not in a customer-contact role needs feedback on performance once a month, the front-line service person needs it once a week." Broadwell adds that front-line people need praise and reinforcement much more frequently as well. "They can take all the praise you can give them. They get all the bullets anyone can take from the customers.

Praise is the bulletproof vest. The supervisor has to be the one to give praise and give it generously."

WHERE'S THE TRAINING?
Though plenty of people agree that service supervision has unique challenges and requires some special skills, it appears that very little specialized training is being offered to service supervisors. A study conducted last year by Zenger-Miller Corp., a training and consulting company in Cupertino, CA, found that only a tiny percentage of organizations provide managers or supervisors with specialized training in service quality. Nancy Cushing, senior researcher on the study, says the vast majority of service training focuses on the front-line employee—not on the employee's manager and not on the management of the service-quality process. Cushing likens this practice to the idea of "making the loading-dock worker responsible for the quality of products." When customer-oriented values are taught only to the front-line people, she warns, there is "considerable risk" of frustrating and alienating them."

One place where training of service supervisors is not neglected is at Walt Disney World Co. in Lake Buena Vista, FL. There, the training of front-line managers is ongoing and intense. It's also very much team-focused. According to Mary Ann Goloversik, manager of HRD for the organization's theme parks, the process of teaching new supervisors and managers to work in teams is critical to service quality. "We get tunnel vision on the front line. It is very easy to miss the big picture and forget that my decisions and actions will affect my neighbor's area."

The instruction begins early. Disney's 10-week, presupervisory training program, called Advanced Skills Development, teaches individual skills—time management, presentation skills, decision making, goal setting, people management and so on—but also assigns trainees to project teams. Each team is assigned the task of selecting a real customer problem—say, improving the park experience for handicapped guests—and presenting a workable solution to senior management at the end of the program. "We want supervisors to think in organizational terms from the very beginning," say Goloversik.

Wagenberg is also concerned that service delivery not be seen as an issue involving only individuals, but as a broad management concern. "It takes longer, but it really is an OD (organization development) thing. You have to get the organization committed and aligned to one common purpose or nothing happens. Service quality isn't something that happens in one department or can happen in only one department. It happens for the organization or not at all."

Or as Whitely puts it, "The goal of a service-quality effort should be to manage your unit so that it creates a predictable, positive, seamless experience for the customer. That requires a team, teamwork and good management."

QUALITY WORK DOESN'T MEAN QUALITY SERVICE

David Maister

Consider the following scenario: You have had your car repaired at a new local garage. A week or two later, your neighbor, curious about whether he or she should also use this new garage, asks, "Did they fix the car?" "I think so," you reply. "It seems to be running smoothly, so I guess they did a good job." Then your neighbor asks an interesting second question: "Did you get good service?" What does this second question mean? Surely, fixing the car is the service, isn't it? Well, yes and no. Fixing the car is part of it, and an important part it is, but by itself it doesn't constitute good service.

Your neighbor is asking about a whole range of other activities that influence your satisfaction with the service providers. Were they accessible? Was it easy to make an appointment? Did they deal with the matter expeditiously? Did they take the time to explain to you, in language appropriate to your level of understanding, what they had found, what, precisely, they did, and why?

When you first approached them, did they ask intelligent questions about symptoms, trying to come up with an informed guess as to the scope of the problem? Or did they just say, "Leave it with us and we'll get back to you," sending you away to worry about how big a problem you had and how much it might end up costing? Did they make you feel as if your car was just one more job to be done, or did they convey the impression that they wanted your business? Did they deal with you with an appropriate mix of respect and friendliness?

If complications arose, did they make strenuous efforts to contact you, inform you of developments, and involve you in the decision as to what to do next? Or did they make all the decisions for you, failing to distinguish between mandatory and precautionary measures and leaving you with a feeling that you might end up paying for work that wasn't truly necessary? Was it easy to settle the bill and understand the charges? Did they provide advice as to how to prevent recurrence of the problem, or to avert other potential problems detected in the course of the repairs?

David Maister is a contributing editor for *The American Lawyer.* This article is republished with permission from the April 1984 issue of *The American Lawyer.* © *The American Lawyer.*

As these questions show, the practical meaning of good service in car repair extends far beyond technical excellence in servicing the car. It is necessary to service not only the *car,* but also the *customer.* Indeed, it may be more important to excel at servicing the customer. Many customers are unable to distinguish between outstanding technical work and the simply competent: In choosing garages, they may pay more attention to the quality of service received than the quality of work performed—which, of course, is not the same thing. And even if the customers *are* sufficiently sophisticated to distinguish between outstanding and competent work their technical needs may call for only the competent: They know that any number of providers can fix the car, and, rather than seek out the most highly qualified (and probably most highly priced) technician in town, these intelligent consumers will appraise providers along a number of dimensions, including responsiveness, attitude, and other nontechnical "service" criteria.

The lessons from this example extend far beyond the car-repair industry. They apply to all service industries, and most significantly to the professions. The markets for legal counsel, tax advice, investment banking services, advertising services, and consulting services all share with our garage mechanic the need to service the client as well as the "car."

The questions posed above could all be equally well asked of a professional service provider, and they provide a useful guide to the client's *perception* of the quality of the professional service. I, the client, may *think* my provider did a good technical job at dealing with the professional matter, but as with the car repair, I am not an expert. The unfolding of time may allow me to find out, as the car does or does not continue to run well, as my legal contracts do or do not result in problems, as my tax arrangements do or do not result in financial benefit, as my merger attempts or stock offerings have a favorable result, and so on.

But even time may not allow me to judge unequivocally whether my professional service provider rendered truly superior advice: A large number of contingencies can cloud my ability to assess the work performed. Even with the most brilliant legal mind on my side, I may lose the case; even the most superior consulting talent available may not prevent me from making what turned out to be a false strategic move. How, then, am I to appraise my service provider?

Whether logical or illogical, sensible or not, even the most sophisticated client will, in such an environment, come to focus more heavily on the quality of service than on the quality of the work. Because of the ambiguity that surrounds technical excellence (and the difficulty the client has in appraising it), the personal relationship between the client and the provider takes on great significance in all of the professions.

Just as with my garage mechanic, when I find a professional service provider whom I trust, in whom I can have confidence, and who provides me with peace of mind and reassurance, I will tend to remain with that provider. Indeed, on most technical or professional matters outside my own area of expertise, I am as much shopping for trust, confidence, peace of mind, and reassurance as I am for "cold" technical expertise. As all clients do, I consider style, manner, and, above all, *attitude* in choosing professional service providers.

John Rathmell, a retired Cornell business school professor, notes in his book *Marketing in the Service Sector:* "Goods are produced, services are performed." My own reformulation is this: Goods are consumed, services are *experienced*. The professional service provider is (or should be) as much in the business of managing the client *experience* with respect to professional services as in the business of executing technical tasks.

Much of the previous discussion can be summarized by what I have come to call "The First Law of Service," expressed as a formula: *Satisfaction = Perception ≤ Expectation*. If the client *perceives* service at a certain level but expected something more (or different), then he or she will be dissatisfied.

The significance of this seemingly simple formula is contained in the observation that neither perception nor expectation necessarily reflects reality. both are experimental, psychological states of mind. Accordingly, the central challenge to service organizations is to manage not only the substance of what they do for clients but also to manage clients' expectations and perceptions. Consider the restaurant chain that consistently overestimates the time it will take for a table to become free. They lose some customers, but those who remain are seated before they expected: a pleasant surprise and a good beginning to the service encounter. Trivial? Perhaps, but a pleased client is easier to keep pleased than one who is in a state of annoyance and impatience because he was led to believe that service would begin earlier than it did.

My colleague Daryl Wyckoff tells the story of checking out of a hotel in San Francisco and commenting to the clerk on the beauty of the view from his room window. The next time he stayed there, he was greeted, "Welcome, Professor Wyckoff. We have assigned you the room with the view that you liked so much." A powerful service experience, and one that is relatively simple to arrange, given the organization's desire to please.

The importance of perceptions and expectations is not restricted to consumer services such as these. It is possible (indeed, all too common in the professional service sector) that the professional does substantively superior work but that this is not perceived by the client. Or, in another case, the professional may invest significant amounts of time and effort in dealing with unforeseen contingencies but, because the client did not expect the contingencies, he or she is irritated by the extra delay and expense rather than thankful for the abilities of the professional.

This isn't solely a matter of unsophisticated clients being unable to appreciate what is truly being done for them. In case after case, I have heard stories (and observed examples) of professionals so completely oriented to their own values (e.g., pride in technical craftsmanship) that the clients' true needs are placed second to the professional desire to create a monument to his or her technical ability. "We could do great work," I have heard frequently, "if the client did not keep getting in the way." Architects run the risk of falling in love with their artistic designs, lawyers with the elegance of their briefs, consultants with the sophistication of their analyses, all to the exclusion of consideration of what the client needs and expects or of how the client perceives the provider's efforts.

The need to be "client centered" is a constant theme of modern management writing (e.g., Peters and Waterman, *In Search of Excellence*). I would assert that it is the professional service sector that is in most urgent need of hearing this message. Because of the proclivity of professionals to become more fascinated with the intellectual challenge of their craft than with being responsive to clients, all too often clients are mocked for their lack of professional knowledge, despised because of their demands, and resented because they control the purse strings and hence the autonomy of the professional.

There is an old saw in the medical profession that the three most important keys to success are availability, affability, and ability—in that order. The same profound insight can be equally well applied to other professions. In all professions, clients gripe that "they do great work, but you can never get hold of them. They don't return my phone calls!" Another common complaint is "I wish they would keep me informed of progress. This may be just another engagement to them, but to me it's critical. I want to know what's going on."

This last statement is particularly telling. People and organizations turn to professional service providers for matters of significant uncertainty, importance, and risk. It is this atmosphere of risk and importance that makes them prepared to pay the traditionally high fees of the professional service sector. Whether it is health, legal concerns, finances, office accommodations, internal organization, or advertising, clients of professional service firms are almost by definition in a state of anxiety and nervousness: They need to be confident that they are in good hands. The slogan of one rapidly growing professional service firm I have studied is "People don't care how much you know until they know how much you care"—a cute phrase but an important one. Clients of professional service firms want to know that they are not being lost in the shuffle. They want to know that their matter is receiving the attention it deserves. The professional service firm that is adept at projecting a *caring* image, and that backs the image up with a substantive reality, will do well in the marketplace.

It should be stressed that, in emphasizing the importance to clients of how they are treated, I am not restricting this observation to unsophisticated buyers. Consider again our car-repair example. To the mechanically unsophisticated, good service may mean clean facilities, a pleasant receptionist, understandable explanations, fast turnaround, and convenient access. To the automobile buff who performs minor repairs himself, good service will mean the opportunity to be involved with decisions, to discuss with the mechanics the intricacies of the problem, and to walk around the repair shop. The technical neophyte might be intimidated by a dirty-fingered engineer speaking technical language, the initiate might be offended by the unnecessary frills of receptionists, free cups of coffee, and nontechnical descriptions. The point is that both types will be concerned with how they are dealt with—how oriented the organization is to their specific needs and preferred style of interaction. Both will be concerned not only with the content of the transaction—getting the car fixed (or the legal matter handled or the accounts audited)—but also with the *process* by which this is accomplished. Each may wish to be treated in a different manner, but each will want to be treated well.

In many professions, the importance of understanding that different clients want to be treated differently is becoming accentuated. Corporations are becoming more sophisticated purchasers of professional services, often with in-house capabilities to handle selected matters. While in the past a lawyer dealt directly with a senior executive, outside counsel now often have to work through in-house counsel. The in-house lawyer is in effect the client and will expect to be dealt with in a different manner than a general manager. Similarly, in investment banking, consulting, and architecture,

chief financial officers, planning departments, and facility-planning committees are, respectively, beginning to act as knowledgeable clients. In all
cases, the message is the same: The nature of the client has changed, and
hence the process of interaction must change. Precise definitions of "good
service" must evolve. The professional can no longer assume that the client
will place trust, confidence, and respect in him or her.

Power, in all professions, is moving from the professional to the client. The
professional firm must increasingly demonstrate a willingness to be
cooperative, responsive, and adaptable in order to win the confidence of
today's client.

What, in concrete terms, can be done? For many firms, a wide range of
seemingly trivial but practically powerful actions are possible. One lawyer
in a large firm relates the following anecdote.

"One of our competitors (in real estate transactions) makes it a common
practice to get a copy of the deal into the hands of their client within
twenty-four hours of the closing of the deal. We think we write better
contracts with more protection for our clients, but there is no denying that
their clients are impressed. We are told that they have a better reputation
for quality of service than we do." A fine example of the gap between
perceptions and reality: If my friend's firm wants to keep its clients,
perhaps it could do a better job of managing the expectations of its
clients—clearly explaining how long it will take to produce a copy of the
deal and why it is in the client's interest to wait the extra few days. The key
is anticipating the client's perceptions and reactions and explicitly dealing
with them in advance. The prescription is clear: Discuss at the earliest
possible point all potential roadblocks, detours, and contingencies that
may arise, and make it clear how your firm will handle them.

There is a danger that in a vigorous attempt to win new clients, excessive
promises may be made, creating expectations that cannot be fulfilled. One
professional I know describes the syndrome this way: "The most depressing day in the office is the day after we have won a new client. We all look
at each other and say, 'How on earth are we going to deliver all we promised
for the budget we agreed to?'"

Client expectations can also be managed by vigorous efforts at keeping the
client informed as to developments, progress, and discretionary decisions.
One professional I spoke with describes his techniques as follows:
"Whenever I reach a decision point, I call the client, lay out the alternatives,
make a recommendation, then ask for his opinion and instructions.

Ninety-nine percent of the time, he tells me to do what I was going to do anyway. But it makes him feel good to be consulted, and he is taking direct responsibility for specific expenditures and time-consuming activities. He is never surprised by what I got up to on his behalf, and he is constantly informed as to what I'm doing for him. if I don't have a decision for him to make, I call him anyway just to let him know what the status is. And every conversation ends with two sentences: I ask if there's anything else he wants me to do, and I tell him when I'll next call him." This may not be an appropriate strategy in all cases: Some clients may interpret constant telephone calls as harassment rather than good service. But it is the preferences of the client, not of the professional, that should determine the manner in which the professional behaves. The professional must discover each client's style preferences and work to communicate the appropriate attitude. The individual quoted above is concerned that he be perceived as responsive: His telephone calls are but a way to symbolize that.

In the October 1983 issue of *The American Lawyer,* Steven Brill, the publisher, tells how pleasantly surprised he was on receiving a letter acknowledging payment of a legal bill and thanking him for his business; an attitude conveyed through a simple, trivial action. The business world is filled with creative examples of this. For example, the hotel room that places a paper strip across the toilet bowl to symbolize that the bathroom has been sanitized—a reassuring touch. Another example: The car-repair shop that hands back the burned-out part that was replaced. Useless, but comforting to know that the part was indeed in need of replacement. Or consider the financial services company that sends a client a clipping from some obscure financial journal about his or her business: The clipping may or may not be useful, but the gesture tells the client that the company cares. Such trivial actions create the *experience* of client satisfaction.

Examples in the professional service sector *can* be found: The firm that consistently follows up client meetings with brief memoranda summarizing the discussion and point agreed to, with a request to the client to call if any misinterpretation has taken place. The firm that routinely explains *in advance* the format of its complex bills so that the client knows what to expect when he arrives. The firm that ensures that all referrals from clients are followed up with a thank-you note, whether or not any new business resulted. The firm that makes the effort to find out the client's real deadlines, and works hard to meet them. The firm that *demonstrates* its trustworthiness by advising clients on how to avoid fees by doing some things themselves, or that demonstrates its integrity, either by admitting areas of weakness and recommending other professionals or by refusing work when it knows it is too busy. Such actions are not matters to be dealt with only by systems and procedures, although these can help. Fundamentally, they are the result of an appropriate firm-wide *attitude* toward clients—an attitude that must be created by the senior professionals of the firm through exemplary personal behavior and role modeling.

Many professional service firms have procedures and mechanisms to assure the quality of the work they produce: review committees, senior-partner oversight, documentation of working papers. However, relatively few have given much attention to improving the quality of *service*. Many firms seek to avoid the increasing price-sensitivity of clients by trumpeting the eternal battle cry of the professional: "We must compete on the superior quality of our work, not on price." An entirely proper sentiment, but one that can easily be misunderstood and misdirected. Improving the quality of work can be costly and hard to demonstrate. Improving the quality of service can be as cheap as instilling more responsive attitudes in professional staff, and it tends to be infinitely more visible to clients.

In a service business, and particularly in the professions, the words of the old song remain true: "It ain't what you do, it's the way that you do it: That's what gets results."

Recognize And Reward Accomplishment

"One hand cannot applaud alone".
Arabian Proverb

Service people are performers. Self-esteem is vital; other-esteem is also very important. While most service people are not solely dependent on applause for affirmation of their worth, acknowledgement from a source outside oneself can be a valuable enhancement to self-acclaim.

Rewards and recognition *are* forms of feedback, echoed by the familiar notion that "I must be doing all right, because they gave me a raise." But their primary role in service excellence is to acclaim, affirm, and acknowledge. Rewards and recognition communicate "this performance is not only good, it adds value to our efforts in the marketplace." Measurement offers the service person confirming and corrective information useful in altering and improving performance. But rewards and recognition are principally tools for evaluation (i.e., valuing). As such; they communicate more about what is good than what is accurate.

Rewards and recognition help energize service people, not in a bribing manner ("If you do well, I will give you a carrot"), but in a manner that symbolizes the effort toward, or achievement of, excellence. Rewards and recognition are more like Olympic medals or Academy Awards and less like commission checks.

People don't work just for the fun of it. They work, first and foremost, for the money they need to buy the necessities and luxuries of life. Money is a powerful motivator—and a very generalized one. It is a means to a vast number of ends, and it makes the fulfillment of an infinite number of dreams possible.

Money, however, is not everything, although many continue to insist that it is way ahead of whatever is in second place. Effective incentive and reward programs can also be created from a combination of dollars, trips to exotic locales, merchandise, and purely psychic payoffs.

Atlanta-based consultant Martin Broadwell is fond of saying, "Service people can take all the praise you can give them. They get all the bullets anyone can take from the customers. Praise is the bulletproof vest. The supervisor has to be the one to give praise and give it generously." Rewards and recognition directly communicate, "Your efforts are important. Keep them up."

We have chosen four articles for this section. The first, "Rewards and Recognition: Yes, They Really Work" by Ron Zemke, appeared in the November 1988 issue of *TRAINING* Magazine. Its central premise is that, if you give service people a paycheck, they will do the job. If you want them to excel, give them more. The form the "more" takes depends upon the company, the performer, and the situation. At a Volvo dealership, getting to use a luxury model off the showroom floor for a month is a big deal. Zemke summarizes various approaches—from jackets to annual celebration meetings to cold cash—and the research that backs the claim that they really work.

The second article, "Rewarding Service Excellence" by Ron Zemke and John Gunkler, was originally titled "Organization-wide Intervention" and appeared in the *Handbook of Organization Behavior Management* (edited by Lee W. Fredrickson), published in 1982 by John Wiley and Sons. It is a case study on the use of a unique rewards system at a major midwestern theme park. Central to the system's success was that it tied rewards (primarily tokens that were accumulated and exchanged for merchandise) to the four key factors of the theme park's service strategy—friendliness, cleanliness, service, and show as determined by the park guests' overall satisfaction with the Country Fair experience.

Celebration is an activity key to service management. And we have included two articles on this aspect of rewards and recognition. Ron Zemke wrote "Faith and Commitment" for the October 1988 issue of *The Service*

Edge newsletter. The article establishes the role celebration plays in service excellence and outlines examples of how celebration has been successfully used in a variety of organizations.

The most complete article we have found on this topic is by an Oakland, California-based consultant named Cathy DeForest. "The Art of Conscious Celebration: A New Concept for Today's Leaders" appeared in *Transforming Leadership: From Vision to Results* (edited by John Adams), published in 1986 by the Miles River Press in Alexandria, Virginia. Celebration not only makes a joyful, public affirmation of effort and achievement; it provides a unique forum for models. Since service is more of an art form, it is often best described through anecdotes. Providing a setting in which someone "tells the success story" can give others a clearer picture of service excellence in action. As DeForest describes it, "The act of celebration provides a way to nourish the spirit of an organization as well as create a moment in time when a glimpse of a transformed organization can be seen and felt."

Finally, our counterpoint is provided by an exchange between Tom Peters and Alfie Kohn in the April 1988 issue of *Inc.* magazine, sparked by an article Kohn wrote for the January 1988 issue of *Inc.* titled "Incentives Can Be Bad for Business." Peters commented on it in a letter to the editor, and Kohn rebuts those comments. We give you all three pieces and let you draw your own conclusions.

We won't spoil the fun by summarizing here their respective points of view. Instead, we encourage you to review these positions in light of your experience and management practices. We found both arguments to be compelling, and we were challenged to sort out our own views about incentives, rewards, and their relationship to subtle coercion and paternalistic control.

REWARDS AND RECOGNITION: YES, THEY REALLY WORK

Ron Zemke

Money may not make the world go around, but managers in exemplary service-sector organizations firmly believe that recognition and rewards are powerful twin engines for employee motivation. In the eyes of managers from 101 such organizations profiled for a new book on service quality, recognizing and praising employees for a job well done isn't superfluous or magnanimous. It's necessary. It confirms accomplishment and reinforces commitment.

In these organizations there is a positive payoff for employees who meet the service standards, and additional financial rewards and psychic accolades for those who exceed them. Employees who go one step further for the customers become "service heroes." They are held up as role models and rewarded accordingly, because their managers know that the celebration of organizational, group and individual service accomplishments is essential if the delivery of high-quality service is to be the norm, not the exception.

COMPENSATION AND MOTIVATION

People don't work just for the fun of it. They work mostly for the money they need to buy the necessities and luxuries of life. Money is a powerful motivator—and a generalized one. It is a means to a vast number of ends and makes possible the fulfillment of any number of dreams.

We need to know, first and foremost, that our paychecks will keep the wolf from the door. But as pay rises, so do visibility, prestige, personal pride and self-esteem. Those attributes can be harnessed to motivate continuing good performance. Consequently, great service organizations often pay above-average wages for their industry. They make that distinction a point of internal pride and a prominent feature in their recruiting efforts.

Exemplary companies in the service sector realize that while pay may ensure attendance, it typically doesn't produce strategic alignment, personal enthusiasm or outstanding performance. So many of them use the carrot of monetary incentives as well. Mississippi Management Corp., an extremely successful hotel management company based in Jackson, MS, pays regular bonuses for such mundane tasks as carving prime rib properly or making more beds (correctly, of course) than the norm. Shuttle-bus drivers for Los Angeles-based SuperShuttle Inc. can earn a paid day off, which is compensated according to a variable rate based on their own typical performance. So the more they hustle and the better they serve, the more they earn on the job and the more valuable their time off becomes.

At First Union National Bank of Charlotte, NC, branch employees are "shopped" by a specialized research company up to three times a quarter. The payoff for an employee who scores a perfect "6" is instant cash in hand, as much as $200. According to First Union Corp.'s chairman and CEO Edward E. Crutchfield Jr., instantaneous rewards are crucial. "Recognition and reward have to be done on a very short-interval basis—given immediately after the service has been rendered. It's not something that you'd get in your pension 35 years from now; it's money you can buy bread with on Monday." Federal Express employees, from the couriers on the street each day to the parcel sorters in the Memphis hub each night, can buy lots of bread. Sorters start at well over $9 an hour, and even part-timers are eligible for profit-sharing bonuses. At Nordstrom Department Stores, salespeople earn about $2 an hour above local retail wages plus a sales commission of 6 percent or more. A top sales associate can gross $50,000 to $60,000 a year, the kind of money usually reserved only for managers in the retail industry.

It's a little puzzling that more companies don't use financial incentives at the front line. Personal pay tied to organizational performance has long been a valued executive perk, generally with sound results. A 1983 McKinsey & Co. study found that in the most profitable companies in the $25 million sales range, for example, 40 percent of CEO compensation and 36 percent of senior management pay is tied to organizational performance. A study conducted in the late 1970s for the National Science Foundation noted that among the 1,100 companies then listed on the New York Stock Exchange, those with formal incentive plans for managers earned an average 43.6 percent more pre-tax profit than companies that did not use incentives.

Executives aren't the only ones who respond well to such programs. The same National Science Foundation report also reviewed 300 studies of productivity, pay and job satisfaction, and concluded that when pay is linked to performance, employees' motivation to work is raised, their productivity is higher, and they're usually more satisfied with their work. One study cited in the report examined 400 companies and found that those that switched from a system that didn't measure work to one that measured work and included performance feedback raised productivity an average of 43 percent. When both performance feedback and *incentives* were instituted, productivity rose 63.8 percent on average.

The study's authors concluded that increased productivity depends on two things. First is motivation: Arousing and maintaining the will to work effectively means having workers who are productive not because they are coerced but because they are committed. Second is reward: Of all the factors that help to create highly motivated and satisfied workers, the principal one appears to be that effective performance is recognized and rewarded in terms that are meaningful to the individuals, whether financial, psychological or both.

That message traditionally has been better understood in manufacturing companies than in service organizations. *People, Performance and Pay,* a recent study by the American Productivity Center in Houston and the American Compensation Association, found that 48 percent of manufacturers, but only 19 percent of service companies, use performance incentive systems. In the service businesses that use these compensation tactics, the most successful techniques are reportedly productivity gain-sharing, pay-for-knowledge and small-group incentives.

Incentives systems aren't automatic performance generators, of course. They can even backfire. Sometimes organizations will "readjust" a system when it becomes obvious that salespeople are going to greatly exceed their sales goals. The excuse is always that the program "needs some fine-tuning." The real reason is that someone in senior management has decided it would be unseemly for some of the troops to earn so much more than others "at *their* level." Translation: "Who do they think they are, earning as much for front-line work as I do as a manager?" Invariably, the front-line people get the message and never again do anything remotely productive enough to get them "rate busted."

It's a natural impulse to make sure the troops' wages don't compare too closely to those of the leaders, says Harvard University's Rosabeth Moss Kanter. "Social psychologists have shown that the maintenance of an authority relationship depends on a degree of inequality," she says. "If the distance between boss and subordinate—social, economic or otherwise—declines, so does automatic deference and respect.

"This is further aided by the existence of objective measures of contribution. Once high performance is established, once the measures are clear and clearly achieved, the subordinate no longer needs the good will of his or her boss quite so much. One more source of dependency is reduced, and power again becomes more equalized. Proven achievement reflected in higher earnings than the boss's produces security. Security produces risk-taking. Risk-taking produces speaking up and pushing back," Kanter concludes.

The instinct to preserve traditional forms of hierarchy and bureaucracy is understandable, but it's worth suppressing when the goal is superior service. Managers are only free to lead when they are able to free their employees to think and act—to understand and do something about the problems encountered in day-to-day business. Nothing signals the sincerity of that message like an incentive for exceptional customer service.

It is vital, however, to think through all the implications of an incentive plan before you institute it. Brokerage houses have long provided incentives to stockbrokers based on their individual performances, typically calculated in terms of sales. Of course, large individual revenues accumulate into large corporate revenues, which can make the organization more hungry for record-breaking quarterly reports than for customer satisfaction.

Even before the October 1987 stock market crash, the business press had begun to question some of the practices in vogue on Wall Street. At some houses, every possible sort of incentive was dangled before the brokers— furs, Mercedes-Benzes, yachts, dinner for two anyplace on the planet, you name it. The question was whether these practices—notable by their absence in firms such as Goldman Sachs and A.G. Edwards & Sons—were causing brokers to work *against* their clients' best interests, churning accounts and pushing people into questionable ventures because those activities boosted the brokers' own compensation and rewards so remarkably.

To be effective over the long term, incentives must be based on the customer's best interests as well as their effects on the individual's paycheck and the company's quarterly revenues. They should emphasize legitimate customer satisfaction. An incentive program that subordinates an organization's long-term relationship with the customer to an individual's short-term gain—whether that individual is a salesperson, a stockholder or a highly placed executive—is a dangerous narcotic.

REWARD AND CORPORATE CULTURE
Reward systems are both a product and an influence on an organization's culture. Professor Jeffrey Kerr of the Edwin L. Cox School of Business at Southern Methodist University, believes that "who gets rewarded and why

is an unequivocal statement of the corporation's values and beliefs." Kerr and his colleagues suggest that there area two opposite extremes in organizational reward "systems." Those extremes illustrate just how heavily various types of systems can influence an organization's culture and its people behavior.

The hierarchy-based reward system, as the name implies, is a top-down model. Supervisors define and evaluate the performance of subordinates. Performance is defined in both qualitative and quantitative terms, with qualitative performance parameters often as important as—or even more important than—quantitative measures. Evaluation of performance is usually quite subjective. Even in quantifiable areas, superiors sometimes use their own knowledge and experiences to interpret the numbers.

That bare-bones description makes working in an organization with a hierarchy-based reward system sound about as pleasant as being a serf on a medieval estate; any alternative would be an improvement, right? Don't be so sure. Hierarchical structures lead to formal salary systems, like a Hay system, that rewards tenure as well as performance. Bonuses tend to represent only a small slice of compensation and are usually based on group and team performance rather than individual performance. Belonging, cooperation, teamwork and loyalty have high value in the hierarchy system. Activities such as employee training, career development, frequent promotions, lateral movement for developmental purposes and the awarding of special perquisites characterize organizations with these reward systems.

The resulting culture, says Kerr, is very much what *Theory Z* author Bill Ouchi describes as a clan: a familial or fraternal group in which all members acknowledge an obligation beyond the contractual exchange of labor for salary. The individual's long-term commitment to the organization is traded for the organization's long-term commitment to the individual. "The relationship," Kerr explains, "is predicated on mutual interests."

At the other extreme of organizational reward systems, says Kerr, is the "performance-based reward system." Numbers are paramount. The qualitative aspects of performance don't affect evaluations, especially at the managerial level. Performance objectives are precise and tend to be primarily numeric. Results matter, and the methods for achieving them are usually up to the local managers and their subordinates. Performance evaluation and feedback focus on the immediate, not the long term. High levels of autonomy and reward characterize the performance-based organization. Concepts such as mentoring, socialization, development promotability and career planning play little part in the performance-based organization.

In Ouchi's scheme of things this is a market culture. Relationships are contractual and mutually exploitive. Level of performance and level of reward are the only guarantees in the contract. When a juicy job opens up, the company is as likely to bring in someone from the outside as to promote an insider.

Are there any pluses in this dog-eat-dog culture? Certainly. For instance, earning potential is unlimited. The profit pool is established among a small number of people, usually a division-sized unit, and is independent of the larger organization. Symbols of rank and status are almost nonexistent, and being a member of the "right clique" or the right family is not a factor in getting ahead.

Kerr also points out that the market culture "does generate personal initiative, a strong sense of ownership and responsibility for operations and decisions, and an entrepreneurial approach to management. The individual is free to pursue goals with a minimum of organizational constraints."

The point of making the distinction between the two systems carries more than mere academic interest. When you are thinking about ways to improve performance through reward and recognition, you must be guided not only by the art and science of incentive motivation but also by an understanding of the culture and values of your organization.

SYMBOLIC REWARD

Money isn't everything—although many continue to insist that it's ahead of whatever is in second place. Still, effective incentive and reward programs can be created from a combination of dollars, trips to exotic locales, merchandise and purely psychological payoffs. American Airlines takes much of the reward methodology of its frequent-flyer program and plugs it into an employee incentive program for individual and small-group service achievements. At Ryder Systems, the Miami-based transportation company, a similar program is in place for rewarding the dealers who rent Ryder's trucks to customers.

Exclusivity can lend appeal to programs whose actual goods range from simple to awe-inspiring. Employees at Southern Bell often ask where they can buy the designer-style jackets and sports apparel the company awards to outstanding service providers. They're told the items aren't for sale—the only way to get a jacket is to earn a jacket. Similarly, executives at Acura's

U.S. headquarters in Gardena, CA, can only envy the limited-edition crystal sculptures awarded to the best dealerships; the contract calls for the artist to produce only enough for the winners.

A little spontaneity is often an effective ingredient in choosing an award or making one out of something at hand. With the St. Louis Cardinals playing in the 1987 World Series, a Citicorp manager in that town knew exactly how to reward the service accomplishments of his branch's people. The cruise-for-two promos accumulated from wholesalers in 1987 by Ukrop's Super Markets in Richmond, VA, became highly sought-after prizes for exceptional front-line performance within the small supermarket chain. Auto mechanics at Don Beyer Volvo, a car dealership in Falls Church, VA, regularly compete for a month's worth of driving around in a luxury model right off the showroom floor.

Little rewards can be as effective as big ones if they're used in the right way. Lapel-style pins and special name tags are tactics common to service leaders such as Federal Express, Citicorp, LensCrafters and First Federal/ Osceola. At Citicorp Retail Services in Denver, good suggestions for new or better ways to serve customers warrant a "Bright Ideas" coffee mug or similar keepsake. The employee who submits the month's best idea wins temporary possession of a circulating trophy—a three-foot-high light bulb.

It's a lighthearted approach, but the underlying thought is what's important. According to Lauren O'Connell, Citicorp's assistant vice president of operations, "The point of these contests and recognition programs and service evaluations and checklists is that they make everyone feel that quality service is his or her individual responsibility. That not only leads to better service quality for the customer, it also means higher morale. People do care about their jobs when they know that their managers consider those jobs to be important. And caring about one's job and knowing that it's important is where service quality really starts."

CELEBRATION

Often entwined with recognition and reward is a sense of celebration. That's clearly apparent when American Express assembles its Great Performers in New York City each year so executives and colleagues can glow upon them for a job exceptionally done. BellSouth, parent of Southern Bell and LensCrafters, also brings its service award winners into corporate headquarters at annual meetings to laud their achievements. Pizza Hut and Domino's Pizza do the same for managers and franchisees at national meetings.

Organization-development consultant Cathy DeForest writes that, like the leaders of an army, managers must "recognize that the act of celebrating provides a way to nourish the spirit of an organization as well as create a moment in time when a glimpse of a transformed organization can be seen and felt."

Recognition and celebrations also are ways of reaffirming to people that they are an important part of something that matters. These little ceremonies can be significant motivators for people in any organization, but especially so in a service organization, where "pride in the product" is essentially pride in personal performance. Two recent studies make the point.

In 1987 *Inc.* magazine and the Hay Group consulting company compared opinions and feelings of employees in the relatively small companies that form the "*Inc. 500*" with those of employees in the large corporations that make up the "*Fortune 500*". Employees in small companies rated their pay and benefits as poorer, their opportunity for advancement as less promising, and company communication as worse than did their counterparts in the larger companies. But surprise! Overall job satisfaction in small companies was significantly, even spectacularly higher.

Why? According to the *Inc.*/Hay survey, employees of the smaller companies tended to believe they were important to their organization and to feel that their organizations were doing something significant. More specifically, people in the smaller companies felt their work was more challenging, said their ideas were more likely to be adopted, reported a higher sense of accomplishment from what they did, and thought they were treated with more respect.

Focus group discussions validated the survey findings, *Inc.* reported: "These are employees who talk about the company in first-person plural, as in 'We may look like we're disorganized, but we're not.' Said another: 'The quality is personal—the product is use.' "

The second confirmation of the importance of feeling involved in something worthwhile comes from a study done by the Forum Corp., a Boston-based consulting company. Forum found that employees who believed their organizations served customers well were much less likely to say they planned to leave their current jobs within the next year than those who felt they worked for a company that was doing a poor job of serving the customer.

The concept of being part of something valuable, worthwhile and important often is expressed most forcefully by the executives at the top of an organization. Fred Smith, founder of Federal Express, has the iron-jawed, fiery look of the true believer when he tells an interviewer, "Our corporate philosophy is people, service, profit. We do something important. We carry the most important commerce in the history of the world." It is no accident that one often hears that sentiment repeated with similar fervor by couriers and managers throughout the FedEx system.

Marriott employees, when asked about their unusual corporate loyalty, say, "We're part of a family here. The name Marriott is a person's name, and it stands for something." That same sense of pride and belonging becomes evident when you talk to people at a lot of organizations that routinely receive high marks from customers for service quality and performance: Lands' End, Dun & Bradstreet, United Van Lines, Southern Bell, Compu-Serve, Delta Air Line, Miller Business Systems, Kinder-Care, Chubb, Northwestern Mutual Life Insurance. Co., 3M, H.B. Fuller, Beth Israel Hospital, the Mayo Clinic . . . the list could stretch on.

But the most memorable way I have heard it expressed was at Walt Disney World, where I asked a young groundskeeper, "How do you like being a street sweeper in a theme park?" He stepped back, stood up tall, looked me square in the eye, and shot back: "I'm not a street sweeper. I'm in show business, I'm part of the Act."

To front-line workers in any organization with ambitions of providing distinctive service to its customers, the feeling of being a part of something important may be the most important motivational principle of all.

REWARDING
SERVICE EXCELLENCE

Ron Zemke and John W. Gunkler

The principles and techniques of organizational behavior management have proved an effective methodology for directing and changing the behavior of individuals, small groups and organizational subsystems. In our experience, it is both possible and practical to treat whole organizations as single entities, using the principles and techniques of organizational behavior management that have proved so useful in suborganizational contexts. There are three prerequisites to treating organizations as single systems:

1. The development of a measurement system that tracks desired organizational results, but that at the same time provides information that can be confirming or corrective of individual and subgroup performance.
2. The development of a system for making organizational performance and outcome information available to subgroups and individuals.
3. The establishment of contingent relationships between organizational results (outcomes) and reinforcement for individual behavior.

These key principles are largely prefigured in the literature on the effects or organizational feedback and token reinforcement systems. Nadler (1976) and Nadler et al (1976) have demonstrated that collecting and feeding back performance data to members of an organization can be an effective approach to changing organizational performance at a variety of levels. Feedback has been associated with changes in employee attitudes and perceptions of the organization (Klein et al., 1971), with changes in specific and observable behavior (Johnston et al., 1978), and with desired organizational results (Emmert, 1978).

Feedback that includes an implied goal has more impact on work performance than explicit goal setting and is as effective as feedback plus explicit goal setting (Dockstader et al., 1977). But the literature also shows that feedback alone is usually much less effective than feedback combined with other organizational intervention techniques (Annett, 1969).

Some of the intervention techniques that have been shown to be highly effective combined with the systematic feedback of performance data include: token reinforcements (see the seminal work by Birnbrauer and Lawler, 1964; Allyon and Azrin, 1965, 1968; Phillips, 1968; Hunt and Zimmerman, 1969; Henderson and Scoles, 1970; and the review by Kazdin and Bootzin, 1972); social approval (Atthowe and Krasner, 1968; Locke, 1969; Kazdin and Klock, 1973; but also see Quay and Hunt, 1965, for a reminder that social approval isn't for everybody).

It is logical, then, that most reported successful organizational behavior management applications tend to be multiple intervention techniques. Komaki et al. (1977) have shown that job description and goal clarification, self-monitoring, posted feedback, and time off can affect worker presence, customer assistance, and maintenance of display products in a retail store. Bourdon (1977) reports increasing employee attendance, efficiency, and product quality in a textile factory using job description clarification, goal setting, training of supervisors in organizational behavior management, a token economy, social reinforcers, and public display of performance data. Connellan and Martin (1981) report substantial changes in employee attendance, machine down time, scrap rates, product quality, customer satisfaction, and job satisfaction measures in the Fisher Body Fleetwood plant of General Motors through the use of performance feedback, goal-setting activities, a social reinforcement strategy, supervisory training, and teambuilding training. And Luthans and Schweizer (1979) showed the impact of contingent time off, feedback, and social reinforcers on productivity, error rate, and quality in a small factory.

We wish to describe how an actual organization-wide intervention works. There is a simple model that may be helpful in understanding the principles. We call this model "the business proposition" (see Figure 20-1), because in any organization there is someone who carries it around in their head as their understanding of how the organization should look when it is functioning well. The business proposition involves several inferential links: "If people PERFORM in a certain manner, we will achieve certain organizational RESULTS, and they will return a profit or VALUE to us." Into the inferential category go both the link between results and value, and the link between behavior and results. Some managers skip a factor and carry around a model that links how people perform directly with profits or value. Others focus only on the results-values link.

As Zemke and Larsen (1981) have discovered, this business proposition is often the standard by which senior management consciously or unconsciously recognizes and rewards the actions of middle managers. Whether those actions actually lead to organizational success, or value, is less important (because it is not made immediately evident) than whether the actions conform to the business proposition (i.e. produce the results). So if the business proposition is that "If we make steel-reinforced buggy whips better than anyone else, we can sell millions of them at 7 cents (12 for 79 cents)," then the message to subsystem managers is clear: You had better find ways to produce the best quality steel-reinforced buggy whips you possibly can! Eventually the business proposition will be tested by the exigencies of the marketplace (we'll actually try to peddle the buggy whips), and those who managed by it will either keep their jobs or be looking for other work.

Most of us who work in organizational behavior management spend our time helping subsystem managers understand and actualize the roles they are to play within the business proposition. We don't usually have the luxury of evaluating that proposition. But if it fails, the line managers won't be the only ones looking for work. In an organizational-wide system, the key is to make organizational results and their values more immediately evident and usable. Then we can use the measures of those results as referents for managing the behavior of employees. This way, either the

Figure 20-1
The Business Proposition

211

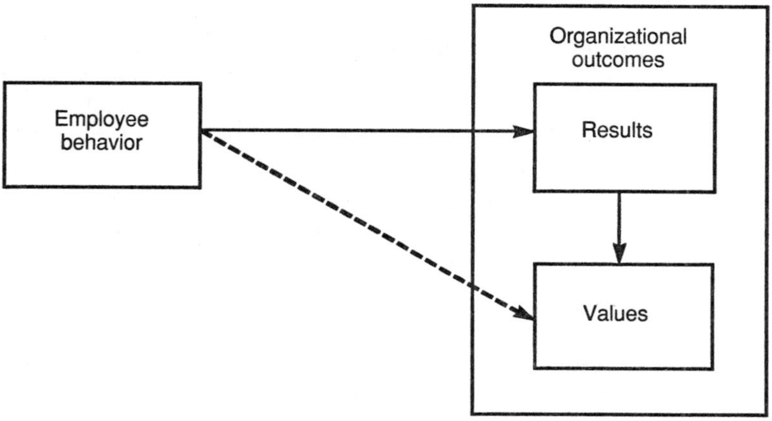

adequacy of the business proposition will become evident, or employee behavior will correct for its errors. Let's look at an example.

CASE STUDY: AN ORGANIZATIONAL-RESULTS-REFERENCED PERFORMANCE MANAGEMENT SYSTEM

Background For three years we acted as consultants to a medium-sized, upper Midwest theme park on the design, development, installation, and management of an organizational-results-referenced performance management system. Theme parks, since the advent of Disneyland, are highly sophisticated, highly profitable, results-oriented businesses. They are made all the more remarkable by the fact that, outside the sun belt, they are staffed primarily by 17- to 20-year-old students working for spending money or tuition. Partly because of their seasonal nature, partly due to heavy turnover, they have to be staffed anew every summer. In addition, theme parks are essentially fixed-market service institutions, so they are dependent upon repeat business for their survival.

The particular theme park we consulted with (we'll refer to it as "Countryfair") employed 800-1000 people at the height of their season. Countryfair is a mixed attraction park; that is, it has a mixture of thrill rides, stage shows, game areas, and food service. Like most theme parks, Countryfair charges a fixed entry fee that entitles guests to free access to all rides, stage shows, and attractions, food, gifts, and games cost extra. The running bottom-line indicator of the industry (and it is quite a sensitive one) is gross dollar revenue divided by guest count, or "pep-cap" (for per capita expenditure). It is a common goal to try to induce the average guest to spend an amount on food, gifts, and games equal to the fixed entrance fee.

Our work with Countryfair began as a training consultancy prior to the first year of actual operation. The management team, veterans of Disney, Marriott and Six Flags parks, brought with them a very strong training-and-development ethic. Such managers are very conscious of guest satisfaction, and are used to spending time and money on the training of front-line employees in customer service and customer relations. And the Disney system veterans especially are quite used to paying close attention to the details of on-the-job behavior of employees, particularly the interactions between guests (customers) and hosts and hostesses (employees). So our consulting work quickly matured beyond training and embraced the more comprehensive goals of assisting management with a complete system for managing performance of employees and organizational results.

Our three-year involvement can be divided into the three Countryfair seasons and labeled: Phase 1-design, develop, test; Phase 2-implement and tune; Phase 3-run and refine. In fact, we are able to report on a fourth season, the years after our involvement ended, which may be labeled: Phase 4-return to baseline.

Phase 1: Design, Develop, Test During our first season, we worked primarily on the design, development and testing of results-referenced feedback system, and the pilot testing of a rudimentary system-wide token economy (reinforcement system).

Among our first actions was to hold a series of lengthy discussions with senior management to specify, behaviorally, their model of what the business looked like when it was operating to their satisfaction. This business proposition was deceptively simple when finally we wrote it down. In part it reads: "Our success depends on repeat business. When guests come to Countryfair, they expect to have a good time, to have fun. When this expectation is met they all tell others and, more importantly, then come back themselves."

We then worked with management to define more precisely what they thought they meant by "fun", so that we could try to develop some measures of this conception of customer satisfaction. Eventually, an operational model coalesced around four keys to guests having fun:

1. *Friendliness*. This meant that customer contact employees were perceived by the guests as smiling and being slightly assertive.
2. *Cleanliness*. When walkways, rest rooms, eating areas, and parking lots were perceived to be neat and clean by guests, this criterion was fulfilled.
3. *Service*. This meant that guests perceived employees to be helpful: food orders taken and delivered in a reasonable time, shop clerks attentive and available when guests arrived, and requests attended to quickly and without rancor.
4. *Show*. This most elusive of the four criteria refers in general to guests' enjoyment of the shows, rides, and attractions. Perceived quality of food and beverages, movement of queues (especially at the rides), and attractiveness of employee costumes all contributed.

Armed with this model, we developed a pool of 48 items to survey guest perceptions of the park's performance. Initial testing over nine days with 222 guests, and factor analysis, resulted in 36 Likert-type items we were confident would reliably measure park results against the four criteria.

When possible, we subsequently tested the validity of these scales by comparing changes in guest perception ratings to measurable changes within the park. For instance, we tested the cleanliness scale by experimentally manipulating the amount of trash allowed to accumulate and by changes in the number of cleanings a specific facility received. We found, in the parking lot, that when the clean-up crew was halved, scores on items asking for guest perceptions of parking lot cleanliness sagged.

The nine days of initial item testing, plus five more days of sampling of guests perceptions using the factor-analyzed scales (we item sampled, so no guest had to answer more than nine questions), formed a baseline for comparison when we began posting organizational feedback and awarding of tokens.

As Figure 20-2 suggests, the display of organizational performance information (feedback alone) had minimal effect on subsequent guest perceptions during this first phase and, by inference, little effect on employee performance. But the institution of a rudimentary token economy did appear to gradually have an effect on guest perceptions and satisfaction. This early token system consisted of providing supervisors and managers with tokens they handed out to employees who they believed were "helping

Figure 20-2
Season 1—Design and Test Phase

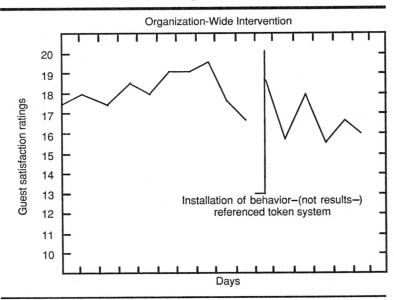

guests enjoy their day." These tokens were redeemable for pizzas, blue jeans and records.

Phase 2: Implement And Tune During the second season of operation at Countryfair, the following procedures were instituted in an effort to make the results-referenced system a viable management tool.

1. A 50-foot-long by 10-foot-high wall next to the time clock was turned into a graph for displaying guest perceptions. On this wall we charted a running average of guest ratings on each of the four factors, as well as an "overall guest satisfaction" measure (the sum of the averages of the four factors). Nearly every employee walked past this wall twice a day. Preceding any display of data, we ran a five-day baseline sampling of guest perceptions.

2. Detailed, item-by-item averages of survey results were also displayed, but in numerical rather than graphic form.

3. The token economy was expanded in a number of ways, and all managers, supervisors, and line employees were trained in the nuances of this new system. A commerical incentives company was retained to provide a point-based menu for redeeming earned tokens.

4. The guest satisfaction measurement system was linked with the token economy. Specifically, each token awarded in the park bore a face value. However, the redemption value of any token depended in a specified way on the level of current overall guest satisfaction. For example, an overall guest satisfaction level of 17 (out of a possible 20 points) multiplied the face value of tokens redeemed that day by 160 percent. So a 10-point token was worth 16 points, but only so long as overall guest satisfaction remained at least at 17.

Employees developed a jargon for talking about the system in which the overall guest satisfaction rating was referred to as the "Countryfair Dow Jones Average." Tokens played the role of "stock" that was traded, bought, sold and otherwise used as the script for an economic subsystem. If anything, this increased the effectiveness of the token economy for its intended purposes.

5. Guest attendance and per-cap figures were also posted publicly. Although they were not attended by so much fanfare as the "Dow Jones," the per-caps became the second half of the results-reference system.

6. A system manager was appointed to manage the token economy and the data gathering and displaying activities. This person become the sole arbiter for disputes concerning token awarding, redemption, and value setting. In addition, we trained the system manager to design and activate suborganizational intervention strategies within the token system to meet short-term needs. He subsequently devised and ran some 30 special performance improvement projects during the second season.

7. Managers and line supervisors were assigned specific token-awarding responsibilities. To insure use of the token system, managers were assigned a minimum number of tokens to award each shift. Line supervisors were given training in the use of tokens to reinforce appropriate behavior and then assigned a criterion level of tokens to be awarded each week. These supervisors were brought together weekly to exchange ideas and experiences related to the use of tokens to foster performance improvement.

8. Multiple backup reinforcement systems were developed and implemented.

- Tokens were modified so that supervisors could write on their backs a description of the specific behavior for which they were being awarded.
- Every fiftieth guest was given an envelope containing two tokens called "Special Thanks Awards." The tokens, small (2 ¾" by 3 ¾") colored cards, asked guests to give the tokens to any employees at Countryfair who made a special effort to make the guest's visit enjoyable.
- Employees were given the right to award their earned tokens to fellow employees and to supervisors.
- As tokens were earned, employees also received small, colored furry balls (or "Fuzzies") to indicate their accumulation of tokens. Different colors represented different totals of token points. These Fuzzies were glued to employees' name tags and employees wore them like badges of excellence, which they were. Later we found that these colored Fuzzies allowed us to tell, at a glance, which employees and which park areas were not being reinforced.
- To address the major management concern about employee absenteeism and turnover, especially toward the end of the summer when the students had a "jingle in their jeans" and saw the start of school looming even larger, we added another wrinkle. Employee time cards were placed in a lottery drum, and prize drawings were held every month. The better your

attendance, the more changes you had to win. The value of lottery prizes was increased over the course of the season. Employees who worked all assigned days for the entire season were eligible for a year-end lottery that had, among other big prizes, an automobile and college scholarships.

As Figure 20-3 shows, the guest perception measures proved to be sensitive to changes in the token economy. We think four features are of special interest.

1. The first 16 data points were gathered prior to data display but with the token system in effect. This pseudo-baseline extends over 32 days of park operation.

2. During the "tokens given and data displayed" period, guest satisfaction ratings grew quite steadily. This period extended over 50 days of park operation.

3. At the point labeled "R1", an accidental reversal of conditions occurred. Because of a glitch in the token accounting method, the system manager suspended all awarding and redemption of tokens for eight operating days.

Figure 20-3
Guest Satisfaction Ratings, Second Year of Park Operations

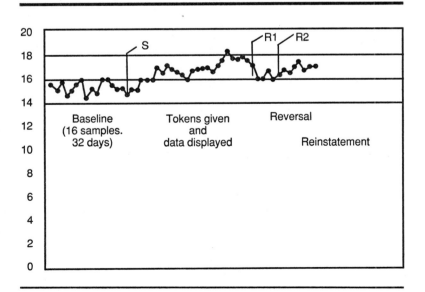

Guest perception data continued to be collected. The accounting problem was resolved and the token system resumed at "R2".

4. The accident reversal between R1 and R2 gave us evidence that the organizational results measures we were using were in fact functionally related to the token economy. We also noted that the results during reinstatement of tokens never again reached the levels attained prior to the reversal. We believe this was due in part to the "run on the bank" that occurred R2, when token redemption was reinstated. Tokens that had been hoarded over the course of the season had been steadily increasing in value because of the upward trend of the Dow Jones. Thus employees had a vested interest in guest perception measures that grew with the number of tokens they owned. When a large number of tokens were redeemed, the amount of vested interest generally decreased across the park.

At the same time we were sensitive to what the guest perception measures were doing, we were paying close attention to the per-cap measures where appropriate. As we mentioned, the per-cap results (values in dollars and cents) were meaningful only for those areas where additional fees were charged after gate admission. These areas were the game areas, gift shops, and food and beverage areas.

Figure 20-4 shows the per-cap results for the games area for a 15-week period. Each data point represents a weekly per-cap average, computed as total dollars taken in at the 10 game area booths, divided by the total park attendance for that seven-day period. As you can see from the graph, during Weeks 2-6 (baseline), per-capita expenditures were almost identical to those in the previous season ($1.08 versus $1.09).

In an effort to increase the per-cap in the games area, the division manager decided to make extra, specially colored tokens available to employees contingent upon the daily per-cap on their shift. These tokens, provided by us, were referred to as "bonus" tokens, because they were earnable above and beyond any other tokens available. This bonus system was put in effect in the seventh week of the park's second season of operation.

During the 10 weeks of the bonus token availability, the per-cap averaged $1.43. The per-cap was never lower than $1.25 during this period, and at one point reached $1.80. (Bonus tokens were not awarded the final four weeks of the season because the park was only open weekends during this period and staffed by part-time people and managers).

While we present the per-cap data in a weekly format in Figure 20-4, bonus tokens were awarded to employees daily. At the beginning of each shift, supervisors announced to employees the previous day's per-cap and awarded tokens. They too only posted results on a weekly basis.

The 35 employees in the games area earned a total of 28,944 bonus points, which were redeemed at an average value of about $.10 a point. So the bonus system cost about $2,894 in redeemed tokens (for an average $82.66 per employee). Payoff was based on improvement over the past year's per-cap. The difference in average per-cap during the bonus period and the past year's per-cap was $1.43 minus $1.09, or $.34. Since the average attendance during the 10-week bonus period was 30,500 people, the improvement in per-capita expenditure was worth $10,375. This translates into better than a 360 percent return on investment in a results-referenced system.

Phase 3: Run And Refine At the end of the third season, the system manager, who was also the personnel manager, made a series of comparisons using personnel costs and attitude measures. Although our focus is, and was then, on organizational results and their primary indicators, these more indirect measures are of interest.

As Figure 20-5 indicates, there were significant changes in a number of personnel measures following the first season, when the system was piloted, and in subsequent seasons. We suppose there are reasonable alternative explanations for these results; however, it can also be argued

Figure 20-4
Per Capita Expenditures by Park Guests

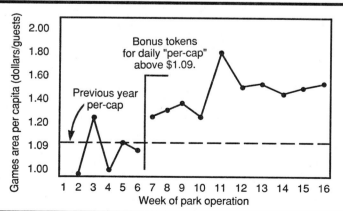

that the results-referenced system was contributory. We'll highlight three features of the system manager's analysis.

1. Employment costs (the costs of finding, employing and retaining employees) were much lower than expected and were budgeted in seasons two and three. Savings in these employment costs (approximately $30,000) offset nearly half the budgeted cost of the results-referenced system (which was $62,000). Such savings almost doubled in the third season, since the increase in proportion of employees requesting to be rehired made college recruiting unnecessary. This savings is not reflected in Season 3 "percent of budget" figures, since the college recruiting efforts did not become a budgeted line item.

2. Typically, employees in the theme park industry sign a contract promising to work a specified part of the season. Because of the high proportion of college students employed, a 5-10% bonus is usually paid for fulfilling the terms of the contract. Just as typically, this bonus is not very effective. While Countryfair shared the industry experience during the first season, they did much better during subsequent seasons after the full results-referenced system went into effect.

3. Low turnover rates during Seasons 2 and 3, employee requests for subsequent season rehiring, and supervisory evaluation of employees' suitability for rehiring suggest that there was a good employee relations climate in the park. The system manager believed this was a result of the "positive nature" of a system geared toward measuring, acknowledging, and rewarding performance and success rather than toward remediating problems.

Figure 20-5
Indirect Measures of System Effectiveness

Case Study	Season 1	Season 2	Season 3
Employment costs (percent of budget)	113%	70%	73%
Hires to jobs	1.83:1	1.25:1	1.28:1
Actual turnover	81%	52%	53%
Employees completing employment contracts	18%	38%	41%
Employees requesting reemployment consideration	18%	35%	44%
Employees judged eligible (desirable) for rehire	42%	82%	81%

Phase 4: Return to Baseline During the fourth season of operation, Countryfair was acquired by an entertainment conglomerate. Though new management expressed interest in the feedback part of the system, the token economy was considered too complicated and unorthodox to be "useful as a management technique". The $62,000 price tag was considered too high for an "employee motivation program," and the results being tracked seemed trivial to the new management team. In our earlier language, they brought with them a different business proposition. This did afford us an unwelcome chance to see a complete reversal of conditions.

The title and labels of Figure 20-6 are somewhat misleading. Season 1, our initial "baseline" period, was not a true baseline. During the brief 35 days, with only 16 measurement periods, guest satisfaction results were displayed and experimented with. And Season 4, the return to baseline, was not exactly a return to baseline. In fact, guests were surveyed for six weeks, 18 measurements of guest perceptions were taken, and the data were displayed in the park. Measurement and display were halted by the new park management when it became evident that guest satisfaction ratings were below those of the previous seasons. But working with the data we have, it is plausible to argue that a management system referenced to overall organizational results deserves consideration as an adjunct to intervention techniques referenced solely to individual or small-group results.

We do not consider an organizational-results-referenced system to be a panacea. It does not obviate the need to train managers in behavior management principles and techniques. Nor is it a substitute for all

Figure 20-6
Four Years of Primary Results Measurement

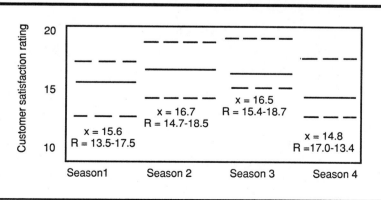

sub-system, small-group, or individual behavior management systems and projects. We view the results-referenced system as a meta-system that provides an arena for suborganizational efforts.

ACTION PLAN: INSTALLING AN ORGANIZATIONAL-RESULTS-REFERENCED PERFORMANCE MANAGEMENT SYSTEM

As we have said, organizations are driven by the conceptions (business propositions) of certain members, usually managers. But they are dependent upon the performance of individuals, groups and subsystems for the fulfillment of that guiding organizational concept. It is the purpose of a results-referenced system to bridge the gap between the critical behavior and the "bottom line" that validates the business proposition. Our experience suggests some guidelines for establishing a results-referenced meta-management system.

1. *Determine the organizational strategy, plan, or model in effect in the organization.* We take our lead from Henry Mintzberg, Robert Doktor, and other strategic thinking and planning experts, who see senior management's most critical responsibility to be holistic, strategic thinking. To further that end, we spend considerable time capturing the business proposition that senior managers hold about what a well-functioning organization (or branch, department, division) looks like—that is, what people will be doing when the organization is being maximally effective.

2. *Negotiate a measurement that reports, on a regular, short-term basis, organizational outcome indicators.* In the theme park case, we negotiated the measurement of overall guest satisfaction and four indicators of that result. In addition, we were able to roll down several direct dollar measures of the value of achieving that result. Our measures in this case happened to be mostly of customer perceptions and satisfaction. We have had equal success in organizations in which the critical organizational measures were less "soft". For instance, key indicators in other instances have been percentage of auto repairs satisfactorily completed the first time, percent of on-time deliveries, and units sold. The trick is to develop significant indicators of organizational performance that are directly related, in management's view, to the primary business proposition.

In the theme park case, we sampled the client population every other day throughout the season. In high-turn public contact organizations, this frequent sampling is useful. When clients come in smaller numbers, or performance cycles are longer, longer schedules work fine. For example, in sales situations we have used weekly and bimonthly cycles for surveying and posting.

3. *Measure key management variables so as to provide information in sizes usable by subunits.* In the theme park case, we were able to develop a pool of customer perception survey items that not only were summed, but individually had utility at the level of small areas within the park and in some cases for individual performers. It is also sometimes possible to work with existing management information systems to break down indicator data already being collected into a size usable by suborganizational units. Regardless of the source, "usable size" has tended to mean that the measure can be noticeably affected by members of the unit and bears a direct, easily inferable (face valid) relationship to unit results or individual behavior.

4. *Make results-indicator data available to all members of the organization.* It is unfortunately nearly axiomatic of organizations that those individuals with least access to performance data are the people who need it most and who, through their individual efforts, can affect it most.

In the theme park, we were able to post organizational performance data in one central location, a locale nearby which all employees passed by twice a day. In this location, near the time clock, results of guest satisfaction surveys were posted every other day, as were daily attendance and per-capita guest expenditure figures. In sales and dispersed manufacturing settings, both unit and organization-wide results have been displayed. The important point is that up-to-date information must be made regularly and widely available.

5. *Establish a "psychoeconomic system" that can reinforce individual performance and organizational results.* In the theme park, individual and subgroup accomplishment garnered tokens for employees, while organizational results levels established the exchange value of the tokens. This approach kept tokens available to sub-system managers for discretionary but contingent reinforcement of individual performance, while maintaining a contingent relationship between token value and organizational results. This dual contingency system increases the reinforcement potential of tokens and maintains a safety factor when creativity in devising suborganizational projects is encouraged.

6. *Get a "multiple-hit" from your reinforcers.* We have often been able to find ways for the system to reinforce one instance of good performance again and again. Perhaps this in some way makes up for the thin schedule necessitated by the economics of token redemption and our inability to notice a large portion of the instances of good performance. In the theme park, one instance of good performance could provide at least five reinforcement occasions:

- When the token was initially given.
- When the Fuzzy earned by the token was displayed on the name tag.
- When guests asked about the Fuzzies on the name tag.
- When the Dow Jones was posted (an occasion when people thought about their own already earned tokens).
- When the tokens were redeemed for prizes.

And, in the case of supervisor-given tokens (because the behavior for which it was earned was written on the back of the token), there was a sixth occasion reported by many employees to be important to them:

- When, perhaps at a time when things where not going so well for you, you took out your hoard of tokens and reread the nice comments on the back.

This multiple hit principle has also been effective for us in manufacturing and sales situations.

7. *Define a clear relationship between organizational results measurement and token values.* Ayllon and Azrin (1968) and Schaefer and Martin (1969) emphasize the necessity for clear, concise rules, not only for how tokens are to be exchanged but for the behavior by which they are to be earned and lost. These rules tie token earning precisely to well-specified behavior. We found, in a results-referenced intervention, that it was effective for token-earning behavior to be left unspecified, in fact, left up to the discretion of supervisors and guests. But it was important that the exchange value of the tokens be clearly and precisely related to the organizational results measures. In the theme park, token redemption values could as much as double if organizational measures improved dramatically, and fall if customer satisfaction fell. This direct tie to organizational results makes it relatively safe to be imprecise in the definition of token-earning behavior. Behavior that does not lead to improved organizational results will be reflected in a lowering of the value of the tokens-a self-correcting effect. Further, the guests who handed out the tokens are the ones who have the best information about (and the most vested interest in) the effectiveness of the behavior that is earning them. This is in contrast to the usual token economy in which the token givers (ward workers in an institution, training people, and so on) are usually people who have no direct vested interest in the resulting behavior of the token earners.

8. *Encourage complexity.* Another rationale for not precisely specifying token-earning behavior is that rigid earn-loss rules rob the manager and supervisor of flexibility and interfere with the organization's ability to adapt to changing conditions and new situations. To make the most of behavior management's power, systems should give managers and super-visors new management options and flexibility. The results-referenced system provides a supportive arena for supervisor-developed short-term behavior change projects. Employees too had flexibility in determining how best to achieve the desired organizational results. The system rewarded their creativity, provided they were effective.

Because our system used a common-based script whose availability was under the control of the system manager, it was also possible to vary the "density" of tokens in areas of the park. We were able to fine tune results by e.g., increasing the density of tokens available in one park area when the previous day's results indicated performance was lagging. Because this "new money" was backed up by a consistent redemption formula (we were on a kind of "gold standard", unlike the U.S. economy), we did not experience any "inflation", but found rather that making more tokens available produced more of the desired behavior. We encouraged creative uses of the power and complexity built into the system, so long as they were consistent with the business proposition of management. Such complexity, which we only began to explore, leads us to believe that calling this a "psychoeconomic system" is not overstating the broad utility and impact it can have.

9. *Program the environment.* Most attempts to influence real work behavior have used artificial settings for the brunt of the intervention (such as by training people in classrooms, or in institutions). This invariably leads to what the literature refers to as the problem of transfer, or generalization, to the work setting (see the review by Kazdin and Bootzin, 1972). The solution offered is to program the environment into which participants will go and in which they are expected to behave differently after the intervention. As should be obvious, in the theme park the brunt of the intervention occurred in the park, with only a little training occurring in artificial settings, such as part of new-employee orientation. And, there was no such thing as "after" the intervention, since so long as the park was running the intervention was running, too.

Even the training that was provided was, as often as possible, done in the park itself rather than in a classroom. While we do not wish to discount the importance of orienting employees and training supervisors and managers in token-awarding and some behavior management principles, most of our efforts went into programming the park itself to provide the feedback and reinforcers necessary to sustain or improve employee performance.

In addition, we used the interactions of park employees with us, during the natural course of things, to contribute to the transfer of behavior onto the job. This was essentially a modeling activity. By training and prompting supervisors to model the use of tokens, using tokens ourselves within job-skills training sessions, and by making sure we and the senior managers gave out tokens within the plain view of others, we sensitized individuals in the environment to the use of tokens.

Ongoing, week-to-week environmental programming focused on keeping the system fresh and attended to by employees. The organization held special small-group training sessions to instruct employees in the niceties of the system: how tokens were likely to be earned, how organizational results measures affected token redemption values, and how tokens could be redeemed. In addition, the company newspaper carried stories of unusual ways individuals earned tokens and how people felt about the system.

10. *Provide a way for people to escape the contingencies.* Another problem typically encountered in token economics is that participants find ways to avoid or escape from the contingencies of the system. This can mean they cheat on the token-earning or losing rules. We did not have rigid rules relating behavior to reinforcers, which made it nearly impossible to cheat in this way. This problem also can mean that participants contrive ways so that they can avoid being subject to the token system. We realized very early that it is unrealistic to expect smiling, cheerful, helpful employees for eight straight hours every day. Therefore, we arranged for off-stage areas within the park. (Places where guests come into contact with employees are referred to as "on-stage" areas.) The off-stage areas were hidden from guests by fences and gates. There employees could go to blow off a little steam, swap "terrible guest" stories with other employees, take scheduled breaks, and generally not be in the public eye nor subject to the token system. We even installed a hanging rubber tire, with "Dump Your Bucket" painted on it and a baseball bat nearby, for taking out aggressions physically.

11. *Prime the system regularly.* Just as people beginning a work day in a skilled job need a set-up period to ready the tools, supplies, and machines of their trade, managers and employees working within a results-referenced structure need some "make ready" activities. In the theme park, the system manager personally reported previous days' results to other managers, suggested targets for the day (goals), and personally modeled token-awarding behavior afresh each day. The system manager would, for example, stand in the hallway near the large "Dow Jones" results chart and engage employees in conversation about the trends at least one morning a week. His role was to congratulate (give social reinforcement) to line employees and line supervisors when results were high or improving, and to solicit improvement ideas when results were below standard. Priming has been a part of sales management's repertoire for years; organizational behavior management brings a new precision to such a routine.

12. *Keep the system fair and clean.* It has been our observation that organizational behavior management systems, be they results-or activity-referenced, tend to experience entropy, or go into eclipse, for one of two reasons: stimulus satiation and system injustice. We addressed the satiation problem through priming, by the variety of ways performance got reinforced, and by encouraging creativity within the complexity of the system. Justice, as fairness, is defined by Homme and Tosti (1972) to mean that the terms of the contract, found on opposite sides of the agreement, must be of relatively equal weight. In general, one must try to relate the amount of reinforcement to the amount of performance."

We have found that disputes over rules and changes in contract conditions can have a highly detrimental effect on system effectiveness. Better to live with a system tipped in favor of line employees, or negotiate adjustments, than to renege on preestablished conditions. In the theme park, only one individual (the system manager) could make any changes in token base values, redemption conditions, or daily token availability (density). The system manager's working guideline was simply to protect the integrity of the system from any suspicion. Hence disputes were negotiated on a case-by-case basis instead of continually rewriting system rules. We learned this "rule" during the second year of the theme park system's operation, when a confusion over redemption rules literally caused a "market panic" and a run on the redemption center.

SUMMARY

As many who have worked within organizations can attest, there are constraints imposed upon what can be attempted, by the business proposition within which intervention strategies take place, and even more constraints on what can be accomplished and what you can take credit for. It is rare in a subsystem intervention to be able to bring to bear the authority of organizational results in designing, testing, verifying, and running behavior management programs. Because of that, the conventional wisdom seems to be: don't take the blame (but of course don't refuse the credit) for bottom-line results. In many situations that is good advice; there are a lot of things under heaven and earth that are not included in your program and that could interfere with the bottom line royally.

What we hope to have shown is how an organization-wide intervention provides an arena within which subsystem, small group, and individual behavior management projects can flourish. Further, with some ongoing feedback of organizational results, and a psychoeconomic system rewarding people on the basis of those results, you have a checks-and-balances system that keeps errant subsystem intervention strategies from going too far astray. This should allow a freer, more creative hand with subsystem intervention strategies. Management who believes in the organizational results is more likely to say, "Sure, try it; just as long as those results keep coming."

In addition, having a results-referenced system permits ongoing evaluation of the efficacy of subsystem projects. This is good news for us who like to do behavior management projects. It is also good news for line managers, who can keep an eye on us through watching the organizational impact of those projects.

The message is simple: don't be afraid to go after organization-wide results to use as referents for behavior management projects. (For example, trust customers to know when they are satisfied or, as Skinner once said, "Trust your pigeon.") Pin down the business proposition and work it. Make sure the outcome measures are credible and widely publicized. Set up contingencies between actions and their organizational results. And believe us, it is a lot more fun out in the job setting than it is in board rooms and other institutions.

FAITH AND COMMITMENT

Ron Zemke

Celebrating success is more than just an excuse for a party. It's an important demonstration of faith and commitment. It reminds everyone in an organization of their purpose and mission, and more importantly, is a way for the organization to loosen up and say to everyone, from front line to mahogany row, "You are important and appreciated. The effort you put forward, your sacrifices, and your results count." Celebration should be an integral part of the way you reward and recognize good performance.

When Bill Daiger of Maryland National Bank wanted his front-line people to know that he and the bank needed and appreciated their efforts to improve customer service, he hired a hall, sent formal invitations, and threw a magnificent party for all employees. The affair was such a hit, the bank regularly takes time to throw parties for its stars.

At Precision Lenscrafters, they celebrate the end of store-level sales contests in a unique fashion. Performance awards are passed out. Customer-compliment letters are read aloud. Individual employees are saluted by the regional manager. Then, the sales person with the contest record closes the meeting by serving a cream pie to the regional manager—straight in the face. Don't ask. Some organizational symbols aren't meant to be understood by outsiders.

At South Memorial Hospital in Oklahoma City, management found a unique way to celebrate the hard work and dedication of hospital staff members. They created a musical comedy, in part a send-up of themselves and their behavior, and performed it for all three shifts of employees, and served up a special meal as well.

In one division of Honeywell Bull, management decided it was past time to recognize the hard work and dedication of the group customer-service staff. Managers and field-service people worked the customer-service desks and phones while the customer-service reps were treated to a catered lunch and recognition ceremony.

Celebration serves a variety of functions in an organization. On the simplest level it is a form of recognition and reward—an important function and worthy purpose. But celebration also reaffirms to people in highly human terms that they are an important part of something that really matters.

Why do people work? Stop paying them for a week or two and you'll have part of the answer soon enough. But people work for recognition as well as reward. A boss who constantly criticizes, and who thinks saying, "Well done." is out of place outside a restaurant, has as tough a time keeping people as the low-pay artist.

For most of us, the feeling of being part of something important and meaningful is a powerful motivator. Being part of a winning team, being seen as the best in the industry, achieving something others admire and respect has a power that can make salary increases, bonuses, and employee-of-the-month plaques seem lackluster by comparison. Celebration reminds everyone that such purposes and goals exist, are exciting, important and attainable. Reconfirming to people at all levels in your organization that they are part of something important, that the service they provide is vital to the organization and the people they serve, may be the most important motivational principle of all.

THE ART OF CONSCIOUS CELEBRATION: A NEW CONCEPT FOR TODAY'S LEADERS

Cathy DeForest

> *"Preoccupied with producing and managing, he [man] has lost touch with vast reaches of reality. His being has been borrowed and depleted. Therefore festivity is not just a luxury of life. It provides the occasion for man to establish his proper relation to time, history, and eternity."*
>
> **Harvey Cox**
> **Feast of Fools**

We have lost our souls. Like those who went in search of the Holy Grail, we of the modern world have gone to the far corners of the earth to bring back profit and treasure to the Court of the Corporate King, while searching for meaning in our personal and work lives. Like those seekers, it is unclear what is illusion and what is reality. Is the creation of new markets, products, and larger profits each year our Grail? Like the knights and women of King Arthur's court, the search has twisted our minds and imprisoned our souls. What is the meaning behind our pursuits? How will the quest end?

We are far from the end of our search. While experiencing a dawning of technological innovation, we are also creating an age of spiritual exploitation and emptiness. While moving closer and closer to understanding how the mind works, we are using our wisdom to build materials that unbalance the ecological systems of the world and nuclear products that make our hearts ache.

Yet along this twisted journey are examples of corporations and leaders who see beyond illusion to a new reality. Their vision sees profit in the context of service and the need to feed the spirit as well as the mind and body. In order to survive the battles of competition, these leaders know they must address the spirit of their modern warriors and kingdoms in order to gain the greatest return on investment.

One element in each of these evolving organizations is leaders who recognize that the art of celebrating provides a way to nourish the spirit of an organization as well as create a moment in time when a glimpse of a transformed organization can be seen and felt. These leaders understand that celebration often portrays a truer reality of their desired culture than the illusions of modern management that have hypnotized our minds.

Like King Arthur's sword, Excalibur, celebrations are founded in sacred energy and therefore have the power to accomplish things that seem impossible by ordinary management means. As we begin a new era, which calls for creativity and innovation, excellence and networking, intuition and change in corporate culture, the spirit of celebration beckons.

WHAT IS CONSCIOUS CELEBRATION?

Organization celebration is the process of honoring individuals, groups, events, achievements, the common and the extraordinary life within an organization in a creative, meaningful, and often festive manner. Celebration brings with it a parade of rich elements—rituals, myths, heroes and heroines, festivity, fantasy, symbols, choreography, story telling—all of which are deeply needed by modern organizations and their leadership in order to balance the pressures of the sometimes uptight corporate world. Celebrations are cause to set aside common everyday menial and strategic tasks. They also encourage fantasy, which invites managers and employees to imagine the impossible and envision new ways to do difficult tasks.

Traditional organization celebrations include: banquets, "roasts," ribbon-cutting ceremonies, and sales awards dinners and trips. The celebrations discussed in this chapter are examples of conscious celebrations—events that mark significant moments that rise the consciousness of the participants to a higher order of reality.

"Conscious" means "knowing oneself," being concerned with "potential," and being aware of inward "psychological and spiritual facts." Conscious celebrations come from a place of self-knowledge and are used to assist people to reach their potential and increase their awareness of the connection between material and spiritual life. They are a modern-day link to the spiritual dimension of an organization. They are also a link to the past—to history and the wisdom of the ages—and a link to the future— visions and dreams. Through these links, organization transformation can take place.

Transformation may occur when the individual and collective consciousnesses of an organization are expanded through celebrating consciously. There is an old saying, "as we think in our hearts, so we become." In conscious celebration our hearts are opened, and we become greater than who we were before the celebration began.

Conscious celebrations can be called "festivals of the spirit," "high touch events for a high tech world," "woven rituals of the soul," and "opportunities to live the vision of an organization." In conscious celebration we create moments that illuminate the deeper meaning of our lives and guide our footsteps into the future.

Conscious celebrations are a chance for us to experience what Harvey Cox (1969) calls the interplay of our specialness with our commonness. Jim Channon, a consultant who has taught the art of ritual to a wide variety of managers, including Army generals, believes that organizations are "run on the fuel of the human spirit" and as such, celebrations are an excuse to kick the juice. They allow the organization to "run on high octane."

The recording of "We are the World" by the USA for Africa organization is an example of a conscious celebration, designed to expand consciousness through celebration and song. In April 1985, thousands of radio stations worldwide played the song at exactly the same moment—an unprecedented event, a true celebration of the human spirit for the human spirit. The result of raising millions of dollars for food, medicine, and self-help is living proof that celebrations can expand consciousness and inspire the human spirit and, through this inspiration, create transformation.

DISTINGUISHING ELEMENTS OF CONSCIOUS CELEBRATION

Celebrations, especially extravagant events, are on the upswing. Coca-Cola Co. staged a Broadway musical at Radio City Music Hall for 5,000 guests in order to introduce Diet Coke to its distributors. Equitable Life Assurance Society spent over 1 million dollars and a year in planning their 125th anniversary extravaganza for 12,000 employees, which included 36 Radio City Rockettes and an orchestra. To ease the tension in the AT&T breakup, that company held a "Super Sports Olympics Day" to create a cohesive family atmosphere within the company.

Are these "industrial theatre" events examples of conscious celebrations or merely modern-type versions of gold watches for retiring salesmen? On the surface they could be classified as the latter. To discern a conscious celebration from a traditional event, each occasion must be examined in depth. Conscious celebrations have five distinguishing characteristics:

1. a specific values base
2. the use of symbols
3. ritual
4. storytelling

5. a special role of leadership in the design and implementation of these celebrations.

Values Conscious celebrations incorporate all or most of these values—authenticity, humor of the heart, play, personal empowerment, elegance and aesthetics, spontaneity, and creativity—and come from a place of love and integrity.

Authenticity. Smart executives know that parties can be seductive and that people often let their defenses down as they relax and enjoy such an event. Some managers capitalize on these occasions in order to manipulate their employees and gain further allegiance to the company. They also patronize them by making people "beholden" to the company for lavish gifts and holiday packages. Conscious celebrations, on the other hand, are events based on genuine appreciation for what people have done as well as who they are as human beings. Leaders of conscious celebrations honestly feel their organization could not exist without the work and dedication of its employees, and they express that feeling sincerely.

Celebrants must also feel that there is desire for their behavior to be authentic. They must not feel forced to contribute to a festive occasion in ways that make them feel uncomfortable or fake. If participants feel forced to mouth insincere words or say things only to impress others, they will not appreciate or enjoy the celebration.

Humor of the Heart. Unlike roasts and hazings, which often are the focus of a celebration, conscious celebrations use humor of the heart. Instead of using sarcasm and caustic jokes, the humor warms the heart and heightens the person's self-esteem rather than tearing it down. The jesting may still poke fun at the person's weaknesses and strengths and people have a lot of fun, but the intention is clear—to honor, not harm.

A group of scientists and engineers from the Department of Energy created a "This is your Tuff Life Roast" for a consultant whose work was completed for a 2½-year association. (Tuff is the substance of a mountain they were studying.) Each manager described his or her appreciation, learning, and feelings through cartoons, poems, songs, and symbolic gifts such as a bottle of aspirin. The roast included teasing, with such statements as "Despite our worst intentions you have guided us over the troubled waters, if not on a direct course, at least on one where we usually remained in sight of the path." The farewell concluded with the presentation of an album of poems, letters, cards and photographs, including a card from the director of the project. Next to the director's signature was a heart drawn with footsteps on it, symbolically acknowledging the footsteps that this consultant had left on his heart.

Play. Deal and Kennedy, authors of *Corporate Cultures,* (1982) note the place of play in releasing tension and encouraging innovation. They state, "despite the fact that it has no real purpose and no rules, play in its various forms (jokes, teasing, brainstorming, and strategizing) bonds people together, reduces conflict, and creates new visions and cultural values." Tandem, IBM, and DEC all provide opportunities for play on company time through workshops, beer busts, and retreats.

Harvey Cox (1969) reminds us that during our industrial era, we grew "more sober and industrious, less playful and imaginative." Often the more creative the frivolity and the more meaningful the play, the more welcome is the balance of the work world.

Personal Empowerment. In traditional, hyped events, money is often used to put on a big production and to stage an event in order to impress the egos of the attendees and sometimes to intentionally bribe them into company loyalty. The main intent of a conscious celebration in not money or expression of power. These events can be elaborate, expensive events or occasions requiring no budget at all. True power empowers others. Conscious celebrations share two of the three basic power commodites Kanter (1983) discusses: *information* (data, technical knowledge, political intelligence, expertise) and *support* (endorsement, backing, approval, legitimacy). When people are informed and legitimized in a celebration, they feel energized and uplifted—empowered. This results in a natural desire to put the best possible skill and expertise into the company, rather than feeling forced or intimidated. They feel grateful to be informed of a company's new direction, if that is the reason for the celebration; inspired and compelled to do their part to achieve the vision of the corporation; and are convinced that the tasks they perform are inherently worthwhile.

On August 6, 1985, the fortieth anniversary of the bombing of Hiroshima men, women and children gathered in a spectacular celebration of peace through individual empowerment. Through the vision of one woman, Justine Merritt, individuals from all walks of life painted, appliqued and wove images of peace on large panels of cloth. Each panel was joined with other panels, first in small towns and then in the capitals of each state, and lastly it was woven for six miles around Washington, D.C. Since that time, the peace ribbon has hung in galleries around the world, continuing to empower those who see it.

Elegance and Aesthetics. Conscious celebrators use the qualities of elegance and aesthetics in the overall design of their celebrations. This charm can range from the casual elegance of an old-fashioned ice cream social, which Syntex Corporation used to mark the achievement of a sales goal, to commissioning an artist to design an art deco poster to mark an anniversary, as did Interaction Associates, a consulting firm.

Elegance can also be experienced in the moment. Most meetings have "strategic moments." Celebrations have moments of "elegance." These are the climactic moments or the magical moments, which, when noted, can move a celebration to the next higher level of meaning. Like an actor's timing or the crescendo of a symphony, these moments can be sensed at the time as well as anticipated in the design of the celebration.

Spontaneity. Harrison Owen (1983) advocates the concept of "open space" in celebration. He believes that "transformation occurs in the open space between what has been, and what shall become." If the open space is there, a transformation can take place in a conscious celebration. However, if every moment of a celebration is orchestrated like a beauty pageant, there will literally be no room for this to occur. This use of open space creates room for surprise, spontaneity, and the unrehearsed meaning of the moment. During a conscious celebration, we cease doing and experience being. People cannot "be" if they are filling every moment "doing." This leader's greatest challenge is to have the courage to create the quiet and allow the space to be open.

Creativity. Each conscious celebration is custom-designed to fit the occasion, organizational norms, and personalities of the participant. This focus calls for creativity. Often the more creative the design of the event, the more honored the persons experiencing the celebration will feel.

One of the most creative celebrations in recent years was conducted through computer terminals. Meta Network is an organization set up to network people around the world in a computer conferencing and electronic mail system. Members of the Meta Network linked together to honor the birthday of the network's founder, Frank Burns. They sent invitations, via the post office, to each member of the Network. When the invitation was opened, small pieces of multicolored confetti fell into the invitee's lap. The creativity continued with the invitation itself:

Shhhhhhh . . . .
You are invited to a surprise birthday party on November 23 for
Frank Burns. We hope as many people as possible will sign on to

*honor Frank. To get to the party—type "join Meta: secret" at any
"Do Next?" prompt. . .*

The uniqueness of the celebration began the moment the invitation was
opened and didn't finish until the secret ended on November 23, when the
party-goers gathered via telecommunications.

Symbols Recent brain research and the writings of such people as Carl
Jung and Jean Houston have raised awareness of the world of symbols.
Celebrations in the past have been rich in the use of symbols, from the
Japanese Noa plays to the Greek Festivals of Dionysus. In today's world
symbols can offer the culminating image that bonds the meaning of a ritual
and enables the celebration to live beyond its temporary existence.

In 1974, Dee Hock, then president of Visa International, gave a symbolic gift
to each member of the International Organizing Committee to heal
differences that at the time seemed irreconcilable (Deal and Kennedy
1982). Hock designed a unique set of gold cuff links for the meeting
knowing that this meeting would determine whether the conflicts within
the organization could be resolved. One cuff link was designed as a relief
map of half of the world and inscribed around it were the Latin words
"Studium Ad, Prosperandum" or "The Will to Succeed." On the second was
the other half of the world surrounded by the words, "Voluntas in
Conveniendum," or "The Grace To Compromise." The die to the casting
was stored in a vault, to be destroyed if the meeting was unsuccessful, or
kept for future sets of cuff links if the directors reached agreements. The
cuff links have become treasured possessions and the symbols, the motto
of Visa International.

Ritual Our culture is built upon ritual. Ritual passed down wisdom
through the ages and translated the mysteries of our material and spiritual
world to the next generation even before the written word was created. In
the Information Age, ritual is necessary in continuing the translation of
known technology and the essence of our cultural ideals. According to
Igelhart (1983) rituals work on two levels: the psychic level (seen and
unseen forces affecting material reality) and the psychological level
(affecting people's actions by affecting their minds). As a result, the energy
of each ritual carries over into other areas of corporate life.

Rituals can be spontaneous or planned, personal or collective. Companies
such as IBM, Dana, Mary Kay Cosmetics, NCR, Holiday Inns, and Procter
and Gamble have made ritual a serious part of day-to-day operations, often
initiating a ritual around such common habits as morning coffee updates.

Yet rituals can easily lose their original meaning, becoming institutional-ized and used to enforce the status quo of stifled behavior rather than to raise consciousness and bring meaning to an organization. At this point, new rituals need to be created and old ones abandoned. Rituals showcase the culture of the organization. If they are meaningful, they dramatize and reinforce the values and beliefs of the organization. If they are stiff or outdated, they telegraph dysfunctional messages to employees.

Ron Green, internal consultant with Alcoa, uses a combination of ritual and symbolism with participants in the corporate training programs. He explains his philosophy behind these events.

> *"Our program uses symbols and rituals to celebrate the skill, awareness, and knowledge gained by each participant. We end our professional development seminars with a graduation dinner, a group class picture, a diploma and a closing ceremony. During the dinners, which are light, playful, fun filled occasions, we present symbols to each participant to help celebrate the most important awareness or skill that he or she gained during the program—giant ears for listening skills, a clown's nose for appreciating the less serious side of themselves, a heart to remind her or him that people are important to a manager. These rituals are often the highlight of the seminar. They serve to bond the group together, become part of the corporate culture and act as a reminder that each member has begun a journey toward greater effectiveness."*
>
> ***(1985, personal communication)***

Storytelling Culture is built on myths and stories. When leaders tell stories in a celebration, they embody the beliefs and values of an organization in a tale that can be easily remembered and repeated. Stories spread like wildfire through an organization. When a story is first told in a celebration, its value becomes heightened, because celebrations are special events that gather people together for public recognition. People inside the organization admire the hero in the story and secretly wish to be that person and have those experiences. Stories inspire people and promote admiration for the storyteller. Storytellers are really modern-day information brokers, and as the world becomes more invested in the Information Age, the value of storytelling will increase.

THE ROLE OF LEADERSHIP
IN THE ACT OF CELEBRATION
What does a leader do to create celebrations that help transform an

organization? An example can shed light on this question (Pyle, personal communication, 1985).

A senior vice president of a major housing company was given the task of turning around 2 of its 12 decentralized organizations, both of which were losing enormous sums of money; were very disorganized; and were experiencing extremely low morale. In spite of the fact that people were working hard, little was being accomplished. The senior vice president knew the employees needed job skills training and organizational help, but he also knew that somehow the people had to become inspired, literally had to have life breathed into them, if they were going to make it. He believed that if he could create a spirit in these companies, they could be turned around and become profitable. He decided to begin a job training program, a management development program, and a series of celebrations.

The first effort, a party quickly and poorly organized by the SVP, was a complete failure. Knowing celebration was the right idea, but that the process of creating it had been all wrong, the SVP called in a consultant for help. They decided to create a contest between the organizations and to involve all of the employees in the planning process. The group designed a picnic as a kickoff event, which included blindfolded piggy-back races, T-shirts, banners, and team names: the "Grizzlies" and "Vultures." The whole event was videotaped and later shown to spouses and participants at the awards banquet at the end of the contest.

Although the vice president was aware that somewhere down the road he wanted to create organizations with a higher purpose than competition, the first step worked toward easing tension, creating some fun, inducing informality, and making it more fun to come to work.

Celebration, in and of itself, became a part of the company philosophy. The values of the company were written into a values constitution and informally and openly discussed throughout the companies. One of the clearly stated values was around celebration:

- We value celebration and believe it enhances work:
- We publicly recognize achievements.
- We encourage spontaneous celebrations.
- We know that if we're having fun, we will work harder, smarter, and longer.
- We evaluate managers on their enthusiasm and ability to create an environment in which it is a pleasure to work.

- Employees who spread gloom will be asked to leave.

Employees started living these values on a day-to-day basis. People began to have fun and began congratulating each other for their accomplishments. Clothes and conversations became more informal.

Deciding that it could be risked, the SVP asked one of the group to meet one evening, have a light meal together, and then spend a few moments saying what they appreciated about each other. He began by telling a story of what one of the members had done that had been especially helpful to him. The response that followed was beyond the leader's wildest dreams. Touching, caring stories were told, laughter filled the room, and there were occasional tears as one by one, every single person was recognized for who they were as well as what they had done.

The group would clearly never be the same again. They had allowed themselves to be vulnerable, to be celebrated and appreciated. Every individual was a valued member of the team. The work which began to be produced by both companies, but especially by the group that had dared to go the farthest in their celebration of each other, was phenomenal. The SVP actually had to issue a policy: "Every employee must take off one day per week and two days back to back, at least once per month." They were inspired. The turnaround had begun.

What did this senior vice president do to create these celebrations? He did what any leader can do to foster the art of celebration—follow a set of principles:

1. Recognize that celebration is an effective tool for reaching the goals and vision of an organization. Know that conscious celebration really is a modern-day link to the spiritual dimension of an organization. Through this link, transformation can be seen and felt.

2. Know what to celebrate. Organizations, like any living system, go through a multitude of changes in their life cycles. Celebrations can be held to mark these moments for many reasons:

- Celebrating stages of organizational change: expansions, reorganizations, closings, mergers, the end of an old technology and the introduction of new one, moves to new locations,
- Celebrating success: financial success, promotion, awards, expansions to new markets,
- Celebrating loss: mourning to let go of old patterns and make

room for new opportunities and new life, loss of old procedures, financial opportunities, contracts, a job, status; death of a colleague; an experiment that failed,

- Celebrating people: teamwork, team successes; founding fathers; winners of sales contests; employee awards; individual birthdays, marriages, reunions, and
- Celebrating events: a company's anniversary, opening day, holidays, articulation of an organization's vision
- Celebrating the unknown: paradox, ambiguity of the marketplace.

3. Use an internal or external consultant if assistance is needed to design or implement a celebration.

4. Lead the first celebrations and model the desired behavior for celebrations. For instance, leaders who avoid sexist and racist language as well as sexual innuendoes in celebrations will set this standard for celebrations throughout the organization.

5. Legitimize celebration within the organization so that others not only know it is okay to celebrate, but that it is a desired part of corporate life. Participate fully in celebrations so others will be encouraged to do the same.

6. When times are hard, don't stop celebrating. Look for small wins. Try celebrations for "The Martyr of the Week" or "The Best Try"—the person who genuinely worked hard, but didn't get results.

7. Once celebrations get rolling, let others lead the way. Keep reinforcing the spirit of celebration, participate in celebration, create some original celebrations, but as the spirit of celebration builds a life of its own, let the spirit take over.

8. Mentor others in the art of celebration. Some people are natural storytellers, entertainers, and, literally masters of ceremony. Create space in the organization for them to use their gifts.

9. Understand that celebration is part of a process for transformative change. When used, it needs to be done with awareness in the context of other tools and change processes.

In addition to following these principles, another way to conceptualize the role of leader in celebration is to describe five different roles: imagineer, artist, shaman, shadow detector, and evocator. Not every role has to be carried out by every leader, nor will every leader feel capable of fulfilling each role. A leader who doesn't feel comfortable with a role or doesn't have the time, can either carefully delegate these roles or work closely with others to jointly fulfill them. However, each role adds to the richness of conscious celebrations.

Imagineer. An imagineer is a person who can imagine the possible and engineer reality to create it. As the saying goes, "If you can dream it, you can create it." Leaders need to envision the potential of a celebration and build those moments into the fabric of organizational life. This is truly the challenge of a transformational leader.

Artist. Artists are the original examples of leaders who transform elements from one state of being to another—clay to pottery, thread to tapestry, acrylic to portraits.

Celebrations are creations. Leaders are the artists behind the creation—the designers, playwrights, choreographers, producers—and have the opportunity to use these experiences to transform their organization into another dimension through their imagination and fantasy. Like any true work of art, however, a leader must follow his or her own creativity and individual personality. A leader who's art is storytelling and humor will create celebrations of that kind; leaders who are shy will use their abilities to empower others to celebrate; leaders who are charismatic and inspirational will themselves become symbols of celebration; and leaders who are dramatic and extravagant will ride an elephant or do the hula down Wall Street.

Shamans. Some leaders are called to be shamans. They are the "spiritual teachers," the elders of a tribe, the old wise ones (Noble 1983). A shaman works with spiritual powers but doesn't seek to have power over others. A shaman brings healing to an organization.

The energy of a celebration creates a positive force that in turn creates an ascending spiral of energy as more people and energy are put in it. Participants talk about being "charged," leaving an event "filled with energy," which will get them over the next hurdle.

Leaders must be aware of the energy force potentially present in celebration and then be able to tap into the energy in an ethical way. Leaders who are drawn to this role need to fully understand the parts they play as shamans, modern-day priests and priestesses. However, unless an individual leader has done his or her homework through developing personally, there is little hope for them to carry out such a special role. This kind of leadership requires ethics, discipline, integrity, skill and alignment with a higher purpose beyond the individual self. Conscious celebrations are a link to the spiritual dimension of an organization, but they are not religious events and should not be used to force religion on someone. They are occasions that allow people to experience their spirituality, which may or may not be connected to any religious philosophy.

Shadow Detectors. To balance their role as shamans, leaders must also be aware of their "shadow side," their dark side, the driver of their unconscious behavior. Leaders must be aware of their individual shadow side so that their unconscious behavior does not creep into a celebration. For instance, leaders who are prone to being the center of attention will probably play out this side of themselves in a celebration, centering more attention on themselves than on the event or people being honored. Leaders who are perfectionists and have high control needs will try to control and choreograph every detail of the celebration "perfectly" and consequently leave no room for spontaneity, surprise, or the natural spirit of the festivity. Leaders who are not in touch with their feelings and are so driven by the hyped part of corporate life will use celebrations as hard sell marketing events, focused on action rather than on occasions where people can relax, play, and appreciate who they are as well as what they do. Since most of the shadow-driven behavior is unconscious behavior, a leader may need to ask colleagues, family members, or consultants for feedback in order to clearly detect their individual shadows. Once discovered, creative ways can be used to control the shadow rather than the shadow running the show.

Evocators. Evocators are leaders who invite others to initiate celebrations on their own. Evoke literally means "to call forth a spirit." Evocators arouse the spirit and emotion of an organization when they use celebration, for celebration is one of the most powerful processes a leader has to breathe spirit into an organization. When an evocator invites others to spend this spirit, people feel pulled to respond as if they are drawn to a magnet, and the spirit of celebration quickly spreads through an organization.

HOW TO CREATE A CONSCIOUS CELEBRATION
Celebration, like any intervention into a living system, can be done in many ways. The following formula is one way to create a successful experience.

Dare To Do It! Celebration is not exactly the norm in most organizations.

Leaders need courage to initiate celebrative ideas and sometimes use faith to implement them. A celebration can fail if it is done half-way or gingerly.

Crocker National Bank has a successful quality circle program called WIN. Courage was required to design and involve traditionally conservative bank managers and employees to participate in a skit called the "Wizard of Win", which celebrated the successes of the improvement program. Most of the employees in attendance had never been to a meeting with their managers or had a chance to hear a division manager or vice-chairman speak. In a time of cutbacks and low morale, the audience experienced managers and employees dressed as a Scarecrow, a Tin Man, a Lion, a Wizard, the Wicked Witch of the Status Quo, the Good Witch of Creativity, and of course, Dorothy.

At one point the Lion sang,

> "Oh, I could listen to all the voices, examine all the choices, make problems go away. I could sort through the confusion and recommend solutions, If I only had a way!"

The Tin Man said, "My problem is that I need a heart badly. You see, I don't feel much involved in my work anymore. I'm just collecting dust and getting rusty." The troupe traveled past Cardholder Corner, Revolving Credit, the Island of General Services, and the Forest of Wire Transfer until they finally reached their destination . . . the Great Wizard of WIN.

From the example of conservative bankers the challenge is there: dare to do it! The wins are significant.

Listen to the Spirit. The words "inspire", "intuition", and "insight" all have a common message for us—to listen within to the powers of our creative minds in order to find guidance for our actions. Current brain research is finally legitimizing for the scientific and rational world what intuitive people have known for ages. Harman and Rheingold (1984) give us instructions for letting inspiration out. "Your unconscious idea processor is awaiting your beck and call. All you have to do is assign it a problem, instruct it, and it will immediately go to work on a problem for you . . . the more clearly, completely, and intently you formulate a question and direct it to the unconscious, the more quickly and effectively the unconscious can come up with an answer to it."

The importance of inspiration cannot be underestimated. David Wolper's inspiration for the 1984 Summer Olympics in Los Angeles was that "at the end of the opening ceremony everyone will feel the same." His inspiration was so strong and so on target with a universal unconscious mind that the athletes broke into spontaneous dancing and celebrating, which carried with it an international feeling of unity extending beyond the patriotism of any given country. When he received the Academy Award almost a year later for the design of that special event, Wolper repeated the inspiration for his vision: "Reach out and touch somebody's hand, Make this world a better place if you can."

Seek Alignment. Since conscious celebrations use and generate sacred energy, it is important for designers, celebrators, and the celebration itself to be aligned with a superordinate goal and a higher purpose beyond individuals. Those purposes might be the vision of the future organization, the connection with the mission of the organization, or evolving the spiritual dimensions of the people gathered. To consider what this purpose is, the entire context for the celebration should be analyzed.

In addition to context and purpose, the energy of a celebration needs to be aligned. To do that, certain questions need to be answered. Examples of these questions are:

- Who should be included in the design of the celebration?
- How can the designers be empowered?
- Who should be included in the celebration?
- What space should be used? (new, old, neutral, inside, outside, etc.)
- How much time should be given to the celebration?
- How much time should be structured? Unstructured?
- What should be the rhythm and pace?
- Who should lead the celebration? In what style?

At St. Joseph Hospital in Kansas City, Missouri, a celebration took place that exemplifies this kind of alignment. The Task Force on Organizational Climate made a presentation to the chief executive officer of a values constitution they had written for the hospital. This constitution was based on the values and mission of the Sisters of St. Joseph and the implicit values of the hospital. Hundreds of employees from all levels of the hospital contributed to the values constitution along with board members and physicians. The designers chose to have each task force member sit in a semicircle with the CEO at the end. Each contributing member held the document and spoke spontaneously about what the constitution meant to him or her. The presentation had a dimension that went beyond handing a report to the CEO. Their work was aligned with a higher goal, a vision of passing on the spirit of a hospital to future employees—a spirit based on the values of "human dignity", "social justice", and "the sacredness of human life". The celebration was a manifestation of these values, and everyone experienced a transformative movement—it seemed as if their vision had already been reached.

Create the Design. Celebrations can occur either spontaneously or with designed intention. Those requiring planning need to have a design with a beginning, a middle, and an end. Within the design, all kinds of materials can be used:

Artwork	**Guests**	**Performers**
Murals	Celebrities	Actors
Paintings	Dignitaries	Clowns
Photography	Founding fathers	Mimes
Sculpture	Retired employees	Tapestry Speakers
Color	**Media**	**Presentation**
	Movies	Awards
	Slides	Certificates
	Video	Diplomas
		Plaques
		Prizes, Trophies
Costumes	**Music**	**Ritual**
Hats, Props	Bands, Dancing,	Applause
	Minstrels	Candles
	Singing	Prayers
		Toasts
Decorations	**Open space**	**Signs**
Balloons		Banners, Flags
Confetti, Favors		Slogans
Lanterns, Scenery		
Wall hangings		
Displays	**Participation**	**Surprises**
Exhibits, Floats	Auctions, Games	
Parades	Skits, Storytelling	
	Tours	
Food	**Plants**	**Symbols**
	Flowers	Mascots, Wands
	Trees	

All of the senses need to be considered in the design phase. The more creative the design, the more special the celebrants will feel.

Signetics, a manufacturer of computer parts and a subsidiary of U. S. Phillips Corporation, has a Zero Defects Program. They created a superb design for a "Zero Defects Day" using an array of these design ideas.

The Zero Defects program has been so successful their customers are constantly reporting zero defects for the Signetics products—a significant fact coming from customers such as Honeywell, Hewlett Packard, DEC, Xerox, and Westinghouse! The celebration of this effort was just as impressive. A high school football field was transformed into a carnival when over 4,000 employees gathered to celebrate and recommit to zero defects. Each division was free to design their own event. The Microprocessor Division dressed up as defect busters to the tune of "Ghost Busters" and came swiftly to the rescue every time a pretend shipment was threatened. A costumed gypsy read the palms of employees and predicted all employees would strive to perform error-free work in the year to come. The climax of the festivity occurred when each member of every division signed a pledge to recommit to zero defects. This celebration, like their everyday work, was designed and performed with zero defects—a true tribute to their spirit, hard work, and the art of celebrating.

The design of a celebration can be easy and simplistic. At an annual meeting of the Walnut Creek Kaiser Medical Center, the internal organization development consultant asked the managers and medical chiefs of staff to reflect on the past year, remembering the times on the job when they appreciated themselves or others. They quickly brainstormed a list, actually refusing to stop because they enjoyed naming these favorite moments. The consultant later went around the medical center photographing each of the people who had been named and posted their pictures and the comments from the meeting for all to see. An easy, quiet moment of celebration spread quickly throughout the Center.

Implement from the Heart. Many of today's organizations are fear driven—employees fear embarrassment, punishment, and loss of job, status, and opportunity. When people are fearful, they cannot give and receive love easily. Before a celebration, leaders may want to ground themselves in a quiet moment of preparation: to relax, release any fears they may have about the celebration, and get in touch with their feelings and the intention of the celebration. At this time, leaders need to let go of any ulterior motives or specific expectations they may have for the celebration. The best results come only if there are no expectations. Leaders can then speak to employees from their hearts.

When meeting with the participants, leaders may need to legitimize fears and honor each person's choice about how much they want to participate in a given celebration. Once people feel safe and comfortable, the passage from the toxins of the work world to the sacred space of the celebration can begin. Then people can begin to open their heart and minds. If they are tight and self-protective, the exchange of heartfelt recognition will not take place. When leaders model being open to giving and receiving love, they create the space for intimacy and bonding to occur. Then, magic can truly happen.

Let Go. Some celebrations need to be planned or they wouldn't occur; but spontaneous celebrations wouldn't occur if they were planned. Consequently, leaders need to learn when to let go. In order to let the spirit or celebration move through an organization, a leader must pass the baton. Spirit, when released, will flourish by its own power. There is an order and power in the universe that is greater than any individual. Leaders must do their part, then get out of the way.

BENEFITS AND RESULTS OF CONSCIOUS CELEBRATION

On the surface, hard-nosed businesspeople may think celebration is trivial, only appropriate if things are going well, or that its proper place is in the home. On the contrary, celebration is tied to the very fabric of corporate culture. The more celebration is woven into the workplace, the more its results can be measured in direct productivity, profit, and people. Celebrations can:

1. Build individual self-esteem—people feel empowered and important;
2. Enhance communication—celebrations foster an open, informal communication where people feel more at ease and consequently share better information;
3. Promote teamwork—because people feel bonded and that their contribution is important;
4. Create energy—people feel renewed, their batteries recharged;
5. Make work more fun—there is a balance between work and play; a climate of festivity instead of a climate of fear or drudgery;
6. Help people through transitions and changes—(e.g., reorganizations, plant closing, leadership changes, job changes);
7. Create a positive outlook—more energy is put into work and less into self-protection;
8. Spawn creativity and innovation;
9. Reinforce and showcase desired norms of behavior;

10. Inspire people and build the faith that their visions can become a reality.

In essence, there are connections between celebration and good business, the human spirit and the bottom line, the spiritual plane and the world of work which produce significant benefits to organizations and their cultures.

SPIRITUAL DIMENSION OF CELEBRATION

Celebration in its highest form is a spiritual experience. Rather than just experiencing an event, individuals experience who they really are— imperfect yet holy beings. Like the snake shedding its skin, like the caterpillar becoming a butterfly, we see our beauty and become more beautiful, we feel our joy and become more joyous, we create our visions and become more visionary.

We experience a transcendance of ourselves, as well as a transcendance of time. We remember the past, experience the present, and live in the future. We are able for a moment to live as Cox says, as if all the things we are struggling for were already accomplished. We see that our visions for the transformation of our organization are already a reality.

This transcendance bonds us in a collective consciousness. We are connected with an energy force beyond ourselves. We realize there are no boundaries between who we are spiritually and our work in organizations. We become beings with purposes larger than material gain, finding meaning more inclusive than work and feeling rewards greater than profit. We allow the spiritual side of ourselves to move within and through our organizations. We experience the deeper meaning of our lives and are guided into the future.

The New Age is calling the festivals of the spirit into the business world. We who are ready to evoke the spiritual dimensions of our work will continue to experience profound shifts in our perception, which will open us to further and greater individual and organizational transcendance. When we experience transcendance once, we can experience it again and again, and then at some point we can begin to create the space in which it can happen for others.

The spirit of celebration cordially invites us to embark on a fantasy of our collective imagination. The place to which we are going is one that is very familiar and at the same time, quite strange. This place is suspended in time, both timeless and a kaleidoscope of all times. We have been there in our dreams and fantasies, and we have also never travelled there before. This invitation is to weave the art of conscious celebration into the fabric of our organizational lives. The journey promises to enable us to rediscover our souls.

INCENTIVES CAN BE BAD
FOR BUSINESS

Alfie Kohn

Whether they know it or not, most executives are Skinnerians. It was Harvard psychologist B.F. Skinner who popularized the theory of positive reinforcement, which holds that presenting a reward after a desired behavior will make that behavior more likely to occur in the future. To our pets we say, "Good dog!" and offer a biscuit. To our employees we say, "Good job!" and offer a performance bonus.

It seems to make sense. But research has been accumulating that shows tangible rewards as well as praise can actually lower the level of performance, particularly in jobs requiring creativity. Study after study has shown that intrinsic interest in a task—the sense that something is worth doing for its own sake—typically declines when someone is given an external reason for doing it.

Author and sociologist Philip Slater put it starkly in his book *Wealth Addiction:* "Getting people to chase money . . . produces nothing except people chasing money. Using money as a motivator leads to a progressive degradation in the quality of everything produced."

The problem is not with money per se, which most of us find desirable. Rather, it is the fact that waving dollar bills in front of people leads them to think of themselves as doing work *only* for the reward. Performance tends to suffer as a result.

In one study, Teresa M. Amabile, associate professor of psychology at Brandeis University, asked 72 creative writers to write some poetry. She gave one group of subjects a list of extrinsic reasons for writing, such as impressing teachers and making money, and asked them to think about their own writing with respect to those reasons. She showed others a list of intrinsic reasons: the enjoyment of playing with words, for example, and satisfaction from self-expression. A third group was not given a list. All were then asked to do more writing.

The results were clear. Those given the extrinsic reasons not only wrote less creatively than the others, as judged by 12 independent poets, but the quality of their work dropped significantly after this brief exposure to the extrinsic reasons.

This effect, according to other studies, is by no means limited to poets. When young tutors were promised free movie tickets for teaching well, they took longer to communicate ideas, got frustrated more easily, and did a poorer job in the end than those who got nothing. In another study, a group of subjects who contracted in advance for a reward made less creative collages and told less inventive stories. Students who were offered a reward for participating in still another experiment not only did more poorly at a creative task, but also failed to memorize as well as the subjects who received no reward.

What's going on here? The experts offer three explanations for such findings, and all of them have important implications for managers.

First, rewards encourage people to focus narrowly on a task, to do it as quickly as possible, and to take few risks. "If they feel, 'This is something I have to get through to get a prize,' they're going to be less creative," says Amabile. The more emphasis placed on the reward, the more inclined someone will be to do the minimum necessary to get it. And that means lower-quality work.

The very fact of turning a task into a means of attaining something else changes the way that task is perceived, as a clever series of experiments by Mark R. Lepper, a professor of psychology at Stanford University, demonstrated. He told a group of children that they could not engage in one activity they liked until they took part in another. Although they had enjoyed both activities equally, the children came to dislike the task that was a prerequisite for the other.

Second, extrinsic rewards can erode intrinsic interest. People who come to see themselves as working for money or approval find their tasks less pleasurable and therefore do not do them as well. "Money may work to 'buy off' one's intrinsic motivation for an activity," says Edward L. Deci, professor of psychology at the University of Rochester and a leading authority on the subject.

What's true of money is also true of competition, which, contrary to myth, is nearly always counterproductive (see "No Contest," Managing People, November 1987). Deci put 80 subjects to work on a spatial-relations puzzle, and he asked some to solve it more quickly than those sitting next to them.

Then each of the subjects sat alone—but secretly observed—in a room that contained a similar puzzle. It turned out that those who had been competing spent less time working on the task voluntarily—and later told Deci they found it less interesting—compared with those who didn't have to compete. The external prod of winning a contest, like that of a bonus, makes a task seem less enjoyable in its own right. Not surprisingly, what's seen as less enjoyable is usually done less well.

But there is a third reason that the use of external motivators can backfire. People come to see themselves as being controlled by a reward. They feel less autonomous, and this often interferes with performance.

There's no shortage of data showing that a feeling of freedom translates into happier and more productive employees. In 1983-84, Amabile and Stan Gryskiewicz, of the Center for Creative Leadership, in Greensboro, NC, interviewed 120 research-and-development scientists, asking each to describe one event from their work experience that exemplified high creativity and one that reflected low creativity. The factor they mentioned most often, by far, was freedom or its absence. Receiving a clear overall direction on a project is useful, the scientists said, but they worked best when they could decide for themselves how to accomplish those goals.

Rewards are often offered in a controlling way, and to that extent, says Deci's colleague Richard Ryan, they stifle productivity. He emphasizes the enormous difference between saying, "I'm giving you this reward because I

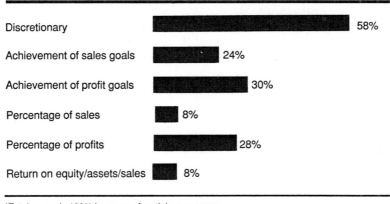

**How Small Companies Allocate
Bonuses to Executives***

Discretionary	58%
Achievement of sales goals	24%
Achievement of profit goals	30%
Percentage of sales	8%
Percentage of profits	28%
Return on equity/assets/sales	8%

*Total exceeds 100% because of mutiple responses.
Source 1987 Inc. Executive Compensation Survey

recognized the value of your work," and "You're getting this reward because you've lived up to my standards." Likewise for verbal feedback: the question isn't whether you give enough of it, or even how positive it is. What matters is how controlling the person perceives it to be.

This point was made in a study conducted by Deci, Ryan, and James Connell. From questionnaires completed by several hundred workers in a corporation that manufactured business machines, they found that those who worked for controlling managers were less satisfied with their jobs and more concerned with pay and benefits. The attitude seemed to be, "If you're going to control me, I'm going to be alienated, and what I'm going to focus on is money." In a related laboratory study, Ryan found that when subjects were praised, told in effect, "Good, you're doing as you should," instead of simply letting them know how well they had done, motivation was low.

Does all this mean that employees should be paid less or ignored when they do good work? Definitely not. Is it an argument for scrapping incentive plans? Probably not. What the research indicates is that all incentive systems—along with verbal feedback—should be guided by two clear principles. Higher-quality work, particularly on jobs requiring creative thinking, is more likely to occur when a person focuses on the challenge of the task itself, rather than on some external motivator, and feels a sense of self-determination, as opposed to feeling controlled by means of praise or reward.

Practically speaking, this means that incentives announced in advance are more likely to undermine performance than are unexpected bonuses that recognize an outstanding job after the fact. Particularly deadly are incentive programs run as contests in which some teams (or individuals) will not receive bonuses no matter how well they perform. Managers need to consider impact of any incentive payment on the workers who *don't* receive it—another hidden cost of rewards.

Provided these conditions are met—and everyone feels the system for awarding bonuses is fair—incentives may not be harmful. But a supportive workplace, one in which workers are allowed autonomy and are not only informed about company goals but help determine them, may not even need incentive systems.

The larger point is that innovation cannot be forced but only allowed to happen. You can help create the conditions that allow it by playing down the significance of rewards and playing up what employees find appealing about the task itself. Effective supervisors take care of their subordinates' financial needs but don't make a big deal about money and its relationship to performance. Instead, they concentrate on the most powerful motivator that exists: the intrinsic interest people have in solving problems. People are most interested when their curiosity is aroused—when discrepancies exist between what they thought was true and what they've just encountered—and when they are challenged by a task that's neither so difficult as to be overwhelming nor so simple as to be boring.

What's more, employees should be matched with the kind of work that they find interesting. "In hiring we almost never look at intrinsic motivation," Amabile observes of most organizations. Yet having someone work on the sort of problem to which he or she is naturally attracted is likely to produce better results than using some artificial means to boost performance.

Of course, some tasks are universally regarded as dull. In these cases, the idea is to get people to internalize the importance of doing them—to transform external reasons into internal incentive. Deci and his colleagues have recently turned their attention to this problem. Their findings suggest that a manager should acknowledge that the task is boring, explain why it needs to be done, and try to maximize a feeling of autonomy.

In another experiment, Deci and graduate student Haleh Eghrari had 90 subjects press a computer-keyboard space bar every time a dot of light appeared on the screen, a task most found uninteresting. the researchers admitted to one group that the activity wasn't much fun, but they explained that it could be useful for learning about concentration. These individuals were praised for their performance afterward. A second group was told that they "should attend to (the task) very carefully . . . since it will be for your own good." Later they were informed that they had done well "as (they) should." The third group was given only instructions without explanation.

As with the competition study, each subject was then left alone in a room and given the option of continuing to play with the computer once the experiment was over. Those in the first group chose to do this more often and also did a better job at the task. "People need to experience a sense of initiation," Deci explains, "so the less you're controlling and demanding, the more they have a chance to feel that initiation themselves."

Self-determination, then, proves decisive with boring tasks as well as with interesting ones. And it isn't only an autocratic environment that wipes out feelings of autonomy. Even well-meaning managers can be controlling in the way they praise or reward. Likewise, financial incentives can come to seem so important that they reduce the attraction of the task itself. Lest managers squelch the very innovation they hope to create, rewards should be used with caution.

ADDITIONAL READING
Amabile, Teresa M. "Motivation and Creativity: Effects of Motivational Orientation on Creative Writers." *Journal of Personality and Social Psychology,* vol. 48, 1985, pp. 393-399.
Deci, Edward L. et al. "When Trying to Win: Competition and Intrinsic Motivation." *Personality and Social Psychology Bulletin,* vol. 7, 1981, pp. 79-83.
Lepper, Mark R. and David Greene, eds. *The Hidden Costs of Reward.* Hillsdale, NJ: Lawrence Erlbaum Associates, 1978.

LETTER TO THE EDITOR

Tom Peters

A recent *New Yorker* cartoon pictures a blackboard bursting with obscure mathematical formulations. One scientist, looking at the board, says to a colleague, "Oh, if only it were so simple." I couldn't help recalling the cartoon as I read Alfie Kohn's article in the January issue of *Inc.*, "Incentives Can Be Bad for Business."

Kohn clearly knows his field. From an academic perspective, his article is superb. He musters compelling evidence to argue that—on the production line or in the research lab—workers will respond most creatively if they have a sense of autonomy, on the one hand, and if they value a task or a job for its own sake, on the other. He is saying that intrinsic motivation is the key to high performance, and I certainly agree.

Kohn further argues that companies can undermine worker creativity by providing the wrong incentives—if, say, they put too much emphasis on extrinsic rewards, such as money, prizes, and positive feedback. These kinds of incentives, he says, lead employees to focus on performance that is quick, riskless (that is, noninnovative), and geared strictly toward

■

volume of output. If a company does use incentives, Kohn recommends that they emphasize quality of output, rather than quantity, and that they encourage self-control (that is, innovation and risk taking). For similar reasons, Kohn argues against establishing a competitive environment in a company. He particularly abhors contests in which some people get no reward because other individuals or groups did better.

On a point-by-point basis, I have no quarrel with any of Kohn's arguments. Moreover, I find him to be a thorough student of the arcane experimental literature on social psychology. But when it comes to the real world of business, I worry that he leaves the wrong impression on a number of scores.

Positive Reinforcement Is Better Than Negative Kohn does a nasty disservice to Harvard psychologist B.F. Skinner by portraying him as a mindless advocate of "waving dollar bills in front of people." To be sure, Skinner is the popularizer of positive reinforcement, but Kohn ignores his most important finding, one with huge implications for business, namely: positive reinforcement is much more beneficial than negative.

That's a key oversight because negative reinforcement (criticism) is far and away the most common means by which American companies try to influence performance. They constantly tell people what they did wrong, rather than what they did right. Yet, as Skinner showed, negative reinforcement—even if well intended—seldom leads to improved performance. More often, it produces convoluted efforts to hide negative results and risk-averse behavior to a much greater degree than that which Kohn describes when criticizing the excesses of positive reinforcement.

Anyone who has spent time observing real-life-business practices knows that Skinner is absolutely right on this point. The great quality advocate, W. Edwards Deming, a statistician who has little truck with psychologists, is adamant in his agreement. He has said that the American propensity for negative performance appraisals is our number-one management problem. Nor is he being totally facetious when he contends that it takes half a year for the average manager to recuperate from his or her performance review.

And, by the way, Skinner would be the first to agree with Kohn that "surprising" positive incentives work best. Skinner, after all, was the one who discovered that aperiodic (random, unexpected) "schedules of reinforcement" are much more powerful shapers of future behavior than periodic (routine, expected) schedules.

Business Problem Number One Is The Almost Total Absence Of Positive Reinforcement Although Kohn is correct about the pitfalls of positive reinforcement, he is arguing in a vacuum. If only American business were having trouble because of too much emphasis on extrinsic motivation, resulting in the denigration of intrinsic motivation. Unfortunately, the much larger problem is the almost total absence of positive reinforcement in the average U.S. company, regardless of size.

Consider these two anecdotal, but typical, examples. One involves Sam Preston, a recently retired executive vice-president at S.C. Johnson & Son Inc., which makes Johnson Wax among other products. Throughout his career, Preston would look for positive acts by employees. Whenever he stumbled on one, he would pen a quick note to the person responsible, concluding with the initials "DWD." Eventually, the recipients figured out the "DWD" stood for "Damned Well Done." When I met Preston, he had just finished his round of retirement parties, and he spoke of his amazement as person after person came up, occasionally verging on tears, to thank him for a single "DWD" that he'd sent as much as 15 years earlier.

I heard a similar story from a man who had recently bought a quarry in New England. Upon learning that a certain quarryman had cut an extraordinary amount of rock the day before, the new owner had impulsively grabbed a walkie-talkie to offer congratulations and praise. Shortly thereafter, he was talking to another employee and learned that the quarryman had been on cloud nine for days. Turns out that this stellar, 25-year veteran of rock blasting had never before received a word of praise from the boss.

The plain fact is that, in America, workers and managers receive far too little positive reinforcement for their contributions. The average employee faces a daunting array of hurdles and uncertainties. Simply to make it through the day is often worth a "well done." But that average person is not likely to receive even a doff of the cap from year to year, or decade to decade, let alone day to day. On a personal note, I must admit to Mr. Kohn that, despite having achieved a modicum of acclaim, I myself can never get enough of that wonderful stuff called positive reinforcement—and if you must schedule your applause in advance, it's jolly well fine with me.

Positive Reinforcement Need Not Be Quantity Based Kohn cautions against rote behavior stemming from positive reinforcement, but the real source of rote behavior is excessive attention to volume. What gets measured gets done, as the saying goes, and—at the vast majority of companies—what gets measured is volume. What gets overlooked is quality. The operative phrase is: "Don't improve it; ship it." That's a big problem, but what else can we expect when volume is all that we try to measure?

The solution, however, is not to abandon incentives, but to base them on nonvolumetric factors as well. In this regard, I was delighted to learn recently that First Chicago Corp. is giving some of its managers bonuses based in part on their success in meeting certain "minimally acceptable performance" goals, as determined by customers.

Similarly, it was quality of service that helped Phil Bressler establish himself as Domino Pizza's top franchisee in the important category of repeat business. Each of his stores would give out a volume-based award for best driver. Before the award was made, however, customers were asked to evaluate the driver's performance. If the quality of service didn't measure up, then no award.

The point is, there are ways to measure what was once thought to be unmeasurable. You can keep score on quality, customer service, responsiveness, innovativeness, even customer listening. Moreover, the sheer act of keeping score will provide a positive stimulant to improvement. Job number two, I'd agree, is to get the right balance between intrinsic and extrinsic motivational factors, but first let's put some of these other missing indicators on the map.

And Then There Is The Little Matter Of Equity, Or Share And Share Alike It's not easy to develop a good incentive system, and there are undoubtedly thousands of ways to construct useless, even damaging, ones. To read Kohn's article, you might think that bad incentive systems are the rule at most companies. The truth, however, is that most companies don't offer any incentives at all to their employees, except to a thimbleful of folks at the top.

A year and a century ago, in 1887, William Cooper Procter, president of Procter & Gamble Co., said that the chief challenge of big business was to shape its policies so that each worker would feel he was a vital part of his company with a chance to share in its success. P&G's landmark profit-distribution plan divided profits between the company and its workers in the same proportion that labor bore the total cost. If wages were 50% of cost, the workers' bonuses would be a whopping one-half of profits. Sadly, P&G's example was not widely emulated, and today only 15% of the U.S. work force participates in such a profit-distribution or gain-sharing plan. A paltry 10% own stock in their companies, despite the generous ESOP incentives available since 1974.

The significance of this appalling record was suggested by a survey that Daniel Yankelovich conducted in the early 1980s. U.S. and Japanese workers were asked to agree or disagree with the statement, "I have an inner need to do the best I can, regardless of pay." The U.S. workers, maligned by so many (especially their managers), outscored the Japanese. Then the two groups were asked a much more practical question: Who did they think would benefit most from an increase in worker productivity? This time, the tables were turned. Some 93% of Japanese workers thought that they would be the prime beneficiaries, while only 9% of the Americans felt that way. In other words, Japanese workers believe that increased productivity is a matter of self-interest—and the facts support them.

So Kohn may be right about the pitfalls of incentive systems, but he's dead wrong in suggesting that bad incentive systems are a major problem for American business. The far greater—and more commonplace—sin is to ignore the worker's incremental contribution altogether.

Competition Is Still The Spice Of Life The ancient philosopher's line is that the world would have no beauty without contrasting ugliness. For better or (sometimes certainly) for worse, comparison—which is to say, competition—is the chief motivator for individuals and groups, whether it takes place in teen beauty pageants, among Nobel-level scientists, or on the shop floor.

Now competition can go too far. I agree with Kohn that competition may cause a worker to focus excessively on speed and what the guy next to him is doing, thereby losing sight of the intrinsic value (that is, quality) of the task at hand. I have seen the disastrous consequences of basing incentive pay on work group competition—especially when workers are not trained adequately, and when the company does not provide the time, the place, and the tools to work creatively on individual and team improvement.

On the other hand, I have also seen group competition work wonders in a plant, under the right conditions. Look at New United Motor Manufacturing Inc. (NUMMI), the extraordinary joint venture between General Motors and Toyota. Its predecessor, a GM plant, was at the bottom of the heap in terms of productivity, quality, absenteeism, and numerous other performance indicators. Now, the 2,500-person operation scores at the top. The dramatic turnaround is mainly a result of employee involvement. Every worker is trained in at least a half-dozen jobs; each person must be good enough to train his or her colleagues; fellow hourly workers are team leaders; and the company provides all the training, tools, time, and space required for problem solving. Competition among teams is sky high, on the job and off, but meticulous preparation came first.

But, group competition aside, I think Kohn is focusing on a secondary issue here. We face enormous business problems today, and they were not caused by too much competition. Rather they reflect the broad deterioration of the national economy—a consequence of the virtual absence of competition from World War II until about 1965. During that period, almost all of our major industries became tidy oligopolies, in no shape to compete with anyone.

Kohn decries the ill effects of copying, and too much distraction with competition. I submit that it is far worse to ignore the competitive reality, and to refuse to copy at all. Consider the Ford Taurus, one of the biggest American product successes in decades. For years, Ford had systematically ignored or denigrated Japanese automobiles and, to some extent, European ones as well. In developing the Taurus, however, it did a complete about-face, purchasing hundreds of vehicles from around the globe. Following a copy-and-exceed strategy, Ford set out to best those vehicles on hundreds of features, from the inner workings of the engine to the ease of gas cap removability. That is, of course, precisely the strategy for which we once scorned the Japanese. Ironically, it is the same strategy with which the American (and then the Germans) surpassed the British in years gone by. The process may not be as creative as Kohn would like, and it certainly reflects an obsession with competition. But it works. And its success demonstrates once again that we have far more to fear from too little than from too much competition.

Let me just add a personal note in conclusion. Many years ago, I was a Ph.D. student of management, and I read with pleasure almost every word of psychologist L. Edward Deci, whom Kohn so reveres. Intrinsic motivation and autonomy have been major, if not dominant, themes in all three of my books. And I acknowledge that the astonishing success of enterprises such as NUMMI are testimony to the importance of intrinsic motivation and self-control. For drawing attention to those issues, Alfie Kohn deserves two full and hearty cheers.

But I must withhold cheer number three, for I feel that, overall, Kohn is addressing matters of secondary concern. Excessive emphasis on incentives and competition is simply not a widespread problem in American business. What we need is a lot *more* positive reinforcement, and a lot less of the negative kind, throughout the corporate landscape. And far from cautioning companies about the dangers of incentives, we should be applauding those that offer their employees a bigger piece of the action. Likewise, we should welcome competition, whatever its source. We have competitive pressure to thank for the positive things that are happening in large companies these days, including the new willingness to copy from the best. Better that than the practices of inward-looking companies and workers, closed to ideas that were Not Invented Here. They are the ones who have made such a bungle of American economic performance worldwide over the past 20 years.

Life ain't simple, as that *New Yorker* cartoon suggested, and neither is business. Kohn has much to say that is thoughtful and wise, and that ought to be heeded. But let's not ignore the forest for the trees.

THE AUTHOR REPLIES
AND REFUSES TO BACK DOWN

Alfie Kohn

When Tom Peters argues that the problem in the real world is too little positive reinforcement rather than too much, he is doing two things at once. He is describing what's going on, and he is prescribing what needs to be done instead. I have no quarrel with the first. But the cartoon phrase "Oh, if only it were so simple ... " seems more appropriate to Peter's prescription—that we should just crank up the positive reinforcement— than to my review of the hidden problems with this tactic.

I do not dispute his argument that praise is better than punishment. Likewise, I say "amen" to his call for more goodies to find their way to workers instead of executives. The research shows quite clearly, however that—when people feel controlled by praise, or when they come to think of themselves as working for extrinsic rewards—quality is likely to suffer. Peters's suggestion that we simply base those rewards on quality rather then quantity will not solve the problem. It may well be true that we have the capability to "keep score on quality," but it is clearly untrue that "the sheer act of keeping score will provide a positive stimulant to improvement."

■

■

Recognize And
Reward Accomplishment

The problem is not just that an artificial incentive for doing a job well is a less effective motivator than intrinsic interest in the job. It's that the incentive can actually do substantial damage by eroding that interest. And the more a task involves creativity, the more a manager must take care in handing out bonuses and praise. All else being equal, concentrating on the score is probably an *obstacle* to improved performance in the long run, at least for tasks more complicated than licking envelopes.

Up to this point in the discussion, though, my differences with Peters are probably more a matter of emphasis than of substance. I agree that workers ought to be recognized more for their efforts, and he agrees that rewards can stifle innovation. But we part company, and I think Peters parts company with the data as well, on the question of competition. As I tried to show in an earlier column ("No Contest," November 1987), the best amount of competition in a company—or anywhere else, for that matter— is none at all.

Even though it's well supported by the evidence, this fact flies in the face of everything we were raised to believe. It's hard to accept the painful truth that we are all made losers by the race to win, that excellence has nothing to do with beating others, that any win/lose arrangement not only is psychologically destructive and ruinous to relationships, but also inherently counterproductive.

A close reading of Peters's examples show that the wonderful results he cites were not really a result of competition at all. Is social comparison or learning by observing useful? In moderation, yes. But benefiting from others' example isn't at all the same thing as trying to defeat them. Does the Toyota-General Motors collaboration seem to be successful? If so, it's because of the employee involvement Peters describes. I'd be willing to bet that the workers (and their productivity) are thriving in *spite* of the additional element of group competition, not because of it.

It baffles me that someone with Tom Peters's expertise would help perpetuate the myth that "we have far more to fear from too little than from too much competition." What we have to fear is too little attention to quality, and competition is to quality, as sugar is to teeth. Its effect on self-esteem is similar.

The research to back this up (which I review in my book, *No Contest: The Case Against Competition*) is so persuasive that I'd say the single most damaging mistake a company can make in devising an incentive plan is to set it up competitively. If a bonus is to be made available to employees, any

263
■

individual (or, better yet, any team) that reaches a certain level of performance should receive that bonus. A contest sets us against one another, so that my success makes yours less likely. In reality, we have a great deal to fear from too much competition, and any amount is too much.

Overcome Customer Disappointment

*"It is easy to smile
   when everything's fine
And life flows along like a song.
But, the man worthwhile
Is the man with a smile
When everything goes dead wrong."*

So goes an old childhood poem. And so, too, goes service. The true test of service wisdom is taken when service falters and the customer is left with disappointment or anger.

This book would not be complete without a segment on service recovery. Recovery is the term we use to identify the efforts made by a service provider to get the injured customer back to normal again. That the word calls to mind the medical field is not accidental. Like medical recovery, all corrections of the customer's negative perception of service require compensating efforts to right the condition—that is, to heal the customer's wounded feelings.

Service recovery is not new. Most of us have early memories of the neighborly merchant who threw in a few extras because of a complaint about the last purchase of apples, beans, carrots, or whatever. Service manners, while unfortunately too rare, are by no means novel. What *is* new is the use of recovery as a part of the strategic service focus of a service provider. The proliferation of service guarantees—once offered only by companies the likes of Sears Roebuck, Rolls-Royce, and L.L. Bean—is indicative of the new status of recovery in

265
■

the service world. The worked-out-in-advance approach to such common breakdown experiences as late pizza deliveries and over-booked airlines telegraph the message that effective recovery is now part and parcel of effective service.

Earlier in this book, we described how customers evaluate service on the basis of how closely their experience in being served matched their expectations. When experience falls short of expectations, the customer immediately has recovery expectations—and from a one-down position. The wise service provider not only tries to understand those expectations but seeks ways to respond that acknowledge that the customer is watching the response from a one-down position.

Falling short of the customer's recovery expectations is like injuring the customer twice. And, since the customer is already aggrieved, simply responding in the way you should have in the first place rarely puts that customer "back to normal." At a minimum, it takes extra care plus acknowledged regret.

We have chosen three articles that offer in-depth views of the issues related to service recovery. The first is one we wrote for the October 1987 issue of *Management Review*. This particular issue of the *Review* was devoted predominantly to service management and contains the Stew Leonard article presented earlier in this book.

Our article, "Service Breakdown: The Road to Recovery," sets up the major issues in effective service recovery, then outlines components the customer must experience in order to return to normal. A key point in the piece is that customers generally experience service breakdown in one of two ways: They are annoyed, or they are victimized. Annoyance is the rather mild form of disappointment caused when service falls somewhat short of the customer's expectations. Victimization, on the other hand, is caused by a major service failure that leaves the customer feeling angered, frightened, or both. The "decibel level" on the customer's emotions dictates what is required for a satisfactory recovery response on the part of the service provider.

The second article, "The Power of Unconditional Service Guarantees" by Christopher W.L. Hart, appeared in the July-August 1988 issue of *Harvard Business Review*. This reading focuses on the growing practice of applying the Sears/L.L.-Bean-type product guarantee to the world of intangible services. Hart offers clear standards for effective service guarantees: 1) unconditional, 2) easy to understand and communicate, 3) meaningful, 4) easy (and painless) to invoke, and 5) easy and quick to collect on. Equally helpful are Hart's suggestions of when inclusion of a service guarantee would add value to a particular service.

Finally, we included an upbeat article from the Winter 1987 issue of *The Quality Review* titled "Setting Priorities for Satisfaction Improvement" (originally appeared as "I Can't Get No Satisfaction"). Authors John Goodman, Arlene Malech, and Theodore Marra, all TARP professionals, summarize some of the research they conducted in 1979 (and updated in 1986) on complaint handling in the United States. Basic to all of TARP's work is the belief that the quickest route to effective recovery is to find ways to get the customer to complain. The resulting feedback provides valuable diagnostic data for service-delivery-system improvement. Customers, for instance, who register complaints report higher satisfaction with service quality than do non-complainers, even if the objects of the formers' complaints are not resolved.

Another key dimension of the TARP approach to effective service management is the use of market-damage studies. Market damage occurs when the customer is unhappy enough not to repurchase or recommend the product. Market damage involves isolating those areas where customers register major that dissatisfaction, calculating the economic impact of dissatisfaction, and then determining the cost-gain ratio of correcting the problem. "Confirmation to top management that 'for each month you do not re-engineer this system, it is costing you $800,000,' " say the authors, "can improve service quality in areas that otherwise might be overlooked."

SERVICE BREAKDOWN—THE ROAD TO RECOVERY

Chip R. Bell and Ron Zemke

> *"You can never find a salesperson when you need one."*
> *"Take a number and be seated."*
> *"What do you mean it can't be fixed?"*
> *"We'll have to send it back to the factory."*

The sound of service breakdown is an all too familiar clatter. It happens every time our experience of service falls painfully short of expectations. The "never-wear-out jeans" wear out; the waitress moves in slow motion; the flight is late again; the laundry cracks a shirt button; the phone goes dead; and we feel the dissonance. While none of us expects service to be always perfect, it seems mediocrity has become the norm.

The winners among service companies, those with the almost mythical reputations, manage the design and deployment of service with laser-like focus on the details. They work as hard at recovery when things go wrong as they work to make things go well the first time out. The Disney-Marriott-American Express formula for success often makes service delivery an art form because of the obsession these organizations have for details, details, details.

"God is in the details," said European architect Mies van der Rohe. And when those service details are managed in perfect sync with consumers' desires, they—and we—walk away feeling a little blessed by the experience.

To understand recovery we first must understand how the customer experiences service. The value received in either case is a function of how close the customers' experiences match their expectations both of *process* and *outcome*. The key word is expectation. Customers' feelings of satisfaction—that "I-got-my-money's-worth" experience—start with their expectations about what getting service should be like, plus the expectation of the final outcome. If the meal was great, but the customer had to go through hell to get it, the customer is left with a bittersweet feeling which nets to a negative. Quality service requires managing the process *and* the outcome.

WHAT IS SATISFACTION?

If customers' experiences exactly match their expectations, they are generally invisible, unnoticed, and essentially taken for granted, customers label such experiences as "satisfaction"—"I got what I expected; no more, no less"—unless, of course, the deliverer takes extra steps to highlight some feature of the service. The print shop that puts a bright red "On Time" sticker on a box ready to be picked up makes visible what might otherwise be taken for granted.

Customer satisfaction is a fickle label. In theory it is the point at which experience exactly matches expectation. However, since the deliverer learns of annoyance through customer feedback and since only 4% of the annoyed customers register that feedback, gauging satisfaction is extraordinarily difficult.

If the experience (process or outcome) deviates from expectation, it is noticed and remembered. Less than expected, the customer is annoyed; more than expected, the customer is pleased. On either side of the neutral zone is a memorable experience. Successful organizations manage to create more memories of delight than disdain. Winning enterprises also view customer satisfaction (no more, no less) as "not good enough."

Clearly, all of us expect deliverers of service to try their best to meet our needs and make things right when foul-ups occur. We call the latter "recovery," and all consumers have recovery expectations they want organizations to meet.

The word "recovery" has been chosen carefully—it means "to return to a normal state; to make whole again." Though many organizations have service departments established to fix what breaks, the deliberate management of the recovery is typically a reactive, damage-minimizing function. We suggest recovery can be as proactively managed for positive outcomes as can service in general.

THE ESSENCE OF BREAKDOWN AND RECOVERY

The key to analyzing service breakdowns begins with understanding how customers experience them. We view breakdown as having at least two distinct levels. Level one we label "annoyance"—the minor feelings of irritation we get when experience falls slightly short of what we hoped for. The second level we label "victimization"—a major feeling of ire, frustration, or "pain." Recovery takes a different form depending on whether the customer feels annoyed or victimized.

The difference between annoyance and victimization is best described through specific examples.

Annoyed: Your flight is one hour late.

Victimized: Your flight is one hour late, causing you to miss the last connection to your destination, resulting in an unplanned overnight stay.

Annoyed: One of your two phones is out of service.

Victimized: Your only phone is out of service and you have a heart condition.

Annoyed: You work in an office downtown and your car breaks down, causing you to have to get a ride to work with a neighbor.

Victimized: You are a traveling salesperson and the car breaks down, causing you to miss several previously scheduled calls on very short notice.

Annoyed: Your car breaks down and you take it to a repair shop.

Victimized: Your car breaks down and you take to a repair shop for the third time for the same problem.

Central to the difference between annoyance and victimization is the way the customer feels about the breakdown. Breakdowns leaving the customer dependant, rather than inconvenienced, and angry, rather than irritated, are victim-level breakdowns. All breakdowns require the deliverer to jump through a few hoops to get the customer back to neutral. More hoops are required for victims to recover.

A RECIPE FOR RECOVERY
At least five ingredients are contained in the recipe for recovery. The first two are imperative for annoyed customers; *all five* are required for the victimized.

1. *Apology.* It might seem like a blinding glimpse of the obvious, but recovery absolutely demands some acknowledgement of error immediately following a breakdown in service.

The flight from Denver to Dallas was more than an hour late taking off. The flight attendant made the FAA speech and the pilot gave the altitude. No mention was made of the lateness. As the plane landed in Dallas, one passenger was over heard remarking, "This airline is so accustomed to being late, they must think it's normal."

Apology is most powerful when delivered in the first person. The corporate "We're sorry" lacks the sincerity and authenticity which comes with a *person* taking responsibility for the infraction—someone acknowledging on behalf of the organization that the customer was mistreated.

2. *Urgent Reinstatement.* As earlier described, the outcome and the process of service delivery must be managed. While a sense of urgency in most customer service is important, it has a new, more critical meaning when applied to recovery.

In some ways, actual reinstatement may not always be required. Sometimes, gallant intent is sufficient. The customer must perceive the deliverer is doing the absolute best job possible to get things back to status quo. There *are* points for good intentions and customer-driven effort. Part of the power of this ingredient is the *demonstration* that the deliverer has the customer's interests at heart.

A flight from Hagerstown to Pittsburgh was delayed for 40 minutes due to a crack in the runway caused by ice. As the pilot told the passengers, they groaned, "this is typical of Mayday Airlines." But every seven or eight minutes the pilot came back on the intercom to describe progress and to predict take-off time. By the fourth announcement, passengers were complimenting the pilot for his "can-do" attitude. As the plane left the repaired runway, passengers applauded.

If the customer is annoyed, the ingredients for recovery are much simpler. Apology and urgent reinstatement, done well, are likely to return the customer to normal. If the customer is victimized, recovery is more complex, and the following three ingredients must be added to the recipe.

3. *Empathy.* Expressing compassion may be the mother lode of all service gold. It is an expression which honors the view that "You are not eligible to change my view or feeling until you first demonstrate that you understand my view or feeling." It is the communication of "I know how you must feel," "I care about you," "I can relate to your misfortune," "I can identify with what has happened." In its highest form, the customer feels heard, affirmed, cared about.

A phone company installed an 800 number for calls about repair for the entire state. Focus group interviews with repair customers revealed great irritation with the system. "How can someone in Chicago understand my situation in Peoria?" The issue seemed to have more to do with perceived empathy than distance.

Sincere expressions of empathy are quite different from expressions of sympathy. Sympathy occurs when one shares another's pain. Empathy is showing compassion for the person in pain without feeling personally in pain—a shoulder to cry on, a source of strength. There are great risks with sympathy: The helper joins the helpee, rather than the other way around. Sympathy is helping someone feel better about being weak; empathy is the kind of understanding that helps someone feel strong. Those who resort to sympathy are themselves one down and add to the "one-downess" of the person in pain. It proves the axiom "Misery loves company."

A Hawaiian woman who spoke limited English was enroute to Roanoke, Virginia, to visit her daughter. After 6000 miles, 18 hours and four stops, she got to Charlotte, only to learn that the Roanoke Airport was closed due to snow and ice. On her last leg of the journey and now only one hour from her destination, she was informed she would have to stay the night in Charlotte. A Piedmont Airlines gate attendant made all arrangements, called her daughter for her, then sat with her for a while, asking the woman questions about Hawaii and her daughter. As tears welled up in the woman's eyes, the gate attendant spontaneously embraced the woman and said, "You've come so far, I know you really want to see her." The woman smiled through her tears and said, "I'm glad you are my friend."

The apology says to the victimized customer, "It matters there was a breakdown"; empathy says, "It matters that YOU were hurt in the process." A wise service expert said, "When service fails, first treat the person, then the problem."

4. *Symbolic Atonement.* The fourth ingredient in the recovery recipe for dealing with victimized customers is some symbol of atonement. At its most basic level, it is a gesture that clearly says, "We want to make it up to you." Key is the symbol or gesture. Atonement is not a pound of flesh, it is a token of sorrow. Atonement is the "It's on us," "Free drink," "No charge," "Here's a coupon worth . . . " type demonstration.

A major phone company had a practice of encouraging customers to take their phones to a shopping center store to have them tested. This made repairs more efficient for the company and potentially less expensive for the customer than home repairs. However, if the instrument checked out as error-free at the phone store, the customer was asked to go to a wall phone in the store and again call for a repair person to schedule a home-repair visit. Customers perceived this practice as saying, "We, the phone company, have now determined that you are not at fault—your telephone instrument is okay. Therefore, it is probably our fault that you have phone problems. That is why you should be further inconvenienced by having to call our repair center and explain our error one more time."

5. *Follow-up.* This ingredient may or may not be critical to quality customer service. The data is mixed. What is unequivocal is the importance of follow-up if the customer is a victim. Not only does it provide a sense of closure, it serves to affirm the authenticity of "We care," and provides a means for feedback.

Follow-up also can be a tool to promote the self-esteem of the service deliverer if properly managed. The service person who takes a beating when things go wrong can "walk away" with a good feeling as a result of the follow-up. "We may have messed up, but things are okay now."

A hotel guest discovered his television was not working as he flipped it on to watch the morning news. As he left for an all-day meeting, he muttered to the house-cleaning woman in the hall that his TV was not working. That evening, he returned prepared to call the hotel engineer. As he entered his room, he noticed a hand written note from the engineer indicating the TV had been repaired. Later that evening the engineer called to find out how the television was working.

MANAGING RECOVERY

It would be oversimplifying a complex process if you concluded that all that was required for recovery was sincerely saying you were sorry, being empathetic, working hard to get things back to normal, showing a gesture of regret, and following up. The business of service management entails a series of systems and processes carefully engineered to produce outcomes consistent with the recipe of recovery. It requires a brand of service leadership which goes beyond pat answers, cue-card responses, and wall banners.

Managing superior recovery entails a commitment to service quality. In general, it is part of a "Let-no-stone-go-unturned" commitment that must exist if service is to be an important strategic force. Recovery is a part of an overall orientation toward identifying and responding to customer needs and expectations. As an executive of a major hospitality company said, "If service is not our top concern day to day, correcting service problems will not happen with much zeal and gusto."

Key to managing superior recovery is giving service delivery people the freedom to make decisions which favor the customer. The fast-food chain example described clearly reflected a service (rather than bureaucratic) orientation. The front line clerk felt empowered to give out a large order of fries. Never mind that the register did not quite match the potato inventory. The deliverer took the license to make a judgment call which helped make the customer feel good again.

Our economy has become a service economy—one more characterized as a performer of service than producer of product. The winning enterprises and the successful departments are those that create distinctive service through their demonstration of commitment, even in those times when one's best intentions fall short of the customer's hopes. The most memorable recoveries are those in which that demonstration far exceeds customer expectations.

THE POWER OF UNCONDITIONAL SERVICE GUARANTEES

Christopher W.L. Hart

When you buy a car, a camera, or a toaster oven, you receive a warranty, a guarantee that the product will work. How often do you receive a warranty for auto repair, wedding photography, or a catered dinner? Virtually never. Yet it is here, in buying services, that the assurance of a guarantee would presumably count most.

Many business executives believe that, by definition, services simply can't be guaranteed. Services are generally delivered by human beings, who are known to be less predictable than machines, and they are usually produced at the same time they are consumed. It is one thing to guarantee a camera, which can be inspected before a customer sets eyes on it and which can be returned to the factory for repairs. But how can you pre-inspect a car tune-up or send an unsuccessful legal argument or bad haircut back for repair? Obviously you can't.

But that doesn't mean customer satisfaction can't be guaranteed. Consider the guarantee offered by "Bugs" Burger Bug Killers (BBBK), a Miami-based pest-extermination company that is owned by S.C. Johnson & Son.

Most of BBBK's competitors claim that they will reduce pests to "acceptable levels;" BBBK promises to eliminate them entirely. Its service guarantee to hotel and restaurant clients promises:

- You don't owe one penny until all pests on your premises have been eradicated.
- If you are ever dissatisfied with BBBK's service, you will receive a refund for up to 12 months of the company's services—plus fees for another exterminator of your choice for the next year.
- If a guest spots a pest on your premises, BBBK will pay for the guest's meal or room, send a letter of apology, and pay for a future meal or stay.
- If your facility is closed down due to the presence of roaches or rodents, BBBK will pay any fines, as well as all lost profits, plus $5,000.

In short, BBBK says, "If we don't satisfy you 100%, we don't take your money."

How successful is this guarantee? The company, which operates throughout the United States, charges up to ten times more than its competitors and yet has a disproportionately high market share in its operating areas. Its service quality is so outstanding that the company rarely needs to make good on its guarantee (in 1986 it paid out only $120,000 on sales of $33 million—just enough to prove that its promises aren't empty ones).

A main reason that the "Bugs" Burger guarantee is a strong model for the service industry is that its founder, Al Burger, began with the concept of the unconditional guarantee and worked backward, designing his entire organization to support the no-pests guarantee—in short, he started with a vision of error-free service. In this article, I will explain why the service guarantee can help your organization institutionalize superlative performance.

WHAT A GOOD SERVICE GUARANTEE IS
Would you be willing to offer a guarantee of 100% customer satisfaction— to pay your dissatisfied customer to use a competitor's service, for example? Or do you believe that promising error-free service is a crazy idea?

Not only is it not crazy, but committing to error-free service can help force a company to provide it. It's a little like skiing. You've got to lean over your skis as you go down the hill, as if willing yourself to fall. But if you edge properly, you don't fall or plunge wildly, you gain control while you pick up speed.

Similarly, a strong service guarantee that puts the customer first doesn't necessarily lead to chaos and failure. If designed and implemented properly, it enables you to get control over your organization—with clear goals and an information network that gives you the data you need to improve performance. BBBK and other service companies show that a service guarantee is not only possible—it's a boon to performance and profits and can be a vehicle to market dominance.

Most existing service guarantees don't really do the job: they are limited in scope and difficult to use. Lufthansa guarantees that its customers will make their connecting flights if there are no delays due to weather or air-traffic control problems. Yet these two factors cause fully 95% of all flight delays. Bank of America will refund up to six months of checking-account fees if a customer is dissatisfied with any aspect of its checking-account service. However, the customer must close the account to collect the modest $5 or $6 per month fee. This guarantee won't win any prizes for fostering repeat business—a primary objective of a good guarantee.

A service guarantee loses power in direct proportion to the number of conditions it contains. How effective is a restaurant's guarantee of prompt service except when it's busy? A housing inspector's guarantee to identify all potential problems in a house except for those not readily apparent? Squaw Valley in California guarantees "your money back" to any skier who has to wait more than ten minutes in a lift line. But it's not that easy: the skier must first pay $1 and register at the lodge as a beginner, intermediate, or expert; the guarantee is operative only if all lifts at the skier's level exceed the ten minutes in any half-hour period; and skiers must check with a "ski hostess" at the end of the day to "win" a refund. A Squaw Valley spokesperson said the resort had made just one payout under the guarantee in a year and a half. No wonder!

What is a good service guarantee? It is 1. unconditional, 2. easy to understand and communicate, 3. meaningful, 4. easy (and painless) to invoke, and 5. easy and quick to collect on.

Unconditional. The best service guarantee promises customer satisfaction unconditionally, without exceptions. Like that of L.L. Bean, the Freeport, Maine retail store and mail-order house: "100% satisfaction in every way ..." An L.L. Bean customer can return a product at any time and get, at his or her option, a replacement, a refund, or a credit. Reputedly, if a customer returns a pair of L.L. Bean boots after ten years, the company will replace them with new boots and no questions. Talk about customer assurance! Customers shouldn't need a lawyer to explain the "ifs, and, and buts" of a guarantee—because ideally there shouldn't be any conditions; a customer is either satisfied or not.

If a company cannot guarantee all elements of its service unconditionally, it should unconditionally guarantee the elements that it can control. Lufthansa cannot promise on-time arrival, for example, but it could guarantee that passengers will be satisfied with its airport waiting areas, its service on the ground and in the air and its food quality—or simply guarantee overall satisfaction.

Easy to Understand and Communicate. A guarantee should be written in simple, concise language that pinpoints the promise. Customers then know precisely what they can expect and employees know precisely what's expected of them. "Five-minute" lunch service, rather than "prompt" service, creates clear expectations, as does "no pests," rather than "pest control."

Meaningful. A good service guarantee is meaningful in two respects. First, it guarantees those aspects of your service that are important to your customers. It may be speedy delivery. Bennigan's, a restaurant chain, promises 15-minute service (or you get a free meal) at lunch, when many customers are in a hurry to get back to the office, but not at dinner, when fast service is not considered a priority to most patrons.

In other cases, price may be the most important element, especially with relatively undifferentiated commodities like rental cars or commercial air travel. By promising the lowest prices in town, stereo shops assuage customers' fears that if they don't go to every outlet in the area they'll pay more than they ought to.

Second, a good guarantee is meaningful financially; it calls for a significant payout when the promise is not kept. What should it be—a full refund? An offer of free service the next time? A trip to Monte Carlo? The answer depends on factors like the cost of the service, the seriousness of the failure, and customers' perception of what's fair. A money-back payout should be large enough to give customers an incentive to invoke the guarantee if dissatisfied. The adage, "Let the punishment fit the crime" is an appropriate guide. At one point, Domino's Pizza (which is based in Ann Arbor, Michigan but operates world-wide) promised "delivery within 30 minutes or the pizza is free." Management found that customers considered this too generous; they felt uncomfortable accepting a free pizza for a mere 5- or 15-minute delay and didn't always take advantage of the guarantee. Consequently, Domino's adjusted its guarantee to "delivery within 30 minutes or $3 off," and customers appear to consider this commitment reasonable.

Easy to Invoke. A customer who is already dissatisfied should not have to jump through hoops to invoke a guarantee; the dissatisfaction is only exacerbated when the customer has to talk to three different people, fill out five forms, go to a different location, make two telephone calls, send in written proof of purchase with a full description of the events, wait for a written reply, go somewhere else to see someone to verify all the preceding facts, and so on.

Traveler's Advantage—a division of CUC International—has, in principle, a great idea: to guarantee the lowest price on the accommodations it books.

But to invoke the guarantee, customers must prove the lower competing price by booking with another agency. That's unpleasant work. Cititravel, a subsidiary of Citicorp, has a better approach. A customer who knows of a lower price can call a toll-free number and speak with an agent, as I did recently. The agent told me that if I didn't have proof of the lower fare, she'd check competing airfares on her computer screen. If the lower fare was there, I'd get that price. If not, she would call the competing airline. If the price was confirmed, she said, "We'll refund your money so fast, you won't believe it—because we want you to be our customer." That's the right attitude if you're offering a guarantee.

Similarly, customers should not be made to feel guilty about invoking the guarantee—no questioning, no raised eyebrows, or "Why me, Lord?" looks. A company should encourage unhappy customers to invoke its guarantee, not put up roadblocks to keep them from speaking up.

Easy to Collect. Customers shouldn't have to work hard to collect a payout, either. The procedure should be easy and equally important, quick—on the spot, if possible. Dissatisfaction with a Manpower temporary worker, for instance, results in an immediate credit to your bill.

What you should not do in your guarantee: don't promise something your customers already expect; don't shroud a guarantee in so many conditions that it loses its point; and don't offer a guarantee so mild that it is never invoked. A guarantee that is essentially risk free to the company will be of little or no value to your customers—and may be a joke to your employees.

WHY A SERVICE GUARANTEE WORKS
A guarantee is a powerful tool—both for marketing service quality and for achieving it—for five reasons.

First, it pushes the entire company to focus on customers' definition of good service—not on executives' assumptions. Second, it sets clear performance standards, which boost employee performance and morale. Third, it generates reliable data (through payouts) when performance is poor. Fourth, it forces an organization to examine its entire service-delivery system for possible failure points. Last, it builds customer loyalty, sales, and market share.

A guarantee forces you to focus on customers. Knowing what customers want is the sine qua non in offering a service guarantee. A company has to identify its target customers' expectations about the elements of the service and the importance they attach to each. Lacking this knowledge of customer needs, a company that wants to guarantee its service may very well guarantee the wrong things.

British Airways conducted a market study and found that its passengers judge its customer services on four dimensions:[1]

1. Care and concern (employees' friendliness, courtesy, and warmth).
2. Initiative (employees' ability and willingness to jockey the system on the customer's behalf).
3. Problem solving (figuring out solutions to customer problems, whether unusual or routine—like multiflight airline tickets).
4. Recovery (going the extra yard, when things go wrong, to handle a particular problem—which includes the simple but often overlooked step of delivering an apology).

British Airways managers confessed that they hadn't even thought about the second and fourth categories. Worse, they realized that if they hadn't understood these important dimensions of customer service, how much thought could their employees be giving to them?

A guarantee sets clear standards. A specific, unambiguous service guarantee sets standards for your organization. It tells employees what the company stands for. BBBK stands for pest elimination, not pest control; Federal Express stands for "absolutely, positively by 10:30 A.M.," not "sometime tomorrow, probably." And it forces the company to define each employee's role and responsibilities in delivering the service. Salespeople, for example, know precisely what their companies can deliver and can represent that accurately—the opposite of the common situation in which salespeople promise the moon and customers get only dirt.

This clarity and sense of identity have the added advantage of creating employee team spirit and pride. Mitchell Fromstein, president and CEO of Manpower says, "At one point, we wondered what the marketing impact would be if we dropped our guarantee. We figured that our accounts were well aware of the guarantee and that it might not have much marketing power anymore. Our employees' reaction was fierce—and it had a lot less to do with marketing than with the pride they take in their work. They said, 'The guarantee is proof that we're a great company. We're willing to tell our customers that if they don't like our service for any reason, it's our fault, not theirs, and we'll make it right.' I realized then that the guarantee is far more than a simple piece of paper that puts customers at ease. It really sets the tone, externally and, perhaps more important, internally, for our commitment to our customers and workers."

A payout that creates financial pain when errors occur is also a powerful statement, to employees and customers alike, that management demands customer satisfaction. A significant payout ensures that both middle and upper management will take the service guarantee seriously; it provides a strong incentive to take every step necessary to deliver. A manager who must bear the full cost of mistakes has ample incentive to figure out how to prevent them from happening.

A guarantee generates feedback. A guarantee creates the goal; it defines what you must do to satisfy your customers. Next, you need to know when you go wrong. A guarantee forces you to create a system for discovering errors—which the Japanese call "golden nuggets" because they're opportunities to learn.

Arguably the greatest ailment afflicting service companies is a lack of decent systems for generating and acting on customer data. Dissatisfied service customers have little incentive to complain on their own, far less so than unhappy product owners do. Many elements of a service are intangible, so consumers who receive poor service are often left with no evidence to support their complaints. (The customer believes the waiter was rude; perhaps the waiter will deny it.) Second, without the equivalent of a product warranty, customers don't know their rights. (Is 15 minutes too long to wait for a restaurant meal? 30 minutes?) Third, there is often no one to complain to—at least no one who looks capable of solving the problem. Often, complaining directly to the person who is rendering poor service will only make things worse.

Customer comment cards have traditionally been the most common method of gathering customer feedback on a company's operations, but they, too, are inadequate for collecting valid, reliable error data. In the first place, they are an impersonal form of communication and are usually short (to maximize the response rate). Why bother, people think, to cram the details of a bad experience onto a printed survey form with a handful of "excellent-good-fair: check-off boxes? Few aggrieved customers believe that completing a comment card will resolve their problems. There fore, only a few customers—usually the most satisfied and dissatisfied—provide feedback through such forms, and fewer still provide meaningful feedback. As a broad gauge of customer sentiment, cards and surveys are useful, but for specific information about customer problems and operational weaknesses, they simply don't fill the bill.

Service companies thus have a hard time collecting error data. Less information on mistakes means fewer opportunities to improve, ultimately resulting in more service errors and more customer dissatisfaction—a cycle that management is often unaware of. A guarantee attacks this malady by giving consumers an incentive and a vehicle for bringing their grievances to management's attention.

Manpower uses its guarantee to glean error data in addition to allaying customer worries about suing an unknown quantity (the temporary worker.) Every customer who employs a Manpower temporary worker is called the first day of a one-day assignment or the second day of a longer assignment to check on the worker's performance. A dissatisfied customer doesn't pay—period. (Manpower pays the worker, however; it assumes complete responsibility for the quality of its service.) The company uses its error data to improve both its work force and its proprietary skills-testing software and skills data base—major elements in its ability to match worker skills to customer requirements. The information Manpower obtains before and after hiring enables its to offer its guarantee with confidence.

A guarantee forces you to understand why you fail. In developing a guarantee, managers must ask questions like these: What failure points exist in the system? If failure points can be identified, can their origins be traced—and overcome? A company that wants to promise timely service delivery, for example, must first understand its operation's capability and the factors limiting that capability. Many service executives, lacking understanding of such basic issues as system throughput time, capacity, and process flow, tend to blame workers, customers, or anything but the service-delivery process.

Even if workers are a problem, managers can do several things to "fix" the organization so that it can support a guarantee—such as design better recruiting, hiring, and training processes. The pest-control industry has historically suffered from unmotivated personnel and high turnover. Al Burger overcame the status quo by offering higher than average pay (attracting a higher caliber of job candidate), using a vigorous screening program (making those hired feel like members of a select group), training all workers for six months, and keeping them motivated by giving them a great deal or autonomy and lots of recognition.

Some managers may be unwilling to pay for an internal service-delivery capability that is above the industry average. Fine. They will never have better than average organizations, either, and they will therefore never be able to develop the kind of competitive advantage that flows from a good service guarantee.

A guarantee builds marketing muscle. Perhaps the most obvious reason for offering a strong service guarantee is its ability to boost marketing: it encourages consumers to buy a service by reducing the risk of the purchase decision, and it generates more sales to existing customers by enhancing loyalty. In the last ten years, Manpower's revenues have mushroomed from $400 million to $4 billion. That's marketing impact.

Keeping most of your customers and getting positive word of mouth, though desirable in any business, are particularly important for service companies. The net present value of sales forgone from lost customers—in other words, the cost of customer dissatisfaction—is enormous. in this respect, it's fair to say that many service companies' biggest competitors are themselves. They frequently spend huge amounts of money to attract new customers without ever figuring out how to provide the consistent service they promise to their existing customers. If customers aren't satisfied, the marketing money has been poured down the drain and may even engender further ill will. (See the sidebar, "Maximizing Marketing Impact.")

A guarantee will only work, of course, if you start with commitment to the customer. If your aim is to minimize the guarantee's impact on your organization but to maximize its marketing punch, you won't succeed. In the long run, you will nullify the guarantee's potential impact on customers, and your marketing dollars will go down the drain.

Phil Bressler, owner of 18 Domino's Pizza franchises in the Baltimore, Maryland area, demonstrates the right commitment to customers. He got upset the time his company recorded its highest monthly earning ever because, he correctly figured, the profits had come from money that should have been paid out on the Domino's guarantee of "delivery within 30 minutes or $3 off." Bressler's unit managers, who have bottom-line responsibility, had pumped up their short-term profits by failing to honor the guarantee consistently. Bressler is convinced that money spent on guarantees is an investment in customer satisfaction and loyalty. He also recognizes that the guarantee is the best way to identify weak operations, and that guarantees not acted on are data not collect.

Compare Bressler's attitude with that of an owner of several nationally franchised motels. His guarantee promises that the company will do "everything possible" to remedy a customer's problem; if the problem cannot be resolved, the customer stays for free. He brags that he's paid, on average, refunds for only two room guarantees per motel per year—a minuscule percentage of room sales. "If my managers are doing their jobs, I don't have to pay out for the guarantee," he says, "If I do have to pay out, my managers are not doing their jobs, and I get rid of them."

Clearly, more than two guests of any hotel are likely to be dissatisfied over the course of a year. By seeking to limit payouts rather than hear complaints, this owner is undoubtedly blowing countless opportunities to create loyal customers out of disgruntled ones. He is also losing rich information about which of his motels need improvement and why, information that can most easily be obtained from customer complaints. You have to wonder why he offers a guarantee at all, since he completely misses the point.

Of course, guarantees may not be effective or practicable for all service firms. Four Seasons Hotels, for example, could probably not get much marketing or operational mileage from a guarantee. With its strong internal vision of absolute customer satisfaction, the company has developed an outstanding service-delivery system and a reputation to match. Thus it already has an implicit guarantee. To advertise the obvious would produce little gain and might actually be perceived as incongruent with the company's prestigious image.

A crucial element in Four Season's service strategy is instilling in all employees a mission of absolute customer satisfaction and empowering them to do whatever is necessary if customer problems do occur. For example, Four Season's Washington hotel was once asked by the State Department to make room for a foreign dignitary. Already booked to capacity, Four Seasons had to tell four other customers with reservations that they could not be accommodated. However, the hotel immediately found rooms for them at another first-class hotel, while assuring them they would remain registered at the Four Seasons (so that any messages they received would be taken and sent to the other hotel). When rooms became available, the customers were driven back to the Four Season by limousine. Four Seasons also paid for their rooms at the other hotel. It was the equivalent of a full money-back guarantee, and more.

Does this mean that every company that performs at the level of a Four Seasons need not offer a service guarantee? Could Federal Express, for example, drop its "absolutely, positively" assurance with little or no effect? Probably not. its guarantee is such a part of its image that dropping the guarantee would hurt it.

In general, organizations that meet the following test probably have little to gain by offering a service guarantee: the company is perceived by the market to be the quality leader in its industry; every employee is inculcated with the "absolute customer satisfaction' philosophy; employees are empowered to take whatever corrective action is necessary to handle complaints; errors are few; and a stated guarantee would be at odds with the company's image.

It is probably unnecessary to point out that few service companies meet these tests.

External Variables. Service guarantees may also be impractical where customer satisfaction is influenced strongly by external forces the service provider can't control. While everybody thinks their businesses are in this fix, most are wrong.

How many variables are truly beyond management's control? Not the work force. Not equipment problems. Not vendor quality. And even businesses subject to "acts of God" (like weather) can control a great deal of their service quality.

BBBK is an example of how one company turned the situation around by analysing the elements of the service-delivery process. By asking, "What obstacles stand in the way of our guaranteeing pest elimination?" Al Burger discovered that clients' poor cleaning and storage practices were one such obstacle. So the company requires customers to maintain sanitary practices and in some cases even make physical changes to their property (like putting in walls). By changing the process, the company could guarantee the outcome.

There may well be uncontrollable factors that create problems. As I noted earlier, such things as flight controllers, airport capacity, and weather limit the extent to which even the finest airline can consistently deliver on-time service. But how employees respond to such externally imposed problems strongly influences customer satisfaction, as British Airways executives learned from their market survey. When things go wrong, will employees go the extra yard to handle the problem? Why couldn't an airline that has refined its problem-handling skills to a science ensure absolute customer satisfaction—uncontrollable variables be damned? How many customers would invoke a guarantee if they understood that the reasons for a problem were completely out of the airline's control—if they were treated with warmth, compassion, and a sense of humor, and if the airline staff communicated with them honestly?

Cheating. Fear of customer cheating is another big hurdle for most service managers considering offering guarantees. When asked why Lufthansa's guarantee required customers to present written proof of purchase, a manager at the airline's U.S. headquarters told me, "If we didn't ask for written proof our customers would cheat us blind."

But experience teaches a different lesson. Sure, there will be cheats—the handful of customers who take advantage of a guarantee to get something for nothing. What they cost the company amounts to very little compared to the benefits derived from a strong guarantee. Says Michael Leven, a hotel industry executive, "Too often management spends its time worrying about the 1% of people who might cheat the company instead of the 99% who don't."

Phil Bressler of Domino's argues that customers cheat only when they feel cheated: "If we charge $8 for a pizza, our customers expect $8 worth of product and service. If we started giving them $7.50 worth of product and service, then they'd start looking for ways to get back that extra 50 cents. Companies create the incentive to cheat, in almost all cases, by cutting costs and not providing value."

Where the potential for false claims is high, a no-questions-asked guarantee may appear to be foolhardy. When Domino's first offered its "delivery within 30 minutes or the pizza is free" guarantee, some college students telephoned orders from hard-to-find locations. The result was free pizza for the students and lost revenue for Domino's. In this environment, the guarantee was problematic because some students perceived it as a game against Domino's. But Bressler takes the view that the revenue thus lost was an investment in the future. "They'll be Domino's customers for life, those kids," he says.

High Costs. Managers are likely to worry about the costs of a service-guarantee program, but for the wrong reasons. Quality "guru" Philip Crosby coined the phrase "quality is free" (in his 1979 book, *Quality Is Free*) to indicate not that quality-improvement efforts cost nothing but that the benefits of quality improvement—fewer errors, higher productivity, more repeat business-outweigh the costs over the long term.

Clearly, a company whose operations are slipshod (or out of control) should not consider offering an unconditional guarantee; the outcome would be either bankruptcy from staggering payouts or an employee revolt stemming from demands to meet standards that are beyond the organization's capability. If your company is like most, however, it's not in that shape;

you will probably only need to buttress operations somewhat. To be sure, an investment of financial and human resources to shore up weak points in the delivery system will likely cause a quick, sharp rise in expenditures.

How sharp an increase depends on several factors: your company's weakness (how far does it have to go to become good?), the nature of the industry, and the strength of your competition, for example. A small restaurant might simply spend more on employee recruiting and training, and perhaps on sponsoring quality circles; a large utility company might need to restructure its entire organization to overcome years of bad habits if it is to delver on a guarantee.

Even though a guarantee carries costs, bear in mind that, as Crosby asserts, a badly performed service also incurs costs—failure costs, which come in many forms, including lost business from disgruntled consumers. In a guarantee program, you shift from spending to mop up failures to spending on preventing failures. And many of those costs are incurred in most organizations anyway (like outlays for staff time spent in planning meetings). It's just that they're spent more productively.

BREAKTHROUGH SERVICE
One great potential of a service guarantee is its ability to change an industry's rules of the game by changing the service-delivery process as competitors conceive it.

BBBK and Federal Express both redefined the meaning of service in their industries, performing at levels that other companies have so far been unable to match. (According to the owner of a competing pest-control company, BBBK "is number one. There is no number two.") By offering breakthrough service, these companies altered the basis of competition in their businesses and put their competitors at a severe disadvantage.

What are the possibilities for replicating their success in other service businesses? Skeptics might claim that BBBK's and Federal Express's success is not widely applicable because they target price-insensitive customers willing to pay for superior service—in short, that these companies are pursing differentiation strategies.

It is true that BBBK's complex preparation, cleaning, and checkup procedures are much more time consuming than those of typical pest-control operators, that the company spends more on pesticides than competitors do, and that its employees are well compensated. And many restaurants and hotels are willing to pay BBBK's higher prices because to them it's ultimately cheaper: the cost of "errors" (guests' spotting roaches or ants) is higher than the cost of error prevention.

But, because of the "quality is free" dictum, breakthrough service does not mean you must become the high-cost producer. Manpower's procedures are not radically more expensive than its competitors'; they're simply better. The company's skills-testing methods and customer-needs diagnoses surely cost less in the long run than a sloppy system. A company that inadequately screens and trains temporary-worker recruits, establishes no detailed customer specifications, and fails to check worker performance loses customers.

Manpower spends heavily on ways to reduce errors further, seeing this spending as an investment that will a. protect its market position; b. reduce time-consuming service errors; and c. reinforce the company's values to employees. Here is the "absolute customer satisfaction" philosophy at work, and whatever cost increase Manpower incurs it makes up in sales volume.

Organizations that figure out how to offer—and deliver—guaranteed, breakthrough service will have tapped into a powerful source of competitive advantage. Doing so is no mean feat, of course, which is precisely why the opportunity to build a competitive advantage exists. Though the task is difficult, it is clearly not impossible, and the service guarantee can play a fundamental role in the process.

MAXIMIZING MARKETING IMPACT

The odds of gaining powerful marketing impact from a service guarantee are in your favor when one or more of the following conditions exists:

The price of the service is high. A bad shoe shine? No big deal. A botched $1,000 car repair is a different story; a guarantee is more effective here.

The customer's ego is on the line. Who wants to be seen after getting a bad haircut?

The customer's expertise with the service is low. When in doubt about a service, a customer will choose one that's covered by a guarantee over those that are not.

The negative consequences of service failure are high. As consumers' expected aggravation, expense, and time lost due to service failure increase, a guarantee gains power. Your computer went down? A computer-repair service with guaranteed response and repair times would be the most logical company to call.

The industry has a bad image for service quality—like pest-control services, security guards, or home repair. A guard company that guarantees to have its posts filled by qualified people would automatically rank high on a list of prospective vendors.

The company depends on frequent customer repurchases. Can it exist on a never-ending stream of new triers (like small service businesses in large markets, or does it have to deal with a finite market? If the market is finite, how close is market saturation? The smaller the size of the potential market of new triers, the more attention management should pay to increasing the loyalty and repurchase rate of existing customers—objectives that a good service guarantee will serve.

The company's business is affected deeply by word of mouth (both positive and negative). Consultants, stockbrokers, restaurants, and resorts are all good examples of services where there are strong incentives to minimize the extent of customer dissatisfaction—and hence, negative word of mouth.

---

1. See British Airways study cited in Karl Albrecht and Ron Zemke, *Service America!* (Homewood, IL, Dow Jones-Irwin, 1985), pp.33-34.

SETTING PRIORITIES FOR SATISFACTION IMPROVEMENT

John Goodman, Arlene Malech,
and Theodore Marra

When is it worthwhile to spend money to improve quality? What is a 5 percent improvement in quality worth to the corporate bottom line? Is one aspect of quality more important than another?

While most companies pride themselves on providing their customers with quality products, few have systematically obtained answers to these questions. Traditionally, the answers have been derived using managerial instinct and intuition. However, research conducted by TARP (Technical Assistance Research Programs) has resulted in a methodology that enables a company to quantify the impact of quality improvements on corporate profits.

The basis of this new methodology is the integration of customer repurchase behavior into quality cost benefit calculations. The analysis is based on the following premises:

- Poor quality is a result not only of manufacturing but also of product design, marketing, and customer education.
- Quality is an intervening variable between the promises made by marketing and the fulfillment of customer expectations measured by satisfaction.
- The best measure of quality is its impact on customer loyalty and purchase of other company products.

Research has shown that, regardless of the industry involved, a substantial segment of customers experience problems with the products and services they purchase. It is this problem experience that initially results in customer dissatisfaction. When defining problems, quality analysts tend to identify problems in manufacturing or accuracy. However, TARP has found that a customer's dissatisfaction with a product typically stems from problems that are employee based, company based, and/or customer based.

Employee-based problems result from the failure of individual employees to follow established policy or procedure. This type of failure could, for instance, lead to a defect in manufacturing, a missing piece in packaging, a billing error, or a misrepresentation of a service or product.

The result of these transactions is likely to be a dissatisfied customer. Furthermore, the customer is apt to translate the dissatisfaction with the service received into a perception of lowered product quality.

Company-based problems are caused by a variety of factors and, in fact, may cause the major portion of dissatisfaction. Product specifications that build unpleasant surprises into the customer experience create company-based problems. For instance, products that are too complex to assemble or operate can lead customers to discard or replace them. TARP has recently found this reflected in connection with cordless telephones, office copiers, and home security systems.

Additionally, marketing often accounts for a large percentage of company-based problems. Customer dissatisfaction results when product capabilities are overpromised, when cautionary notes are not provided, and/or when a product made according to specifications does not fulfill the customer's reasonable expectations. When there is a discrepancy between expectations and reality, the customer becomes just as dissatisfied as if the product were defective.

The final cause of dissatisfaction is the *customer-based problem*. This type of problem encompasses unreasonable customer expectations, customer errors, and customer failure to follow company procedures due to a lack of information/education. To the extent that the customer is unpleasantly surprised, the perception of product quality is lowered. While this cause of customer unhappiness is not directly attributable to the company, it can be mitigated and often even prevented. Accurate product-service information, clearly written manuals, and plain English contracts can help to eliminate customer-caused problems.

Customers who experience problems (regardless of the cause) become dissatisfied. A dissatisfied customer is less likely to repurchase the product than a satisfied customer; less likely to recommend the product to friends and associates; less likely to purchase other products made by the offending company; and more likely to spread negative word of mouth, which discourages others from buying the product.

Research conducted by TARP Institute from 1981 to 1986 documents the fact that the negative word of mouth generated by dissatisfied customers is double the positive word of mouth spread by satisfied customers. And a study done by General Electric in 1982 found that the impact of word of mouth on a consumer's repurchase decision is twice as important as corporate advertising.

However, it is possible for a company to mitigate the market damage caused by a consumer's problem experience. Merely getting the dissatisfied customer to complain (many customers who experience problems do not complain at all) increases repurchase intention, and satisfactorily resolving the problem can restore virtually all the lost loyalty while minimizing negative word of mouth (see charts below). Moreover, an

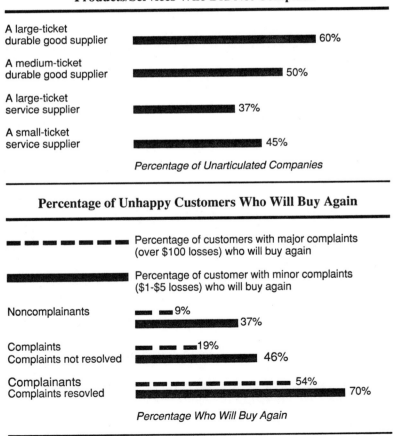

Percentage of Customers Experiencing Problems With Selected Products/Services Who Did Not Complain

A large-ticket durable good supplier — 60%

A medium-ticket durable good supplier — 50%

A large-ticket service supplier — 37%

A small-ticket service supplier — 45%

Percentage of Unarticulated Companies

Percentage of Unhappy Customers Who Will Buy Again

— — — — — — — Percentage of customers with major complaints (over $100 losses) who will buy again

■■■■■■ Percentage of customer with minor complaints ($1-$5 losses) who will buy again

Noncomplainants — — 9%
37%

Complaints
Complaints not resolved — — —19%
46%

Complainants
Complaints resovled — — — — — — — — — 54%
70%

Percentage Who Will Buy Again

effective complaint-handling unit can become a corporate profit center rather than a cost center.

How satisfied is a satisfied customer, or when is "good" good enough? Unfortunately, the company that asks its customers how satisfied they are but has failed to conduct basic research into customer expectations cannot answer these questions. This is a primary failing of much of the customer satisfaction measurement currently being conducted within the business community. Furthermore, many corporations do not realize that any satisfaction rating below "completely satisfied" implies significant levels of market damage. Therefore, market-damage or market-action questions should always be included in satisfaction measurement.

Satisfaction cannot be considered in a vacuum. What is critical to the long-term success of a company are the market actions that are related to customer satisfaction. Thus, a cause of dissatisfaction that does not translate to market damage is not as important as one that does.

Regardless of the type of industry involved, quality assurance has traditionally depended on systematic inspections as a source of information. Additionally, quality assurance has seen its responsibility as ending when the customer receives a product that meets internal product specifications. Therefore, problems in design, installation, distribution, and after-sale use and maintenance often have not been fully addressed.

Recently it has been recognized that customer complaints provide a valuable additional source of quality assurance data. Using complaints in this manner is less costly than systematic sampling and inspection and provides more timely information than that available from warranty data. Furthermore, complaint data provide the ability to diagnose the root cause(s) of the customer's problem. By combining problem-experience reports with other information from a comprehensive complaint classification system, it is possible to differentiate causes such as manufacturing defects from those connected with product design, sales, distribution, and after-sale use and maintenance. Thus, complaint data can serve to improve the ability of quality assurance to provide rapid feedback into the system to enhance the customer's overall perception of product service quality.

There are three cautionary notes that must be highlighted for quality assurance personnel who want to use complaint data:

1. Complaints are not directly projectable to the marketplace, and the fact that there is a new complaint on a product/service does not prove there is a real problem in the marketplace.

2. If complaints increase, the problem incidence may not have risen. It may be that customers have a more readily accessible channel of communication with the company.

3. Complaint data are not a substitute for market research. A sample of customers must be surveyed to assure that estimates are correct. Complaint data are only a short-term indication of what may be going on.

TARP has found that in the absence of a routinized approach to setting priorities, the quality assurance/improvement process can consume substantial resources in areas that provide little demonstratable payback. In the early 1980s Johnson & Johnson, Xerox, and AT&T sponsored research to develop a methodology to quantify the value of quality improvements as a means for setting priorities. A major benefit of the methodology is that it addresses not only improvements in physical quality but in marketing and service quality as well. This methodology is described below.

Step 1: Identify major sources of customer dissatisfaction in terms of frequency. The universe examined should include presale and sales experience as well as postsale product performance and service.

The problem experience can be estimated in one of two ways. First, a random sample of customers can be asked if they have encountered problems. Second, customer complaints to headquarters can be extrapolated to the marketplace by estimating the percentage of customers who do not complain, the percentage who complain to retailers or the field, and thereby the ratio of complaints at headquarters to the total number of problems that have been experienced. TARP's experience is that the ratio of headquarters complaints to problems experienced by customers is usually between 1:20 and 1:100.

Step 2: Identify the market damage resulting from a single occurrence of the problem. Market damage occurs when the customer is unhappy enough not to repurchase or recommend the product or to buy other products made by the same company. The quality analyst must therefore determine what percentage of customers encountering a problem will not repurchase because of their experience. This information is best gathered via a survey, ideally the same survey that gathered problem frequency data for Step 1.

Quality analysts often assume that all problems have equal impact. TARP has found that human interaction problems, such as failure to return phone calls, can cause as much as four times the market damage as a product problem such as excessive machine downtime. Thus, market damage must be determined by problem type. Likewise, an unclear explanation of a bill or claim payment has more negative impact than a shipment with a short count or a somewhat slower response (within limits).

Step 3: Determine the overall market damage. Once one knows the problem prevalence and its market damage, it is possible to calculate the current market damage for each major problem that customers are encountering. The process involves simply multiplying the customer base by the problem frequency and by the percentage of customers lost if the problem is encountered.

Step 4: Rank order problems in terms of market damage. Once this is done, it will become clear that the problem that causes the most complaints or that is most prevalent in inspections may not be causing the most market damage.

Step 5: Determine the cause and cost of the mitigation/elimination of each problem. The cause of the problem is determined by examining all possible alternatives. These alternatives include individual employee actions, product specifications, selling and delivery practices, and unexpected customer behavior.

Step 6: Perform cost benefit calculation to determine priority for action. The cost of correcting each problem as determined in Step 5 is then balanced with the resulting reduction in market damage. One counterintuitive finding will be that moderately damaging problems with minor cost of correction will result in much higher cost benefits than very serious problems that require total product redesign or re-engineering. Given quality assurance's limited resources, it will often be more intelligent to tackle the intermediate, high-payback problems rather than the huge, long-term problems. At the same time, it will now be possible to tell management, "For each month you do not re-engineer this system it is costing you $800,000" rather than saying, "It is a severe problem but it will cost a lot to fix."

Achieving product quality means more than minimizing manufacturing defects. To the customer, every interaction with the company is a reflection on quality. Any perception of lowered product quality decreases customer repurchase intention. The innovative company, therefore, will expand its definition of quality and will concentrate its efforts on those areas that cause market damage. Such action will result in customer loyalty and increased profitability.

VIEWING SERVICE QUALITY AT METROPOLITAN LIFE

How do you define and measure the customer's view of service? At Met Life, John Falzon, senior vice president, quality and planning, turned for answers to some original research conducted by Texas A&M professors A. Parasuraman, Valarie A. Zeithaml, and Leonard Berry, who have developed "a conceptual model" of service quality. Working with one of the researchers, Falzon developed a special seminar for senior officers of Met life, and each of the company's various departments is now constructing appropriate survey instruments to measure customer satisfaction. Among the major findings of the Texas A&M research:

1. There are several distinctions that set services apart from goods. First of all, services are intangible—they cannot be measured, tested, or verified in advance of sales to assure quality. Second, services have a high labor content—they reflect the behavior of the service personnel who are intrinsic to service delivery. Therefore, performance of the service varies from provider to provider, from customer to customer, and from day to day. Third, the consumption of many services is inseparable from their production—and the customer often participates in the service delivery process. Finally, services are perishable—they cannot be saved or inventoried. Once the opportunity is missed, there is no second chance to sell a service to a customer.

Obviously, these four characteristics of service pose problems to firms who desire to deliver high quality services. They also lead to the conclusion that because of the people-intensive nature of service, the process of delivering a service is as important as the outcome, and non-routine transactions deserve as much—if not more—attention as routine transactions.

"This is an extremely important point," Falzon says, "Too often, and I know it's true in our case, the measurements of performance for service transactions are built around the routine actions and are concerned primarily with outcomes. Somehow the non-routine transaction is excluded—perhaps we view it as the exception. Similarly, the process of delivery does not lend itself to easy measurement, and therefore we tend to exclude it from examination."

2. As a basis for measurement, the research was able to identify the most significant factors influencing the overall evaluation. These factors fall within five generic classifications: *reliability*—the ability to perform the promised service dependably and accurately: *responsiveness*—the willingness to help customers and provide prompt service; *tangibles*—physical facilities, equipment, and appearance of personnel; *assurance*—knowledge and courtesy of employees and their ability to convey trust and confidence; *empathy*—caring, individualized attention provided to customers.

3. The researchers developed a survey instrument, based upon the foregoing factors, that was able to quantify service performance. Moreover, the instrument was designed within a system that enables management to identify and isolate problem areas.

4. One of the most significant findings of the research was that a rather precise definition could be applied to the measurement of quality in the service sector. Quality of services is measured by the difference between the expectation levels of the customer on the one hand, and the customer's perceived level of service delivery on the other. The gap between these two points represents the size of the service problem.

Create A Service Culture

"Corporations have values and beliefs to pass along—not just products. They have stories to tell—not just profits to make. They have heroes whom managers and workers can emulate—not just faceless bureaucrats. In short, they are human institutions that provide practical meaning for people, both on and off the job."

Terence Deal and
Allan Kennedy
Corporate Cultures

So what is culture? Pigmy eating habits. *National Geographic.* Margaret Mead's *Coming of Age in Samoa* and *Growing up in New Guinea.* Richard Leaky's *On the Origin of Species.* The stuff of Anthropology 101? For some, yes, that's what the word *culture* still calls to mind. But today the study of culture as a social science is no longer a remote, exotic, arcane pursuit. Thanks to writers like Deal and Kennedy, Peters and Waterman, Kouzes and Posner, culture is as much a boardroom topic as are leveraged buyouts and hostile takeovers.

Organizational culture is formally defined by MIT professor Edgar Schein as "the pattern of basic assumptions that a given group has invented, discovered, or developed in learning to cope with its problems of external adaptation and internal integration, and that have worked well enough to be considered valid and, therefore, to be taught to new members as the correct way to perceive, think, and feel in relation to those problems." Vijay Sathe, a professor at the

Claremont Graduate School Management Center, defines organizational culture more succinctly as "... the set of important understandings (often unstated) that members of a community share in common."

While writers may quibble over the best set of words to communicate the meaning of the concept, they all agree that corporate culture typically has a more compelling influence on employee actions than policies, standards, and directives. It is culture that guides employees to make decisions and judgments when required to act in the absence of relevant policies, standards, or directives.

This book so far has assembled the six major building blocks required to construct an organization or unit remarkable for its distinctive customer service. We end the book with a section on the mortar needed to bind the blocks together. A strong service culture is consistently found in those organizations known for superior customer service. Organizations like Disney, Federal Express, IBM, Quad Graphics and Marriott have developed a set of values, beliefs, and norms that make service excellence a way of life. Sometimes it has happened by chance but mostly by careful planning. Regardless of how it developed, everyone involved works at preserving a culture that is unstintingly committed to customer care.

Professor Sathe suggests that the essence of corporate culture is expressed through shared things (e.g., shirt sleeves or open offices), shared sayings (e.g., "Our customer is 'the boss,'" or "Service makes the difference"), shared doings (e.g., managers talk with customers, frequent celebrations, or shop the competition), and shared feelings ("We are the company that cares" or "This organization treats me like a professional"). This things-sayings-doings-feelings recipe for assessment of a service culture provides guidelines for creating such a culture in all organizations.

We have chosen four articles to help tell the culture story. The first is a short overview by Ron Zemke titled "Creating Service Cultures." that appeared in the November 1988 issue of "The Service Edge" newsletter. The article translates Vijay Sathe's culture research into the language of service. And it distills five management actions necessary to transforming an organization's culture into one that values distinctive service.

Next, we offer the classic research work of University of Maryland Professor Benjamin Schneider that appeared as "The Service Organization: Climate Is Crucial" in the Autumn, 1980 issue of *Organizational Dynamics*. Schneider's initial premise is this: By typically concentrating on the easily countable, relatively short-run indices of human effectiveness—a manufacturing mentality and orientation—management risks grave consequences in the service sector. Since service performance is directed at animate (human) objects rather than nonresponsive raw materials, the relevant assessors of effective performance should be those served.

Schneider used a major bank as the context for his research, specifically examining the relationship between the employee's perception of an organization as having a customer-service orientation and the level of satisfaction experienced by customers. A key finding of the study was that employee relations were a major variable affecting customer relations. Schneider asserts, "Management emphasis in a service organization cannot be hidden from those who are served: climate shows in service organizations."

"If you are not serving the customer, your job is to be serving someone who is," said Jan Carlzon, CEO of SAS Airlines. With that philosophy in mind, Carlzon helped transform the debt-ridden loss leader into a profitable, respected industry leader. In the third article, titled "The Manager As Servant," Ron Zemke uses the Carlzon credo to posit the view that, until managers accept "serving" and "supporting" employees as their principal role, a true service culture is not likely to evolve. "Managing is a performing art," said George Washington University Professor Peter Vaill in a 1989 book bearing that title. We earlier described service in the same terms. Is there no real difference between serving and managing? And what about deference? Where does assertive, directional leadership end and supportive, enabling service on the part of the manager begin? The Zemke article may prompt you to reexamine your ideas about supervision of employees.

The final article of the book is Edward Tenner's "The Meaning of Quality," an editorial piece from the first issue (Winter 1986) of *Quality* Magazine. We could say we closed with it because we liked the philosophy it advocated, but that would be only partially true. The article attempts to convey the very essence of quality: a vital belief in the pursuit of excellence for its own sake. While the focus of Tenner's article is on product quality rather than service quality, the concept of "crafting a product (or creating a performance) better than it has to be" is axiomatic to distinctiveness. As Tenner describes his version of the quest for quality, he raises quality paradoxes that zero in on the challenges of managing its creation.

Service wisdom is a term that suggests inspirational attributes like courage, creativity, curiosity, passion, and a reverence for the honor of serving another. Like the field mouse's act of thorn removal from the aching paw of the mighty lion, service is an act of giving. And *distinctive* service is a special gift in that it surprises the receiver by exceeding expectations while being, at the same time, consistent with those expectations. Service wisdom is a tool for creating special gifts. This book is our gift to all who find pleasure in serving.

CREATING
SERVICE CULTURES

Ron Zemke

Organizational culture. You can't touch it or explain it to your kids. Yet work in an organization for more than a day and you learn there are things you do and don't do, say and don't say, that are organizationally proper and improper.

Making a fundamental change in an organization's culture, like making service quality a prominent part of the permanent value system when technology or inventions have been the banner in the past, is no mean task. You can change your advertising as easily as you change your underwear. You can update your look, your logo type, and literature with equal dispatch. But changing your core corporate culture takes time, strategic and tactical thought, and considerable energy.

Professor Vijay Sathe of the Graduate Management Center in Claremont, CA, has frequently pointed out that changing the culture of an organization is no trivial matter, but is by no means impossible. The key is to know what to attend to. Sathe suggests there are five management musts to changing a major facet of an organization's culture.

1. *Specifying the behavior that members are expected to exhibit—both internally and externally.* At Riverside Methodist Hospital in Columbus, OH, CEO Erie Chapman works with his staff to eliminate behaviors that communicate the feeling, "You are my hostage." Chapman says the emphasis should be on keeping patients informed about their treatment and status. One of the hospital's service-focused rules: Emergency room patients wait no more than 15 minutes.

At Tacoma General Hospital in Tacoma, WA, management has published and trained employees in a set of behaviors referred to as the hospital's "12 Caring Actions." They are part of the hospital's MERCI program—Medical Excellence Requires Concern for the Individual—a permanent program that encompasses a philosophy of customer service.

2. *Create explicit justifications for the valued behaviors; that is, develop a* *plausible explanation for the necessity of the new, required behavior.* At Federal Express they talk about carrying the most important cargo in history, and remind employees they are not only entrusted with mail and machine parts, but with human organs destined for transplants, vital medicines, and other life-giving cargo.

3. *Create "cultural communications"—develop rituals, ceremonies, stories, metaphors, heroes, logos, and symbols of the new culture and its values.* At J.C. Penney and LensCrafters good service is rewarded with pins and points, awarded in very public ceremonies. At First Union National Bank in Charlotte, NC, retail branches are shopped three times a quarter, and the results made available throughout the system. Those employees who receive a perfect score on a "shop" are instantly rewarded. And that information circulates in the system.

4. *Socialize newcomers in the ethos of the new culture soon after they're hired.* The Disney organization sets the standard for communicating its values, philosophies, and history to newcomers through a training program called "Traditions" that intertwines a detailed company history lesson with corporate conduct, customer relations, and job training.

Chicago-based ServiceMaster Corp., a cleaning and maintenance company, takes an unconventional approach to creating loyalty and inculcating company values. The company offers a wide variety of job-skills programs designed to upgrade not only the career potential of front-line employees, but to enhance their self-esteem as well. The key, say ServiceMaster execs, is that people who take pride in themselves, who see real career potential in what they had assumed to be nothing jobs, also take pride in the work they do for company customers.

5. *Remove members of the group who deviate from, or who will not accept, the new culture.* It is difficult for most managers to fire an employee for cause, let alone figure out how to divest the organization of an employee who can't get with the new way of doing things. But as the new, deregulated phone companies have learned, in the long run it makes more sense, and is more humane, to open an early out avenue for employees who are unwilling or unable to deal with a drastic change in focus, values, and culture.

At Longo Toyota, El Monte, CA, salespeople who turn a deaf ear to customers who have post-sale service problems assure themselves a short stay on the payroll. General Manager John Clark perpetuates founder Don Longo's belief that moving iron is only half of a salesperson's job. Ensuring that customers have an A-plus experience with the dealership is the half that leads to repeat sales. Removing a heavy hitter from the payroll for inattention to that belief—that corporate value—is a heavy reinforcer of the message.

While it is possible to change the focus and practices of an organization's culture, it is critical to preserve to a considerable extent what has gone before and build on it to make the change. As management researchers Alan Wilkins and Nigel Bristow point out, you can't "ape" your way to excellence. Distinctive service competence and service quality will come from shaping the inherent genius of your organization, not from trying to become some wholly different organization. Honoring and learning from the past doesn't mean we have to be trapped by it.

So go slow. Make incremental change. Treat cultural transition the same way you treat any important organizational objectives—set intermediate targets, and realize that as powerful as culture is, it is also fragile. It resides in people and their perceptions, and changing it rests on the most fragile and difficult of acts: changing people.

THE SERVICE ORGANIZATION: CLIMATE IS CRUCIAL

Benjamin Schneider

Behavioral science studies of work have generally concentrated on those outcomes of worker participation in the organization that can easily be counted—for example, days absent—particularly in manufacturing when production levels, absenteeism, and turnover are the "bottom line" in evaluating the usefulness of the behavioral sciences.

I think this emphasis on the "bottom line" is based on the fact that our theories and models about organizational dynamics come from the manufacturing sector. Thus, because the score is kept by accountants, organizations tend to monitor the easily identifiable cost. It has not been noticed that this focus on "easily countables" gives a short-run perspective and cuts down, or even eliminates, attention paid to organizational constituencies that aren't directly involved with financial matters. Accountants, economists, and financial analysts provide the data on which decision makers base their decisions so the only constituencies that influence decisions are stockholders and banks; customers, suppliers, employees, or the families of employees are given scant attention.

The emphasis on easily countable, relatively short-run indices of human effectiveness may be shortsighted in the manufacturing sector; in the service sector, it is myopic. Yet service organizations tend to adopt a straight short-run, accounting-oriented, productivity frame of reference when they evaluate employee performance and determine organizational effectiveness. In banks, for example, tellers are evaluated on how they "prove out" at the end of each day, rather than on how courteous they are to the bank's customers; the competence of airline reservation clerks is judged on the number of paperwork errors they make when they book passengers, rather than on the goodwill they generate when they handle a transaction to the satisfaction of the customer; and life insurance managers monitor salespersons' dollar volume rather than their "bedside manner" as a basis for rewards. The primary measure turns out to be a short-run concern for easily countable performance standards that are relevant to short-run financial concerns.

It would be useful if the definition of "productivity"—especially in service industries—was broadened to include at least courtesy and style of performance—particularly because the long-term effectiveness of the organization depends on service. Because the performance of employees in service organizations is directed at animate (human) objects rather than the nonfeeling, nonresponsive raw materials handled in the manufacturing world, the appropriate judges of performance should be those who are served.

The underlying thesis of this article is that in service organizations, organizational dynamics have a direct impact on the people the organization serves, as well as on employee performance and attitudes. This article focuses on the nature of employees who work in service organizations, how management's orientation to service affects employees, how management's orientation to service affects customers, and the relationship between employee and customer views of the service orientation of the organization. The project that illustrates these concerns was conducted in 23 branches of an East Coast commercial bank.

WORKING FRAMEWORK

The working framework is based on research from two viewpoints—the employee's and the customer's. Let's look at the research background from each of these vantages.

Research Background: The Employee Side As I've already noted, our models of organizational dynamics have been developed in, and concentrate on, manufacturing organizations—that is, organizations that transform raw materials into consumable products. Employees' efforts in such organizations are aimed at essentially nonreactive targets. In contrast, service organization employees have face-to-face contact with customers; their work involves much greater interpersonal interaction than manufacturing work. This type of work seems to result in increased stress and strain because employees try to meet conflicting demands from management and customer. Management ought to try and reduce this stress. But how? To answer this question, we must identify the types of people likely to be employed in customer contact jobs in service organizations.

We assumed that an individual's choice of occupation or organization wasn't a random process and that people choose the kinds of jobs they have and the kinds of organizations in which they work. Research literature on occupational and organizational choice suggests that people who choose service jobs in for-profit organizations probably have strong desires to give good service, to work with people in face-to-face relationships and, interestingly, they are probably concerned with organizational success. Therefore, management can potentially manage employee stress by establishing a climate in which employees' desires to give good service are made easier and encouraged; a climate in which service, as proved by management word and deed, is an organizational imperative.

When managers in service organizations establish policies and procedures, and otherwise engage in behaviors that show concern for the organization's clients, they are service enthusiasts. Service enthusiasts engage in activities designed to satisfy the organization's customers. Service bureaucrats, on the other hand, are interested in system maintenance, routine, and adherence to uniform operating guidelines and procedures. The most important difference between these orientations is the service enthusiast's emphasis on the importance of interpersonal relationships at work, concern for the customer, and flexible application of rules as opposed to the bureaucrat's avoidance of interpersonal issues and stress on rules, procedures, and system maintenance. When employee opinions about how their organization should function are not congruent with what they perceive the organization is actually emphasizing, role stress and strain— that is, role ambiguity and role conflict—usually result. Employees' role stress and strain would also manifest itself in other negative outcomes such as dissatisfaction, frustration, and plans to leave the organization. This framework is shown in Figure 1.

Research Background: Customer Side Consumers who make decisions about the goods or services offered by an organization are the ultimate judges of the quality of those goods and services in the American free-market system. What is surprising is that (1) researchers and businessmen have concentrated far more on how to attract consumers to products and services than on how it retain those customers, (2) there is almost no published research on the retention of service consumers, and

Figure 1
How Employees-Management Incongruence Leads
to Employees' Negative Feelings

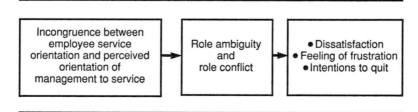

(3) consumer evaluation of products or services have rarely been used as a criterion or index of organizational effectiveness. The study of organizational behavior has left relatively unexplored the questions of why consumers continue to utilize the services of a bank, an airline, a hospital, a university, an insurance agency, and so on, and of how the dynamics or processes of these organizations are related to consumer evaluation of services they receive.

In an earlier study, I hypothesized that service consumers are responsive to the same kinds of organizational practices and procedures that affect employees. I suggested that consumers would be better served if service organizations were structured to meet and satisfy the needs of their employees. The logic for the hypothesis is quite simple: Employees in service organizations desire to give good service and when those desires are made easier by management's support, both employees and consumers are likely to react positively—that is, employees should have feelings of satisfaction, not frustration, and so on; customers should feel good about the quality of the service they receive.

It is important to note that positive outcomes for both customer and employee are a direct function of the same set of organizational dynamics—namely, the extent to which the organization, through its practices and procedures, demonstrates a "climate for service". Of course, positive employee outcomes are in a totally different realm from customer outcomes; the former involve the largest chunk of daytime hours (employees' total work experiences); the latter involve only a fleeting or transient relationship (a three-or four-minute visit every now and then to a bank, for example). However, these two groups share an experience with the same organizational behavior; this suggests that the way customers perceive their treatment when they use the organization's services should be positively related to what employees say about the organization's service practices and procedures. These ideas are portrayed schematically in Figure 2.

Note also that these thoughts about the impact on customers of managerial orientation to employees represent, in fact, a "boundary-spanning" or "spillover" concept. This suggests that human resources processes and procedures established for customer-contact employees in service organizations have unintentional consequences because they cannot be hidden from the consumer; there is no room for "quality control" between the employees' behavior and the customer's "purchase". The climate for service "shows" to those who are served.

It could be no different. Service organizations are established to attract and retain customers through service; their reason for being is (or should be) the customer. In fact, this logic indicates that when employees feel their service organization is not customer-oriented, both employees and customers should report the customer has less positive experiences. Conversely, in organizations where employees report that management displays characteristics of the service enthusiast and establishes customer-oriented policies and procedures, customers should report higher levels or quality of service and they should be more likely to keep their service accounts with the organization.

The Research Process Data for this project were collected in three distinct phases: preparation of the organization for the data collection process, interviews with bank branch employees and customers, and survey development and administration to employees and customers.

Preparation Of The Organization It took the researcher five years to find a bank in which to test these hypotheses because banks, like most service organizations, separate their employee "attitude" research from their customer "opinion" research; this thwarted any opportunity to examine relationships between employees and customers. Fortunately, the management of the bank that eventually cooperated (financially as well as psychologically) realized that while customer opinions about quality were an index of branches effectiveness, actual attempts to change branch practices and procedures would be nonproductive unless techniques were

Figure 2
Antecedents and Consequences of
"Climate For Service" in Banks

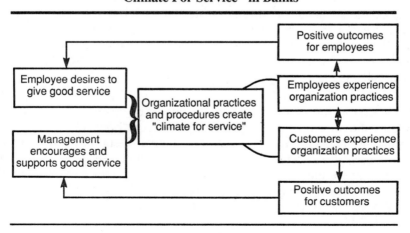

available for measuring how higher-quality differed from lower-quality branches. My research framework provided a technique for identifying the relationships, if any, between customer opinions about service and employee descriptions of branch practices and procedures. Because these descriptions referred specifically to actual branch routine and the research provided diagnostic data that were useful for organizational change, the bank finally agreed to participate.

Both parties to the project took on specific responsibilities. The bank was expected to:

- *Arrange a meeting with branch managers to solicit their cooperation.* This gave those branch managers who would participate in the study an opportunity to meet and observe the research team and to ask questions about their roles.
- *Arrange corporate newspaper announcements describing the research and research team.* This alerted the whole organization to the research effort and help allay false rumors.
- *Arrange for all customer and employee interviews and conduct the customer interviews after the research team trained the interviewers.* The idea of using bank employees to conduct the customer interviews was to get nonbranch people (especially marketing types) to speak to actual customers.
- *Appoint a liaison team to work with the research team.* The liaison team acquainted researchers with some of the language of the organization (every organization has its own language) and specified "obvious" ways to conduct the research. This team was used as a sounding board and critic and was particularly valuable in critiquing the proposed surveys.
- *Print and mail surveys to all sampled customers and employees, and select the customer samples (all employees in the relevant branches were asked to respond).*

The research team had the duty to:

- *Explain the research effort to participating bank employees*—on a face-to-face basis with bank branch managers and in writing to other branch employees.
- *Interview branch employees.*
- *Develop the survey drafts for both customers and employees, and check them with the liaison team.*
- *Analyze data and write reports.*
- *Feed data back to branch managers and employees.*

Manager And Employee Interviews As preparation for the employee survey, the branch manager, one nonteller, and one teller were interviewed from each branch. Some interviews were "one-on-one", while others were conducted in groups. Groups were always composed of employees holding jobs at the same level—all managers or all tellers, for example. These interviews were tape-recorded and concentrated on the following issues:

- What happened to and around them on a typical day that made them feel particularly good or particularly bad about their work.
- What came to mind when they thought about customer service and the bank.
- What they thought giving good service involved; what are the components of good service.
- How they felt when they weren't giving good service; what prevented them from providing good customer service.

Customer Interviews Customers were interviewed from each of the branches by randomly selecting three account holders from mailing lists, telephoning them, and asking them to participate in an interview for which they would be paid $15. Interviews were conducted at a branch convenient to the customer and were conducted "one-on-one". Customers were asked the following questions:

- In a few words, how would you describe the service you generally receive at the branch where you do most of your banking?
- Can you tell me about a time you went to your branch and received service you thought was particularly good? Please tell me what happened, who was involved, how you felt, and why you think you were treated well.
- Now tell me about a time when service was particularly bad.

Survey And Development And Administration Based on an informal analysis of the interviews, one survey was designed for employees and one for customers. The survey differed from the interviews in the level of the detail of the questions and, very importantly, in the number of people from whom we were able to collect data. The latter difference permitted more systematic, quantitatively based exploration of the hypotheses.

In all, survey responses came from 263 employees and 1,657 customers from 23 branches of the bank; about 70 customers and about 11 employees per branch.

Results Of Employee Interviews The employee interviews suggested a complex set of issues in the service orientation of branches. At a more general level, as expected, employees responded to our questions with the themes of both enthusiasts and bureaucrats. The issues that reflected an enthusiastic orientation referred to the branch's philosophy of a flexible and interpersonally open form of involvement with the branch's customers and the community in the delivery of service. In the survey, the enthusiastic orientation was measured by these items, for example: keeping a sense of "family" among branch employees, having the branch involved in community affairs and giving customer service in new and creative ways. In contrast, the bureaucratic orientation was measured by constraints on giving good service—for example, stress on rules, procedures, and system maintenance that, we were told, often diverted energy away from providing good customer service. Other measures of the bureaucratic theme included strict adherence to rules and procedures, routine performance of one's job, and the use of only established methods for solving customers' problems.

On an everyday activity level, employees said that the activities that represented good service included the degree to which the branch manager assumed the traditional managerial functions of giving good service (planning, coordinating, goal setting, establishing routine), the extent to which extra effort in serving customers was rewarded and appreciated, and the degree to which there was an active attempt to retain customers in the branch.

Employees also told us about some primarily central bank-controlled (as compared with predominantly branch-controlled) support systems that would help them give better or poorer customer service. Four apparently independent and identifiable support systems were noted:

- *Personnel support* ("The employees sent by Personnel are not able to do their jobs well.")
- *Central processing support* ("Having all customer records in a central location makes it easier on the branch.")
- *Marketing support* ("We are well-prepared by Marketing for the introduction of new products and services.")
- *Equipment/supply support* ("Equipment and machinery in the branch are well-serviced and rarely break down.")

The managerial functions scale is presented in Figure 3 as an illustration of the kinds of items in a complete scale from the employee survey.

Parenthetically, it is worth noting that the three interviewers were remarkably unanimous in their agreement about the very strong desire of the employees in this system to give customers good service. Indeed, a central theme coming out of the interviews was a sense of frustration—that is, the feeling that "the system" set up obstacles that frustrated their desire to provide the best possible customer service.

Results Of Customer Interviews In response to the open-ended questions about service, customers identified ten issues associated with the climate for service at their branch. These ten, with an example of the kind of statements used in the customer survey, are:

1. *Teller courtesy* ("Tellers care about customers as people in my branch.")
2. *Officer courtesy* ("Some officers in the branch know me by name.")
3. *Teller competence* ("Tellers in the branch are well-trained and knowledgeable.")
4. *Adequate staff* ("My branch seems to have enough employees to handle its customers.")
5. *Branch administration* ("It sometimes seems to me that tellers have to walk all over the place to get things done.")
6. *Handling services* ("Deposits are promptly credited to my account(s).")

Figure 3
Items Composing the Managerial Function Scale
From the Employee Survey

Item Number	Item
4	My branch manager supports employees when they come up with new ideas on customer service.
7	My branch manager sets definite quality standards of good customer service.
9	My branch manager meets regularly with employees to discuss work performance goals.
13	My branch manager accepts the responsibilities of his/her job.
20	My branch manager gets the people in different jobs to work together in serving branch customers.
21	My branch manager works at keeping an orderly routine going in the branch.
29	My branch manager takes time to help new employees learn about the branch and its customers.

7. *Convenience* ("I like the fact that the bank has a large number of branches.")

8. *Employee turnover* ("There seems to be a high turnover of employees in my branch.")

9. *Selling* ("Officers of the bank have tried to get me to open new accounts.")

10. *Employee attitudes* ("My impression is that the branch employees really try to give the customers good service.")

Statements from the branch administration scale from the customer survey are presented in Figure 4.

SURVEY FINDINGS

Results of the survey will be presented in two parts: 1. data on employee desires to give good service, and what happens when the stress of customer vs. management demands is encountered, and 2. data on the relationships between the way employees and customers experience service.

Employee Desires To Give Good Service To explore employee desires to give good service, we took a two-pronged approach: First we asked employees to tell us how essential both the enthusiastic approach and the bureaucratic approach were to good service. Then we asked the same employees to tell us how essential they felt management thinks both

Figure 4
Items Involved in the Branch Administration Scale
From the Customer Survey

Item Number	Item
-33	An officer (or someone else) takes charge of things when the bank becomes overcrowded.
-4	It sometimes seems to me that tellers have to walk all over the place to get things done.
-12	When I've opened new accounts or had to change old ones, something usually got messed up.
34	My branch has an adequate supply of deposit and withdrawal tickets.
-36	I sometimes feel lost in the branch, not knowing where to go for a certain transaction.
-39	It is difficult to know who to call or where to write when I need specific kinds of bank-related information.

NOTE: A minus sign before the item number indicates that the item was reverse-scored.

the enthusiastic and the bureaucratic approaches are to giving good service.

Ascertaining employees' perceptions of management's perspective, as well as their own, permitted the examination of two interesting questions: First, do service employees generally see themselves emphasizing different approaches to service than they believe management wants? As shown in Figure 5, the answer is "Yes"; employees see themselves more as enthusiasts and less as bureaucrats than they believe management is. The second question is considerably more subtle: it asked for the consequences of a discrepancy between the way employees believe service should be given and the way they think management wants service provided.

Answers to the second question provided information that enabled us to calculate, for each employee, the discrepancy employee emphases and perceived management emphases and then to relate that discrepancy to employee report of role stress—that is, of role conflict and ambiguity, job dissatisfaction, frustration over being unable to give good service, and intentions to change jobs. Following the logic presented earlier, it was assumed that the larger the discrepancy, the more negative feelings employees would experience. In fact, as shown in Figure 6, this was the case. This means that a host of negative consequences follow when employees think customer service should be handled in ways that differ from the way they believe management wants service given.

Additional analyses, not shown here, revealed that the service orientation discrepancy first creates role conflict and ambiguity, and then the other negative outcomes. Thus incongruence between employee and desires and the perceived orientation of management first seems to lead to role stress;

Figure 5
Employee Views on Own
and Management's Service Orientation

Approach to Service	Average Employees' Own Views	Average Employees' Views of Managemen.
Bureaucrat	1.92	2.33
Enthusiast	2.48	2.35

NOTE: All responses were made on a three-point scale. The differences between employees' own views and employees' views of management are both statistically significant.

it is this stress that then seems to result in frustration, dissatisfaction, and intentions to quit.

Relationship Between Customer And Employee Views Of Service

It is one thing to be aware that employees may suffer feelings of conflict or frustration when they disagree with management's orientation to service, but it is another thing to find out that management's orientation to service is related to other indices of organizational success. The present study defines organizational success in terms of customer evaluations of the level or quality of service rendered by their bank branch.

At this point our frame of reference switched from how individual employees experience their work world to the ways in which employees and customers, as groups, experience their bank branches. Thus, the reference is not to individuals but to organizations—that is, bank branches. Therefore, the focus shifts from the 263 branch employees, to the 23 branches. This change was necessary because organizations are really aggregates of people and, in evaluating organizational effectiveness, meaningful aggregates constitute the appropriate frames of reference.

Customer data combined with employee data provided the answer to the question: Are employees' descriptions of customer service in their branch related to what customers have to say about the service they receive? Once again, the answer is yes.

For example, Figure 7 shows how customer views of service are related to employee views of service in the 23 branches. The dots in the figure each represent a branch.

Figure 6
Correlations Between Service-Orientation Discrepancy and Employee Outcomes

Employees' Negative Feelings	Correlation
Role conflict	.45
Role ambiguity	.20
Dissatisfaction	.42
Frustration	.33
Turnover intentions	.32

NOTE: A large discrepancy means less agreement; all correlations are significantly different from zero.

The data for employees were based on their responses to the question: "How do you think the customers of your branch view the general quality of the service they receive in your branch?" Customers were asked to: "Describe the general quality of the service you receive in your branch." Both groups graded service on the following six-point scale: outstanding, excellent, good, not so good, bad, terrible. The analysis showed that customers report better service in branches when employees report that:

- There's a more enthusiastic service emphasis.
- The branch manager emphasizes service as he or she carries out the role of the branch manager.
- There's an active attempt to retain all customer account holders, not only large accounts.
- The personnel department provides a sufficient number of well-train tellers.
- Equipment is well-maintained and supplies are plentiful.

In fact, the correlation of the data from the analyses of employee and customer responses was so consistently strong that it was possible to

Figure 7
**Relationship Between Customer and Employee Perceptions
of Customer Service**

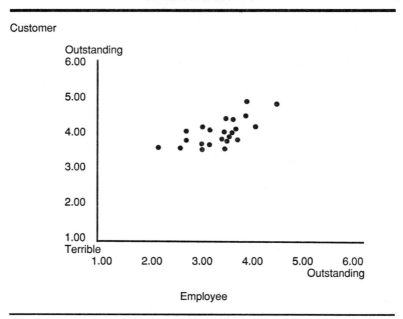

isolate a few customer perceptions that warrant particular note—that is, it was possible to identify which facets of service from the customer's view were most strongly related to selected facets of service as described by employees.

For example, when employees describe their branch as one in which the manager emphasizes customer service as he or she carries out the traditional managerial role, customers report not only generally superior service but, more specifically, that:

- The tellers are courteous.
- The tellers are competent.
- The staffing level is adequate.
- The branch is administered well.
- Teller turnover is low.
- The staff has positive work attitudes.

Similar findings were observed when branches were described by employees as having more of an enthusiastic approach and also when employees reported they worked in a branch that actively tried to retain all categories of account holders.

SUMMARY
These results may be summarized as follows: When branch employees perceive a strong orientation in their branch, the customers of those branches report not only that they receive generally superior service, but that specific facets of service are handled in a superior manner. In addition, employees themselves experience less negative consequences at work when their branch has more of an enthusiastic orientation to service. Thus, employees are less dissatisfied and frustrated, more likely to plan to remain in their branch, and they experience less role conflict and role ambiguity when the branch is more like employees feel it should be—that is, more enthusiastic in its approach to service.

A major conclusion from this study: Employees and customers of service organizations will each experience positive outcomes when the organization operates with a customer service orientation. This orientation seems to result in superior service practices and procedures that are observable by customers and that seem to fit employee views of the appropriate style for dealing with customers.

More specifically, this research supports the following assumptions:

1. Employees perceive themselves to be more enthusiastic and management to be more bureaucratic to service orientation. This suggests gaps between the goals of employees vis-a-vis service and the management goals that employees perceive. It is important for organizations to be aware of where these differences exist so they can take steps to remedy them. Figure 8 pinpointed these differences for the branch employees in this study and, thus, where the bank needed to change to be more congruent with the employees' more enthusiastic, less bureaucratic orientation to service.

2. Employees who work in settings that are more congruent with their own service orientation experience less role ambiguity and role conflict and, as a result, are generally more satisfied, experience less frustration in their efforts to give good service, and are more likely to report they intend to keep working for the organization. This assumption was clearly supported; it also suggests that what management frequently perceives as employee disinterest or lack of motivation is really employees' lack of enthusiasm for carrying out management policies that are incongruent with their own desires. In fact, employees in this study seemed very interested in meeting customer service needs, but less interested in satisfying management's bureaucratic needs.

3. Even though they view service from a different perspective, employee and customer perceptions of organizational effectiveness are positively related. Support for this assumption was quite strong; that is, when employees report that their branch emphasized service by work and deed, customers report superior banking experiences. These data, and my earlier work with bank customers also show that customers who report a more positive service climate are less likely to switch their accounts to other banks. These findings clearly indicate that management emphasis in a service organization cannot be hidden from those who are served: climate shows in service organizations.

This idea of an organization's climate being apparent to customers goes to the heart of issues presented in the introduction about the determination of organizational effectiveness. A finance-oriented conspiracy seems to promote a short-run productivity orientation rather than a more long-term, wholistic perspective to determine organizational effectiveness. A more succinct way of summarizing this issue is through the concept of "goodwill".

An organization accrues goodwill over long periods of time by varied behaviors. Goodwill is reflected in the way people who have direct (that is,

Figure 8
Discrepancies Between Employee and Management
Perceptions of Service Facets

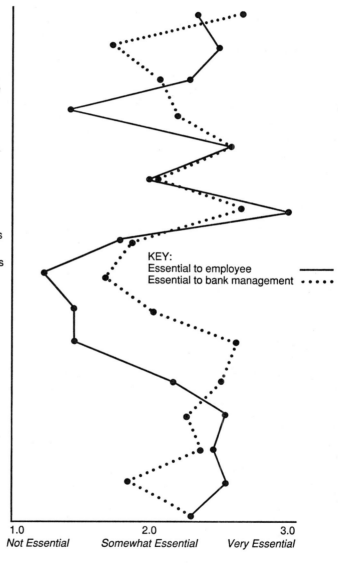

Strictly following all
rules and procedures

Keeping a sense of
"family" among the
employees within a branch

Being able to know and
address customers by name

Giving customers special
treatment based on size
of their accounts

Being able to perform
different jobs in the branch

Doing one's job in a
routine fashion

Having cooperation
among branch employees

Having bank branches
involved in community affairs

Checking identification of all
(even well-known) customers

Using only established
methods for solving
customers' problems

Meeting sales quotas set
by bank management for
the branch at all costs

Performing more than
assigned job duties

Showing personal concern
for any customer's
banking problem

Taking the time to give
detailed explanations of
services to customers

Maintaining an emphasis
on quality rather than
quantity of service

Giving customer service
in new and creative ways

KEY:
Essential to employee ——————
Essential to bank management ·····

1.0 | 2.0 | 3.0
Not Essential | Somewhat Essential | Very Essential

employees), indirect (that is, employees' families), and in-between (that is, customers, suppliers) contact with an organization think and speak about it; goodwill is the organization's reputation—that is, the way it is viewed by the multiple constituencies it affects and which by it is affected.

While the present study concentrated on the goodwill perceptions of customers, there probably would have been similar results from research concentrated on other branch constituencies. Thus suppliers to the branches could have been asked for their opinions about the branch, and branch employees could have been asked about how suppliers are treated. Or employees' families could have reported their opinions about the way the bank affects their spouse/parent and so on, and employees might have reported on the general quality of consideration given them as employees. Perhaps more interestingly, potential branch employees could have been surveyed about what they think it would be like to work in a particular branch, and those perceptions could have been related to what incumbents report it is like to work there.

In each of these hypothetical research efforts, the interesting issue would be the way in which climates created in the branch are "picked up" by the various groups important to the long-term survival of the organization. I suspect these questions are infrequently asked, and rarely if ever pursued systematically. Yet, organizations need the good will of families when an employee is making turnover decisions; they need to have a positive reputation as a place to work in order to attract good employees, and, especially in a time of strife (for example, in a situation like that of the Chrysler Corporation), they need the good will of suppliers.

A very general conclusion, then, culled from this research effort: It is just as important for the organization to be interested in its relationships with the many groups that affect its long-term viability as it is for it to be concerned with the short-run financial considerations affecting stockholders and creditors, and so on.

THE MANAGER AS SERVANT

Ron Zemke

I love it when people mess with my mind. I like nothing better than to have my preconceived notions and self-evident truths tampered with. A gold star for stirring it up this time goes to Jan Carlzon, president of Scandinavian Airline Systems.

Carlzon is a puckish, outgoing sort with a penchant for quotable quotes and a flair for personal publicity. He has been the cover boy of several European business publications and both Tom Peters and John Naisbitt mention him in their new books. His credibility isn't hurt by the fact that between early 1981 and late 1982 he turned SAS from a red ink embarrassment into an on-time, first-rate, moneymaking, customer-pleasing success. When Carlzon speaks a lot of people listen.

My favorite bit of Carlzonia is a verbal touchstone he believes helped guide his management team in turning SAS around: "If you're not serving the customer, you had better be serving someone who is".

As I see it, Mr. Carlzon's little homily cuts through 50 years of management-school obfuscation and goes to the heart of what management is really about: giving aid and comfort to those who do the organization's work, serving those who serve the company's customers.

Yes, of course, management is also about maintaining fiscal responsibility, making deals, beating back "greenmailers", flying around the country satisfying stockholders, planning, controlling and fighting the thousand-and-one battles intrinsic to the manager's way of life. In this sense, too, management is service, Service to stockholders, financiers and Wall Street analysts. Service to customers and clients.

But first and foremost, management is service to those who, day in and day out, go about the business of acquiring, satisfying and retaining customers; service to the people who make the product, sell the goods, generate the goodwill, inspire the repeat business and make the profit possible.

■

Create A
Service Culture

Does that sound more like a bromide than like the shattering of a self-evident truth? Then suppose I point out that another way to say it is: The primary function of managers is to serve their subordinates. And suppose I assert that Peter Drucker, the patron saint of modern management, was pointing to a universal neglect of that very principle when he said, "Most of what we call management consists of making if difficult for people to get their work done." Later Drucker suggested that once a year all managers should stop and ask the front-line troops what they (the managers) are doing that keeps the troops from serving the customers—and then stop doing it.

When asked what his responsibilities are as CEO of the nation's ninth largest retailing organization, Bill Marriott, president of the Marriott hotel chain, replied without hesitation, "My job is to motivate them, teach them, help them, and care about them." The "them" are Marriott's 120,000 employees. The job description is that of a support person.

Granted that planning, organizing and controlling are important things for managers to know how to do, the question is, Why are we spending all of our time teaching managers to plan, organize and control, and none of our time teaching them to identify and serve their real customers: the people who serve the people who consume the organization's products and services?

Next time you have a lull in a management training program, write this sentence on the flipchart and see where the discussion goes: *"If you're not serving the customer, you'd better be serving someone who is"*.

If your group doesn't reach the conclusion that "management-service", I'll fold my tent and go back to repairing typewriters instead of pounding on them.

THE MEANING
OF QUALITY

Edward Tenner

Quality, or the absence of it, can pierce like a knife. When this happened to me the knife was real. It belonged to a cobbler. As a student in Heidelberg in the late '60s, I took my shoes for repair in the picturesque? decaying old town where I lodged. I had bought the American-made shoes from an American retailer that had a prestigious image, but the heels had worn more quickly than I had expected. Through a courtyard where smudgy blond children played I reached an ill-lit shop run by a small gray, middle-aged man, an apparition from the Weimar-era photography of August Sander, smoking a cheap Rhine-Rubr cigar. He pried off the offending heel, uncovering a wooden inset presumably used to skimp on rubber, and cackled triumphantly, " Ami!" In Heidelberg the word was not French for friend; it was German for Yankee and about as chummy as jerry or kraut.

Unlike his fictional countryman in John Galsworthy's story *Quality*, set in Edwardian London, he was not starving to death as he finished his last order of superlative boots. But he knew his shoemaking; his knife had probed other American foot gear, and his suspicions were confirmed. A civilization, *my* civilization, had been tried and convicted of contempt for quality.

Long after the shoes were discarded, the feelings remained: wounded national pride, yes, but also interest in how complex and even paradoxical an idea quality can be. I watched as America (and the rest of the world) began to deal with quality more seriously in everything from urban design to consumer safety. Quality is now a goal of civilized life. But trying to measure quality too exactly can be useless and even harmful in the absence of an inner will to strive for it, to make things better than they have to be.

Quality has become an American issue since the second World War, as we have lost confidence in our products and services. The critique of quality began with a persnickety few and spread over decades to Middle America. When the writer Bernard DeVoto announced in *Fortune* in 1951 that business regularly forces on the consumer products of lower quality than it knows how to make, he still spoke self-consciously for the academic and professional. In the 1950s and early 1960s, liberals pointed to deteriorating product quality in attacking business for hucksterism and planned obsolescence. Meanwhile, cultural conservatives argued that Johnny couldn't read because the public school establishment put buildings and attendance ahead of academic standards.

In the late '60s and '70s, inflation, the rusting snow belt, the new environmental consciousness and the triumph of well-made imports all helped to make quality an issue for most of us. Schlock passed from garment-district argot to mainstream slang by the mid-'60s. Robert Pirsig's autobiographical *Zen and the Art of Motorcycle Maintenance* (1974) brought a philosopher's search for the meaning of quality, metaphysical and mechanical, to the bestseller lists. By 1980, Barbara Tuchman's essay "The Decline of Quality" needed to make no excuses for affirming traditional high culture against mass tastes.

Quality can be a sensory experience. To see, hear or taste quality is to discover something that has been fashioned with love. Quality can be felt in the balance of a fine chef's knife made in Oregon and the silky focusing of a pair of German binoculars. It can be heard in the two-stage click of an Italian sports-car door latching shut after a gentle push and in pianist Alfred Brendel playing Liszt. It can be seen in the mellow glow of a pair of bench-made English brogues after five years of professional shining or the sharply visible impression, the "bite," of the letterpress printing and the creamy paper of a volume of the *Oxford English Dictionary* in perfect condition after five decades of use. It can be sensed even in the elegance of a mathematical proof as it is demonstrated by a gifted teacher.

But since we value quality so much, why isn't there more of it? One reply to this question is that we don't always know how to look for it. We take the appearance of some part of the quality of the whole, judging not only the book by its cover and the wine by its label, but the Delicious apple by its knobby bottom and waxed surface. Ever since Eberhard Faber coated its Mongol pencils yellow in the 1890s to proclaim the Asian source of their premium Siberian graphite, yellow has been the color of most American pencils; to this day, whenever some intrepid pencilmaker paints an identical product green, complaints pour in about defects.

Another reply is that there is more quality around than we think. Nostalgia clouds our judgement. While many people believe in a golden age of pre-industrial artisanship, in fact our ancestors complained of poor quality too. A few fastidious Renaissance scholars shunned early printed books as crude imitations of genuine calligraphy. Nineteenth-century English critics doubted that the great railroad stations of their day, now regarded as masterpieces of design and construction, could be considered architecture at all.

Prophets of deterioration often ignore past mediocrity and present achievement. Lamenting the Checker taxi, no longer in production, they remember the leg room but forget the rattles. Deploring the thinner steel of today's cars, they overlook the tougher paint and lesser need for maintenance. And they disregard the large number of people still willing to pay more for the durability of American classics like Kirby vacuum cleaners, Snap-on tools and Fuller brushes.

Yet we can't take American quality for granted, even in something as simple as a children's cartoon. The crude animation of today's Saturday morning fare makes *Daffy Duck* and *Road Runner* look like *Fantasia*. Even some of America's most respected hardback publishers use bindings that will fall apart on the nation's bookshelves. If, that is, the nation's bookshelves will hold them. A Los Angeles magazine recently published a bitter article by two Soviet emigrés, once worshipers of the label MADE IN THE U.S.A., whose newly ordered bookshelves "rejected Euclidean geometry . . . so that parallel lines intersected and generally did whatever they felt like doing".

In international trade, problems with quality have hurt us at least as much as high wages and a strong dollar. As recently as 1983, a Harvard Business School study of the U.S. and Japanese room-airconditioner industries show that the worst Japanese maker had a failure rate that was half that of the best American maker. Our oil tanker fleet is 32nd out of 65 countries ranked for reliability by a New York-based research group.

If the reality of quality is close to the perception, then America definitely has some catching up to do. A majority of U.S. workers polled in 1985 believed their Japanese counterparts worked harder, more attentively and with higher standards. Evidently they think the same about many Europeans. Are German automotive engineers really the lab-coated *Ubermenschen* in the TV commercials? Millions of American viewers seem to think so.

The public sector has been even more depressing. America's space program, once the symbol of technological excellence, is in shambles. Two major satellite-launching failures have followed the explosion of the

Challenger space shuttle in January 1986. Five percent of young adults are illiterate and 80% of 17-year-old students cannot write an "adequate persuasive letter", according to reports of the U.S. Department of Education and the National Assessment of Educational Progress. The once esteemed Tennessee Valley Authority has not been allowed to operate any of its nuclear reactors for more than a year because of safety violations.

Having put our trust in professionalization and specialization, we have made it harder for any single individual to take responsibility for the quality of a project. Before two suspended walkways in the Kansas City Hyatt Regency Hotel collapsed in 1981, neither the general contractor, the construction manager, the testing and inspection laboratory, the architect's resident inspector or city inspectors noticed a faulty connection between a threaded rod and a beam, according to Forrest Wilson, a professor of architecture at Catholic University who has studied the accident. Apparently no one regarded it as his job to notice such a flaw.

If even testers and inspectors have no system for assuring quality, is it any wonder that it puzzles the rest of us? We think we know quality when we encounter it, but when we try to analyze it, we find not a unified concept but a series of paradoxes.

Paradox No. 1. Opposing quality and quantity seems logical but it is just as natural to link them. The legal historian F.W. Maitland wrote that "there are some thoughts which will not come to men who are not tightly packed." In higher education, "critical mass" . . . shorthand for the size an academic department must reach to attract the best faculty and students. Busy parents like to plan what they call "quality time" with children. But research by David Stern, a psychiatrist at Cornell Medical College, has shown that the moments most important to a child's development often come unexpectedly. Thus quality time can depend on a parent's simply being around a lot.

Quality is sometimes real to us only after we have assigned quantitative grade, score or rank to it. The ancient Olympic Games recognized no second-or third-place winners. There were no time distance records. The Greeks regarded quality qualitatively. According to Stanford historian Amos Funkenstein, it was during the Middle Ages that people first believed that quality could be made a science. The circles of Dante's *Inferno* are carefully graded. Ranking the pupils in a class was a medieval innovation that led to our present grade-point averages and percentiles.

In the U.S., as quality became a public concern, we began to handout stars and merit badges as never before. People eagerly sought out ratings of the best; not only hotels and restaurants but films, colleges, hardware, software and corporations as employers. Researchers began to weigh the quality of life (a phrase first used in the U.S. in 1955) of communities and whole countries; a recent survey at the University of Pennsylvania, for example, ranks Denmark first and the U.S. 27th.

Necessary as quantification of quality seems, it has a price. It makes us magnify insignificant differences in performance. The pressure of standardized test scores brings a cram-school mentality into the classroom. The importance of quarterly earnings reports discourages companies from long-term investment in product improvement. Yet how can we be fair without measurement?

Paradox No. 2. We want quality to be both priceless and purchasable, to be above mere ostentation yet to be available to the highest bidder. Once this was no paradox at all. Quality was what upper-class patrons said it was. Many of the old masters had to sign contracts specifying their paintings' dimensions and content in detail. Until well into the 18th century, there was no professional music criticism and no set of musical classics, as the music historian William Weber has shown; patrons did not quite call the tune, but their tastes mattered. One musical patron of the late 15th and early 16th centuries, Isabella d'Este, Marchesa of Mantua, had instruments constructed to measure, as we might have a suit or dress tailored. The composers she supported wrote pieces expressly for her voice and even developed new musical forms at her direction. According to the *Oxford English Dictionary*, a quality horse in the 18th century simply meant one suitable for a person of quality. It is only since the 19th century that quality has meant an inherent degree of excellence in a product or service.

In the last hundred years, we have loosened the connections between buying habits and social position. Anybody with a job paying above the minimum wage can buy a diamond or rent a limousine at least occasionally. A recent advertising agency study shows many heavy buyers of premium goods to be younger middle-class people who can't always afford more basic items like a house. Meanwhile, upper-class taste now often tends to the folk arts-weather vanes, Navajo blankets, Shaker chairs and decoy ducks, all made superbly but (originally, at least) for everyday use and not for display or prestige.

Still, the concept of quality has an aristocratic heritage that makes it divisive. "I am too disdainful of shoddy goods," humorist Russell Baker wrote recently. "The word for this condition is 'elitist'. It is a bad word which is meant to make the person to whom it is applied seem despicable." In fact fastidiousness and ostentation are not easy to separate from the drive for quality. The rarity of fish may make it desirable as much as its taste; when salmon was still abundant, medieval London apprentices are said to have protested being fed so much of it. Adam Smith, in his *Theory of Moral Sentiments* (1759), smiled at the connoisseur of watches willing to pay a premium for a useless minute or two of accuracy.

Before the invention of electrolytic extraction in the 1890s, aluminum was so difficult to produce that it had the cachet of present-day platinum; Emperor Napoleon III of France and Empress Eugenie set the places of their most illustrious guests with knives, forks and spoons of the precious metal. In the past few years, as Japan has lowered restrictions on some food imports and prices have fallen, the once costly box of grapefruit has disappeared as a prestigious business gift there, though the flavor of the produce has surely not changed. No wonder so many social scientists, since Thorstein Veblen's if not since Smith's day, have seen quality as a doctrine for defending privilege.

Paradox No. 3. Quality usually depends on many qualities and increasing one may reduce another. Thus traditional all-cotton American men's blue chambray shirts, which are comfortable because they are absorbent, are now shunned by their original industrial clientele. Reason: one quality (comfort) conflicts with another (practicality). Today's working man prefers the easy care of polyester-blend shirts, which were first introduced in 1953 by Brooks Brothers as a specialty item for traveling executive. Work shirts, meanwhile, have become upscale leisure wear, selling for $36 and more. Our class metaphor should not be blue collar and white collar but natural collar and synthetic collar.

Paradox No. 4. Quality can also imply the limitation of excellence. Within a market economy and a democratic society, compromises are inevitable. When U.S. industry developed quality control, as the historians Eugene S. Ferguson and Daniel J. Boorstin have shown, it was to maintain predictable—not necessarily the highest possible—quality at a low cost. This statistical approach does not always support what Veblen called "the instinct of workmanship." The marketplace is just as likely to demand low price with so-so quality as high price with high quality.

Likewise, quality control in education is ambiguous. The scientific study of children's reading levels, begun with the commendable goal of systematic progress for all pupils, has helped reduce the vocabulary of textbooks so drastically that it is hard to find the word "because" in elementary school readers. The apple on the teacher's desk and the text on the pupil's were both meant to be of high quality in a certain way: bland, inoffensive, standardized, tested, nationally transportable. Quality as uniform goodness drives out quality as peak performance-or rather it drives some of us from supermarkets and public schools to farmers' stands and private academies.

In fact, a shift to premium goods and services does not necessarily show the prevalence of quality in a society; rather it can be a warning sign. The political economist Albert O. Hirschman has suggested that the middle range of quality is unstable. Once it worsens, those who can afford to defect pay more for better things. Most upwardly mobile people leave a sinking neighborhood, for example, rather than fight for improvement. Their pursuit of quality reduces further the quality of life of those who can't leave.

Quality, then, is not completely rational. We cannot increase it in our lives merely by making it into a science. Efforts to measure quality and regulate its creation do not, we have seen, always succeed. No, we have to grant quality its moral dimension. Too often we expect excellence to result from something else: the pursuit of money, say, or fame. But instead it should be recognized as a virtue—something to be sought for its own sake—not just a profitable strategy. To the Swiss, with their passion for grace and precision in everything from pocket knives to highway bridges, quality is second nature. Can we import not just Swiss products but the attitudes behind them?

Whatever Swiss clockwork—or Danish furniture or Swedish automobiles— have to teach us, we still must follow our own path to quality. We must not restrict our idea of it to a museum-store, anodized-steel designer grail for a discerning few. Our definition of equality has instead to recapture the idea of mass-produced excellence that we gave the Japanese and others.

Certainly there is plenty of evidence that we can do just that. Our aircraft, business and professional schools, industrial research laboratories, computers, steaks and ready made suits are still the world standard. Black marketeers the world over covet our blue jeans, cigarettes and videos. Humble American baked beans line the shelve of Piccadilly's specialty grocers. Vintage Detroit iron still cruises the streets of Havana. Furthermore, we can excel at traditional crafts. The violins handmade by a 33-year-old Michigan artisan lead to international prizes. And young apprentices keep the medieval stonemason's skills alive as they work on New York City's Cathedral of St. John the Divine.

Years after my visit to the Heidelbery shoemaker, I took one of the last runs of the old Southern Crescent, the train carrying passengers between New York and New Orleans, before the Southern Railway turned the route over to Amtrak. The meals were among the finest I had ever enjoyed on any train. Then a few months later I read a newspaper report about a cook on the Crescent killed in a derailment. He was described as having been a perfectionist, bringing his own mixing bowls and pans when the railroad's did not meet his standards. Of course there must have been several cooks on the Crescent, but somehow I was sure he had been mine. Here was America's answer to the shoemaker, a man who spent his life doing something better than it had to be done, for passengers whom he might never see. Some will still think that quality is a mask for privilege, others that it takes a patience and pride of place that are beyond the capacity of the vain and lazy *Amis*. Yet the example of that cook on the Southern Crescent remains, I think we will find ourselves returning to something strong in our past, best expressed by the critic who described an individual who embodies the ideals of Ralph Waldo Emerson as someone who likes "a good barn as well as a great tragedy."

Bibliography

Albrecht, Karl, ACHIEVING EXCELLENCE IN SERVICE, **Training and Development Journal,** December 1985, pp. 64-67.

Albrecht, Karl and Ron Zemke, THE CLEAR MODEL OF SERVICE: A SUCCESS STORY OF THE NEW ECONOMY, **Training News,** August 1985.

Bacas, Harry, MAKE IT RIGHT FOR THE CUSTOMER, **Nation's Business,** November 1987, pp. 49-52.

Beckham, J. Daniel, GETTING A GRASP ON QUALITY, **Healthcare Forum,** March-April 1987, pp. 12-20.

Berry, Dick and Carol Surprenant, DEFUSING THE COMPLAINT TIME BOMB, **Sales & Marketing Management,** July 11, 1977, pp. 40-42.

Berry, Leonard L., BIG IDEAS IN SERVICES MARKETING, **Journal of Consumer Marketing,** Spring 1986, pp. 47-51.

Berry, Leonard L., COMMUNICATION CENTRAL TO CUSTOMER SERVICE, **American Banker,** March 1987, pp. 4-5.

Berry, Leonard L., SERVICE STRATEGIES IN THE 1980'S, **Journal of Retail Banking,** Vol. 1, No. 2, 1979, pp. 1-10.

Berry, Leonard L., SERVICES MARKETING IS DIFFERENT, **Business,** May-June 1980, pp. 24-28.

Berry, Leonard L., THE EMPLOYEE AS CUSTOMER, **Journal of Retail Banking,** March 1981, pp. 33-40.

Birch, David L., NO RESPECT, **Inc.,** May 1987, pp. 22-24.

Blanding, Warren, TARGETING THE TEN TOP SOURCES OF STRESS IN CUS-

TOMER SERVICE, **Customer Service Newsletter,** October and November 1986, pp. 2-4.

Blessing, Buck, SUPPORT YOUR SUPPORT STAFF, **Training and Development,** November 1986, pp. 22-25.

Blessing, Buck, THE MUSCLES BEHIND THE SMILES, **TRAINING Magazine,** October 1986, pp. 85-92.

Bowen, David E., MANAGING CUSTOMERS AS HUMAN RESOURCES IN SERVICE ORGANIZATIONS, **Human Resource Management,** Fall 1986, pp. 371-383.

Bowen, David E., THE SERVICE INDUSTRY PLAY BOOK, **New Management,** Vol. No., 2 1987, pp. 44-47.

Bowen, David E. and Gareth R. Jones, TRANSACTION COST ANALYSIS OF SERVICE ORGANIZATION-CUSTOMER EXCHANGE, **Academy of Management Review,** Vol. 11, No. 2, 1986, pp. 428-441.

Burris, Mike, COMPLAINTS: TURNING LEMONS INTO LEMONADE, **The Sporting Goods Dealer,** January 1980, pp. 139-142.

Chase, Richard B., THE CUSTOMER CONTACT APPROACH TO SERVICES: THEORETICAL BASES AND PRACTICAL EXTENSIONS, **Operations Research,** Winter 1981, 37-43.

Chase, Richard B., WHERE DOES THE CUSTOMER FIT IN A SERVICE OPERATION? **Harvard Business Review,** Vol. 56, 1978, pp. 137-142.

Chase, Richard B., Gregory B. Northcraft, and Gerrit Wolf, DESIGNING HIGH-CONTACT SERVICE SYSTEMS: APPLICATION TO BRANCHES OF A SAVINGS AND LOAN, **Decision Sciences,** Fall 1984, pp. 542-55.

Chase, Richard B. and David A. Tansik, THE CUSTOMER CONTACT MODEL FOR ORGANIZATION DESIGN, **Management Science,** September 1983, pp. 1037-1049.

Crosby, Philip B., **Quality is Free: The Art of Making Quality Certain,** N.Y.: New American Library, 1979.

Desatnick, Robert L. BUILDING THE CUSTOMER-ORIENTED WORK FORCE, **Training and Development Journal,** March 1987, pp. 72-75.

Elbeck, Matt, AN APPROACH TO CLIENT SATISFACTION MEASUREMENT AS AN ATTRIBUTE OF HEALTH SERVICE QUALITY, **Health Care Management Review,** Summer 1987, pp. 47-52.

Farmer, John, Anthony Alleyne, Balteano Duffus, and Mark Downing, CONTROLLING SERVICE QUALITY, **Business Quarterly,** Winter 1985.

Garner, A. and Reissman, F., **The Service Society and the Consumer Vanguard,** NY: Harper and Row, 1974.

Hawken, Paul, THE EMPLOYEE AS CUSTOMER, **Inc.,** November 1987, pp. 21-22.

Heskett, James L., LESSONS IN THE SERVICE SECTOR, **Harvard Business Review,** March-April 1987, pp. 118-126.

Hochschild, A. **The Managed Heart: Commercialization of Human**

Feeling, Berkeley, CA: University of California Press, 1983.

Hostage, G. M., QUALITY CONTROL IN A SERVICE BUSINESS, **Harvard Business Review,** July-August 1975, pp. 100-108.

Howard, James S., QUALITY: TAKES U.S. BUSINESS BY STORM, **Dun and Bradstreet Reports,** July 1985, pp. 31-44.

Kirkland, Richard, ARE SERVICE JOBS GOOD JOBS? **Fortune,** June 10, 1985. p. 38.

Klein, Linda, SUPERIOR AMBULANCE CHASES THE CLIENTS IT WANTS, **Business Atlanta,** July 1986, p. 122.

Koepp, Stephen, PUL-EEZE! WILL SOMEBODY HELP ME?, **Time,** February 2, 1987, pp. 48-57.

Kutcher, Ronald and Jerome Mark, THE SERVICE SECTOR: SOME COMMON MISPERCEPTIONS REVIEWED, **Monthly Labor Review,** April 1983, pp. 21-27.

Labovitz, George H., KEEPING YOUR INTERNAL CUSTOMERS SATISFIED, **The Wall Street Journal,** July 6, 1987.

Landvater, Darryl, CLOSE TO THE CUSTOMER: BUILDING A REPUTATION FOR SUPERIOR CUSTOMER SERVICE CAN BOOST SALES AND PROFITS, **Infosystems,** September 1985, p. 86.

Lee, Chris, TRAINING THE FRONT LINE TO TRAIN THE FRONT LINE, **TRAINING Magazine,** March 1987, pp. 77-81.

Levitt, Theodore, THE INDUSTRIALIZATION OF SERVICE, **Harvard Business Review,** Vol. 54, 1976, pp. 41-52.

Linden, Fabian, VALUE OF THE DOLLS, **Across the Board,** December 1985, pp. 55-60.

Lovelock, Christopher H. (Ed.), **Services Marketing,** Englewood Cliffs, NJ: Prentice-Hall, 1984.

Maister, D.H., BALANCING THE PROFESSIONAL SERVICE FIRM, **Sloan Management Review,** Vol. 24, No. 1, 1982, pp. 15-29.

Manning, Shaun, SERVICE CRISIS OR TRAINING VACUUM? **Food and Service,** November 1988.

McCallum, J. Richard and Wayne Harrison, INTERDEPENDENCE IN THE SERVICE ENCOUNTER, in **The Service Encounter,** by John A. Czepiel, Michael R. Soloman, and Carol F. Suprenant, (Eds.), Lexington, MA: D.C. Heath, 1985.

McGinnis, V.J., THE MISSION STATEMENT: A KEY STEP IN STRATEGIC PLANNING, **Business,** November-December 1981, pp. 39-43.

Mills, Peter K. and James H. Morris, CLIENTS AS 'PARTIAL' EMPLOYEES OF SERVICE ORGANIZATIONS: ROLE DEVELOPMENT IN CLIENT PARTICIPATION, **Academy of Management Review,** Vol. 11, No. 4, pp. 726-735.

Moccardi, Sal, OTIS ELEVATOR DISPATCHES PEACE OF MIND, **Inbound/Outbound,** August 1988, pp. 20-28.

Northcraft, Gregory B. and Richard B. Chase, MANAGING SERVICE DEMAND AT THE POINT OF DELIVERY, **Academy of Management Review,** Vol. 10, No. 1, 1985, pp. 66-75.

Parasuraman, A., Valarie A. Zeithaml and Leonard L. Berry, A CONCEPTUAL MODEL OF SERVICE QUALITY AND ITS IMPLICATIONS FOR FUTURE RESEARCH, **Journal of Marketing,** Fall 1985, pp. 41-50.

Pearce, John. A., THE COMPANY MISSION AS A STRATEGIC GOAL, **Sloan Management Review,** Spring 1982, pp. 15-24.

Pearce, John A. and Fred David, CORPORATE MISSION STATEMENTS: THE BOTTOM LINE, **Academy of Management Executive,** Vol. 1, No. 2, 1987, pp. 109-116.

Peters, Thomas J. and Waterman, Robert H. **In Search of Excellence: Lessons from America's Best-Run Companies,** NY: Harper and Row, 1982.

Quinn, James B. and Christopher E. Gagnon, WILL SERVICE FOLLOW MANUFACTURING INTO DECLINE?, **Harvard Business Review,** November-December 1986, pp. 95-103.

Richman, Tom, MISSISSIPPI MOTIVATORS, **Inc.,** October 1986, pp. 83-87.

Sathe, Vijay, IMPLICATIONS OF CORPORATE CULTURE: A MANAGER'S GUIDE TO ACTION, **Organizational Dynamics,** Autumn 1983, pp. 5-23.

Schneider, Benjamin, THE PERCEPTIONS OF ORGANIZATIONAL CLIMATE: THE CUSTOMER'S VIEW, **Journal of Applied Psychology,** Vol. 57, 1973, pp. 248-256.

Schneider, Benjamin and David E. Bowen, EMPLOYEE AND CUSTOMER PERCEPTIONS OF SERVICE IN BANKS: REPLICATION AND EXTENSION, **Journal of Applied Psychology,** Vol. 70, 1985, pp. 423-433.

Seller, Patricia, HOW TO HANDLE CUSTOMERS' GRIPES, **Fortune,** October 24, 1988, pp. 88-100.

Shetty, Y. K. and Joel E. Ross, QUALITY AND ITS MANAGEMENT IN SERVICE BUSINESSES, **Industrial Management,** November-December 1985, pp. 7-12.

Shostack, G. Lynn, BANKS SELL SERVICES—NOT THINGS, **Bankers Magazine,** Winter 1977, pp. 40-45.

Shullman, Robert R., Mark D. Willard and Joel Perelmuth, THE IMPACT OF SERVICE QUALITY IS MEASURABLE—AT THE BOTTOM LINE, **Mobius,** Fall 1987, pp. 3-5.

Staples, W. A. and K. U. Black, DEFINING YOUR BUSINESS MISSION: A STRATEGIC PERSPECTIVE, **Journal of Business Strategies,** Vol. 1, 1984, pp. 33-39.

Stern, Louis W. and Frederick D. Sturdivant, CUSTOMER-DRIVEN DISTRIBUTION SYSTEMS, **Harvard Business Review,** July-August 1987, pp. 34-39.

Thomas, Dan R. E., STRATEGY IS DIFFERENT IN SERVICE BUSINESSES, **Harvard Business Review,** July-August, 1978, pp. 5-12.

Vredenburg, Harrie and Chow-Hou Wee, THE ROLE OF CUSTOMER SERVICE IN DETERMINING CUSTOMER SATISFACTION, **Journal of the Academy of Marketing Science** (Can), Summer 1986.

Zeithaml, Valerie, HOW CONSUMER EVALUATION PROCESSES DIFFER BETWEEN GOODS AND SERVICES, in **Marketing of Services,** J.H. Donnelly and W.R. George (Eds.), Chicago: American Marketing Association, 1981, pp. 191-199.

Zemke, Ron, CUSTOMER EDUCATION: THE SILENT REVOLUTION, **TRAINING Magazine,** January 1985, pp. 26-39.

Zemke, Ron, HEALTH CARE REDISCOVERS PATIENTS, **TRAINING Magazine,** April 1987, pp. 40-45.

Zemke, Ron, SCANDINAVIAN MANAGEMENT—A LOOK AT OUR FUTURE? **Management Review,** July 1988.

Zemke, Ron and Karl Albrecht, SERVICE MANAGEMENT: A NEW GAME PLAN FOR THE POST-INDUSTRIAL ERA, **TRAINING Magazine,** February 1985, pp. 54-62.

About The Authors

Ron Zemke is a management consultant, journalist, and behavioral scientist. As senior editor of Minneapolis-based *TRAINING* Magazine and editor of *The Service Edge* Newsletter, he has covered the emergence of the nation's growing service sector as well as other major issues in American business and management. Ron formed his own consulting group, Performance Research Associates, Inc., in 1972. Before that he was manager of training for Olivetti Corporation and the director of education and training at Citicorp. He is the author or co-author of eight books. Among them are: *The Service Edge: 101 Companies that Profit from Customer Care,* and the best selling *Service America!: Doing Business in the New Economy.* In addition, he has published numerous articles in professional journals and acts as host on four films on the service management process.

Chip R. Bell is a nationally-known trainer and independent consultant based in Charlotte, North Carolina. His consulting practice focuses on leadership training and service management consulting. He was formerly a partner with LEAD Associates, Inc., a training and consulting firm. Prior to that he was vice president and director of Management and Organization Development for NCNB Corporation, a large bank holding company. Additionally, he was on the staff of the Department of Instruction for the U.S. Army Infantry School. He holds graduate degrees in organizational psychology and human resource development from Vanderbilt University and George Washington University. Chip is the author of *Influencing: Marketing the Ideas that Matter* as well as numerous journal articles; he is co-author of *Understanding Training, The Trainer's Professional Development Handbook, Instructing for Results, Clients and Consultants* and *Managing the Learning Process.*

About The Contributors

Karl Albrecht is an internationally-known management consultant, seminar presenter, speaker, and a prolific author. He concentrates on pioneering new concepts for increasing individual and organizational effectiveness and has consulted with major corporations on strategic planning, organization development and service management. He is author or co-author of eleven books including *Service America!, Stress & the Manager, Brain Power* and *The Creative Corporation.*

Gary F. Bargatze is vice president of service strategy development for Technical Assistance Research Programs (TARP), a research and consulting organization specializing in customer service. He has co-authored articles and working papers discussing quality improvement implementation strategies and is a senior examiner for the Malcolm Baldridge National Quality Award.

Dr. Leonard L. Berry is Foley's/Federated professor of retailing and marketing studies and director of the Center for Retailing Studies in the College of Business Administration, Texas A&M University. He writes and lectures extensively on services marketing, financial services marketing, retailing strategy and quality of service. Dr. Berry is the author of many books, articles, and papers. His most recent book is *Service Quality—A Profit Strategy for Financial Institutions.*

David Bowen is assistant professor of

management and organization, graduate school of business administration, University of Southern California. He received his Ph.d. in business administration from Michigan State University. Mr. Bowen has published numerous articles on organizational behavior in the service sector and has consulted with many clients on issues of service quality. He is co-editing a book tentatively titled *Service Management Effectiveness: An Interdisciplinary Perspective.*

Cathy DeForest, Ph.d. is an organization development consultant who has worked with major corporations, universities, government and non-profits. She is in private practice in California and is adjunct faculty to the MBA program at John F. Kennedy University and the California Institute of Integral Studies. Dr. DeForest is currently writing two books, *Strategic Visioning for the 21st Century* and *Conscious Business: The Key to the Next Millennium.*

Matt Elbeck is an associate professor in the Department of Marketing, University of North Dakota, Grand Forks. He has published 16 articles in the health services marketing field.

John A. Goodman is president of Technical Assistance Research Programs (TARP), a research and consulting organization specializing in customer service. He has managed more than fourscore separate customer service studies, including TARP's White House sponsored evaluation of complaint handling practices in government and business.

John Gunkler is president of Decision Futures, a provider of consulting services and related computer software to companies in need of strategic change. He is also a partner in Option Technologies, Inc., where he creates and applies technology that helps people work better together. Some of the organizations Mr. Gunkler has consulted with include CitiBank, Bank of America, Ford Motor Company, ALCOA, AT&T and Mead Corporation.

Christopher W.L. Hart is an assistant professor in the department of production and operations management at the Harvard University Graduate School of Business. His recent work is concentrated in the areas of quality and productivity improvement, particularly in service businesses. Dr. Hart is the author or co-author of two books, more than 20 articles, over 20 case studies and many other reports and special publications.

Alfie Kohn is author of *No Contest: The Case Against Competition* (published in paperback by Houghton Mifflin), and *Beyond Selfishness: Altruism, Empathy and the Brighter Side of Human Nature* (to be published in 1990 by Basic Books). He is a contributing editor to *Psychology Today* and has written for *The Atlantic, The Nation,* and many other publications. Mr. Kohn lives in Cambridge, Massachusetts.

Rikard Larsson is presently a double doctoral candidate at the University of Lund in Sweden and at the School of Business, University of Southern California. His research has principally focused on mergers and acquisitions.

Stew Leonard is the founder and chairman of Stew Leonard's of Norwalk, CT, an enterprise that began as a small dairy store in 1969 and today has sales approaching 100 million dollars a year, encompasses over 10 acres, and serves 100,000 shoppers each week. He built his organization on a foundation of teamwork and a firm belief in and commitment to the philosophy that the customer is always right.

Theodore Levitt is professor of business administration at Harvard and editor of the *Harvard Business Review.* His most recent book is *The Marketing Imagination,* (The Free Press 1986).

David Maister formed Maister Associates in 1985 and is a full-time consultant to professional service firms. Previously he was on the faculty of the Harvard Business School. He has authored or co-authored seven books including a collection of 25 of his own articles titled *Professional Service Firm Management.*

Arlene R. Malech, Ph.d. is a senior research associate with Technical Assistance Research Programs (TARP) and has been involved in a number of projects to assess existing corporate complaint handling departments. She was project director for the United States Office of Consumer Affairs' *Consumer Complaint Handling in America* update study.

Theodore Marra is vice president of Technical Assistance Research Programs (TARP), a research and consulting organization specializing in customer service. He has assisted such firms as Xerox, IBM, Shell and many others in improving the quality of their customer service activities and in facilitating the cultural change necessary to become more customer focused.

A. "Parsu" Parasuraman is Foley's/Federated professor of retailing and marketing studies at Texas A&M University. His research interests include services marketing, sales management, and marketing strategy. He has written numerous articles for professional journals and has authored a textbook titled *Marketing Research*.

Tom Peters is a business management expert and author of three bestsellers: *In Search of Excellence,* (co-authored with Robert Waterman), *A Passion for Excellence*, (co-authored with Nancy Austin), and *Thriving On Chaos*.

Benjamin Schneider is professor of psychology at the University of Maryland, College Park. He has published more than 75 articles and co-authored several books including *Organizational Climates and Careers: The Work Lives of Priests* and *Staffing Organizations*. He edited *Facilitating Work Effectiveness* and *Organizational Climate and Culture*.

Karl Schoenberger was formerly deputy bureau chief—Asian (Tokyo) for *The Wall Street Journal*. After completing a degree in Chinese from Stanford University, he became a staff reporter for the Associated Press. Following that he worked for the *Hartford Courant* before joining *The Wall Street Journal*. Mr. Schoenberger currently resides in Tokyo.

Benson P. Shapiro is a professor of business administration at the Harvard Business School. He is currently performing research on product line planning, interfunctional coordination, and strategic account selection and management. He is author and co-author of six books, 16 *Harvard Business Review* articles, and numerous other material. His books include *Segmenting the Industrial Market, Sales Program Management,* and a three-volume series on marketing management.

Edward Tenner, Ph.d. is an executive editor at Princeton University Press. A writer and consultant, he currently is the visiting lecturer of the Council of the Humanities of Princeton University. Mr. Tenner is author of *Tech Speak* (Crown Publishers).

Valarie Zeithaml is associate professor at the Fuqua School of Business, Duke University. Her primary teaching interests are in the areas of service marketing, advertising, and marketing strategy. Her research interests include services marketing, consumer perceptions of price, and information processing. Professor Zeithaml has published numerous articles in her field and she serves on the editorial review board of the *Journal of Marketing* and the *Journal of Consumer Research*.

THANKS!!

Kristin Anderson, Philip Jones,
Julie Swiler, Helen Spielberg,
Klay DeVries, Sherry Knowles,
and Jim Knowles.

REQUIRED READING FOR HUMAN RESOURCES PROFESSIONALS

Please send me the following publications.

Qty.	Title	Amount
_____	Adult Learning In Your Classroom. $19.95.	_____
_____	Creative Training Techniques Handbook. By Bob Pike. $45.50.	_____
_____	Designing and Delivering Cost-Effective Training—And Measuring the Results. Second Edition: $68.95.	_____
_____	Effective Training Delivery. $19.95.	_____
_____	Evaluating Training. $19.95.	_____
_____	Instructing for Results. By Fredric Margolis and Chip R. Bell. $17.95.	_____
_____	Performance Technology. $19.95.	_____
_____	Service America! By Karl Albrecht and Ron Zemke. Dow Jones Irwin. $19.95.	_____
_____	The Service Edge: 101 Companies That Profit From Customer Care. By Ron Zemke with Dick Schaaf. NAL Books. $19.95.	_____
_____	Service Wisdom: Creating and Maintaining the Customer Service Edge. By Ron Zemke and Chip R. Bell. $19.95.	_____
_____	The Training Directors' Forum Guide To Selling Training To Management. $14.95.	_____
_____	The Training Directors' Forum Guide To Training Consultants. $14.95.	_____
_____	Training Terms. $19.95.	_____
_____	Understanding Training: Perspectives and Practices. By Fredric Margolis and Chip R. Bell. $17.95.	_____
_____	What Works at Work: Lessons From the Masters. By George Dixon. $39.95.	_____
_____	**Add $3.00 per book for shipping and handling.** **Add S/H**	_____
_____	Creative Training Techniques Newsletter. 12 issues per year. $89 subscription.	_____
_____	Front-Line Service Newsletter. 12 issues per year. $69 subscription. Discounted bulk subscriptions available.	_____
_____	The Service Edge Newsletter. 12 issues per year. $98 subscription.	_____
_____	Training Directors' Forum Newsletter. 12 issues per year, plus four quarterly supplements. $96 subscription.	_____
_____	**TOTAL** **Total $**	_____

Allow 4-6 weeks for delivery. Offer expires 12/31/92.

☐ Check or money order is enclosed. Make check payable to Lakewood Publications.

☐ Government purchase order is enclosed.

☐ Please charge: ☐ VISA   ☐ MasterCard   ☐ American Express

Card # _____ Exp. _____ Signature _____

(Required for Credit Card use)

NAME _____

TITLE _____

COMPANY _____

ADDRESS _____

CITY _____

PROV./STATE   POSTAL/ZIP CODE

PHONE _____ - _____

AREA CODE

SW2

ORDER FORM MISSING?
Call 800-328-4329
or 612-333-0471
and ask for up-to-date catalog of
Lakewood books and publications for
managers and human resources professionals.

Mail Your Order Form
and Payment Today To:

Lakewood Books
50 South Ninth Street
Minneapolis, MN 55402